X GENDER

1

Story and Art by
Asuka Miyazaki

CONTENTS

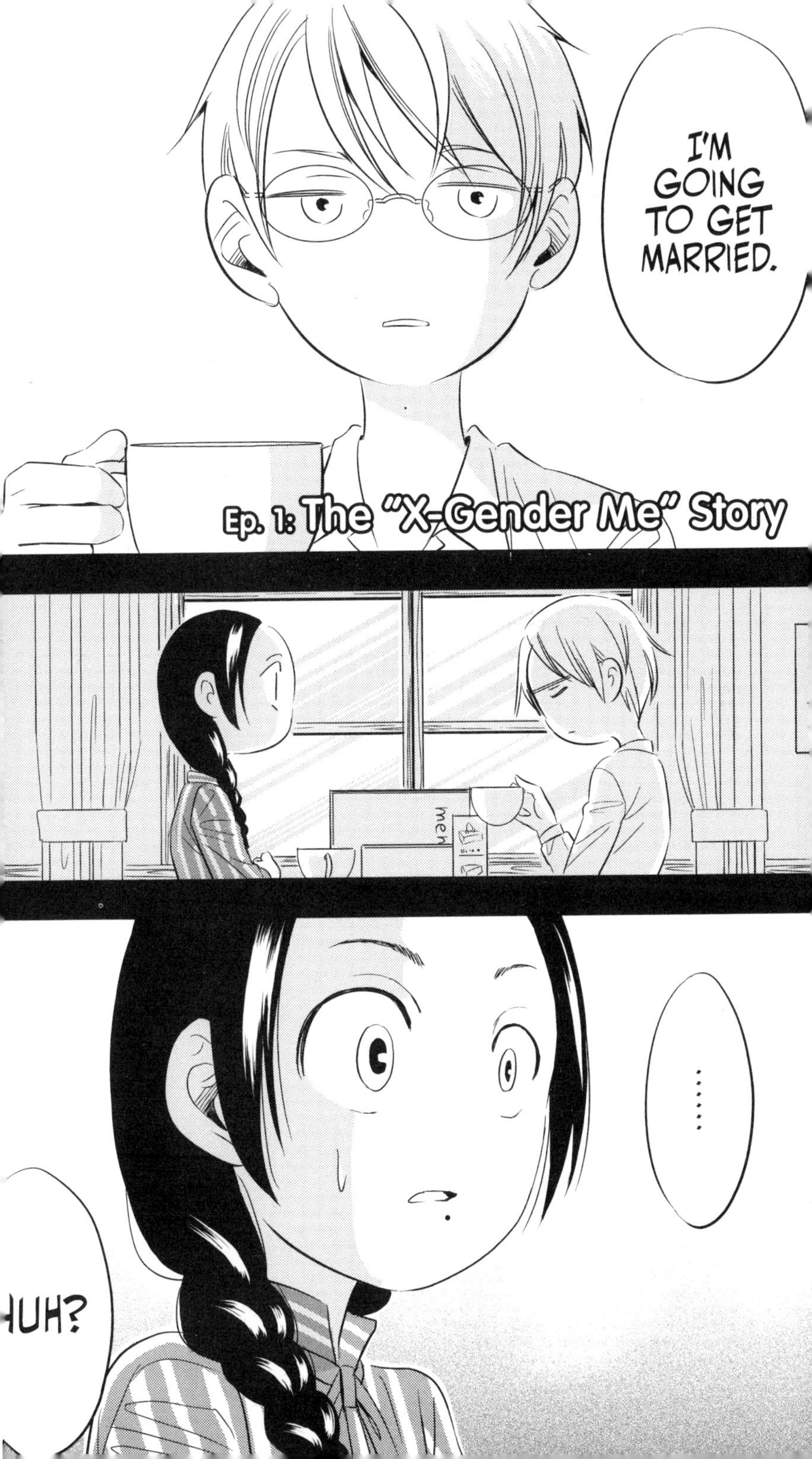
I'M GOING TO GET MARRIED.
Ep. 1: The "X-Gender Me" Story
......
HUH?

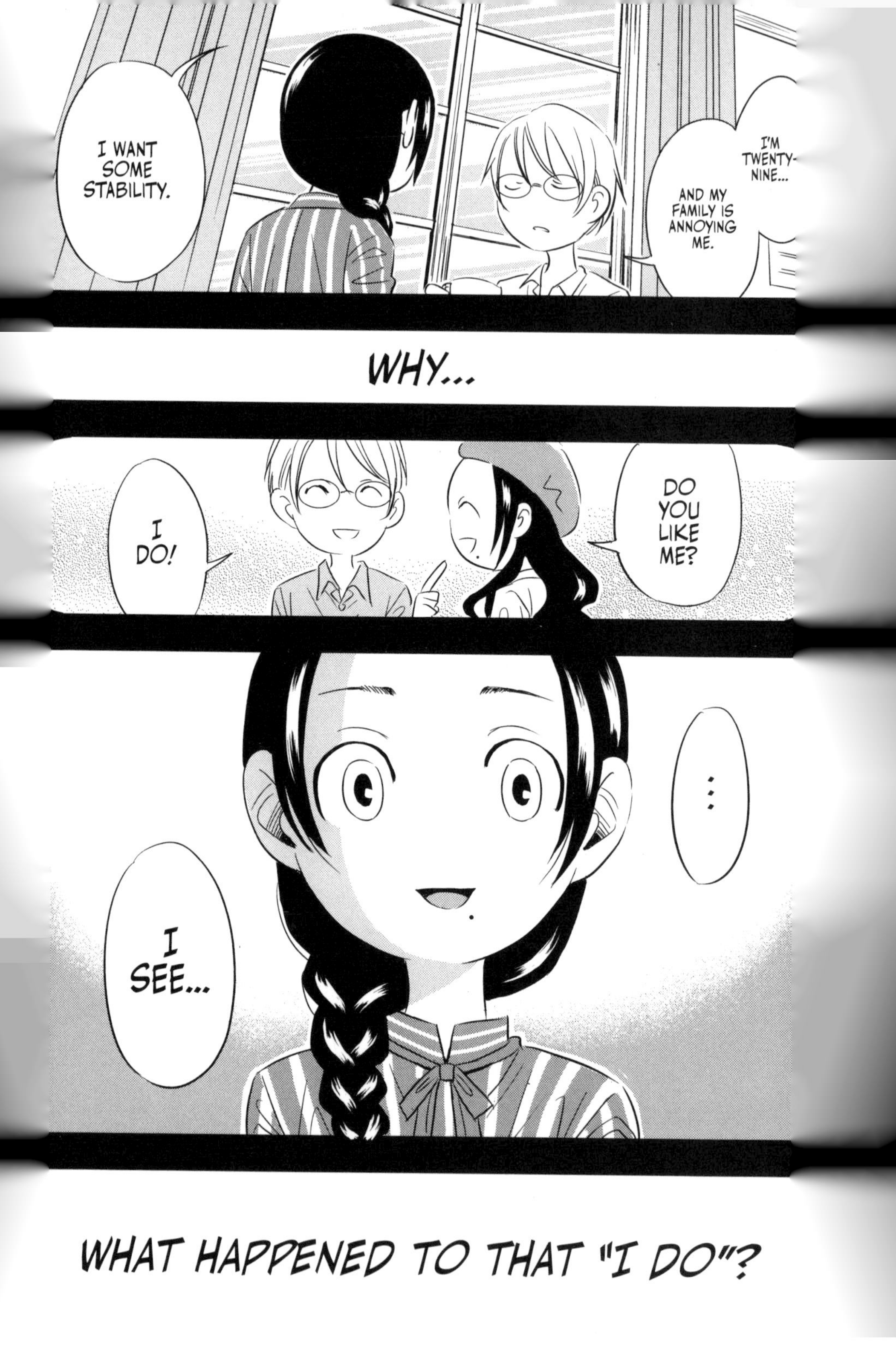
I'M TWENTY-NINE...
AND MY FAMILY IS ANNOYING ME.
I WANT SOME STABILITY.
WHY...
DO YOU LIKE ME?
I DO!
...
I SEE...
WHAT HAPPENED TO THAT "I DO"?

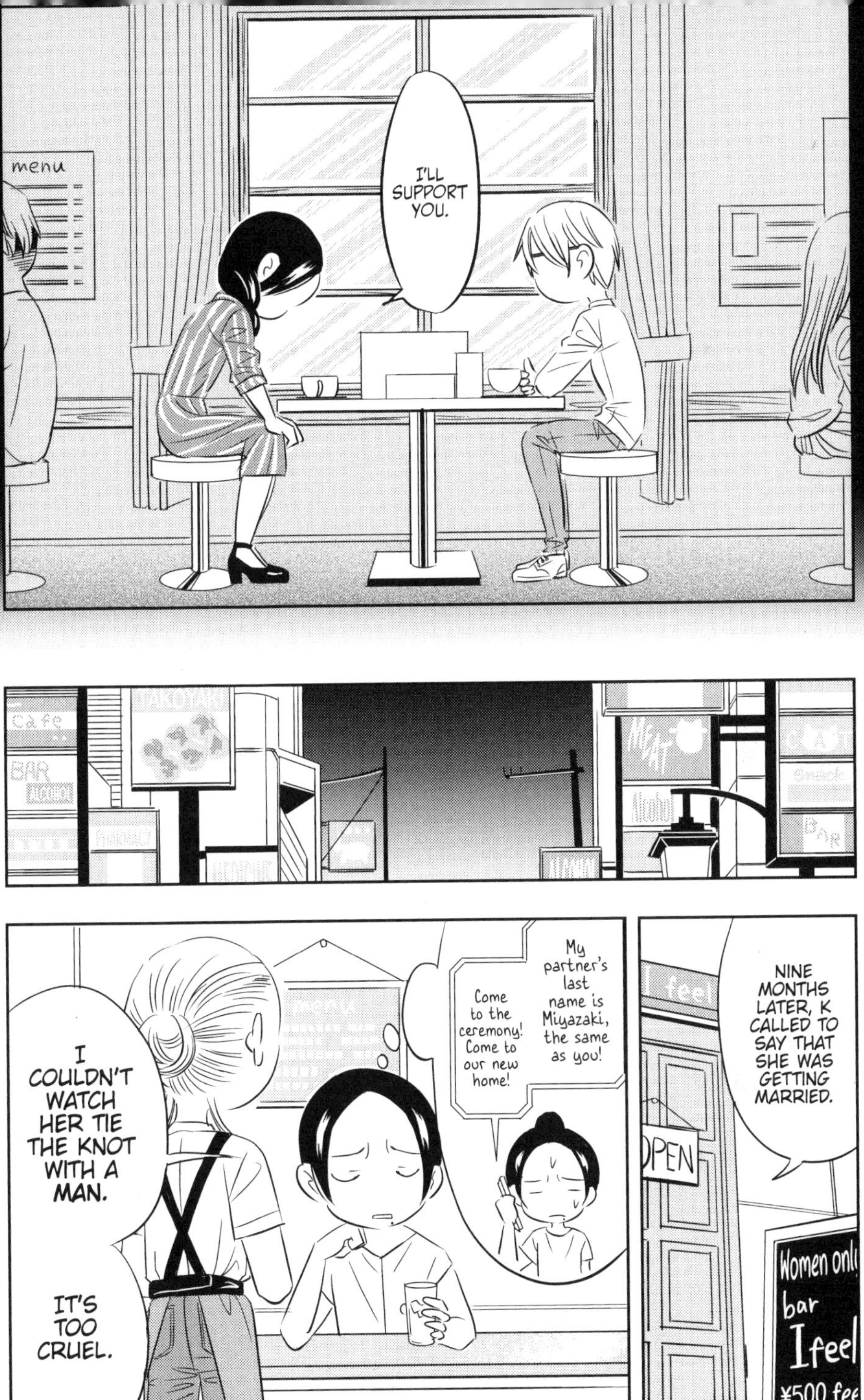
menu
I'LL SUPPORT YOU.
TAKOYAKI
Cafe
BAR
MEAT
NINE MONTHS LATER, K CALLED TO SAY THAT SHE WAS GETTING MARRIED.
OPEN
Women only bar
I feel
¥500 fee
My partner's last name is Miyazaki, the same as you!
Come to the ceremony! Come to our new home!
I COULDN'T WATCH HER TIE THE KNOT WITH A MAN.
IT'S TOO CRUEL.

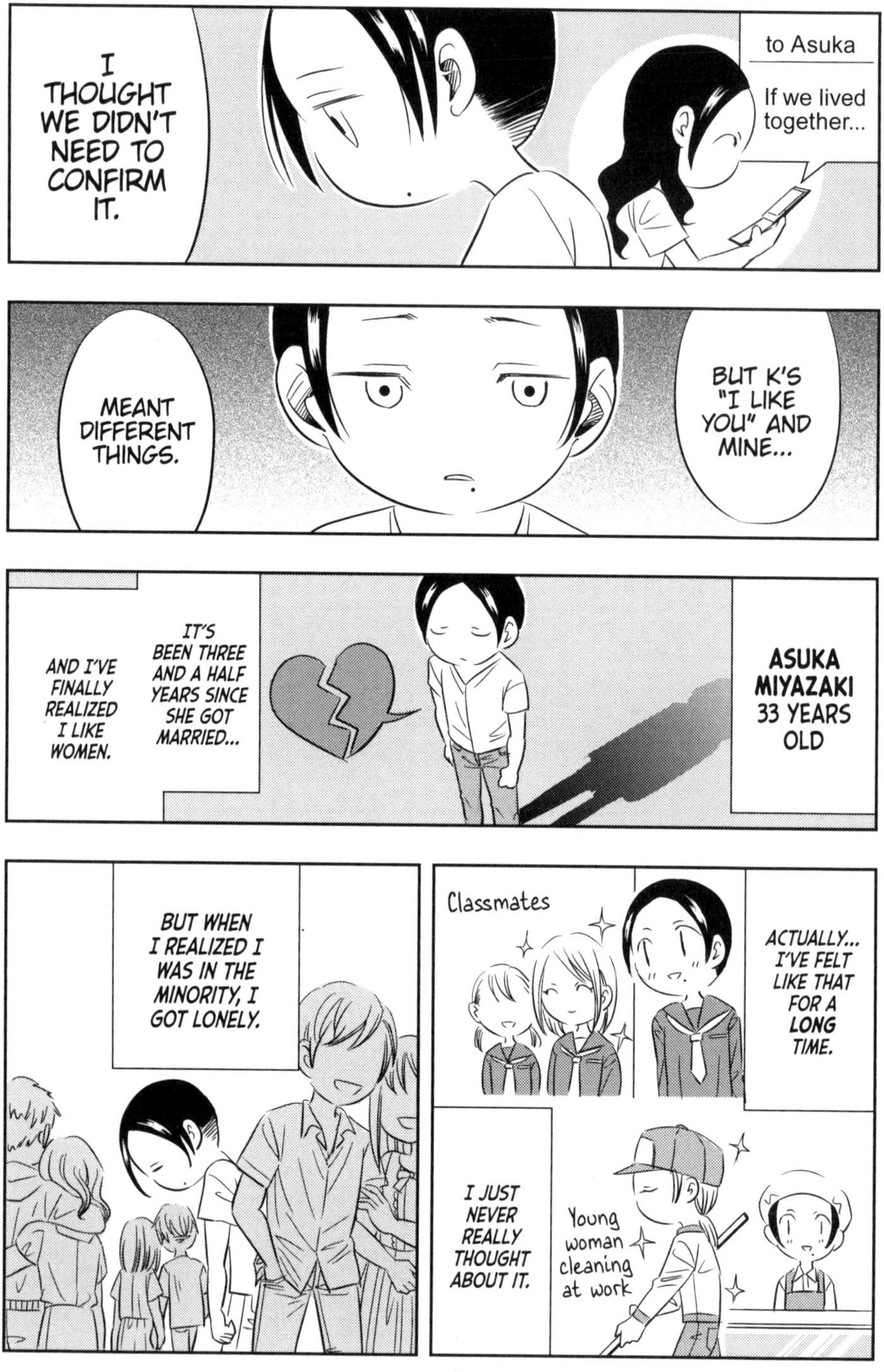
to Asuka
If we lived together...
I THOUGHT WE DIDN'T NEED TO CONFIRM IT.
BUT K'S "I LIKE YOU" AND MINE...
MEANT DIFFERENT THINGS.
ASUKA MIYAZAKI 33 YEARS OLD
IT'S BEEN THREE AND A HALF YEARS SINCE SHE GOT MARRIED...
AND I'VE FINALLY REALIZED I LIKE WOMEN.
ACTUALLY... I'VE FELT LIKE THAT FOR A LONG TIME.
Classmates
Young woman cleaning at work
I JUST NEVER REALLY THOUGHT ABOUT IT.
BUT WHEN I REALIZED I WAS IN THE MINORITY, I GOT LONELY.

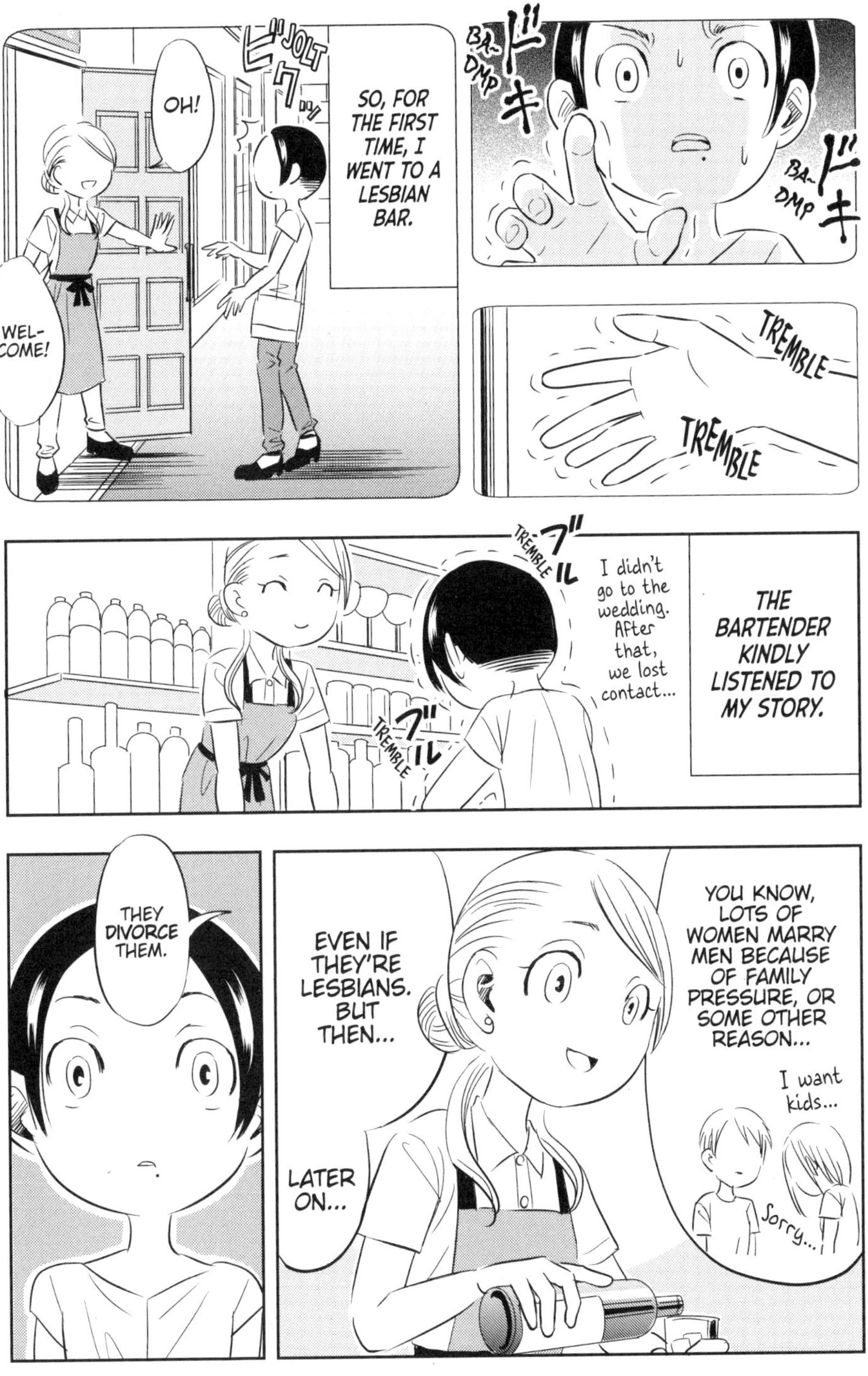
BA-DMP ドキ
BA-DMP ドキ
TREMBLE
TREMBLE
SO, FOR THE FIRST TIME, I WENT TO A LESBIAN BAR.
JOLT ビクッ
OH!
WEL-COME!
THE BARTENDER KINDLY LISTENED TO MY STORY.
I didn't go to the wedding. After that, we lost contact...
TREMBLE ブル
TREMBLE ブル
YOU KNOW, LOTS OF WOMEN MARRY MEN BECAUSE OF FAMILY PRESSURE, OR SOME OTHER REASON...
I want kids...
Sorry...
EVEN IF THEY'RE LESBIANS. BUT THEN...
LATER ON...
THEY DIVORCE THEM.

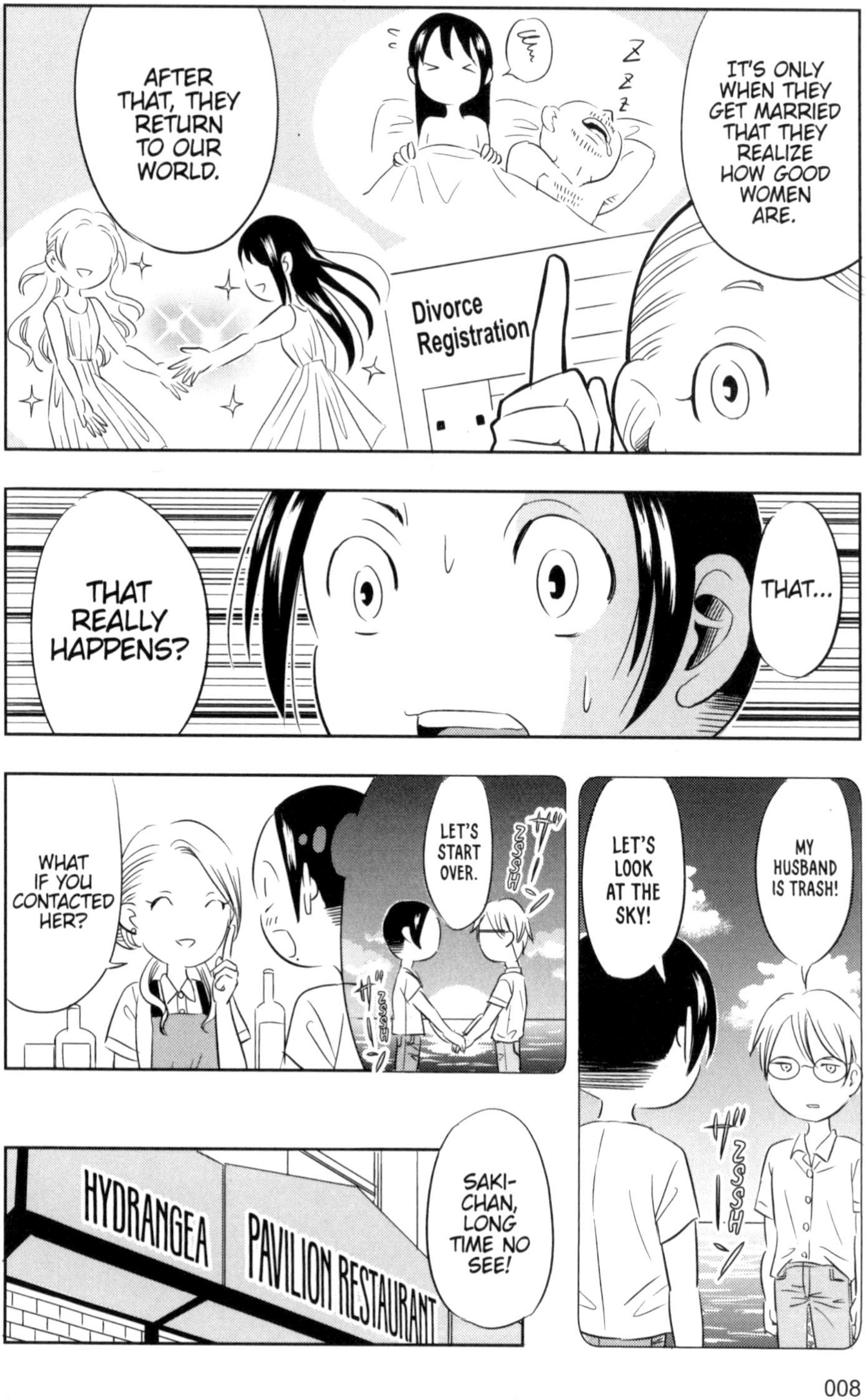
IT'S ONLY WHEN THEY GET MARRIED THAT THEY REALIZE HOW GOOD WOMEN ARE.
Divorce Registration
AFTER THAT, THEY RETURN TO OUR WORLD.
THAT...
THAT REALLY HAPPENS?
MY HUSBAND IS TRASH!
LET'S LOOK AT THE SKY!
LET'S START OVER.
WHAT IF YOU CONTACTED HER?
SAKI-CHAN, LONG TIME NO SEE!
HYDRANGEA PAVILION RESTAURANT

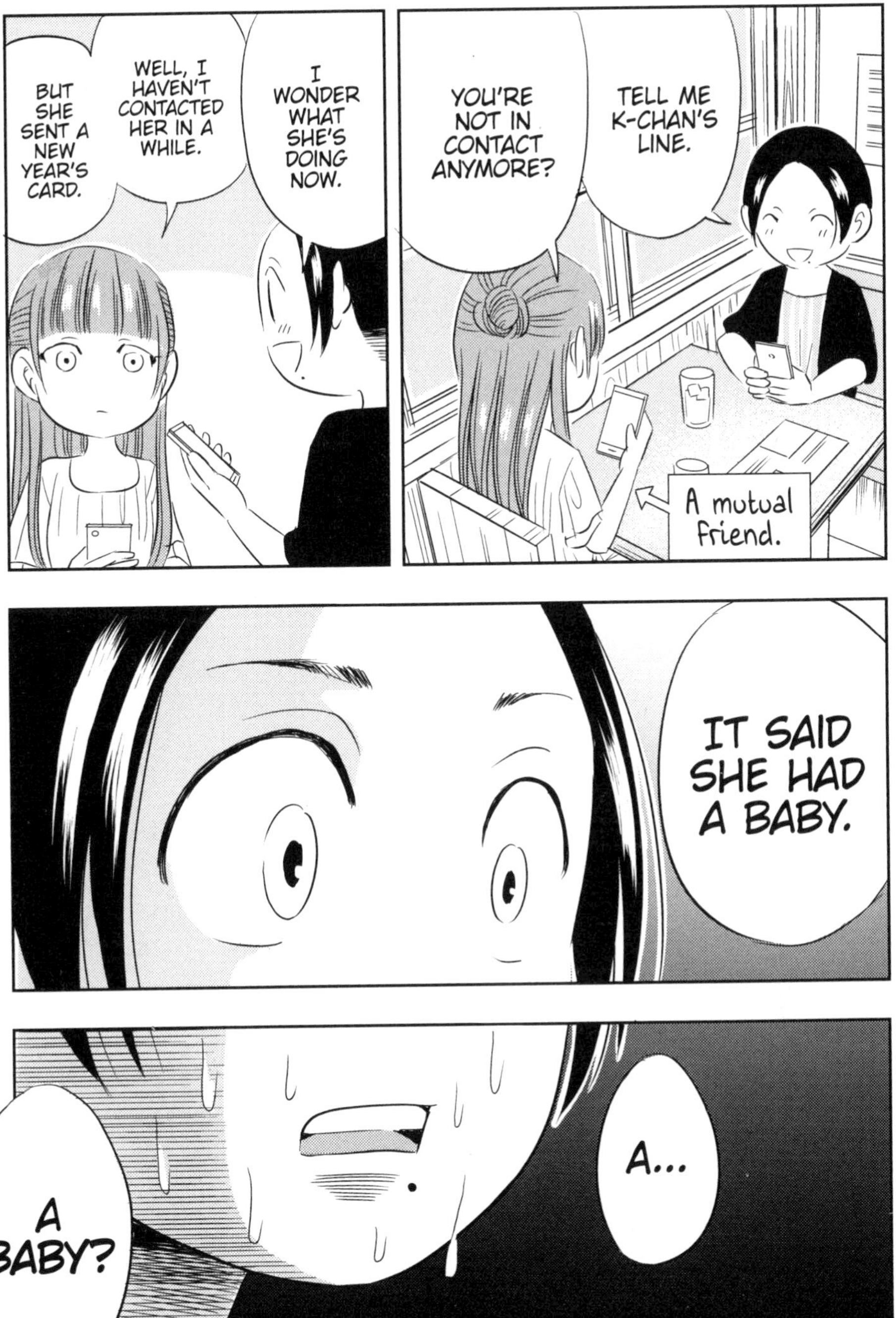
TELL ME K-CHAN'S LINE.
YOU'RE NOT IN CONTACT ANYMORE?
A mutual friend.
I WONDER WHAT SHE'S DOING NOW.
WELL, I HAVEN'T CONTACTED HER IN A WHILE.
BUT SHE SENT A NEW YEAR'S CARD.
IT SAID SHE HAD A BABY.
A...
A BABY?

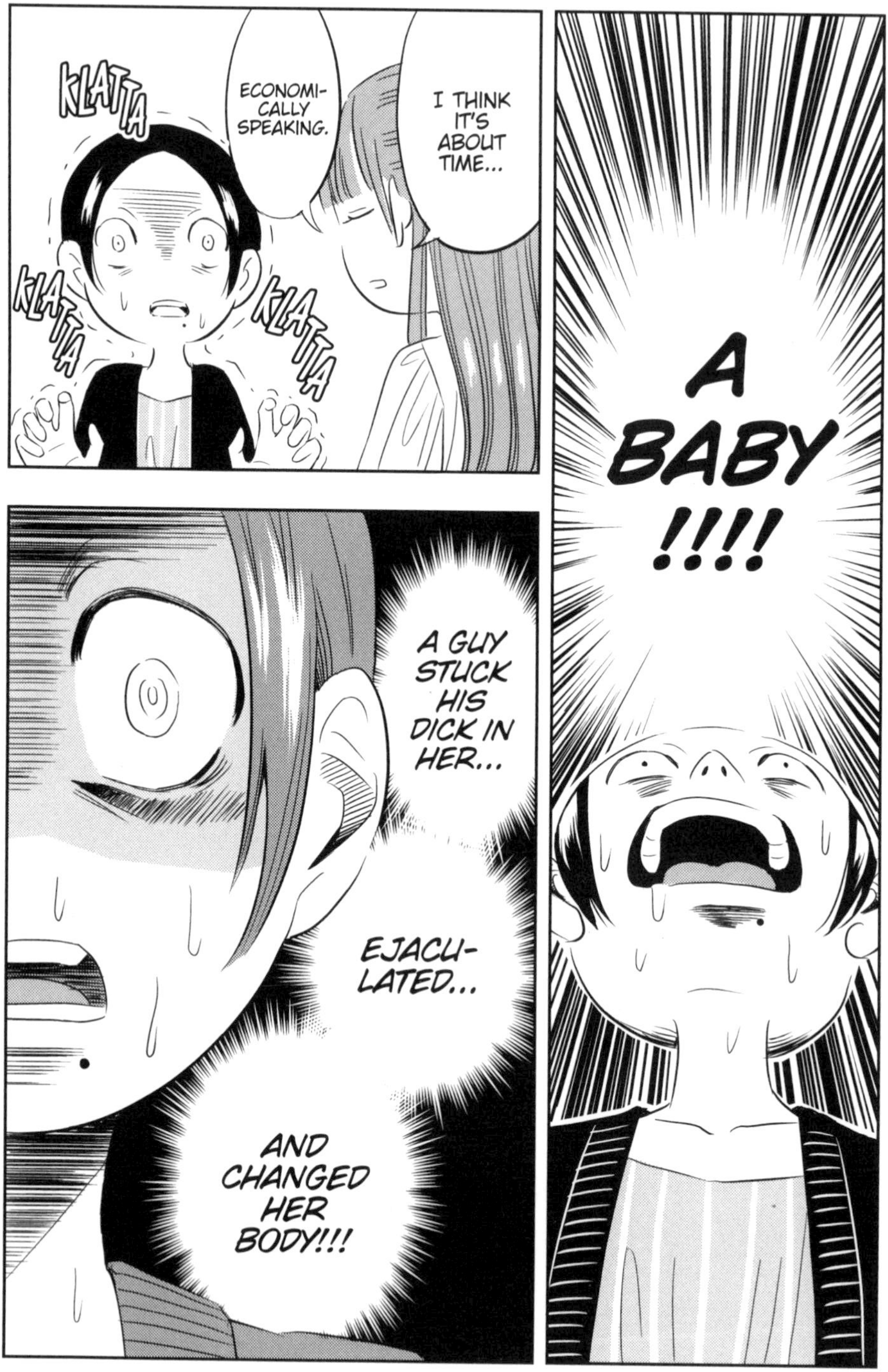
A BABY!!!!
I THINK IT'S ABOUT TIME...
ECONOMICALLY SPEAKING.
KLATTA
KLATTA
KLATTA
A GUY STUCK HIS DICK IN HER...
EJACULATED...
AND CHANGED HER BODY!!!

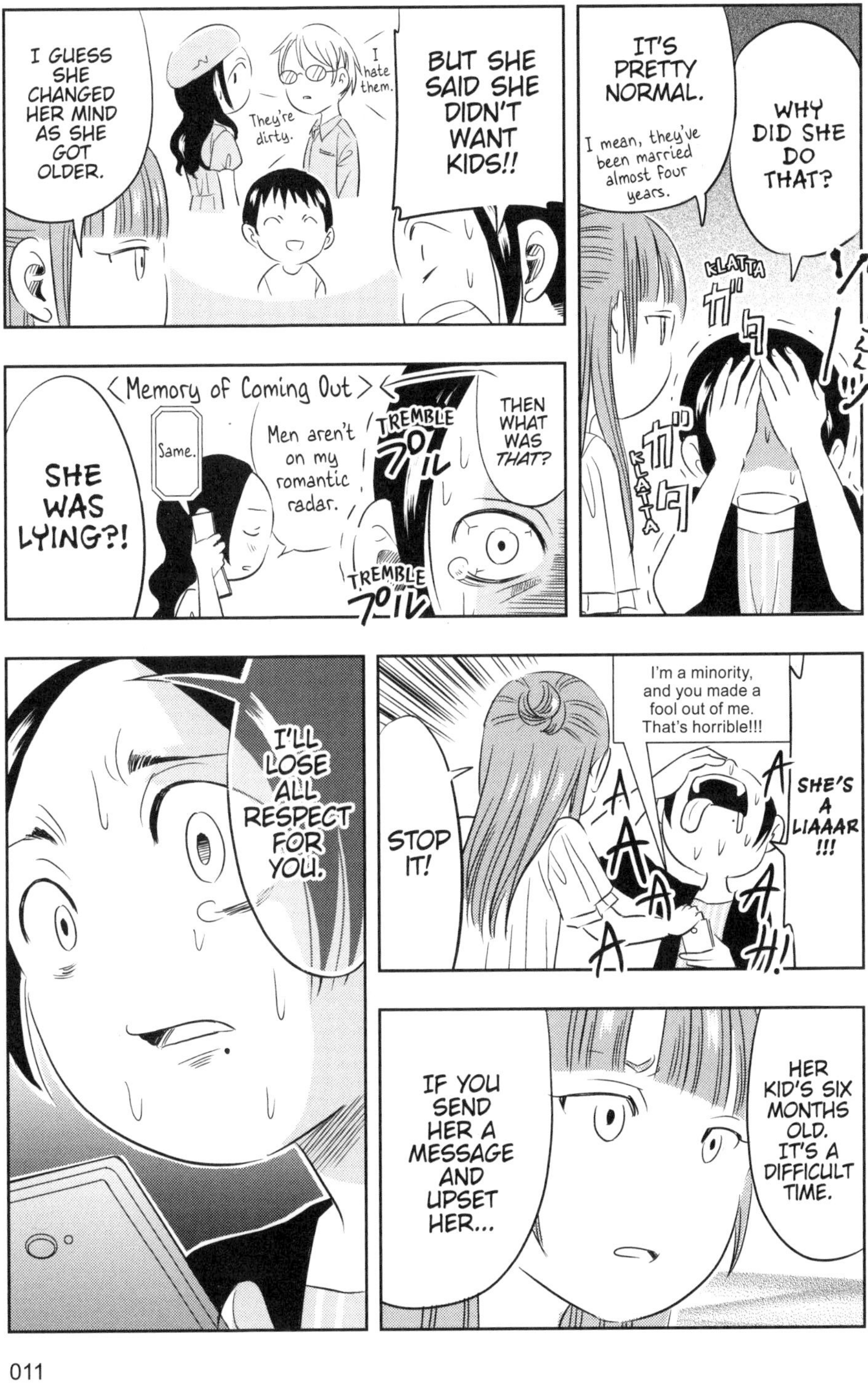
WHY DID SHE DO THAT?
IT'S PRETTY NORMAL.
I mean, they've been married almost four years.
CHILL!!
KLATTA
KLATTA
BUT SHE SAID SHE DIDN'T WANT KIDS!!
I hate them.
They're dirty.
I GUESS SHE CHANGED HER MIND AS SHE GOT OLDER.
〈Memory of Coming Out〉
THEN WHAT WAS THAT?
TREMBLE
Men aren't on my romantic radar.
Same.
TREMBLE
SHE WAS LYING?!
SHE'S A LIAAAR!!!
I'm a minority, and you made a fool out of me. That's horrible!!!
AAAAAAAAAH!
STOP IT!
HER KID'S SIX MONTHS OLD. IT'S A DIFFICULT TIME.
IF YOU SEND HER A MESSAGE AND UPSET HER...
I'LL LOSE ALL RESPECT FOR YOU.

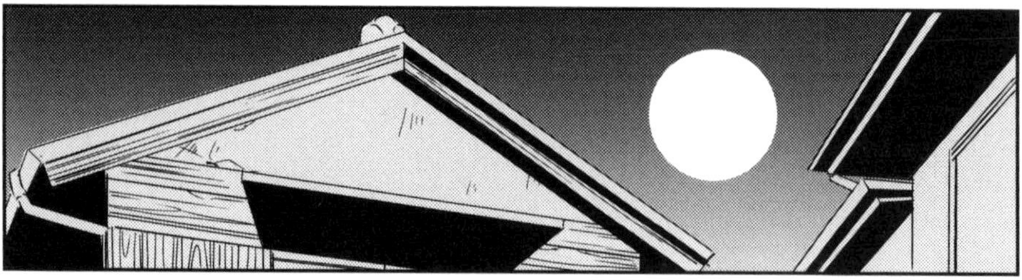

I heard from Saki-chan! Congrats on the baby!

Thanks! They'll be six months old soon.

I'm praying for your happiness, K-chan |

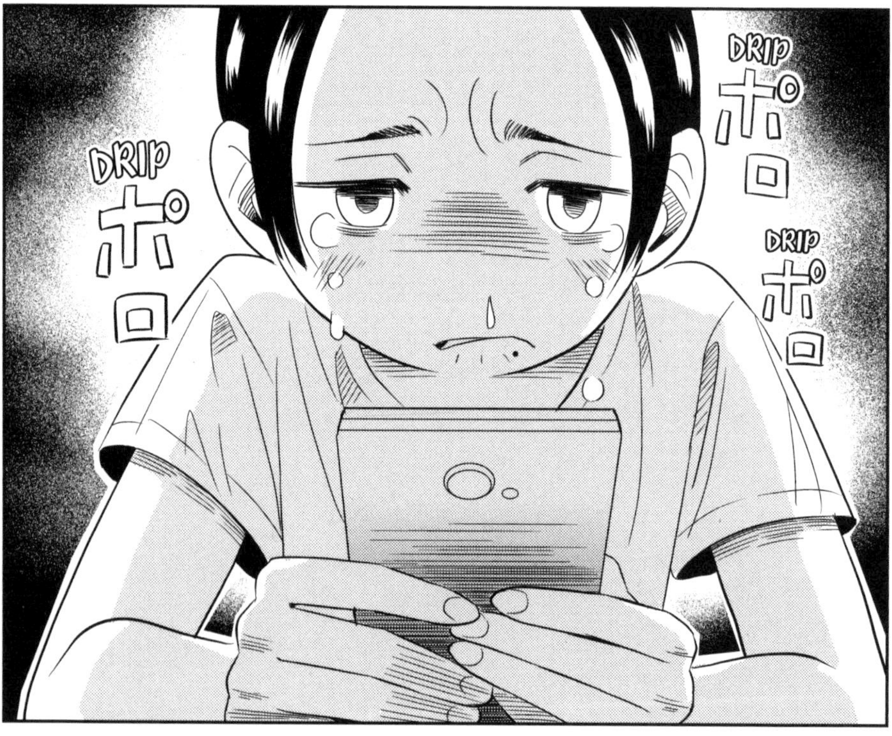
DRIP
ポロ
DRIP
ポロ
DRIP
ポロ

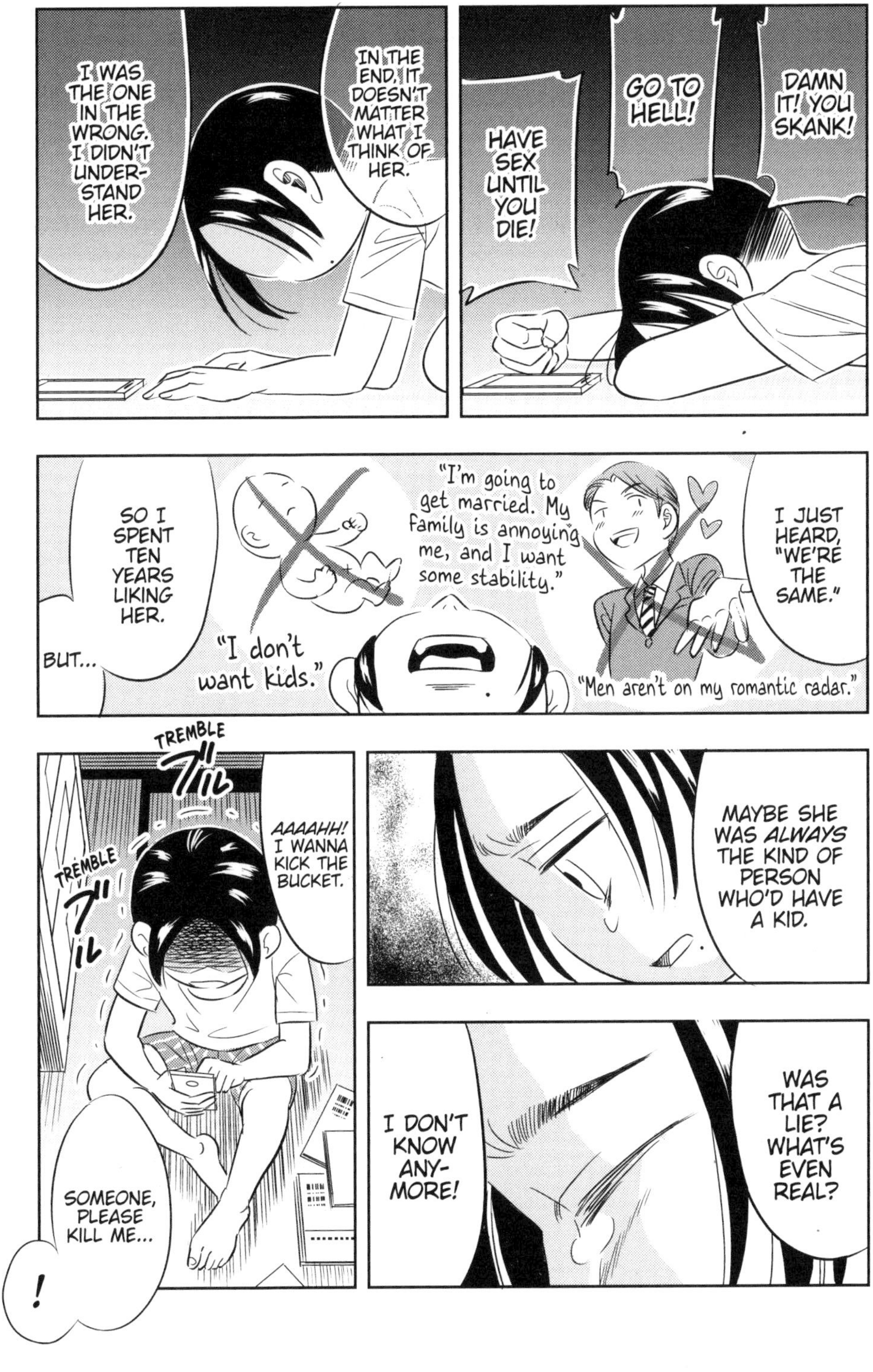
DAMN IT! YOU SKANK!
GO TO HELL!
HAVE SEX UNTIL YOU DIE!
IN THE END, IT DOESN'T MATTER WHAT I THINK OF HER.
I WAS THE ONE IN THE WRONG. I DIDN'T UNDER-STAND HER.
I JUST HEARD, "WE'RE THE SAME."
"Men aren't on my romantic radar."
"I'm going to get married. My family is annoying me, and I want some stability."
"I don't want kids."
SO I SPENT TEN YEARS LIKING HER.
BUT...
MAYBE SHE WAS ALWAYS THE KIND OF PERSON WHO'D HAVE A KID.
WAS THAT A LIE? WHAT'S EVEN REAL?
I DON'T KNOW ANY-MORE!
TREMBLE
AAAAHH! I WANNA KICK THE BUCKET.
TREMBLE
SOMEONE, PLEASE KILL ME...
!

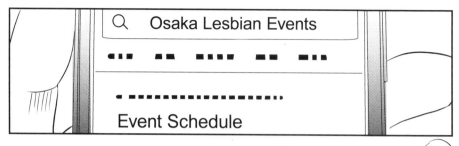

Q Osaka Lesbian Events

Event Schedule

OH?

THERE ARE QUITE A FEW PLACES TO MEET WOMEN.

I'LL TRY IT.

AN IRL MEETUP AT A BAR...

Meetup support!

SKRITCH

ALL RIGHT!

IRL Meetup

IRL Mee

SKRITCH

JUST YOU WATCH, K!

I'LL FIND A WOMAN AND BE HAPPY!

Diary

X-GENDER

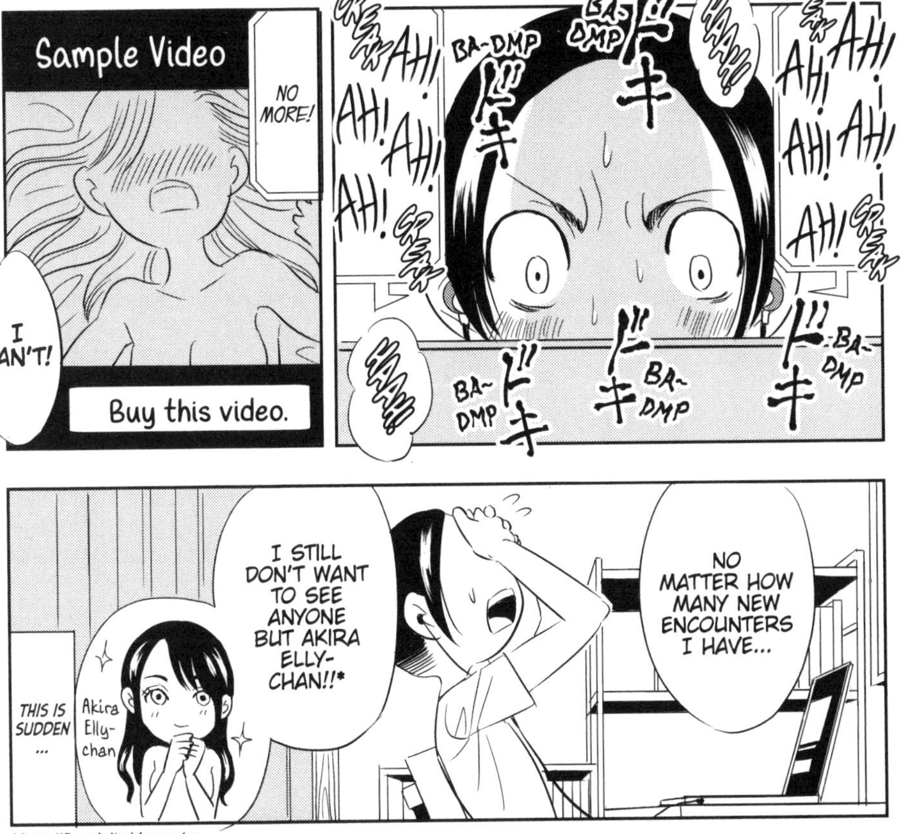
CREAK
AH! AH! AH! AH!
CREAK
AH! AH! AH! AH! AH!
BA-DMP ドキ
HAAH!
BA-DMP ドキ
BA-DMP ドキ
BA-DMP ドキ
BA-DMP ドキ
HAAH!
CREAK
CREAK
Sample Video
NO MORE!
I CAN'T!
Buy this video.
NO MATTER HOW MANY NEW ENCOUNTERS I HAVE...
I STILL DON'T WANT TO SEE ANYONE BUT AKIRA ELLY-CHAN!!*
Akira Elly-chan
THIS IS SUDDEN ...

*A prolific adult video actor.

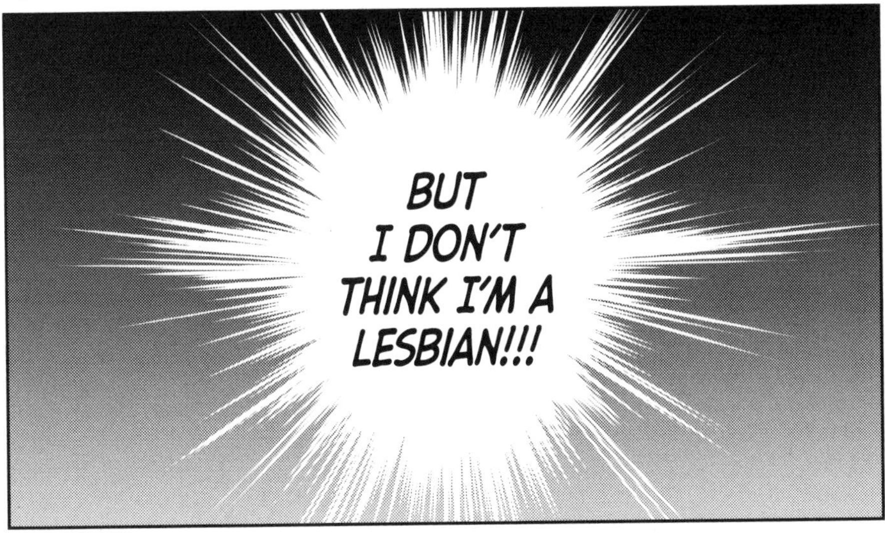
BUT I DON'T THINK I'M A LESBIAN!!!

Ep. 2: The "What I Want You to Know About Gender" Story

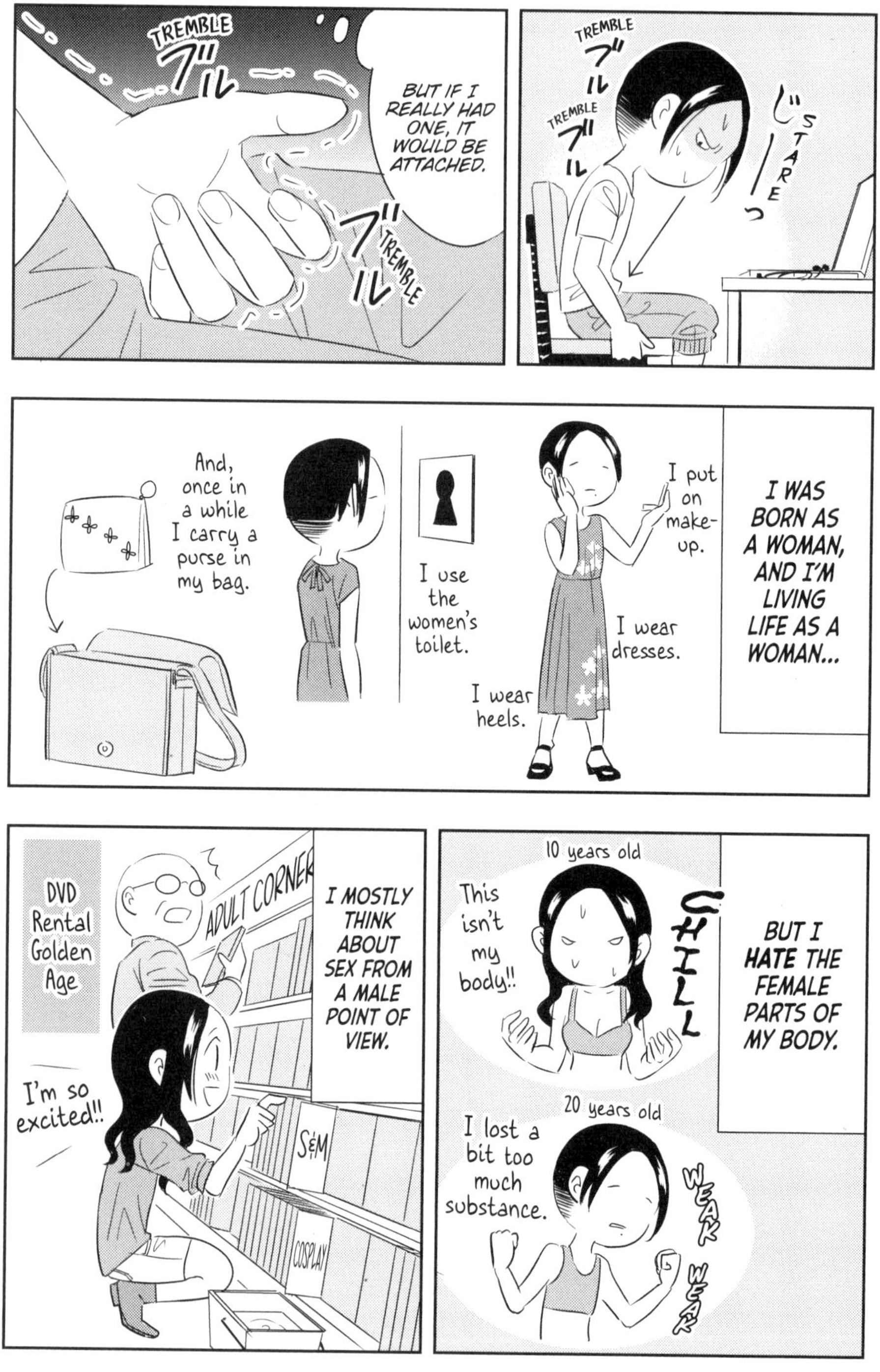
TREMBLE ブル
TREMBLE ブル
じーっ STARE
BUT IF I REALLY HAD ONE, IT WOULD BE ATTACHED.
TREMBLE ブル
TREMBLE ブル
I WAS BORN AS A WOMAN, AND I'M LIVING LIFE AS A WOMAN...
I put on make-up.
I wear dresses.
I wear heels.
I use the women's toilet.
And, once in a while I carry a purse in my bag.
BUT I HATE THE FEMALE PARTS OF MY BODY.
10 years old
CHILL
This isn't my body!!
20 years old
WEAK WEAK
I lost a bit too much substance.
I MOSTLY THINK ABOUT SEX FROM A MALE POINT OF VIEW.
ADULT CORNER
DVD Rental Golden Age
S&M
COSPLAY
I'm so excited!!

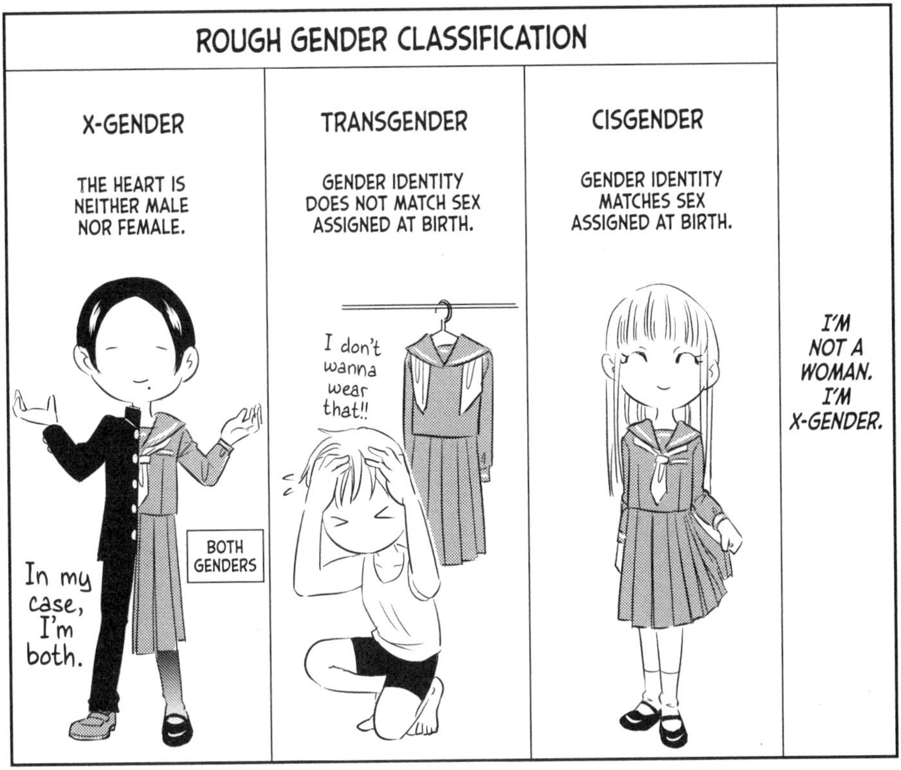
I'M NOT A WOMAN. I'M X-GENDER.
ROUGH GENDER CLASSIFICATION
CISGENDER
GENDER IDENTITY MATCHES SEX ASSIGNED AT BIRTH.
TRANSGENDER
GENDER IDENTITY DOES NOT MATCH SEX ASSIGNED AT BIRTH.
I don't wanna wear that!!
X-GENDER
THE HEART IS NEITHER MALE NOR FEMALE.
BOTH GENDERS
In my case, I'm both.

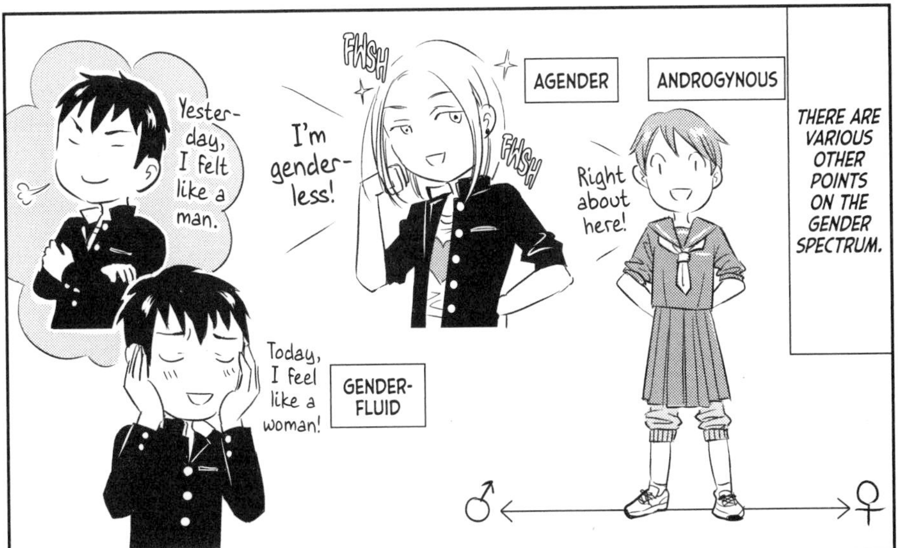
THERE ARE VARIOUS OTHER POINTS ON THE GENDER SPECTRUM.
ANDROGYNOUS
Right about here!
AGENDER
FWSH
FWSH
I'm genderless!
Yesterday, I felt like a man.
Today, I feel like a woman!
GENDER-FLUID

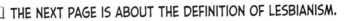

THE NEXT PAGE IS ABOUT THE DEFINITION OF LESBIANISM.

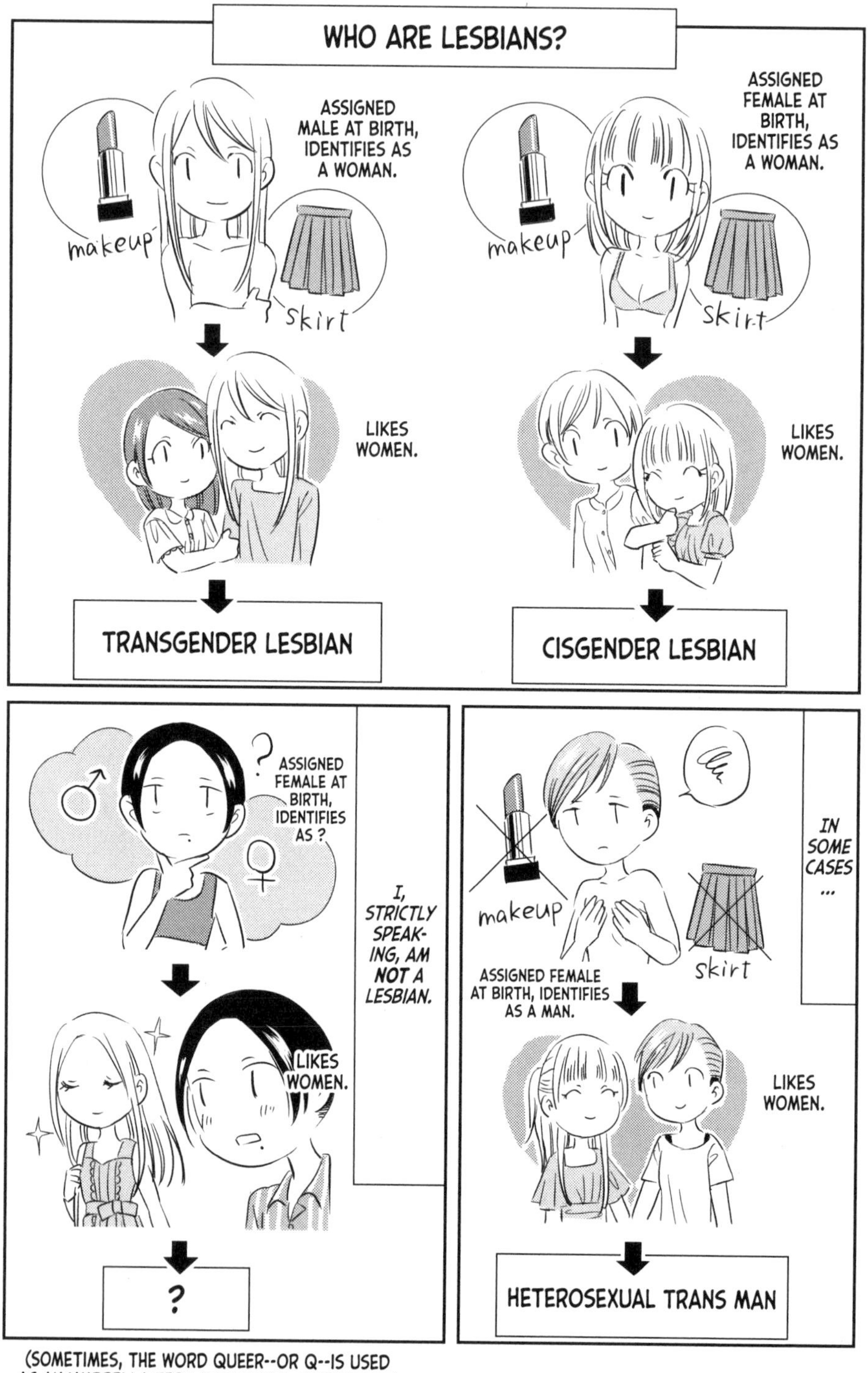
WHO ARE LESBIANS?
ASSIGNED FEMALE AT BIRTH, IDENTIFIES AS A WOMAN.
makeup
skirt
LIKES WOMEN.
CISGENDER LESBIAN
ASSIGNED MALE AT BIRTH, IDENTIFIES AS A WOMAN.
makeup
skirt
LIKES WOMEN.
TRANSGENDER LESBIAN
IN SOME CASES...
makeup
skirt
ASSIGNED FEMALE AT BIRTH, IDENTIFIES AS A MAN.
LIKES WOMEN.
HETEROSEXUAL TRANS MAN
I, STRICTLY SPEAKING, AM NOT A LESBIAN.
ASSIGNED FEMALE AT BIRTH, IDENTIFIES AS ?
LIKES WOMEN.
?

(SOMETIMES, THE WORD QUEER--OR Q--IS USED AS AN UMBRELLA TERM FOR SEXUAL MINORITIES.)

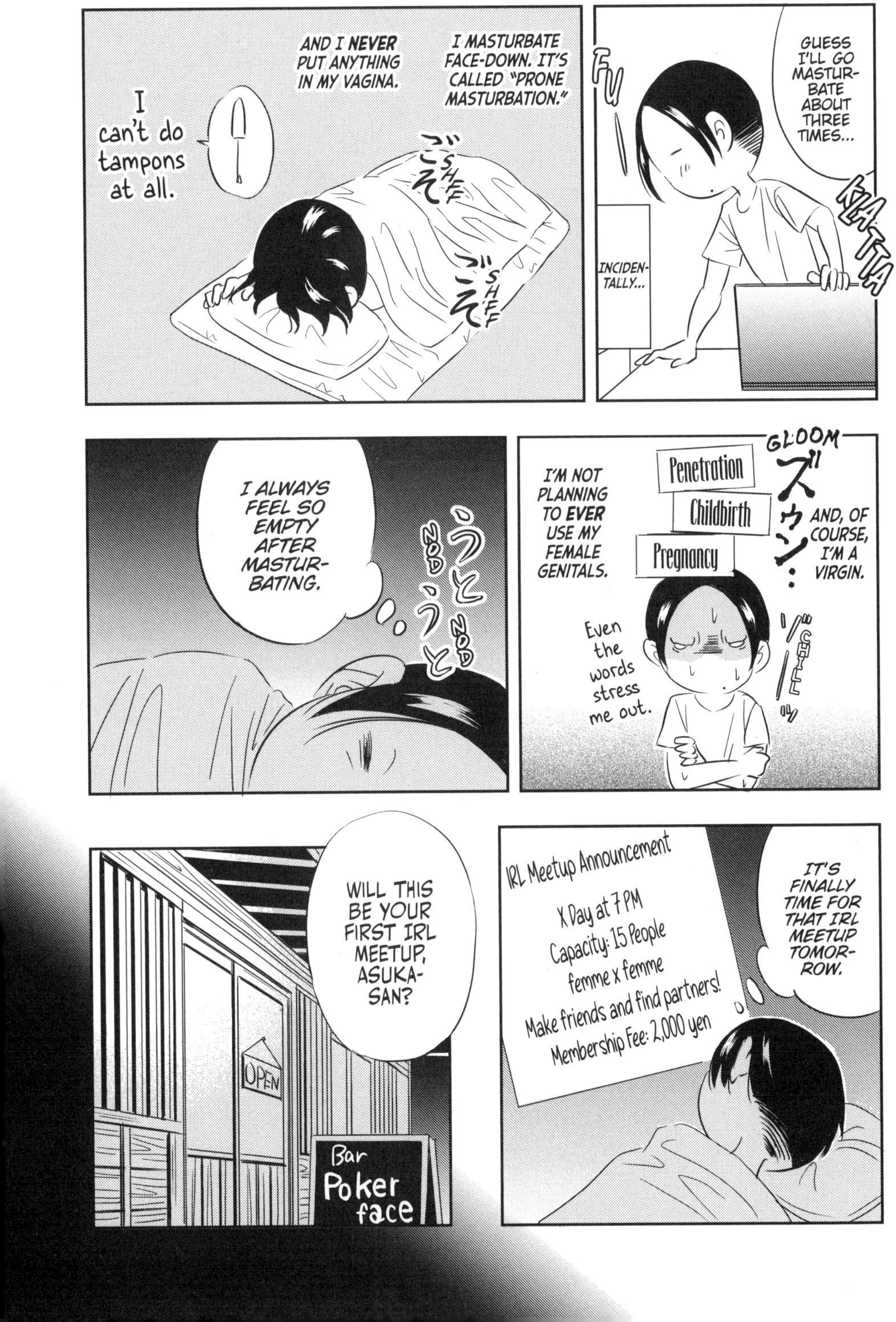
GUESS I'LL GO MASTURBATE ABOUT THREE TIMES...
FU
KATTA
INCIDENTALLY...
I MASTURBATE FACE-DOWN. IT'S CALLED "PRONE MASTURBATION."
AND I **NEVER** PUT ANYTHING IN MY VAGINA.
SHUFF
SHUFF
I can't do tampons at all.
GLOOM
ズゥン
AND, OF COURSE, I'M A VIRGIN.
Penetration
Childbirth
Pregnancy
I'M NOT PLANNING TO **EVER** USE MY FEMALE GENITALS.
CHILL
Even the words stress me out.
うと NOD うと NOD
I ALWAYS FEEL SO EMPTY AFTER MASTURBATING.
IT'S FINALLY TIME FOR THAT IRL MEETUP TOMORROW.
IRL Meetup Announcement
X Day at 7 PM
Capacity: 15 People
femme x femme
Make friends and find partners!
Membership Fee: 2,000 yen
WILL THIS BE YOUR FIRST IRL MEETUP, ASUKA-SAN?
OPEN
Bar Poker face

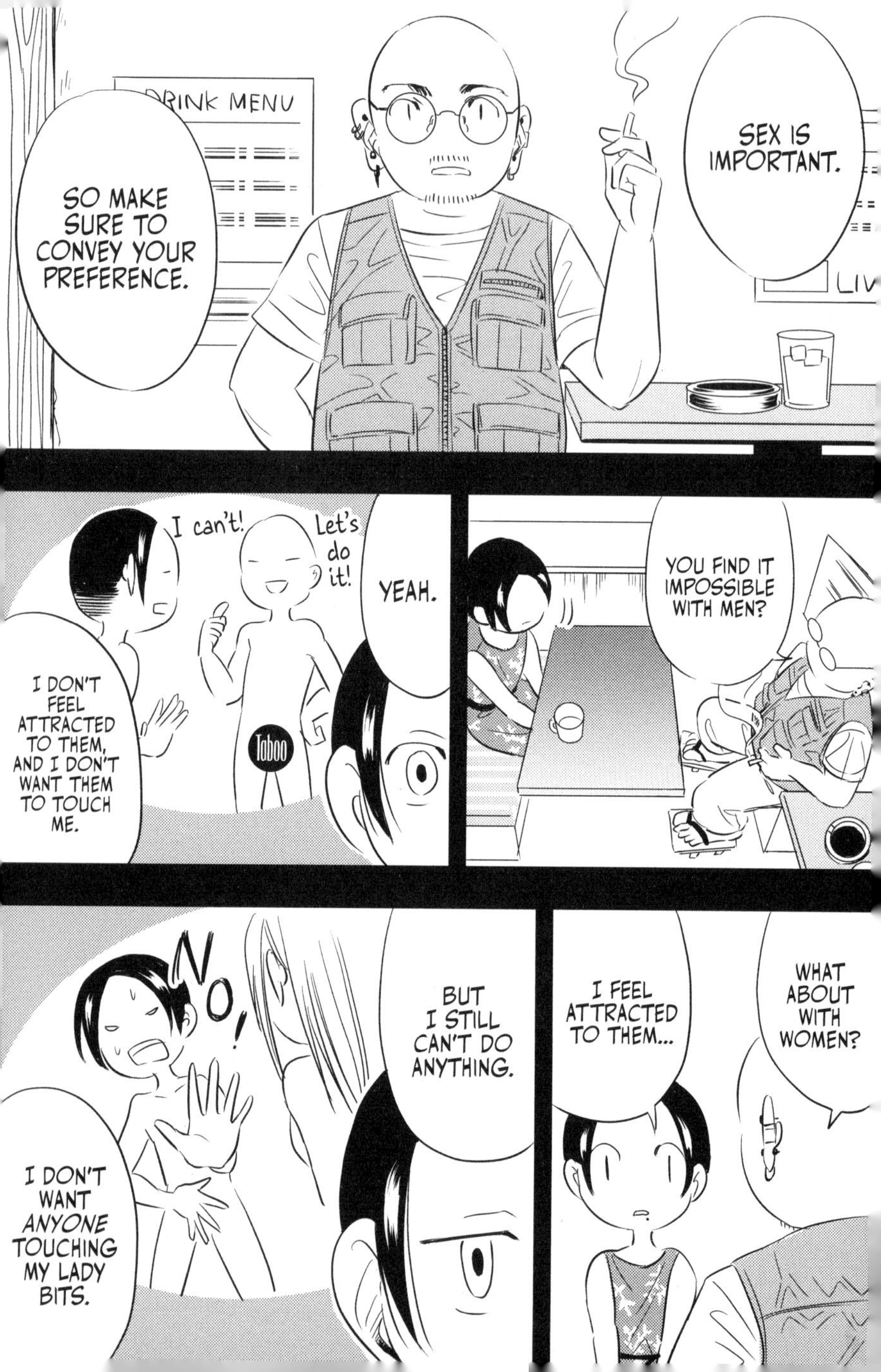

SEX IS IMPORTANT.
DRINK MENU
SO MAKE SURE TO CONVEY YOUR PREFERENCE.
YOU FIND IT IMPOSSIBLE WITH MEN?
YEAH.
Let's do it!
I can't!
Taboo
I DON'T FEEL ATTRACTED TO THEM, AND I DON'T WANT THEM TO TOUCH ME.
WHAT ABOUT WITH WOMEN?
I FEEL ATTRACTED TO THEM...
BUT I STILL CAN'T DO ANYTHING.
NO!
I DON'T WANT *ANYONE* TOUCHING MY LADY BITS.

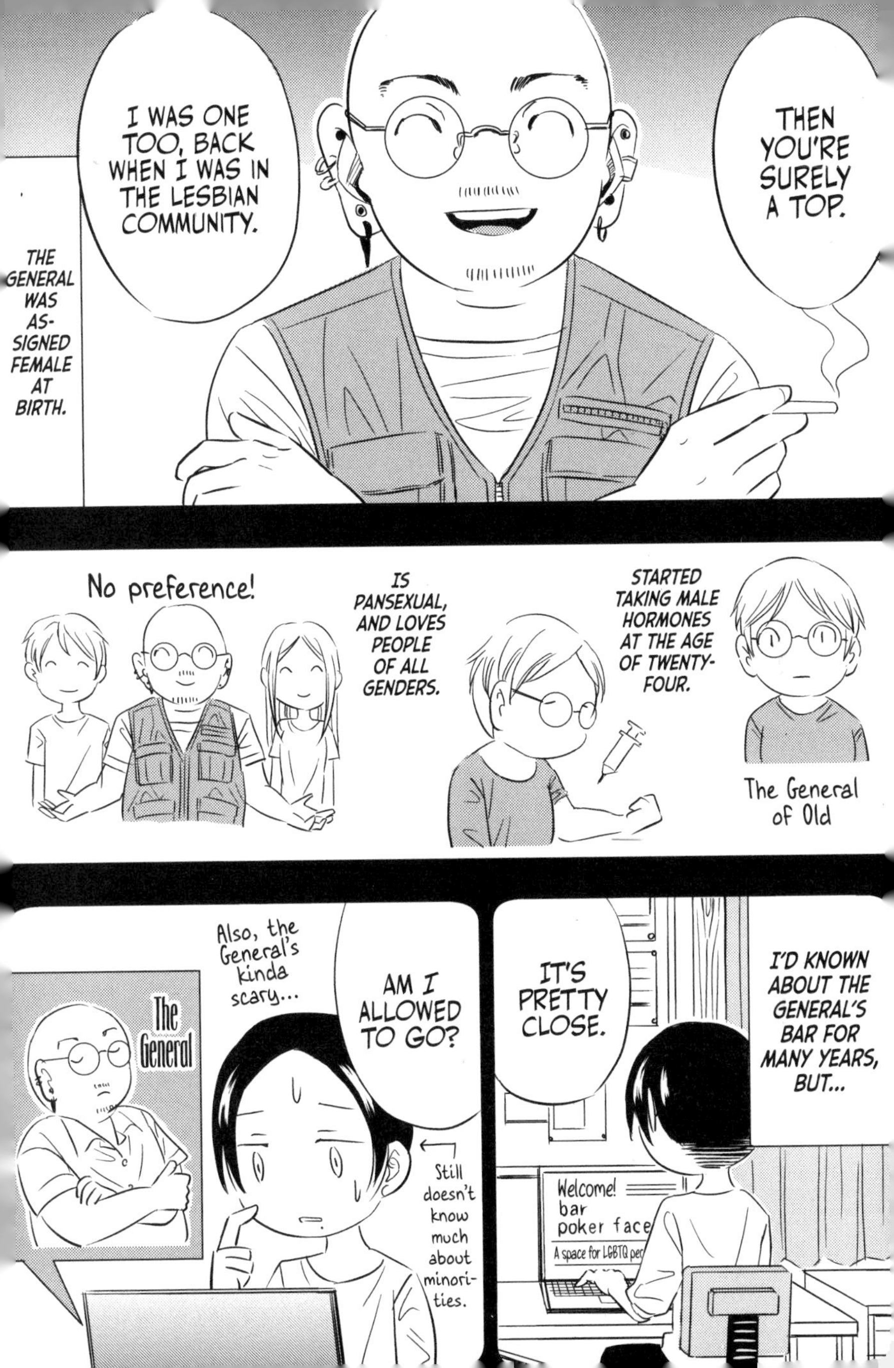
THEN YOU'RE SURELY A TOP.
I WAS ONE TOO, BACK WHEN I WAS IN THE LESBIAN COMMUNITY.
THE GENERAL WAS AS-SIGNED FEMALE AT BIRTH.
STARTED TAKING MALE HORMONES AT THE AGE OF TWENTY-FOUR.
The General of Old
IS PANSEXUAL, AND LOVES PEOPLE OF ALL GENDERS.
No preference!
I'D KNOWN ABOUT THE GENERAL'S BAR FOR MANY YEARS, BUT...
IT'S PRETTY CLOSE.
Welcome!
bar poker face
AM I ALLOWED TO GO?
Also, the General's kinda scary...
The General
Still doesn't know much about minori-ties.

bar Poker face
I SEE.
SO, YOU'RE X-GENDER, RIGHT?
The General's younger brother.
BA-DMP
ドキ
ドキ
BA-DMP
X-GENDER?
YO!
NICE TO MEET YOU!
THE GENERAL SEEMS SURPRISINGLY KIND.
AH!
I'M PLEASED TO MEET YOU, TOO!
THIS WAS ONE MONTH AGO.
IN THE PAST, TOPS WERE CALLED "BOYS"...
BUT A LOT HAS CHANGED IN THE PAST TEN YEARS.
LET ME GIVE YOU A SHORT EXPLANATION OF THESE WORDS AS THEY'RE USED HERE IN JAPAN.

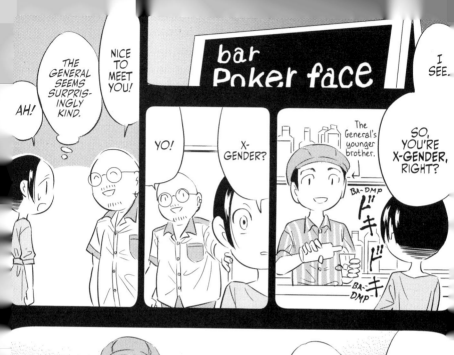

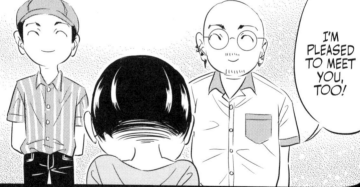

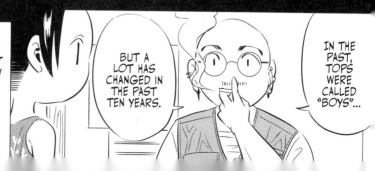

LESBIAN TERMINOLOGY

REGARDING APPEARANCE

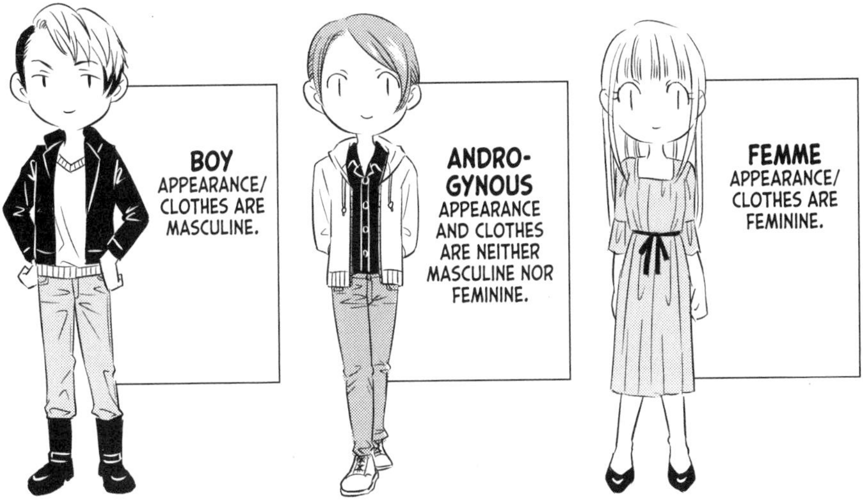

BOY
APPEARANCE/ CLOTHES ARE MASCULINE.

ANDROGYNOUS
APPEARANCE AND CLOTHES ARE NEITHER MASCULINE NOR FEMININE.

FEMME
APPEARANCE/ CLOTHES ARE FEMININE.

REGARDING SEXUALITY

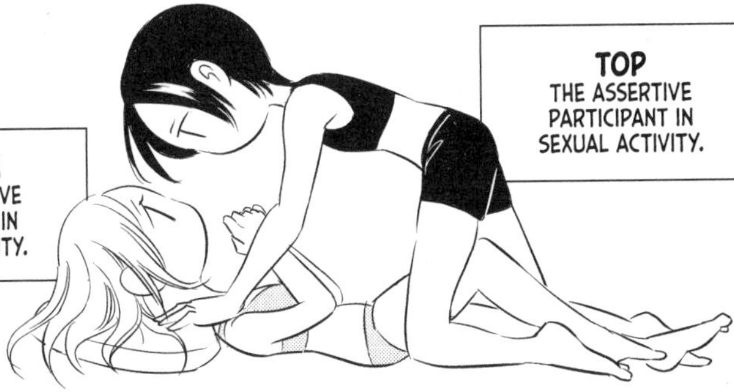

TOP
THE ASSERTIVE PARTICIPANT IN SEXUAL ACTIVITY.

BOTTOM
THE SUBMISSIVE PARTICIPANT IN SEXUAL ACTIVITY.

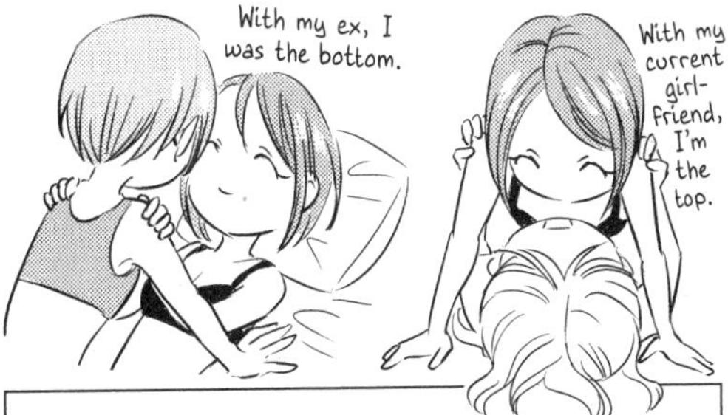
With my ex, I was the bottom.
With my current girlfriend, I'm the top.

VERSATILE
SOMEONE WHO CAN BE BOTH A TOP *AND* A BOTTOM.

TOTAL TOP
SOMEONE WHO IS ALWAYS THE TOP IN SEXUAL ACTIVITY.

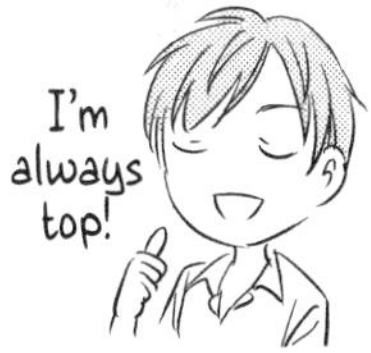
I'm always top!

TOTAL BOTTOM
SOMEONE WHO'S ALWAYS THE BOTTOM IN SEXUAL ACTIVITY.

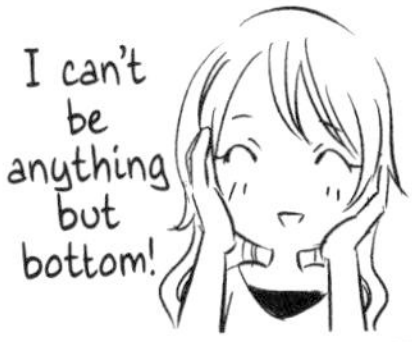
I can't be anything but bottom!

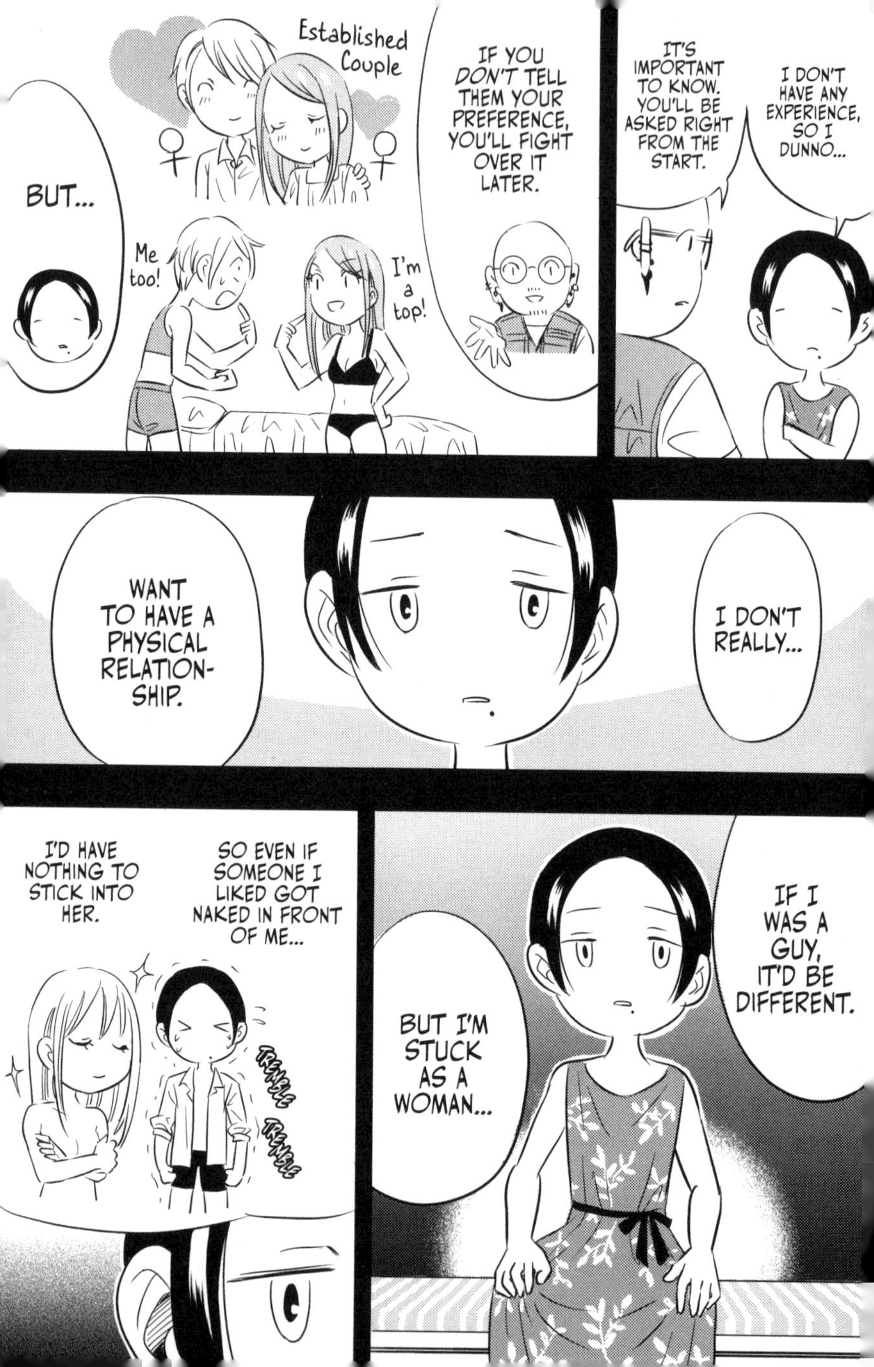
I DON'T HAVE ANY EXPERIENCE, SO I DUNNO...
IT'S IMPORTANT TO KNOW. YOU'LL BE ASKED RIGHT FROM THE START.
IF YOU DON'T TELL THEM YOUR PREFERENCE, YOU'LL FIGHT OVER IT LATER.
Established Couple
I'm a top!
Me too!
BUT...
I DON'T REALLY...
WANT TO HAVE A PHYSICAL RELATION-SHIP.
IF I WAS A GUY, IT'D BE DIFFERENT.
BUT I'M STUCK AS A WOMAN...
SO EVEN IF SOMEONE I LIKED GOT NAKED IN FRONT OF ME...
I'D HAVE NOTHING TO STICK INTO HER.
TREMBLE
TREMBLE

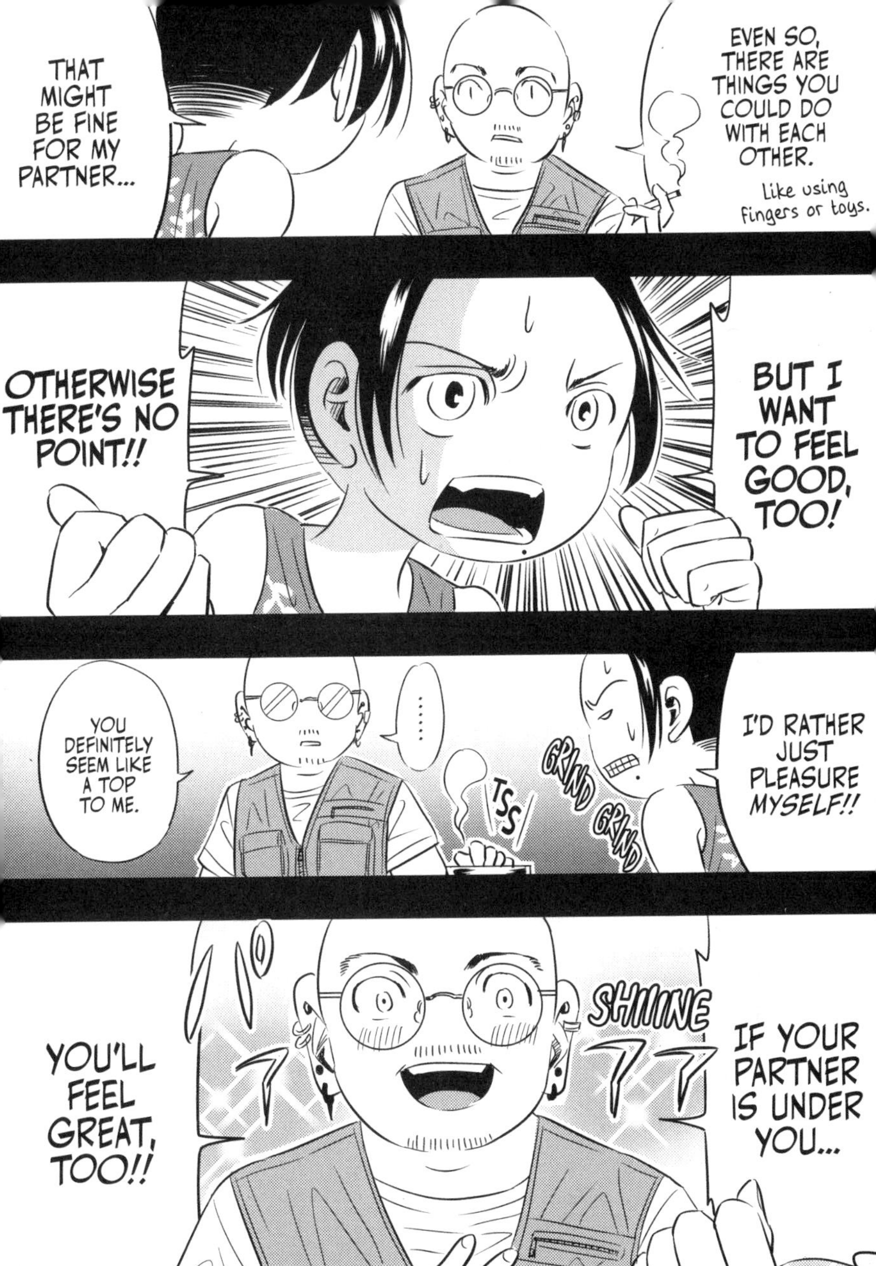
EVEN SO, THERE ARE THINGS YOU COULD DO WITH EACH OTHER.
Like using fingers or toys.
THAT MIGHT BE FINE FOR MY PARTNER...
BUT I WANT TO FEEL GOOD, TOO!
OTHERWISE THERE'S NO POINT!!
I'D RATHER JUST PLEASURE MYSELF!!
GRIND GRIND
TSS
......
YOU DEFINITELY SEEM LIKE A TOP TO ME.
SHIIINE
IF YOUR PARTNER IS UNDER YOU...
YOU'LL FEEL GREAT, TOO!!

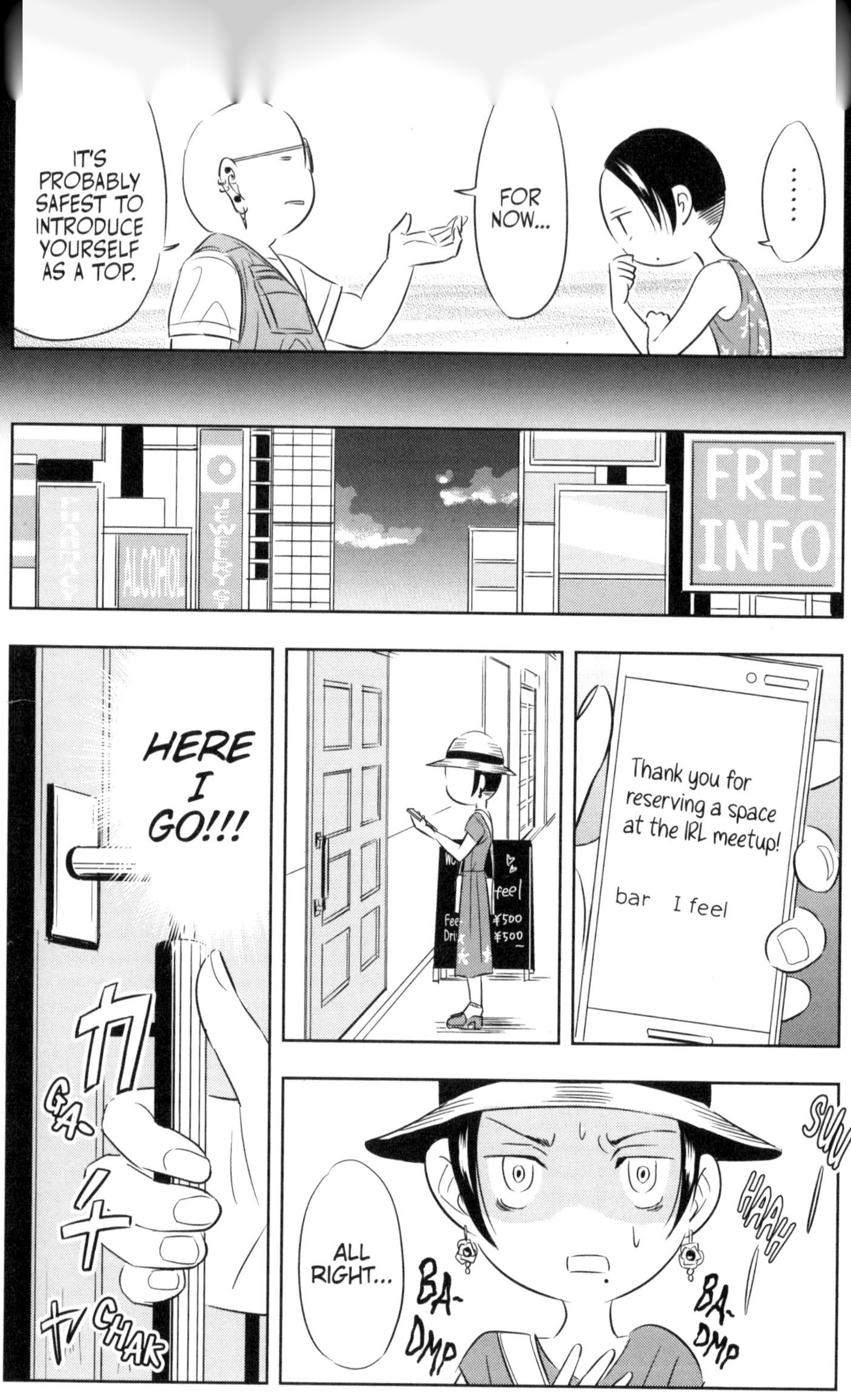
......
FOR NOW...
IT'S PROBABLY SAFEST TO INTRODUCE YOURSELF AS A TOP.
FREE INFO
JEWELRY
Thank you for reserving a space at the IRL meetup!
bar I feel
feel
¥500
¥500
SUU- HAAH-
BA-DMP
BA-DMP
ALL RIGHT...
HERE I GO!!!
カチャ
GA-CHAK

Ep. 3: The "First IRL Meetup" Story

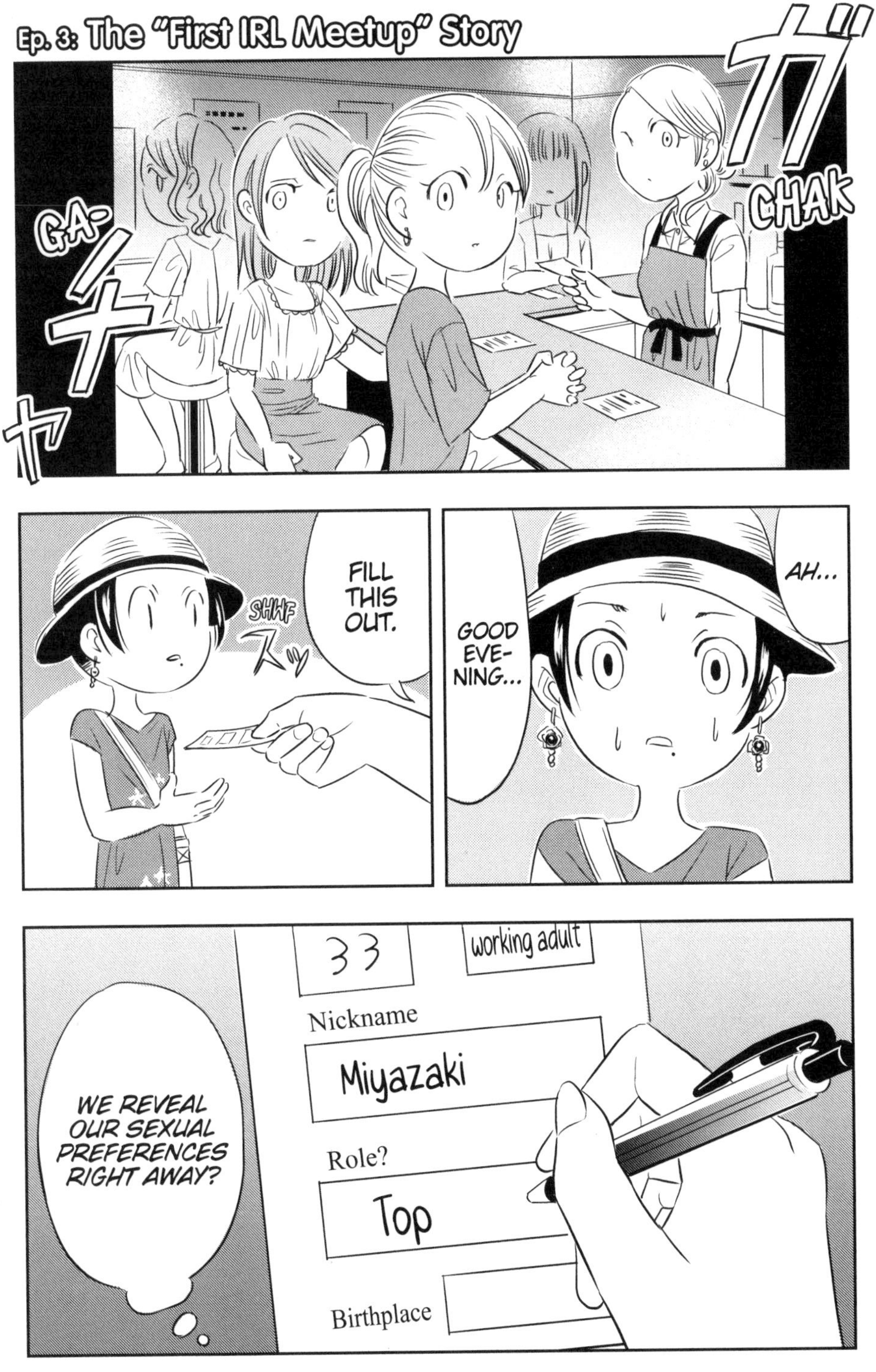
ガ
CHAK
GA-
AH...
GOOD EVE-NING...
FILL THIS OUT.
SHWF
スッ
33
working adult
Nickname
Miyazaki
Role?
Top
Birthplace
WE REVEAL OUR SEXUAL PREFERENCES RIGHT AWAY?

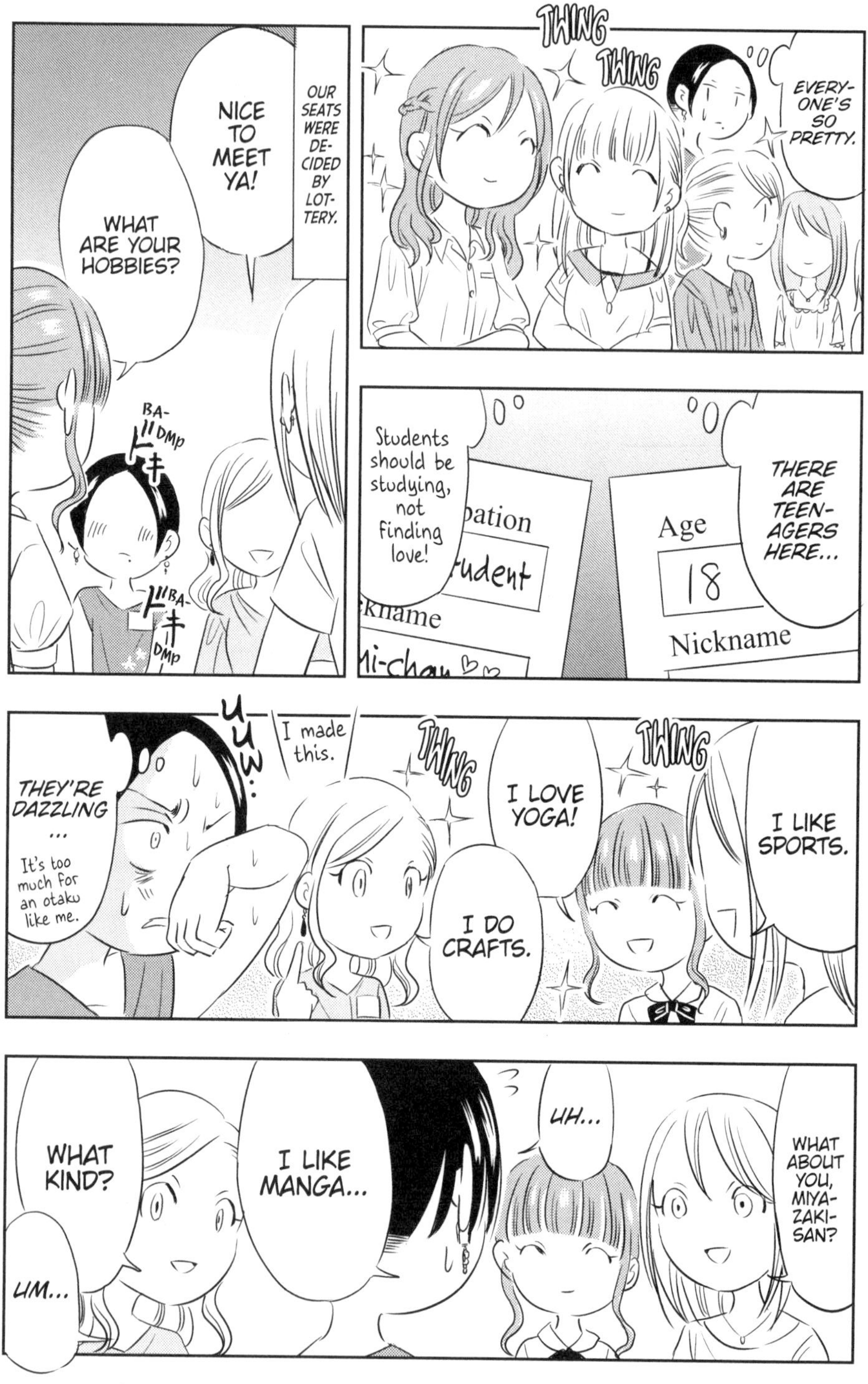
THING
THING
EVERY-ONE'S SO PRETTY.
THERE ARE TEEN-AGERS HERE...
Students should be studying, not finding love!
Age
18
Nickname
pation
tudent
kname
Mi-chan
OUR SEATS WERE DE-CIDED BY LOT-TERY.
NICE TO MEET YA!
WHAT ARE YOUR HOBBIES?
BA-DMP
BA-DMP
THING
I LIKE SPORTS.
I LOVE YOGA!
THING
I DO CRAFTS.
I made this.
UUW...
THEY'RE DAZZLING...
It's too much for an otaku like me.
WHAT ABOUT YOU, MIYA-ZAKI-SAN?
UH...
I LIKE MANGA...
WHAT KIND?
UM...

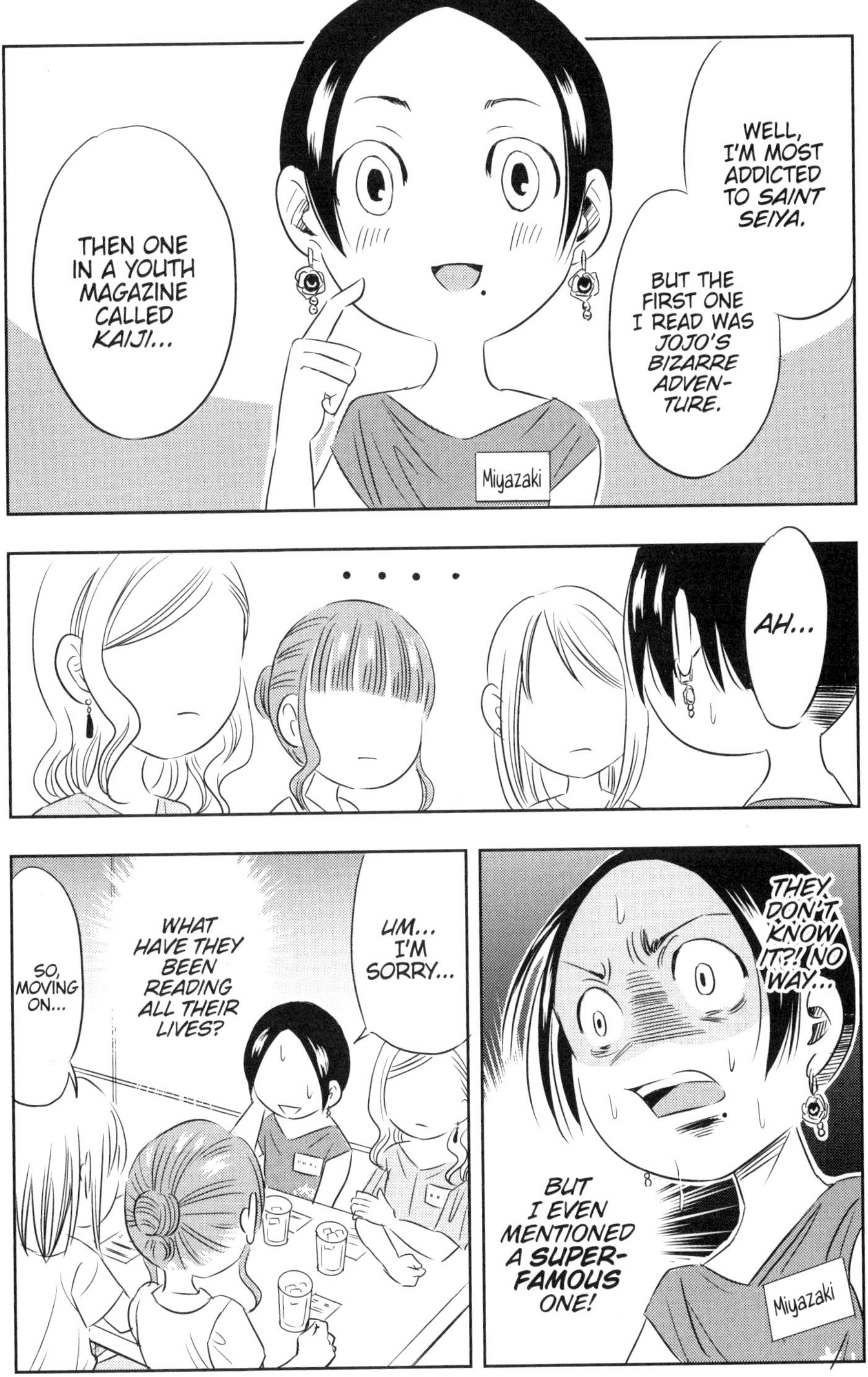
WELL, I'M MOST ADDICTED TO SAINT SEIYA.
BUT THE FIRST ONE I READ WAS JOJO'S BIZARRE ADVEN-TURE.
THEN ONE IN A YOUTH MAGAZINE CALLED KAIJI...
Miyazaki
AH...
THEY DON'T KNOW IT?! NO WAY...
BUT I EVEN MENTIONED A SUPER-FAMOUS ONE!
Miyazaki
UM... I'M SORRY...
WHAT HAVE THEY BEEN READING ALL THEIR LIVES?
SO, MOVING ON...

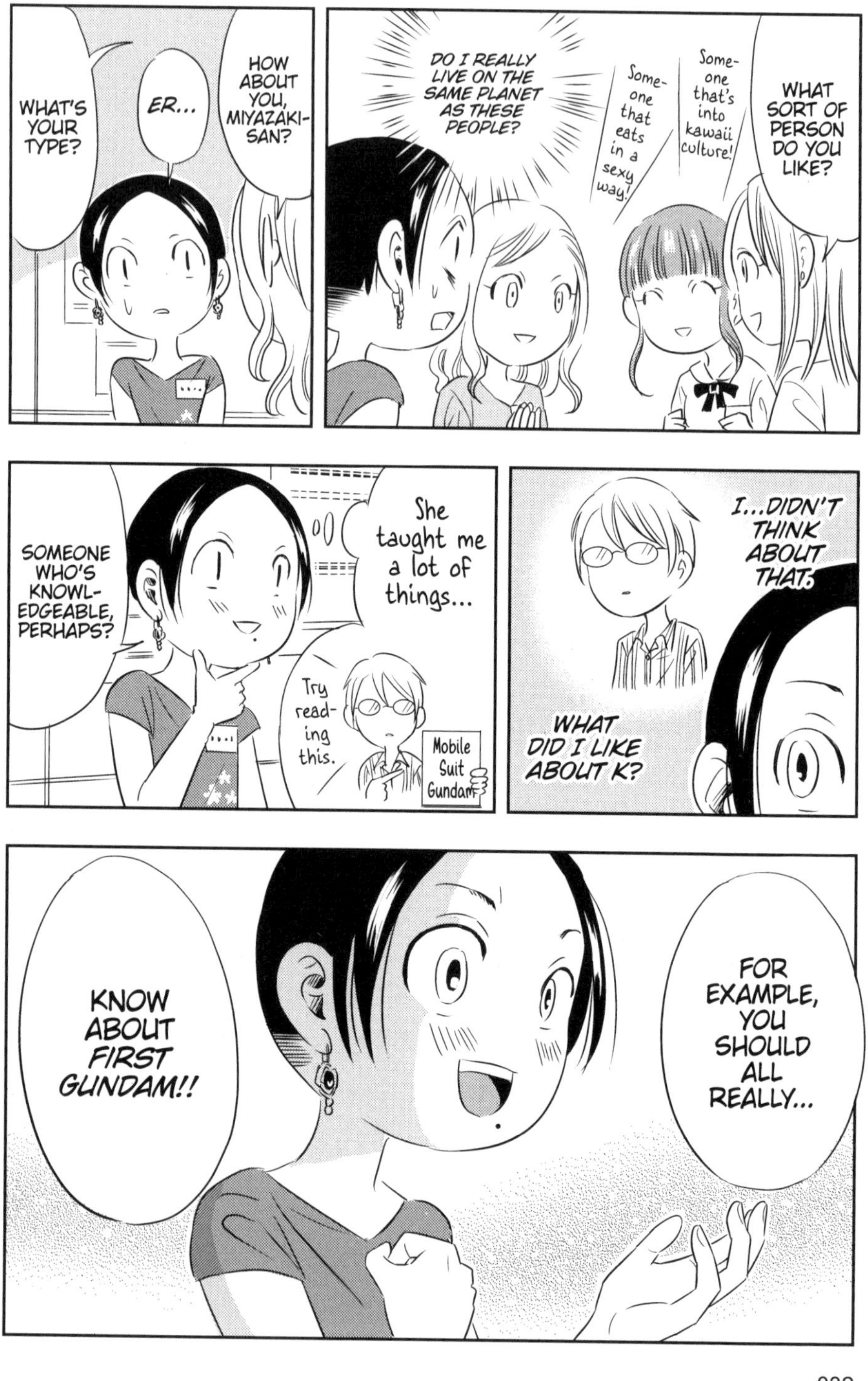
WHAT SORT OF PERSON DO YOU LIKE?
Someone that's into kawaii culture!
Someone that eats in a sexy way!
DO I REALLY LIVE ON THE SAME PLANET AS THESE PEOPLE?
HOW ABOUT YOU, MIYAZAKI-SAN?
ER...
WHAT'S YOUR TYPE?
I...DIDN'T THINK ABOUT THAT.
WHAT DID I LIKE ABOUT K?
She taught me a lot of things...
SOMEONE WHO'S KNOWLEDGEABLE, PERHAPS?
Try reading this.
Mobile Suit Gundam
FOR EXAMPLE, YOU SHOULD ALL REALLY...
KNOW ABOUT FIRST GUNDAM!!

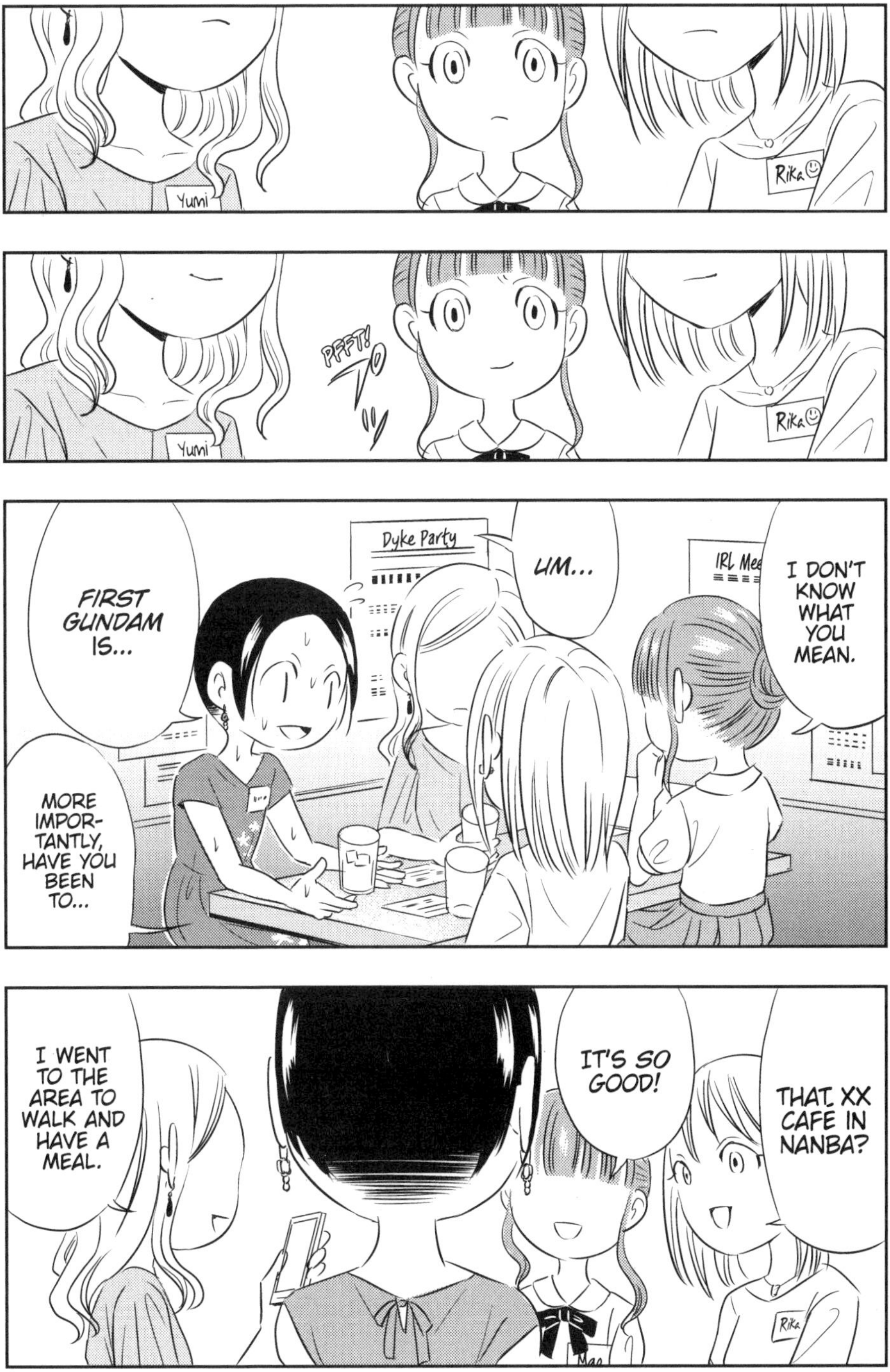
Rika
Yumi
Rika
PFFT!
Yumi
Dyke Party
I DON'T KNOW WHAT YOU MEAN.
UM...
FIRST GUNDAM IS...
MORE IMPORTANTLY, HAVE YOU BEEN TO...
THAT XX CAFE IN NANBA?
IT'S SO GOOD!
I WENT TO THE AREA TO WALK AND HAVE A MEAL.
Rika

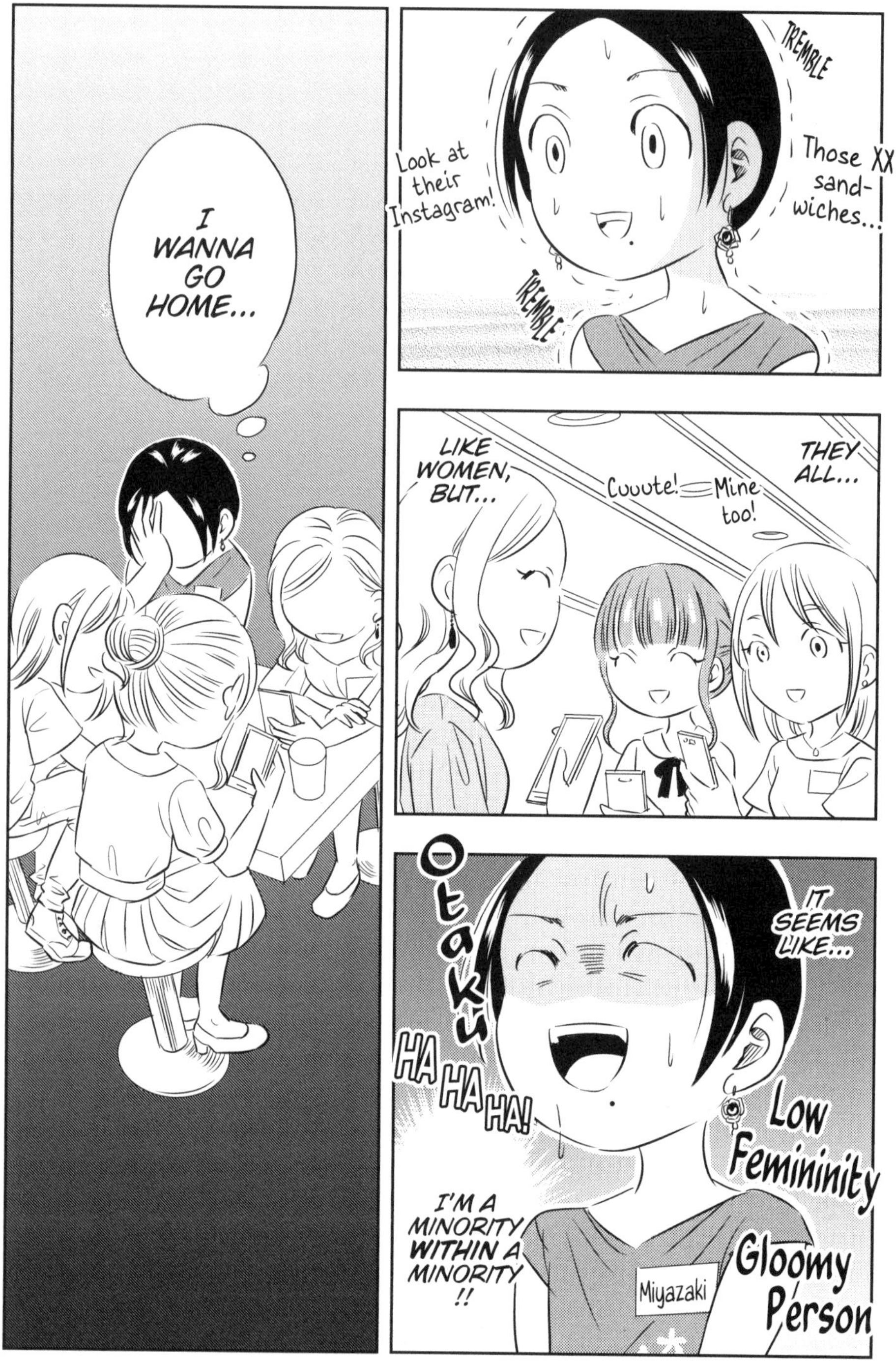
TREMBLE
Those XX sandwiches...
Look at their Instagram!
TREMBLE
THEY ALL...
Mine too!
Cuuute!
LIKE WOMEN, BUT...
IT SEEMS LIKE...
Otaku
HA HA HA!
Low Femininity
Gloomy Person
Miyazaki
I'M A MINORITY WITHIN A MINORITY!!
I WANNA GO HOME...

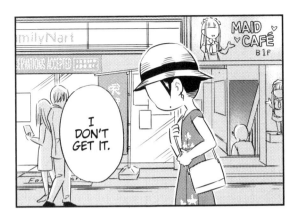

bar I feel
THE IRL MEETUP IS OVER!
Women Only
bar I feel
Fee: 500 ¥
MAID CAFÉ
B1F
I DON'T GET IT.
Alcohol
WHY DID WE TALK FOR FIFTEEN MINUTES ABOUT TRENDY-LOOKING DRINKS?
IS IT REALLY *THAT* MUCH FUN TO POST PHOTOS OF THEM ONLINE?
GAME
BUBBLE TEA WON'T LAST THE YEAR...
BUT *GUNDAM* HAS LASTED FOR FORTY YEARS!
THE ARCADE.
I USED TO COME HERE WITH K.

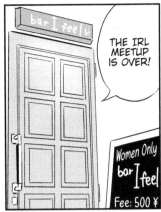

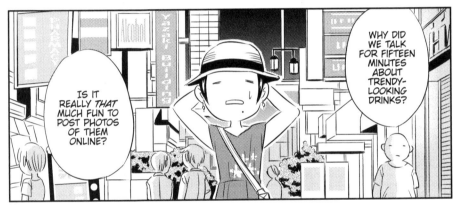

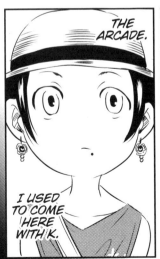

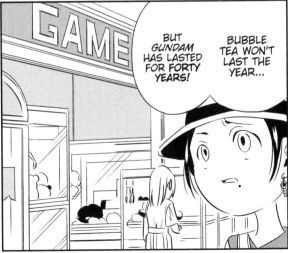

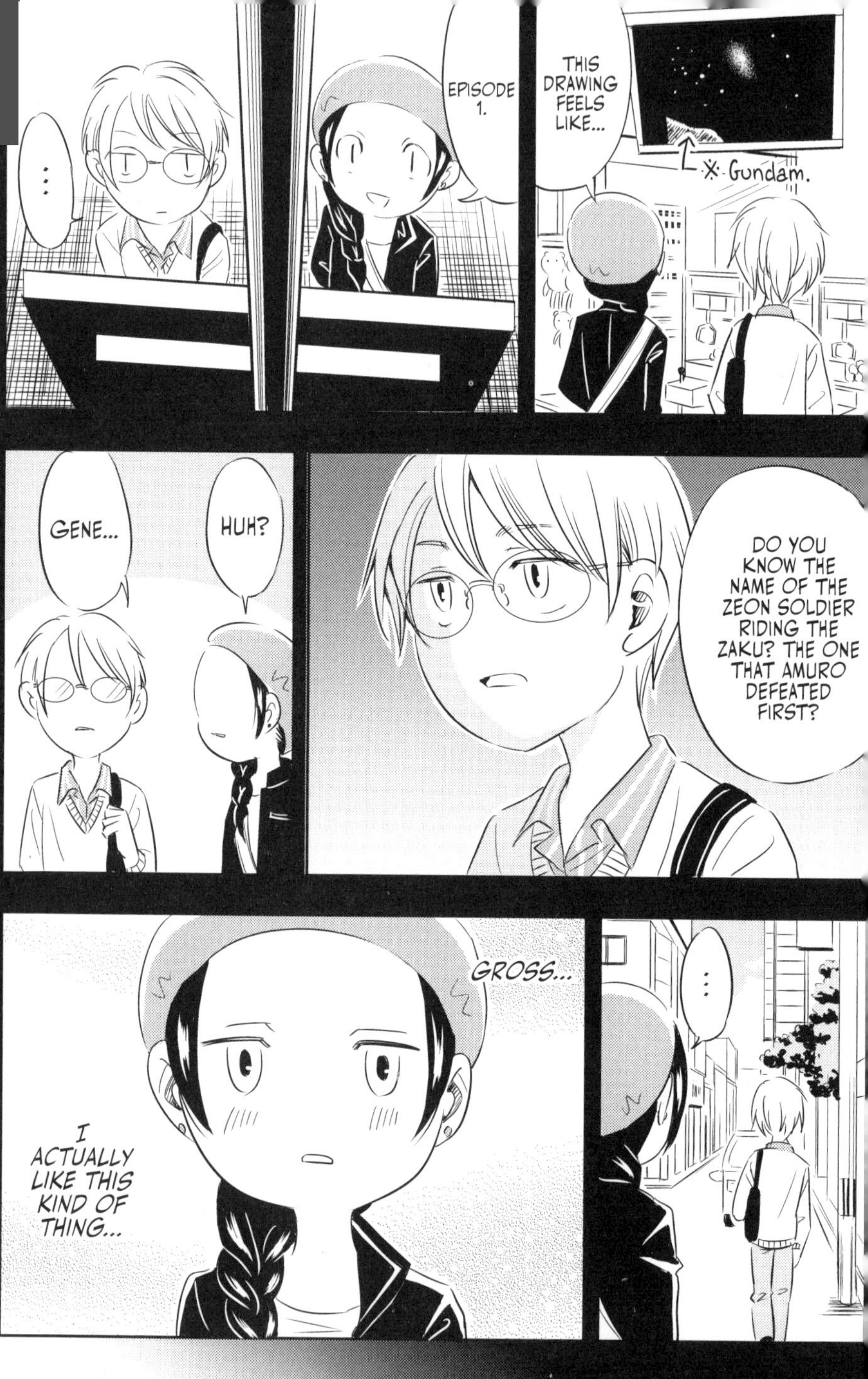
THIS DRAWING FEELS LIKE...
※ Gundam.
EPISODE 1.
...
DO YOU KNOW THE NAME OF THE ZEON SOLDIER RIDING THE ZAKU? THE ONE THAT AMURO DEFEATED FIRST?
HUH?
GENE...
...
GROSS...
I ACTUALLY LIKE THIS KIND OF THING...

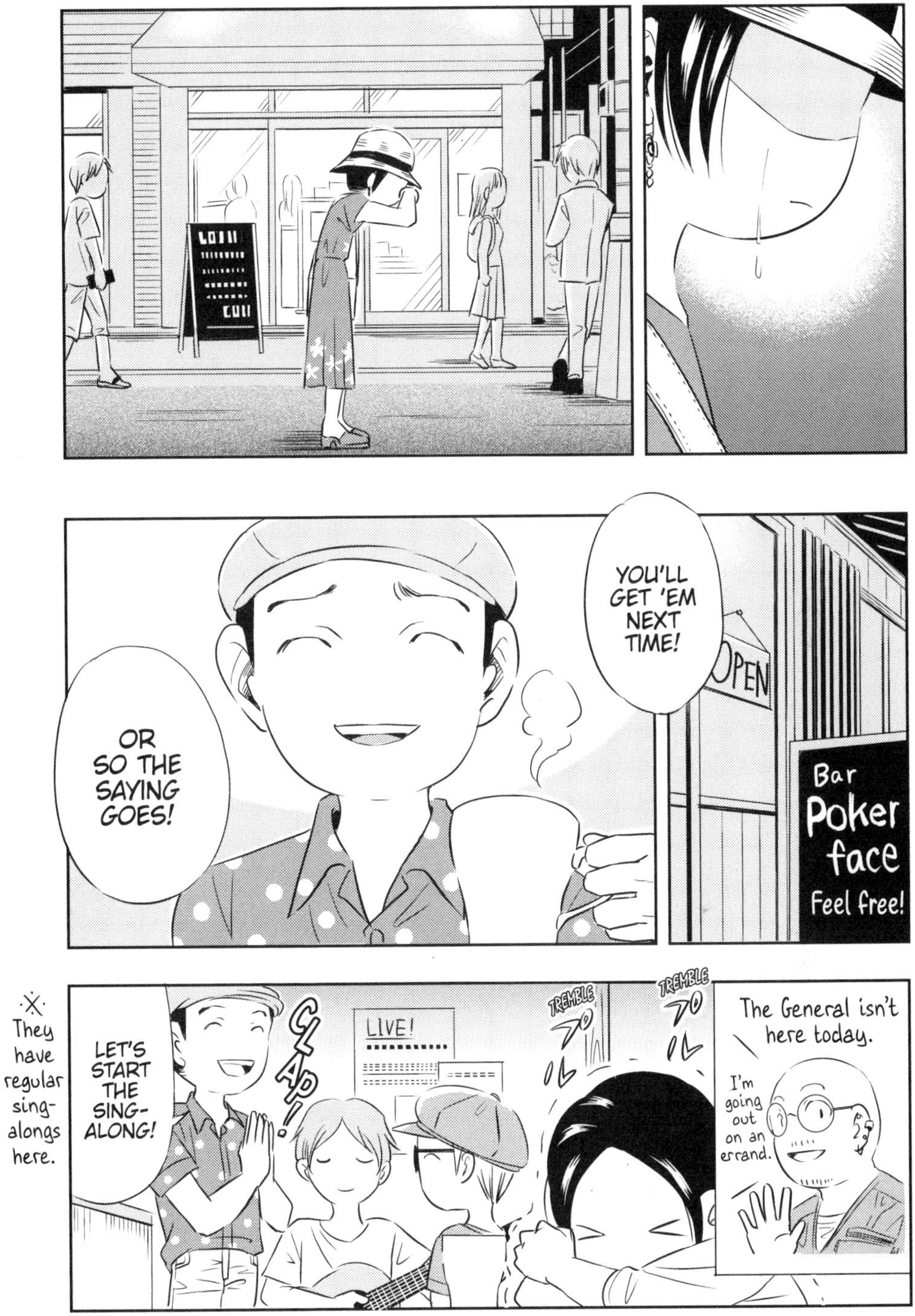
YOU'LL GET 'EM NEXT TIME!
OR SO THE SAYING GOES!
OPEN
Bar Poker face Feel free!
The General isn't here today.
I'm going out on an errand.
TREMBLE
TREMBLE
CLAP!
LIVE!
LET'S START THE SING-ALONG!
※ They have regular sing-alongs here.

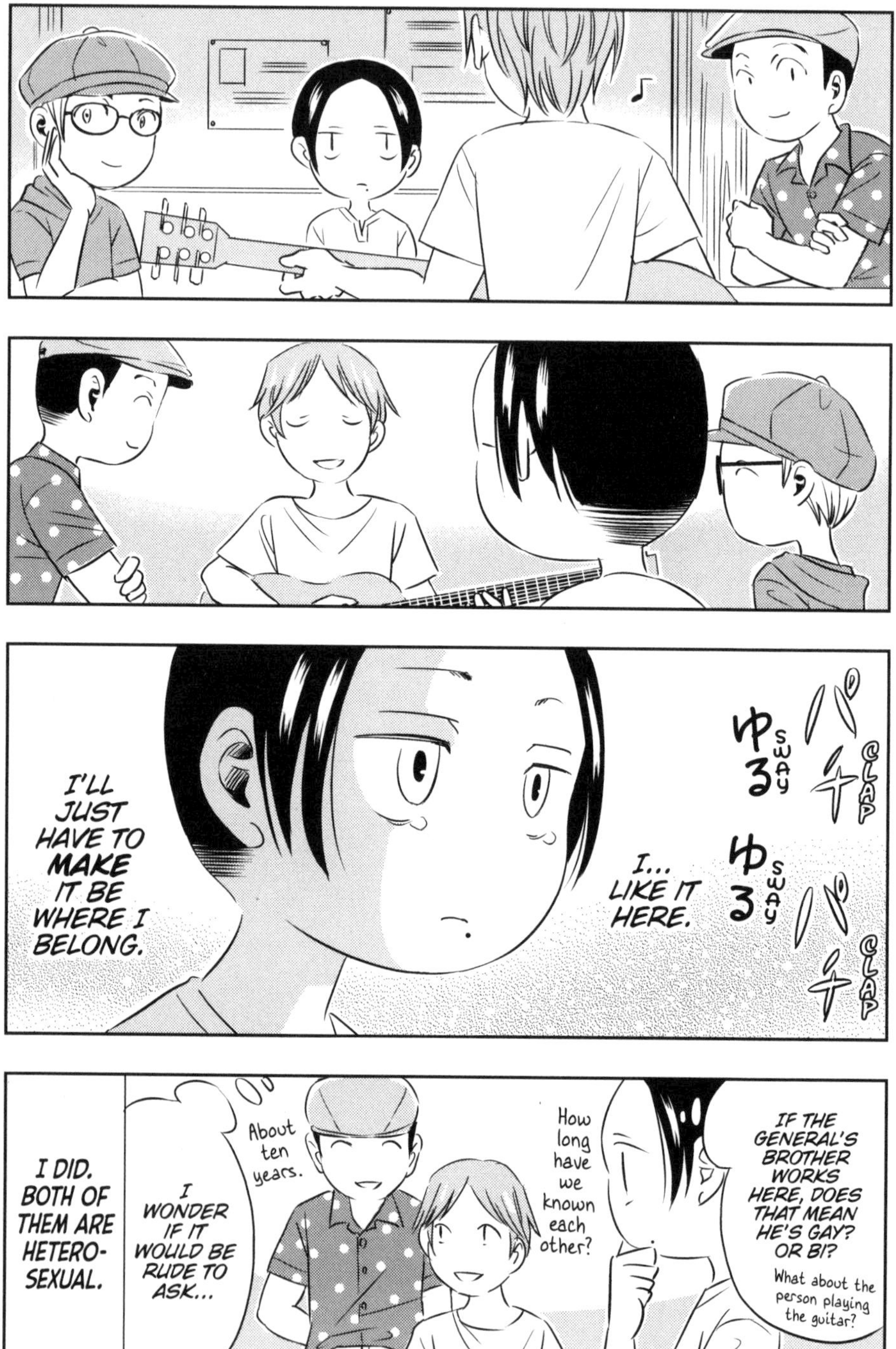
パチ CLAP
パチ CLAP
ゆる SWAY
ゆる SWAY
I... LIKE IT HERE.
I'LL JUST HAVE TO MAKE IT BE WHERE I BELONG.
IF THE GENERAL'S BROTHER WORKS HERE, DOES THAT MEAN HE'S GAY? OR BI?
What about the person playing the guitar?
How long have we known each other?
About ten years.
I WONDER IF IT WOULD BE RUDE TO ASK...
I DID. BOTH OF THEM ARE HETERO-SEXUAL.

Ep. 4: The "Watching Porn Because I Can't *Do It*" Story

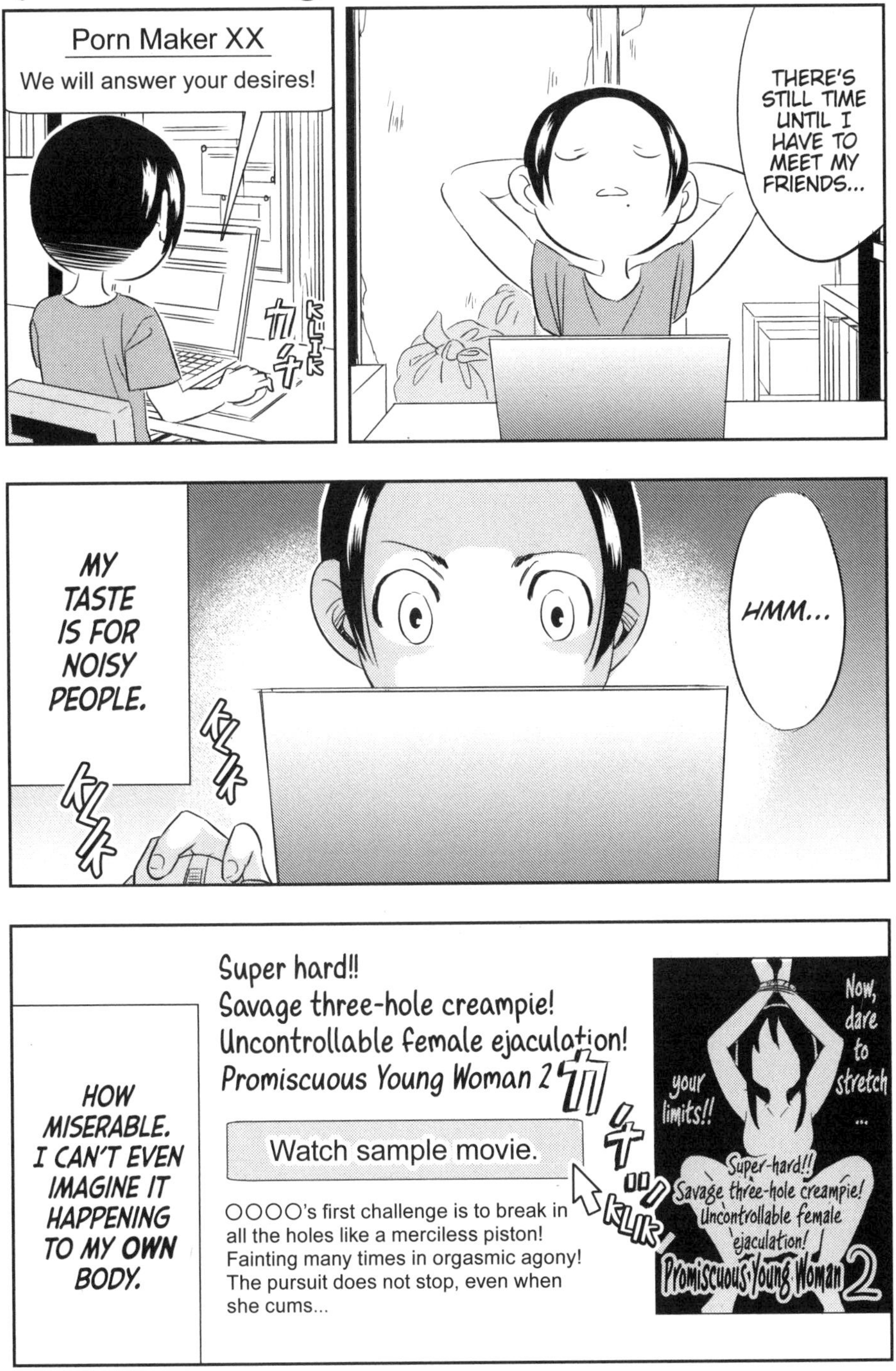
THERE'S STILL TIME UNTIL I HAVE TO MEET MY FRIENDS...
Porn Maker XX
We will answer your desires!
KLIK
HMM...
MY TASTE IS FOR NOISY PEOPLE.
KLIK
KLIK
Now, dare to stretch your limits!!
Super-hard!! Savage three-hole creampie! Uncontrollable female ejaculation!
Promiscuous Young Woman 2
KLIK
Super hard!!
Savage three-hole creampie!
Uncontrollable female ejaculation!
Promiscuous Young Woman 2
Watch sample movie.
○○○○'s first challenge is to break in all the holes like a merciless piston! Fainting many times in orgasmic agony! The pursuit does not stop, even when she cums...
HOW MISERABLE. I CAN'T EVEN IMAGINE IT HAPPENING TO MY OWN BODY.

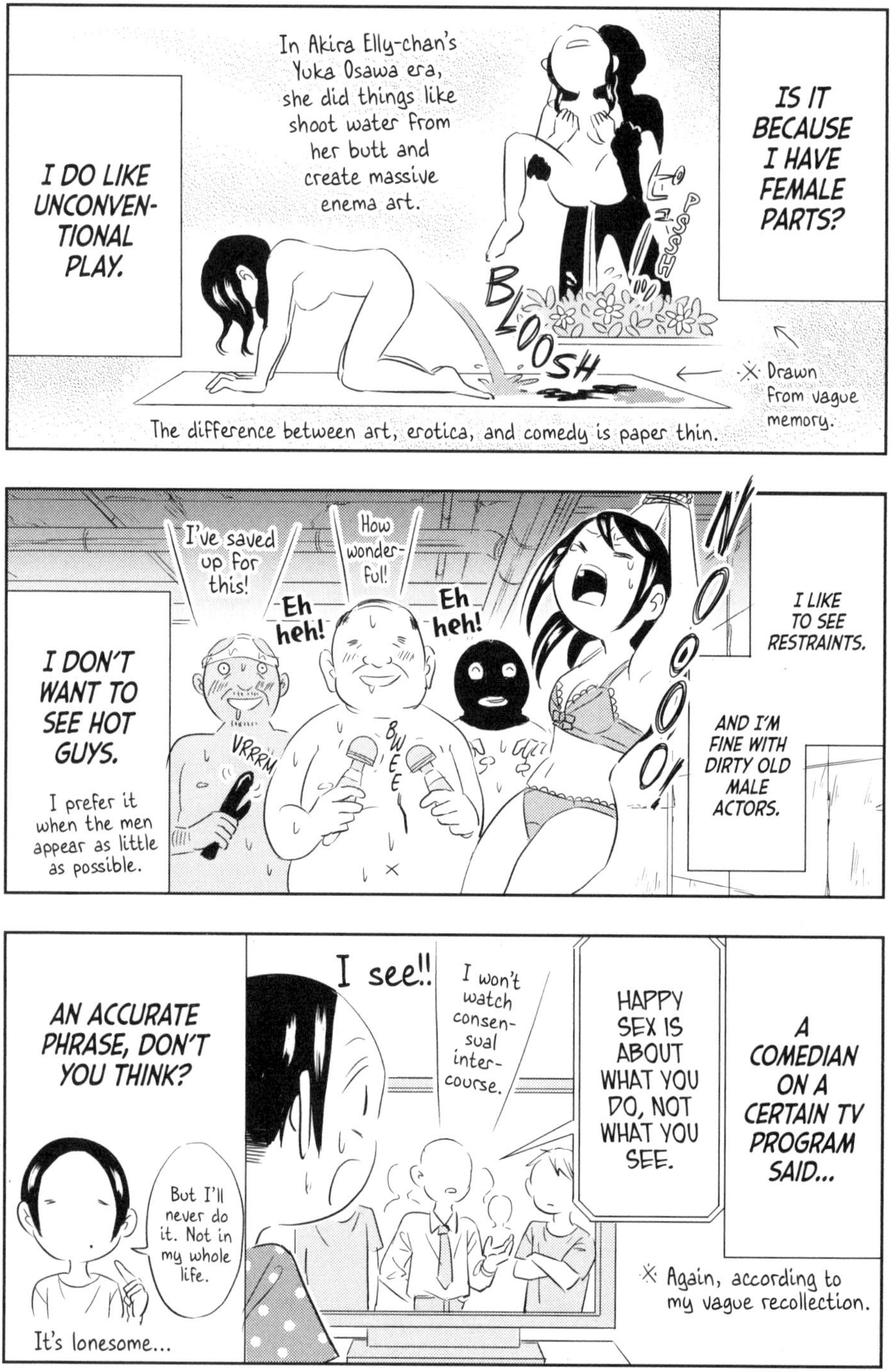
IS IT BECAUSE I HAVE FEMALE PARTS?
In Akira Elly-chan's Yuka Osawa era, she did things like shoot water from her butt and create massive enema art.
PSSSH
BLOOSH
I DO LIKE UNCONVEN-TIONAL PLAY.
※ Drawn from vague memory.
The difference between art, erotica, and comedy is paper thin.
I LIKE TO SEE RESTRAINTS.
AND I'M FINE WITH DIRTY OLD MALE ACTORS.
NOOOOOO!
Eh heh!
How wonder-ful!
Eh heh!
I've saved up for this!
BWEE
VRRRM
I DON'T WANT TO SEE HOT GUYS.
I prefer it when the men appear as little as possible.
A COMEDIAN ON A CERTAIN TV PROGRAM SAID...
HAPPY SEX IS ABOUT WHAT YOU DO, NOT WHAT YOU SEE.
I won't watch consen-sual inter-course.
I see!!
※ Again, according to my vague recollection.
AN ACCURATE PHRASE, DON'T YOU THINK?
But I'll never do it. Not in my whole life.
It's lonesome...

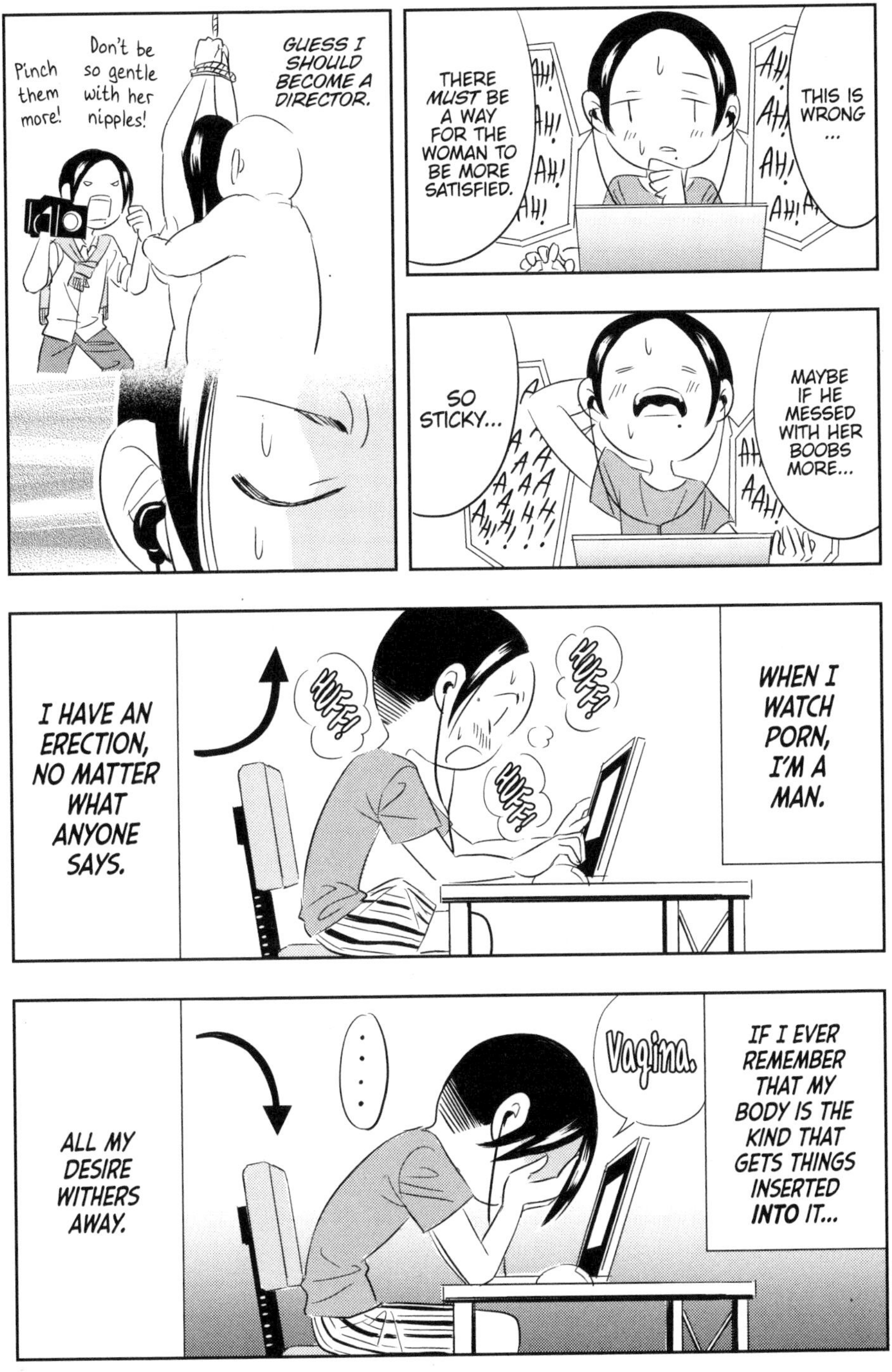
THIS IS WRONG ...
AH! AH! AH! AH! AH!
THERE MUST BE A WAY FOR THE WOMAN TO BE MORE SATISFIED.
AH! AH! AH! AH!
MAYBE IF HE MESSED WITH HER BOOBS MORE...
AH! AAH!
SO STICKY...
GUESS I SHOULD BECOME A DIRECTOR.
Don't be so gentle with her nipples!
Pinch them more!
WHEN I WATCH PORN, I'M A MAN.
HUFF!
HUFF!
HUFF!
I HAVE AN ERECTION, NO MATTER WHAT ANYONE SAYS.
IF I EVER REMEMBER THAT MY BODY IS THE KIND THAT GETS THINGS INSERTED INTO IT...
Vagina.
....
ALL MY DESIRE WITHERS AWAY.

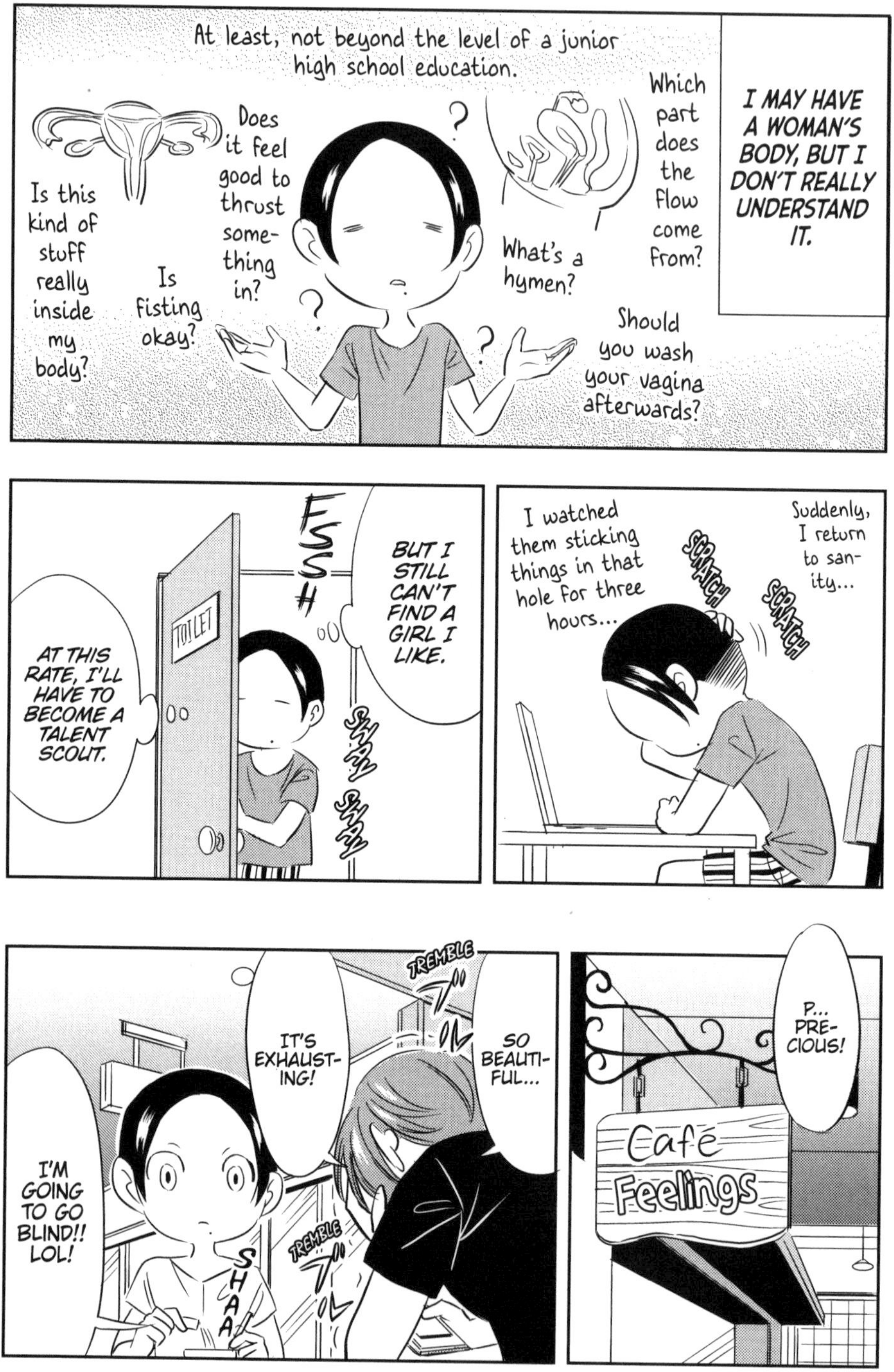
I MAY HAVE A WOMAN'S BODY, BUT I DON'T REALLY UNDERSTAND IT.
At least, not beyond the level of a junior high school education.
Which part does the flow come from?
Does it feel good to thrust some-thing in?
What's a hymen?
Is this kind of stuff really inside my body?
Is fisting okay?
Should you wash your vagina afterwards?
Suddenly, I return to san-ity...
I watched them sticking things in that hole for three hours...
SCRATCH
SCRATCH
FSSH
BUT I STILL CAN'T FIND A GIRL I LIKE.
SWAY SWAY
TOILET
AT THIS RATE, I'LL HAVE TO BECOME A TALENT SCOUT.
P... PRE-CIOUS!
Cafe
Feelings
SO BEAUTI-FUL...
TREMBLE
IT'S EXHAUST-ING!
TREMBLE
SHAA
I'M GOING TO GO BLIND!! LOL!

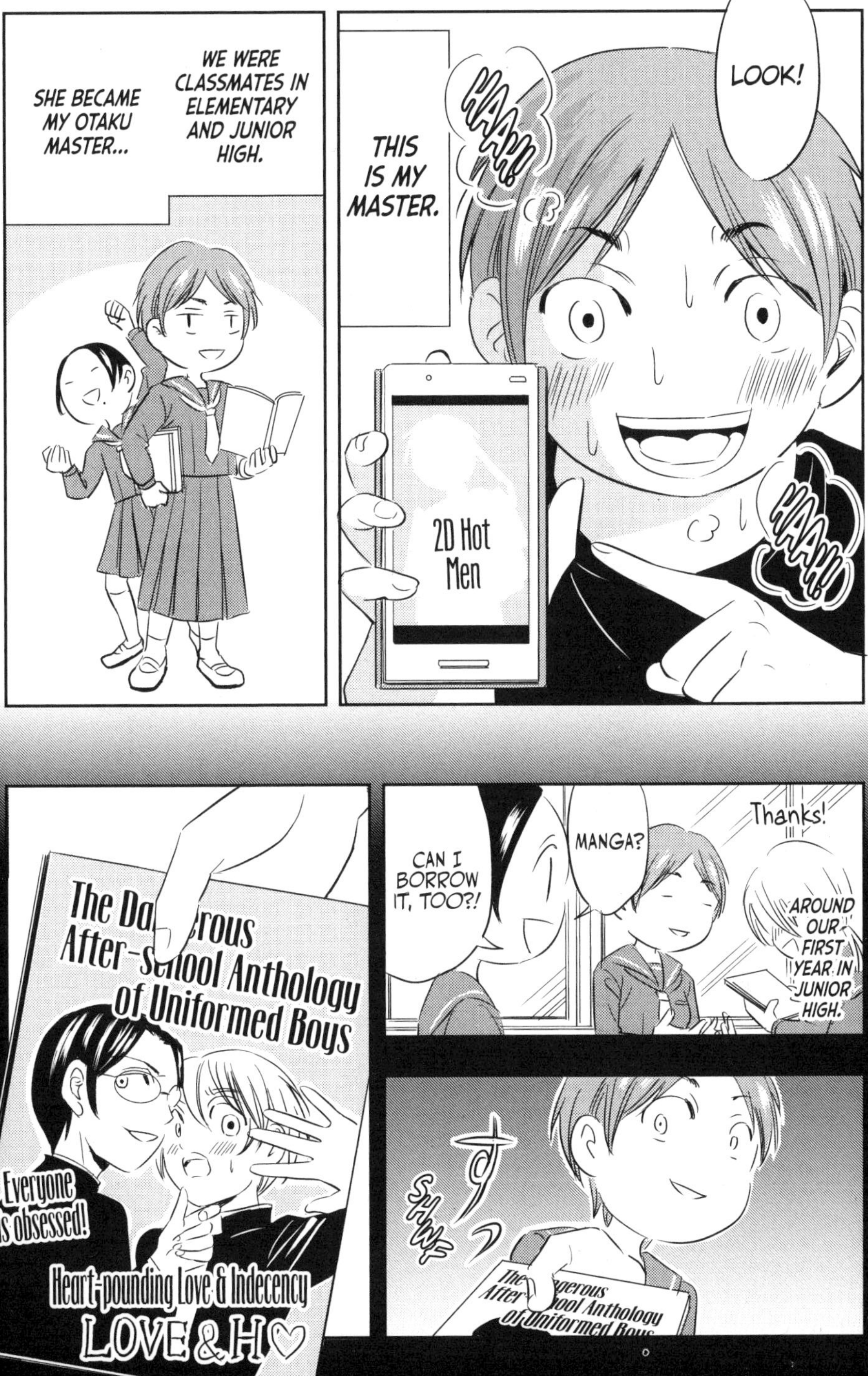
LOOK!
HAAAH
THIS IS MY MASTER.
2D Hot Men
HAAAH
WE WERE CLASSMATES IN ELEMENTARY AND JUNIOR HIGH.
SHE BECAME MY OTAKU MASTER...
Thanks!
AROUND OUR FIRST YEAR IN JUNIOR HIGH.
MANGA?
CAN I BORROW IT, TOO?!
SHWF
of Uniformed Boys
The Da gerous
After-s ool Anthology
of Uniformed Boys
Everyone is obsessed!
Heart-pounding Love & Indecency
LOVE & H♡

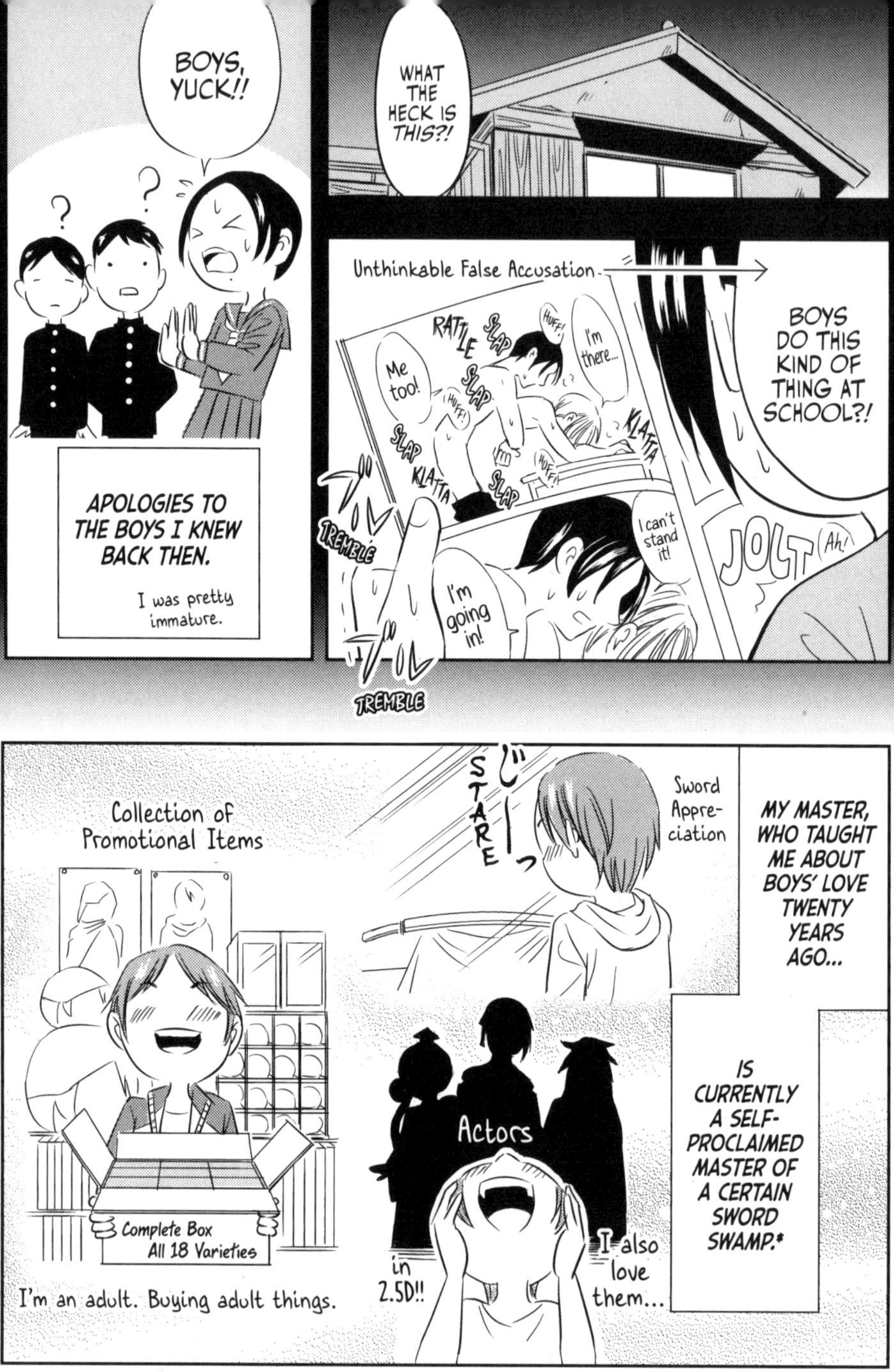
WHAT THE HECK IS THIS?!
BOYS DO THIS KIND OF THING AT SCHOOL?!
JOLT
(Ah!)
Unthinkable False Accusation
I'm there...
(HUFF!)
SLAP
RATTLE
SLAP
Me too!
(HUFF!)
SLAP
KLATTA
(HUFF!)
SLAP
KLATTA
SLAP
I can't stand it!
I'm going in!
TREMBLE
TREMBLE
BOYS, YUCK!!
APOLOGIES TO THE BOYS I KNEW BACK THEN.
I was pretty immature.
MY MASTER, WHO TAUGHT ME ABOUT BOYS' LOVE TWENTY YEARS AGO...
Sword Appreciation
STARE
Collection of Promotional Items
IS CURRENTLY A SELF-PROCLAIMED MASTER OF A CERTAIN SWORD SWAMP.*
I also love them...
Actors
in 2.5D!!
Complete Box All 18 Varieties
I'm an adult. Buying adult things.

*In internet lingo, "swamp" refers to being so addicted to something that you sink into it and can't get out. A master of a certain sword swamp is someone who's addicted to an anthropomorphic game where swords become beautiful youths.

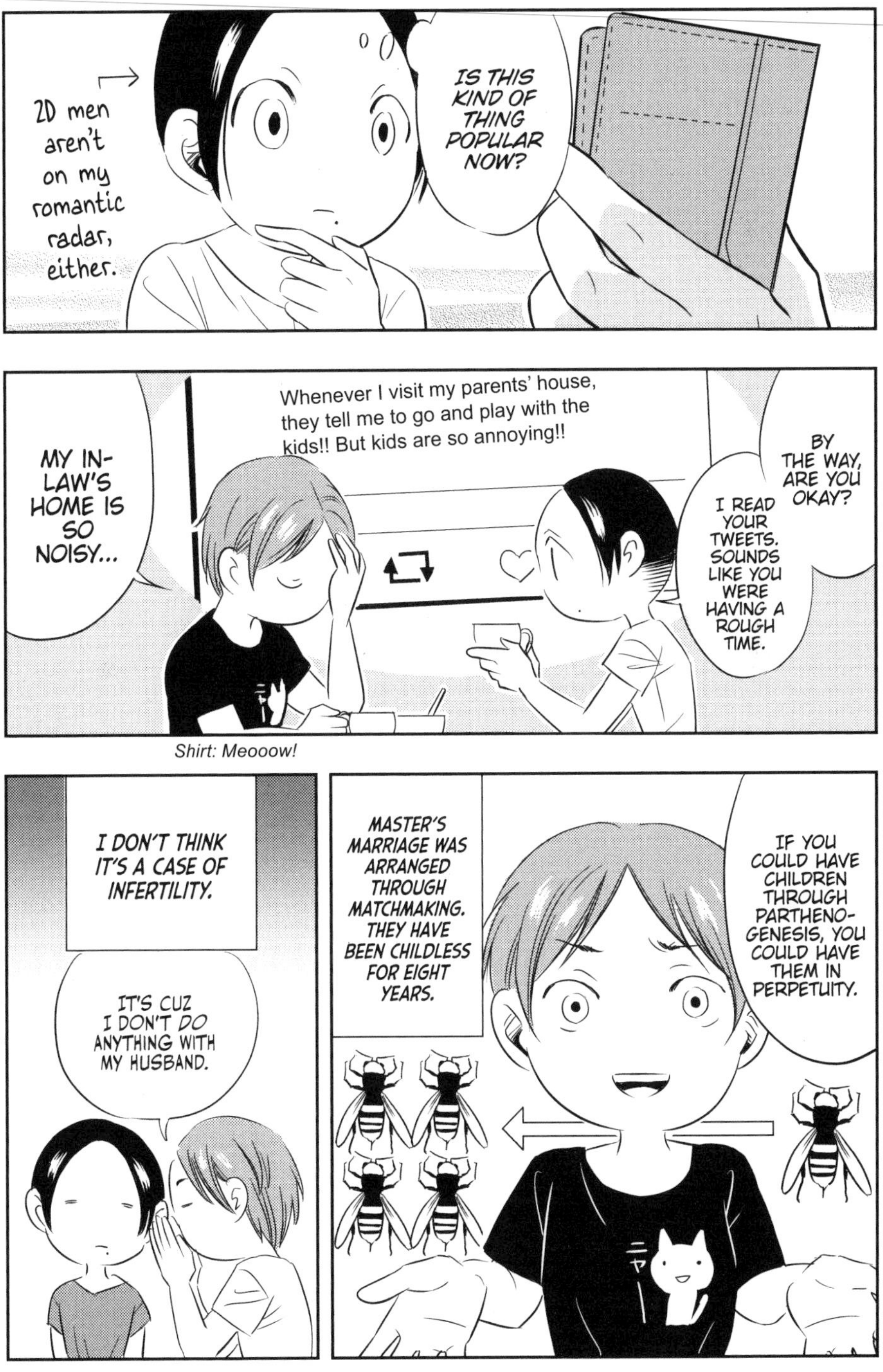
IS THIS KIND OF THING POPULAR NOW?
2D men aren't on my romantic radar, either.
BY THE WAY, ARE YOU OKAY?
I READ YOUR TWEETS. SOUNDS LIKE YOU WERE HAVING A ROUGH TIME.
MY IN-LAW'S HOME IS SO NOISY...
Whenever I visit my parents' house, they tell me to go and play with the kids!! But kids are so annoying!!
Shirt: Meooow!
IF YOU COULD HAVE CHILDREN THROUGH PARTHENO-GENESIS, YOU COULD HAVE THEM IN PERPETUITY.
MASTER'S MARRIAGE WAS ARRANGED THROUGH MATCHMAKING. THEY HAVE BEEN CHILDLESS FOR EIGHT YEARS.
I DON'T THINK IT'S A CASE OF INFERTILITY.
IT'S CUZ I DON'T *DO* ANYTHING WITH MY HUSBAND.

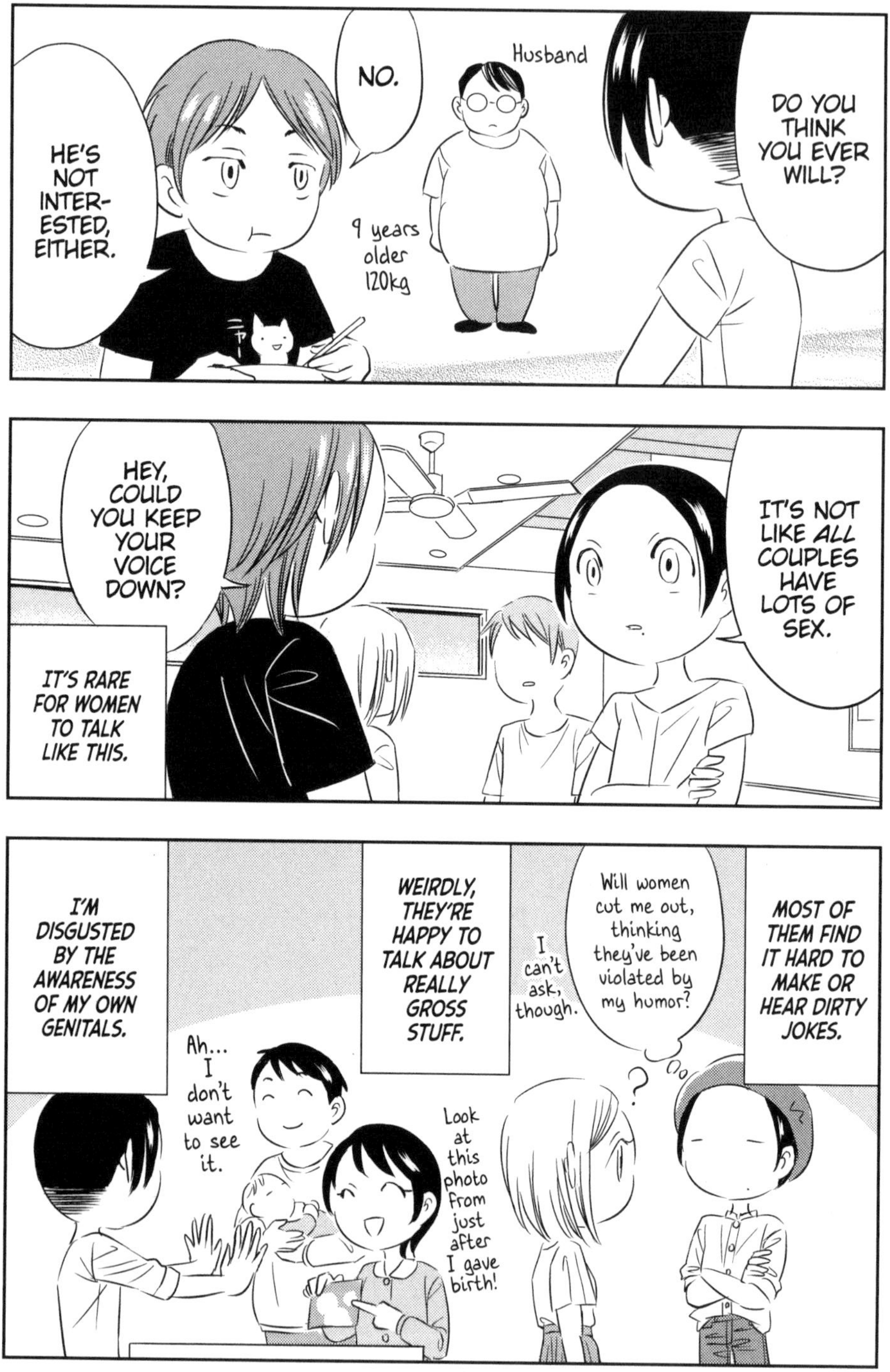
DO YOU THINK YOU EVER WILL?
Husband
9 years older 120kg
NO.
HE'S NOT INTER-ESTED, EITHER.
ニャー
IT'S NOT LIKE ALL COUPLES HAVE LOTS OF SEX.
HEY, COULD YOU KEEP YOUR VOICE DOWN?
IT'S RARE FOR WOMEN TO TALK LIKE THIS.
MOST OF THEM FIND IT HARD TO MAKE OR HEAR DIRTY JOKES.
Will women cut me out, thinking they've been violated by my humor?
I can't ask, though.
WEIRDLY, THEY'RE HAPPY TO TALK ABOUT REALLY GROSS STUFF.
Look at this photo from just after I gave birth!
Ah... I don't want to see it.
I'M DISGUSTED BY THE AWARENESS OF MY OWN GENITALS.

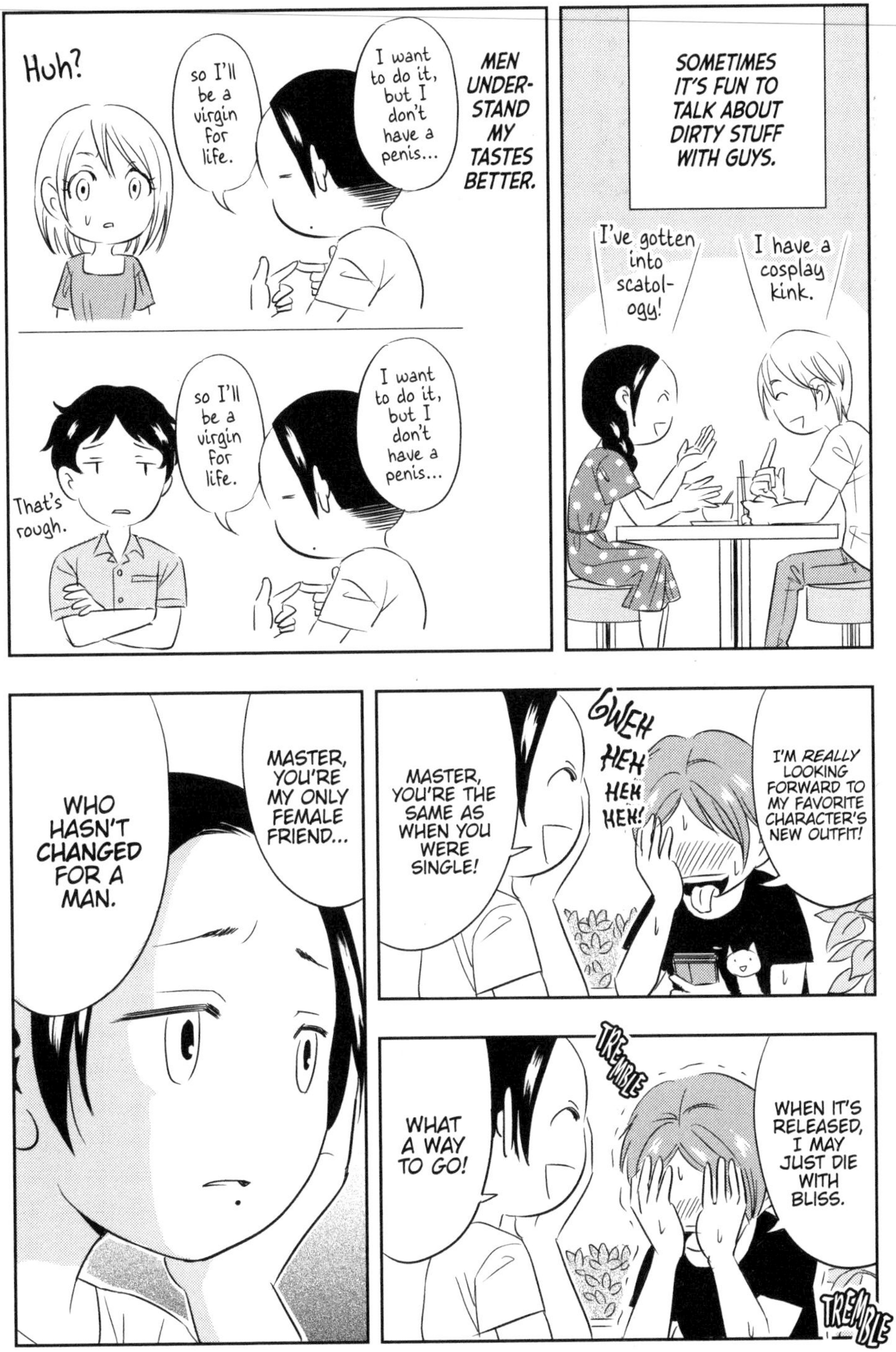
SOMETIMES IT'S FUN TO TALK ABOUT DIRTY STUFF WITH GUYS.
I have a cosplay kink.
I've gotten into scatol-ogy!
MEN UNDER-STAND MY TASTES BETTER.
I want to do it, but I don't have a penis...
so I'll be a virgin for life.
Huh?
I want to do it, but I don't have a penis...
so I'll be a virgin for life.
That's rough.
I'M REALLY LOOKING FORWARD TO MY FAVORITE CHARACTER'S NEW OUTFIT!
GWEH HEH HEH HEH!
MASTER, YOU'RE THE SAME AS WHEN YOU WERE SINGLE!
WHEN IT'S RELEASED, I MAY JUST DIE WITH BLISS.
TREMBLE
TREMBLE
WHAT A WAY TO GO!
MASTER, YOU'RE MY ONLY FEMALE FRIEND...
WHO HASN'T CHANGED FOR A MAN.

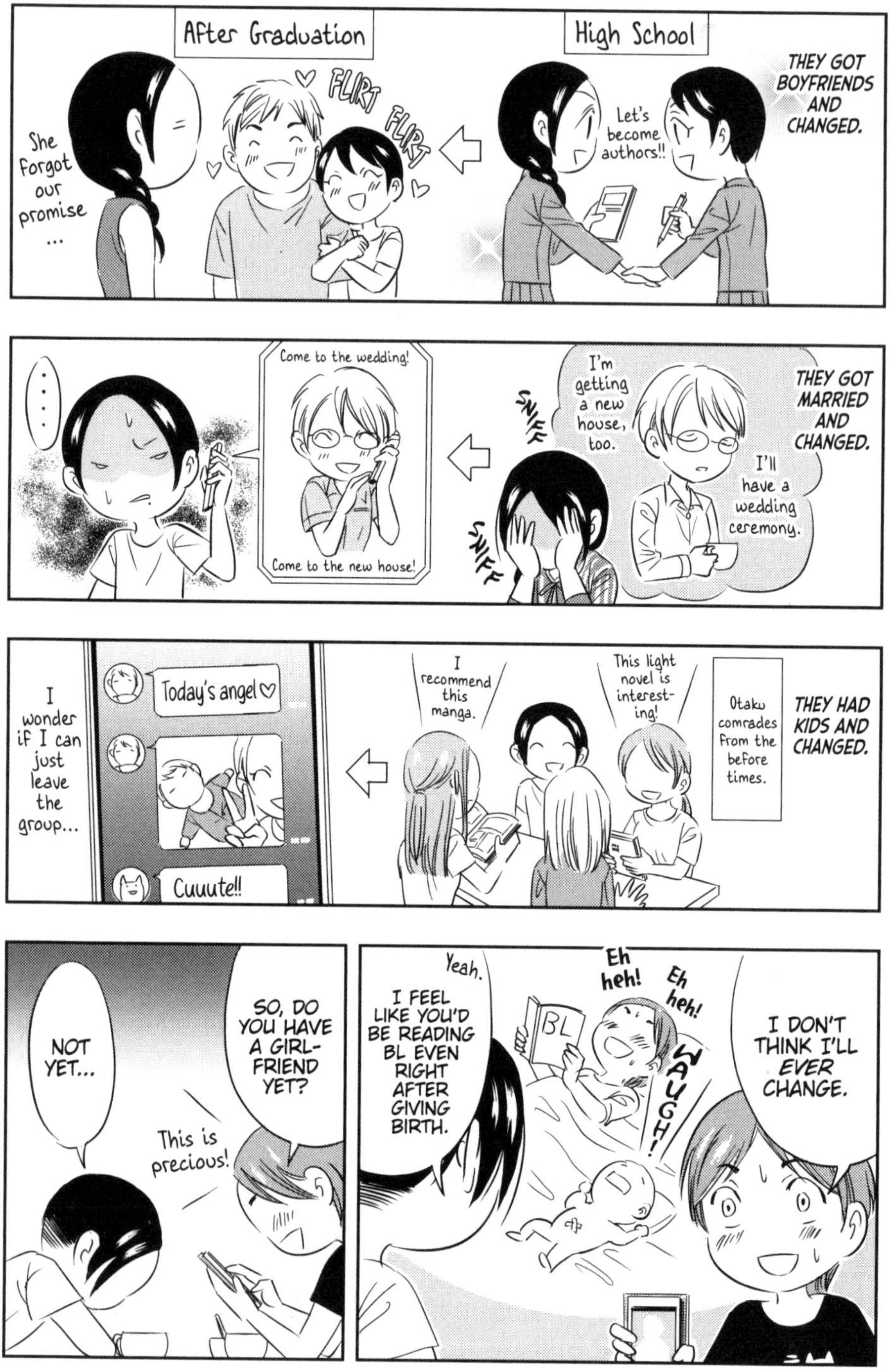
THEY GOT BOYFRIENDS AND CHANGED.
High School
Let's become authors!!
After Graduation
FLIRT
FLIRT
She forgot our promise ...
THEY GOT MARRIED AND CHANGED.
I'm getting a new house, too.
I'll have a wedding ceremony.
SNIFF
SNIFF
Come to the wedding!
Come to the new house!
.....
THEY HAD KIDS AND CHANGED.
Otaku comrades from the before times.
This light novel is interest-ing!
I recommend this manga.
Today's angel ♡
Cuuute!!
I wonder if I can just leave the group...
I DON'T THINK I'LL EVER CHANGE.
Eh heh!
Eh heh!
WAUGH!
BL
Yeah.
I FEEL LIKE YOU'D BE READING BL EVEN RIGHT AFTER GIVING BIRTH.
SO, DO YOU HAVE A GIRL-FRIEND YET?
This is precious!
NOT YET...

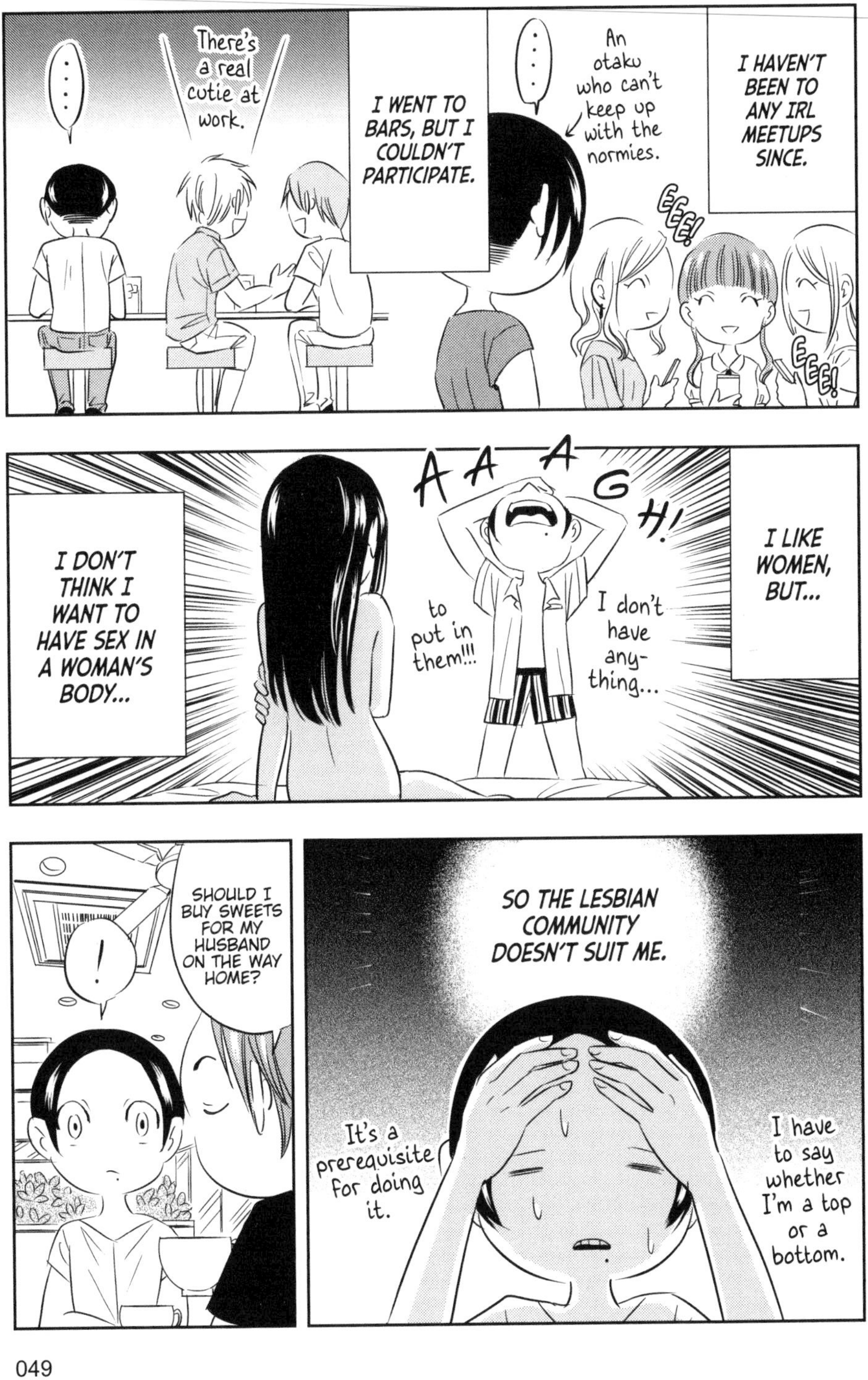
I HAVEN'T BEEN TO ANY IRL MEETUPS SINCE.
EEE!
...
An otaku who can't keep up with the normies.
EEE!
I WENT TO BARS, BUT I COULDN'T PARTICIPATE.
There's a real cutie at work.
...
I LIKE WOMEN, BUT...
AAAGH!
I don't have any-thing...
to put in them!!!
I DON'T THINK I WANT TO HAVE SEX IN A WOMAN'S BODY...
SO THE LESBIAN COMMUNITY DOESN'T SUIT ME.
I have to say whether I'm a top or a bottom.
It's a prerequisite for doing it.
SHOULD I BUY SWEETS FOR MY HUSBAND ON THE WAY HOME?
!

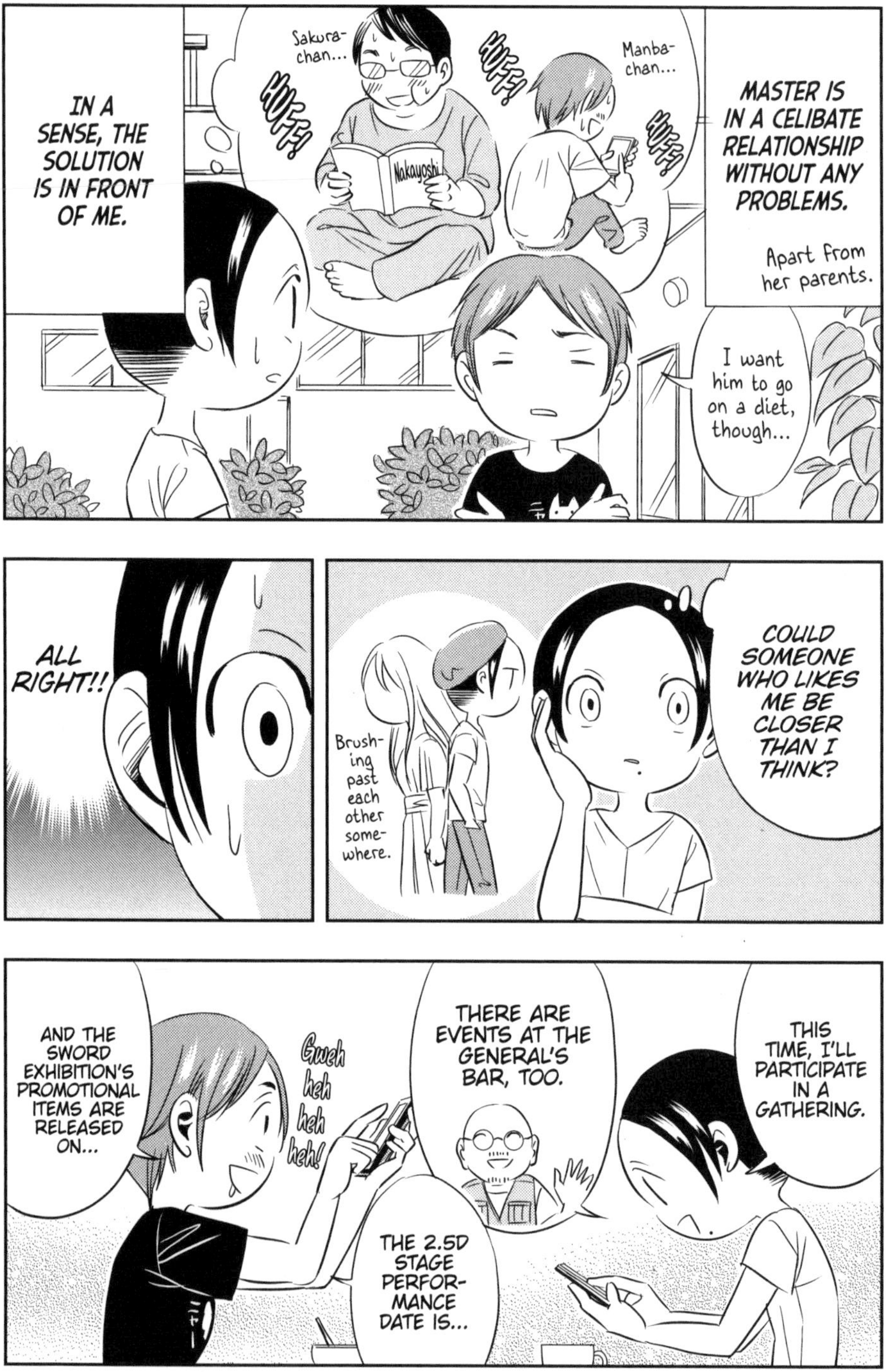
MASTER IS IN A CELIBATE RELATIONSHIP WITHOUT ANY PROBLEMS.
Apart from her parents.
Manba-chan...
Sakura-chan...
Nakayoshi
IN A SENSE, THE SOLUTION IS IN FRONT OF ME.
I want him to go on a diet, though...
COULD SOMEONE WHO LIKES ME BE CLOSER THAN I THINK?
Brushing past each other somewhere.
ALL RIGHT!!
THIS TIME, I'LL PARTICIPATE IN A GATHERING.
THERE ARE EVENTS AT THE GENERAL'S BAR, TOO.
THE 2.5D STAGE PERFORMANCE DATE IS...
Gweh heh heh heh!
AND THE SWORD EXHIBITION'S PROMOTIONAL ITEMS ARE RELEASED ON...

Ep. 5: The "Penis" Story

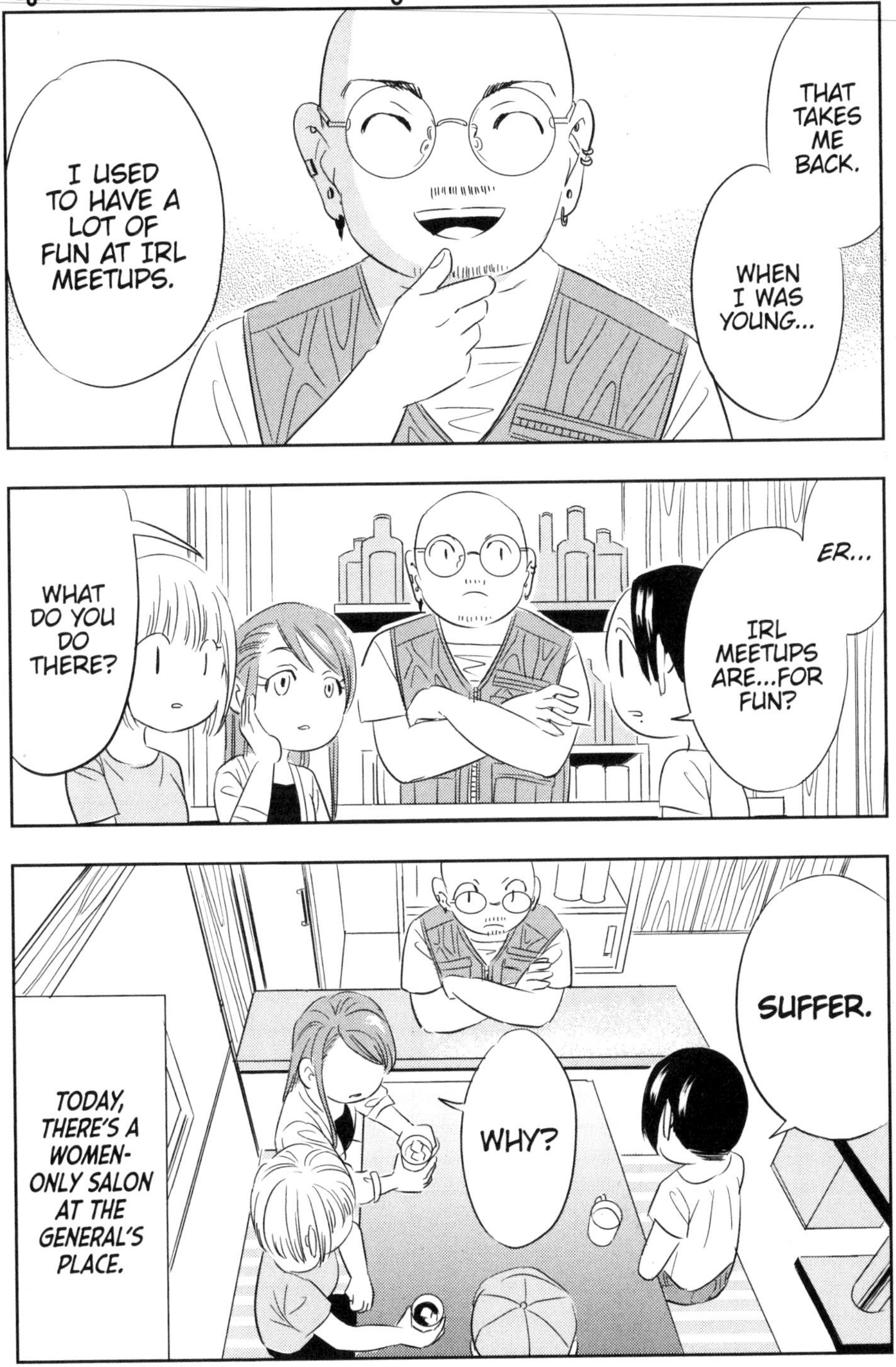

THAT TAKES ME BACK.
WHEN I WAS YOUNG...
I USED TO HAVE A LOT OF FUN AT IRL MEETUPS.
ER...
IRL MEETUPS ARE...FOR FUN?
WHAT DO YOU DO THERE?
SUFFER.
WHY?
TODAY, THERE'S A WOMEN-ONLY SALON AT THE GENERAL'S PLACE.

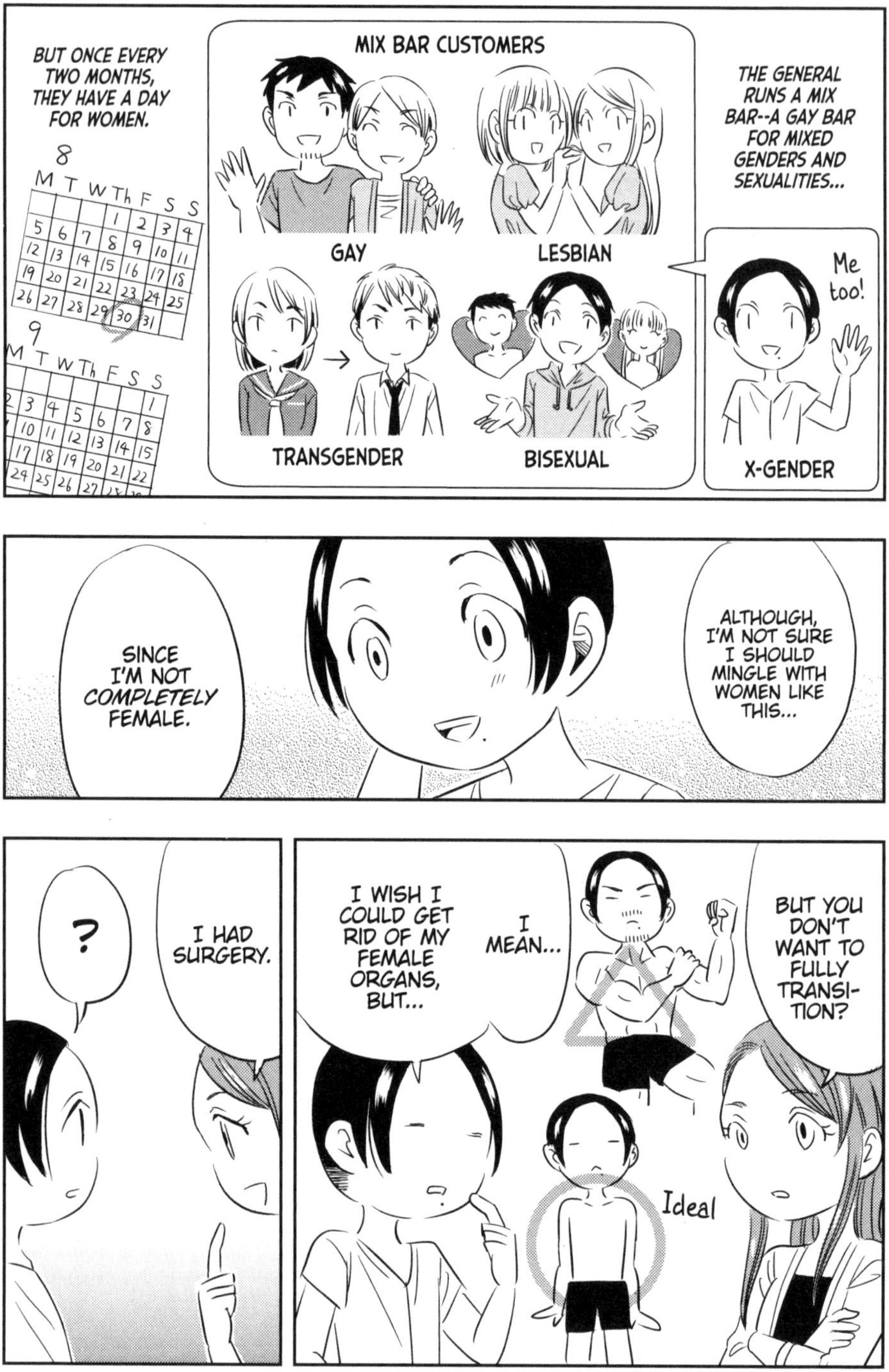
THE GENERAL RUNS A MIX BAR--A GAY BAR FOR MIXED GENDERS AND SEXUALITIES...
Me too!
X-GENDER
MIX BAR CUSTOMERS
GAY
LESBIAN
TRANSGENDER
BISEXUAL
BUT ONCE EVERY TWO MONTHS, THEY HAVE A DAY FOR WOMEN.
ALTHOUGH, I'M NOT SURE I SHOULD MINGLE WITH WOMEN LIKE THIS...
SINCE I'M NOT *COMPLETELY* FEMALE.
BUT YOU DON'T WANT TO FULLY TRANSI-TION?
I MEAN...
I WISH I COULD GET RID OF MY FEMALE ORGANS, BUT...
Ideal
I HAD SURGERY.
?

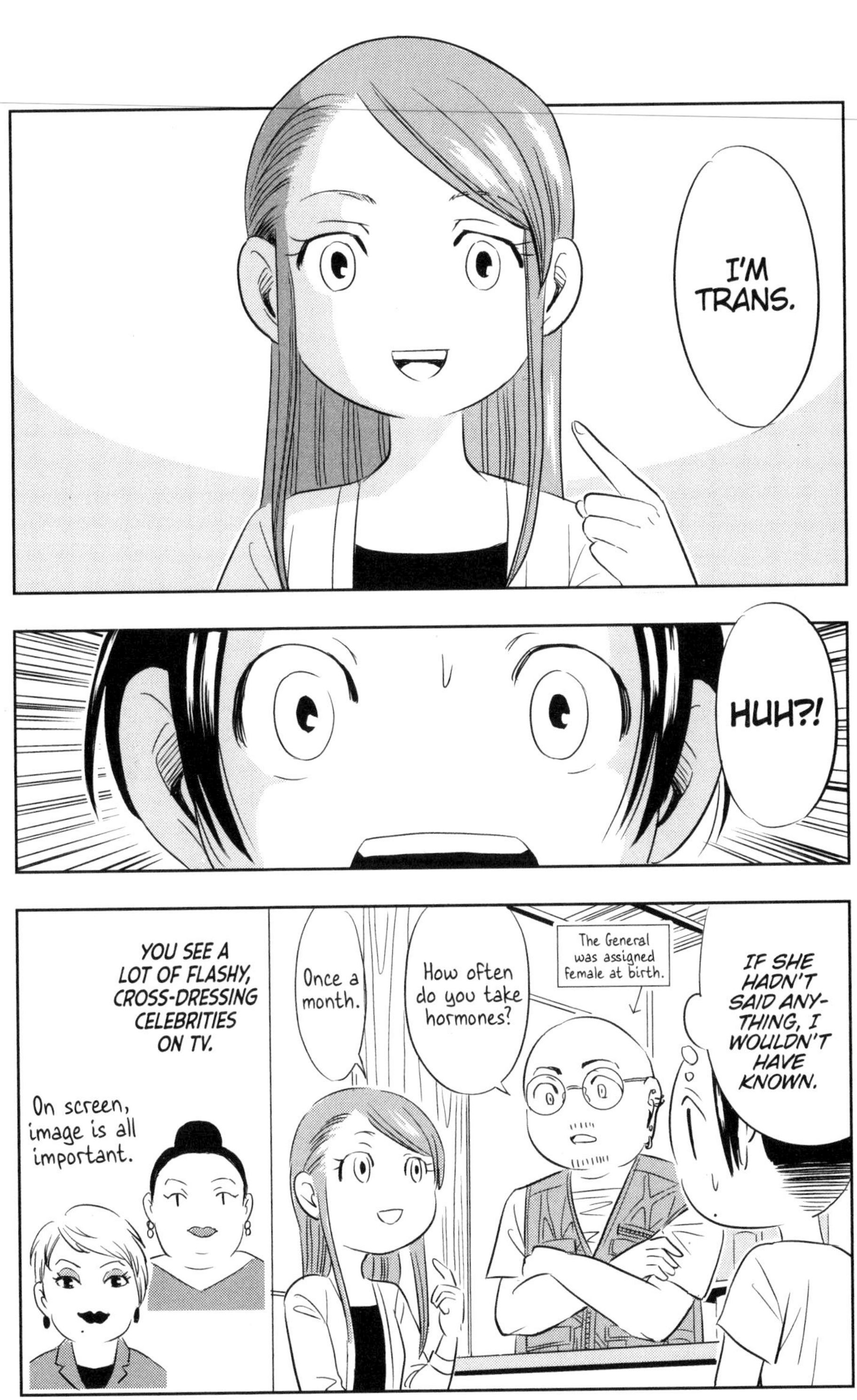
I'M TRANS.
HUH?!
IF SHE HADN'T SAID ANYTHING, I WOULDN'T HAVE KNOWN.
The General was assigned female at birth.
How often do you take hormones?
Once a month.
YOU SEE A LOT OF FLASHY, CROSS-DRESSING CELEBRITIES ON TV.
On screen, image is all important.

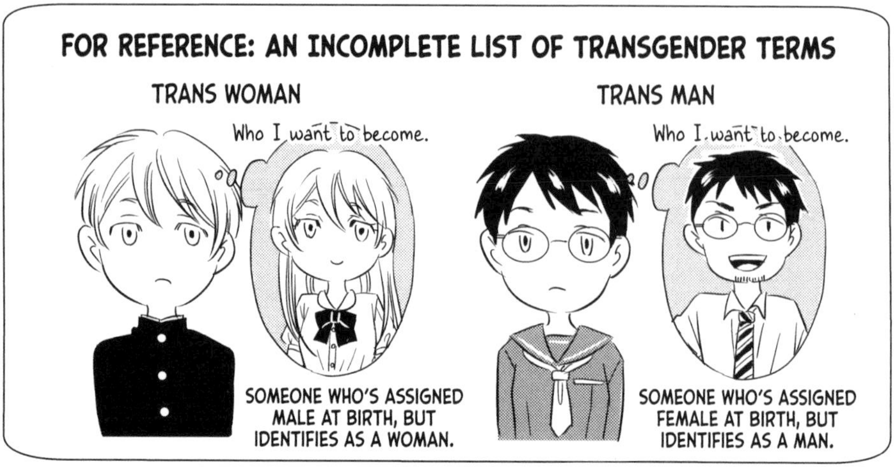
FOR REFERENCE: AN INCOMPLETE LIST OF TRANSGENDER TERMS
TRANS MAN
Who I want to become.
SOMEONE WHO'S ASSIGNED FEMALE AT BIRTH, BUT IDENTIFIES AS A MAN.
TRANS WOMAN
Who I want to become.
SOMEONE WHO'S ASSIGNED MALE AT BIRTH, BUT IDENTIFIES AS A WOMAN.

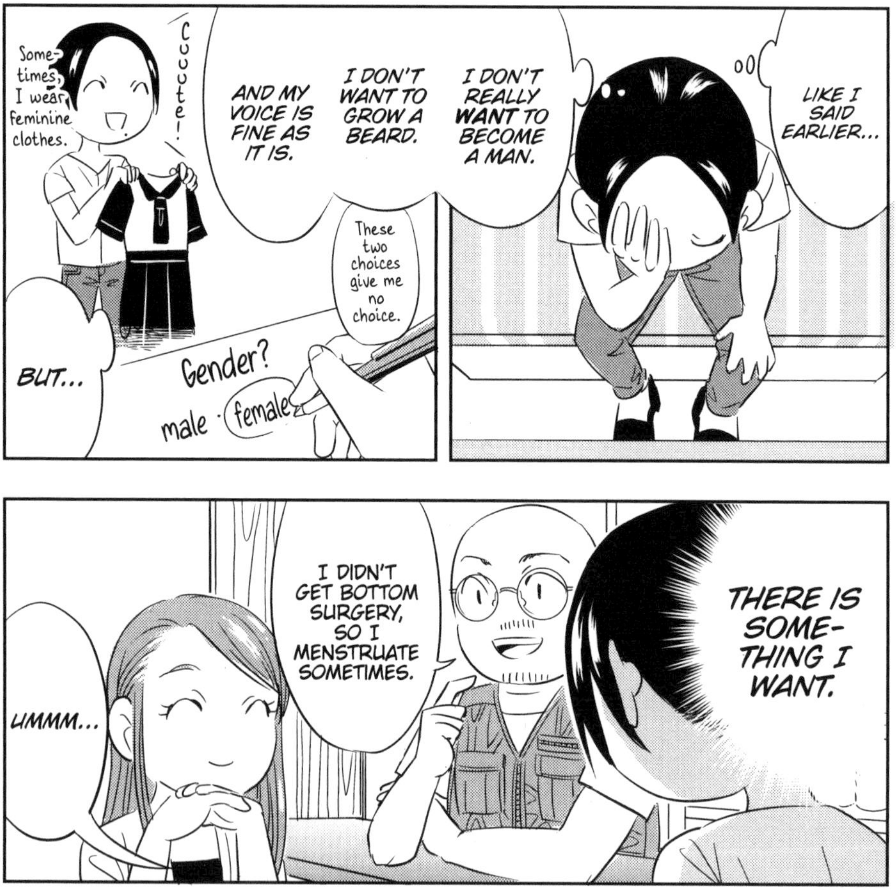
LIKE I SAID EARLIER...
I DON'T REALLY WANT TO BECOME A MAN.
I DON'T WANT TO GROW A BEARD.
AND MY VOICE IS FINE AS IT IS.
Cuuute!
Sometimes, I wear feminine clothes.
These two choices give me no choice.
BUT...
Gender?
male · female
THERE IS SOMETHING I WANT.
I DIDN'T GET BOTTOM SURGERY, SO I MENSTRUATE SOMETIMES.
UMMM...

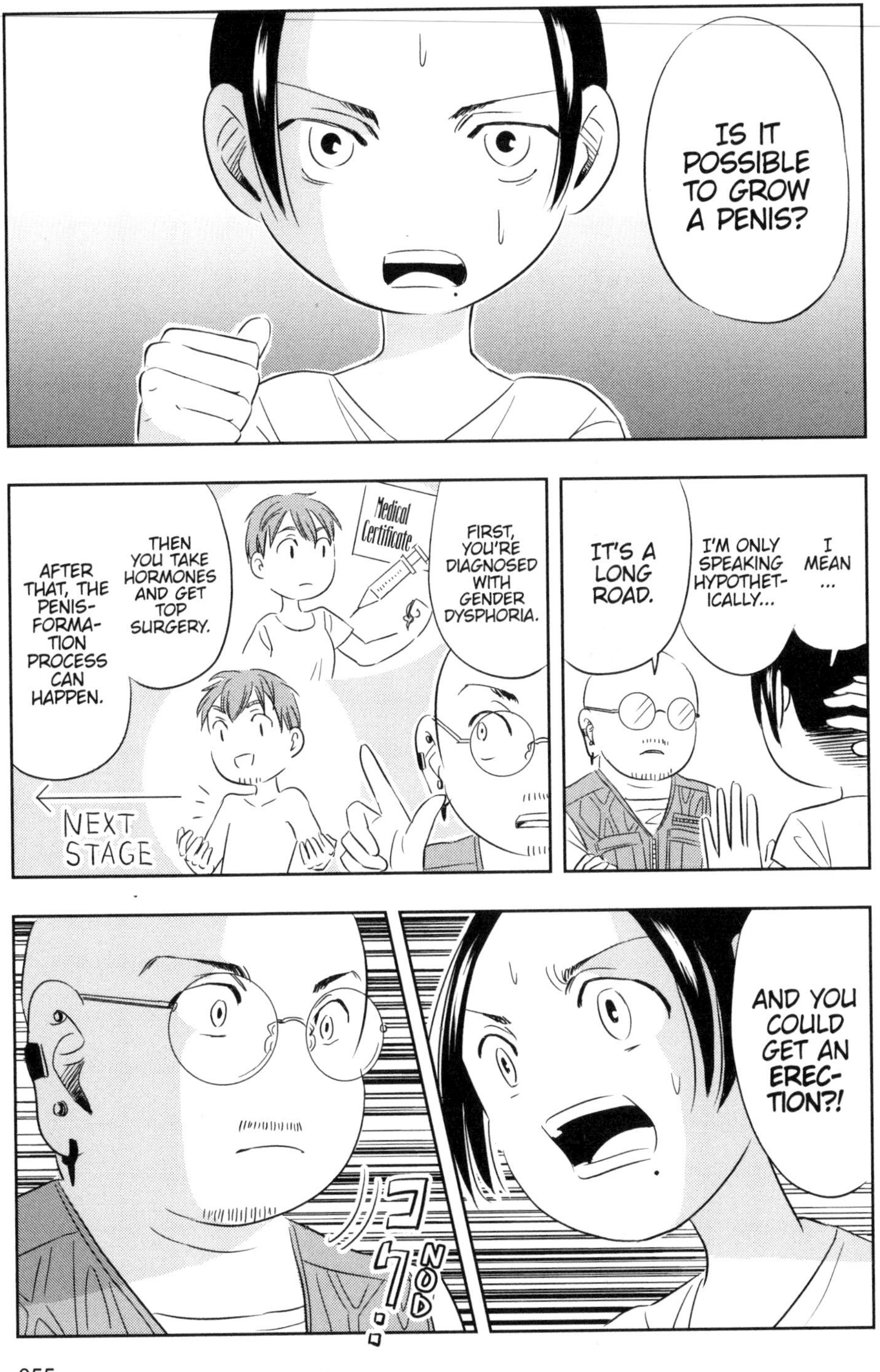
IS IT POSSIBLE TO GROW A PENIS?
I MEAN ...
I'M ONLY SPEAKING HYPOTHETICALLY...
IT'S A LONG ROAD.
FIRST, YOU'RE DIAGNOSED WITH GENDER DYSPHORIA.
Medical Certificate
THEN YOU TAKE HORMONES AND GET TOP SURGERY.
AFTER THAT, THE PENIS-FORMATION PROCESS CAN HAPPEN.
NEXT STAGE
AND YOU COULD GET AN ERECTION?!
NOD

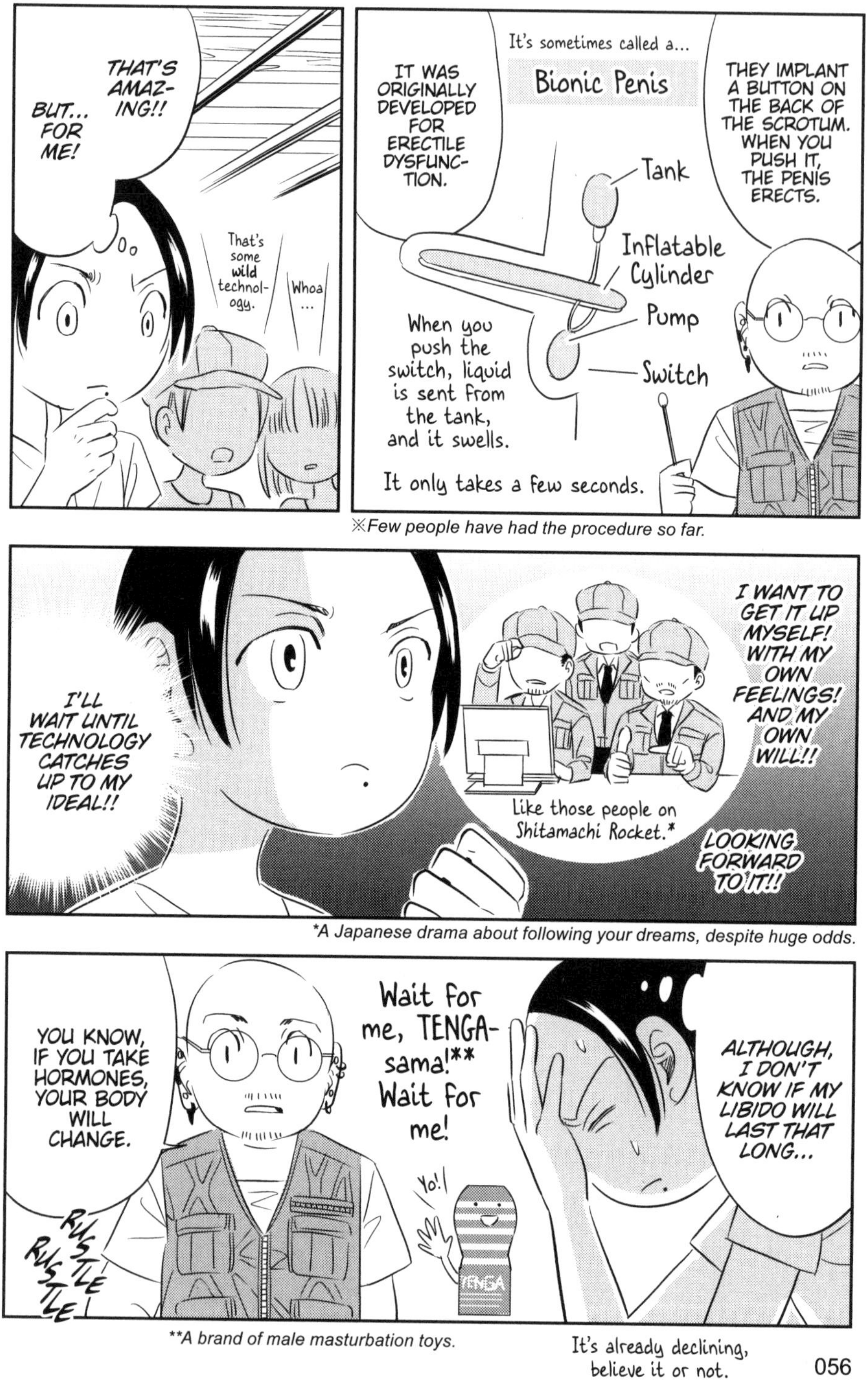

THEY IMPLANT A BUTTON ON THE BACK OF THE SCROTUM. WHEN YOU PUSH IT, THE PENIS ERECTS.
It's sometimes called a...
Bionic Penis
IT WAS ORIGINALLY DEVELOPED FOR ERECTILE DYSFUNCTION.
Tank
Inflatable Cylinder
Pump
Switch
When you push the switch, liquid is sent from the tank, and it swells.
It only takes a few seconds.
THAT'S AMAZING!!
BUT... FOR ME!
Whoa...
That's some wild technology.
I WANT TO GET IT UP MYSELF! WITH MY OWN FEELINGS! AND MY OWN WILL!!
Like those people on Shitamachi Rocket.*
LOOKING FORWARD TO IT!!
I'LL WAIT UNTIL TECHNOLOGY CATCHES UP TO MY IDEAL!!
ALTHOUGH, I DON'T KNOW IF MY LIBIDO WILL LAST THAT LONG...
Wait for me, TENGA-sama!** Wait for me!
Yo!
TENGA
YOU KNOW, IF YOU TAKE HORMONES, YOUR BODY WILL CHANGE.
RUSTLE RUSTLE
It's already declining, believe it or not.

※Few people have had the procedure so far.

*A Japanese drama about following your dreams, despite huge odds.

**A brand of male masturbation toys.

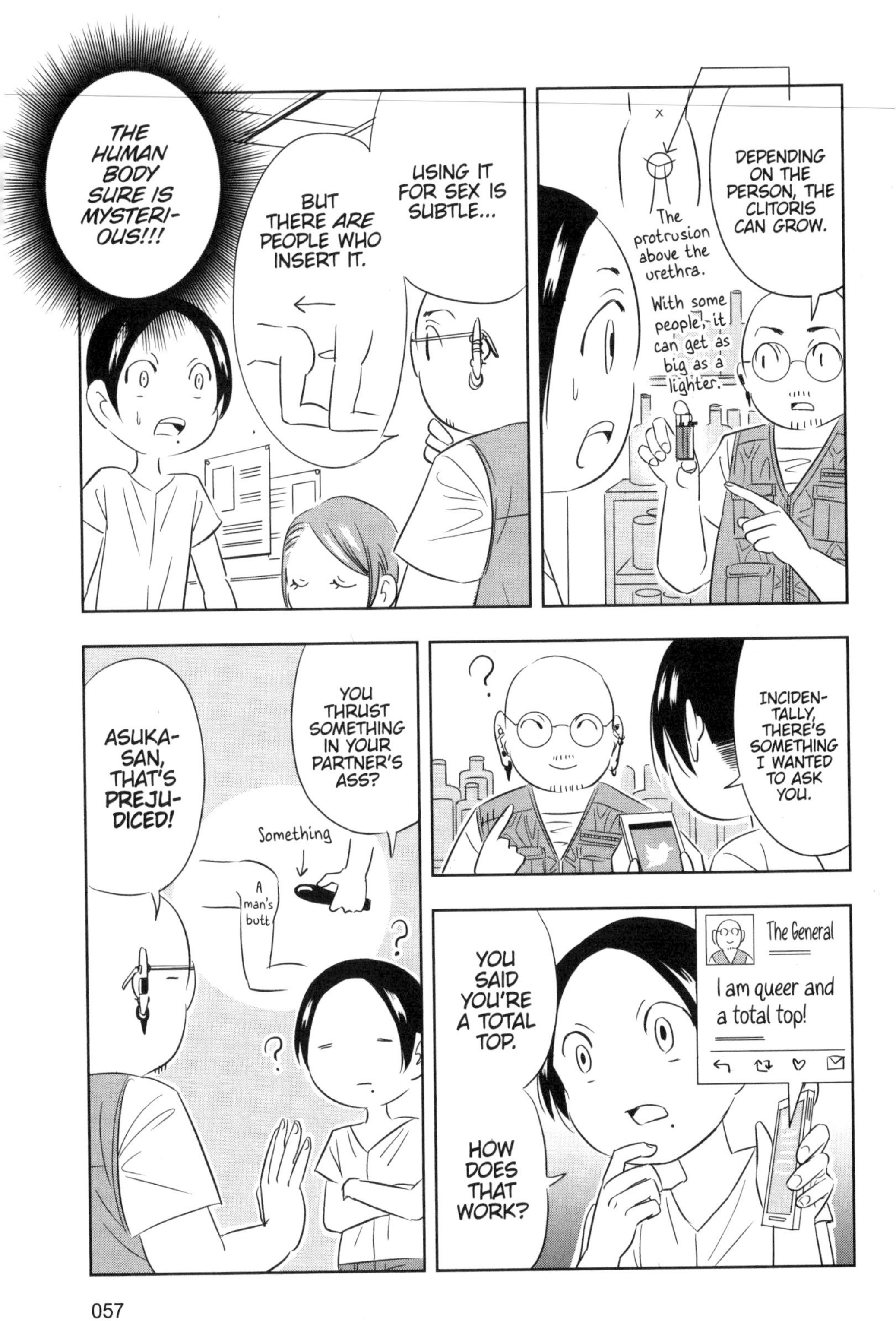

DEPENDING ON THE PERSON, THE CLITORIS CAN GROW.
The protrusion above the urethra.
With some people, it can get as big as a lighter.
USING IT FOR SEX IS SUBTLE...
BUT THERE ARE PEOPLE WHO INSERT IT.
THE HUMAN BODY SURE IS MYSTERIOUS!!!
INCIDENTALLY, THERE'S SOMETHING I WANTED TO ASK YOU.
The General
I am queer and a total top!
YOU SAID YOU'RE A TOTAL TOP.
HOW DOES THAT WORK?
YOU THRUST SOMETHING IN YOUR PARTNER'S ASS?
Something
A man's butt
ASUKA-SAN, THAT'S PREJUDICED!

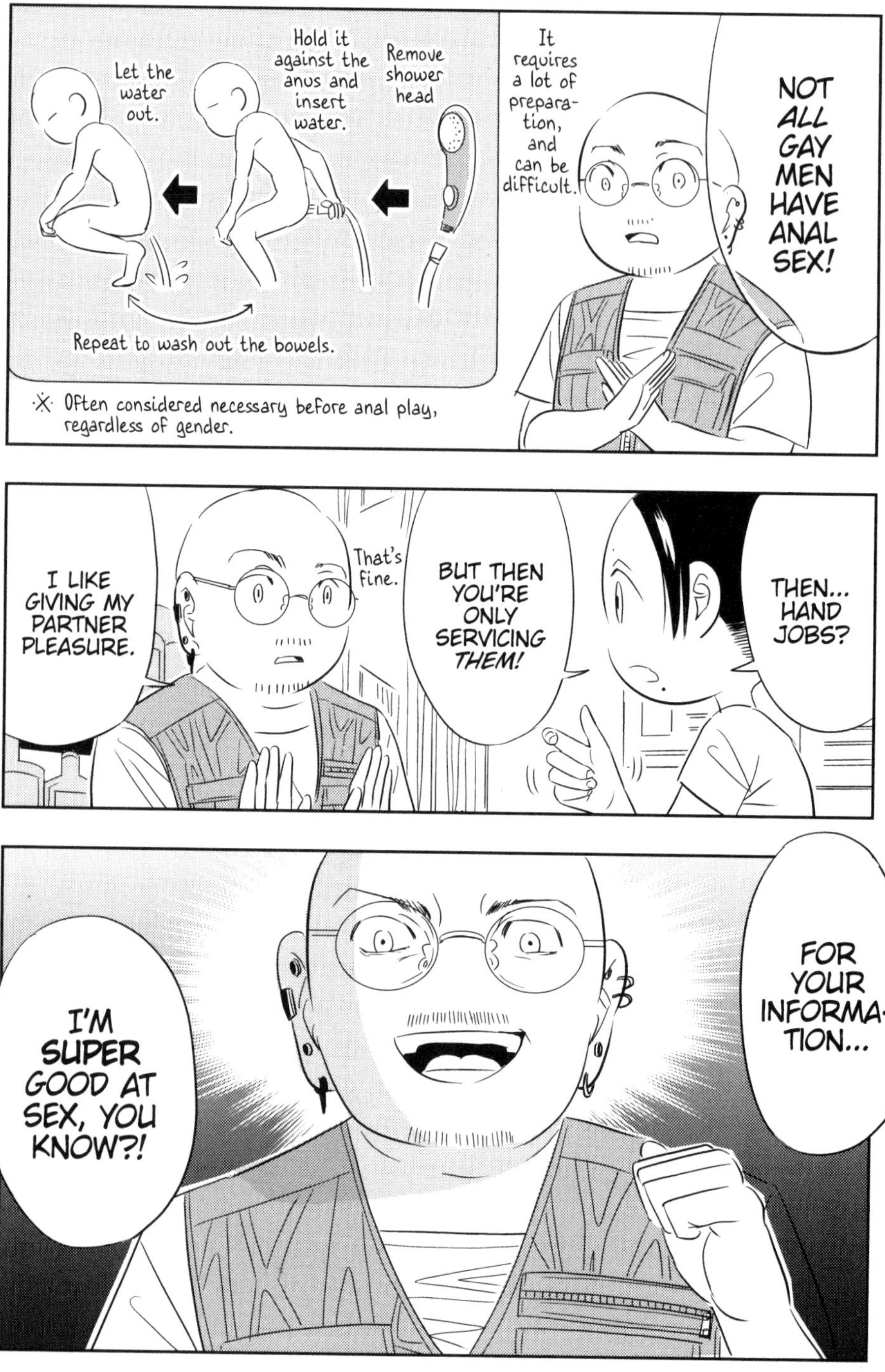
NOT ALL GAY MEN HAVE ANAL SEX!
It requires a lot of preparation, and can be difficult.
Remove shower head
Hold it against the anus and insert water.
Let the water out.
Repeat to wash out the bowels.
※ Often considered necessary before anal play, regardless of gender.
THEN... HAND JOBS?
BUT THEN YOU'RE ONLY SERVICING THEM!
That's fine.
I LIKE GIVING MY PARTNER PLEASURE.
FOR YOUR INFORMATION...
I'M SUPER GOOD AT SEX, YOU KNOW?!

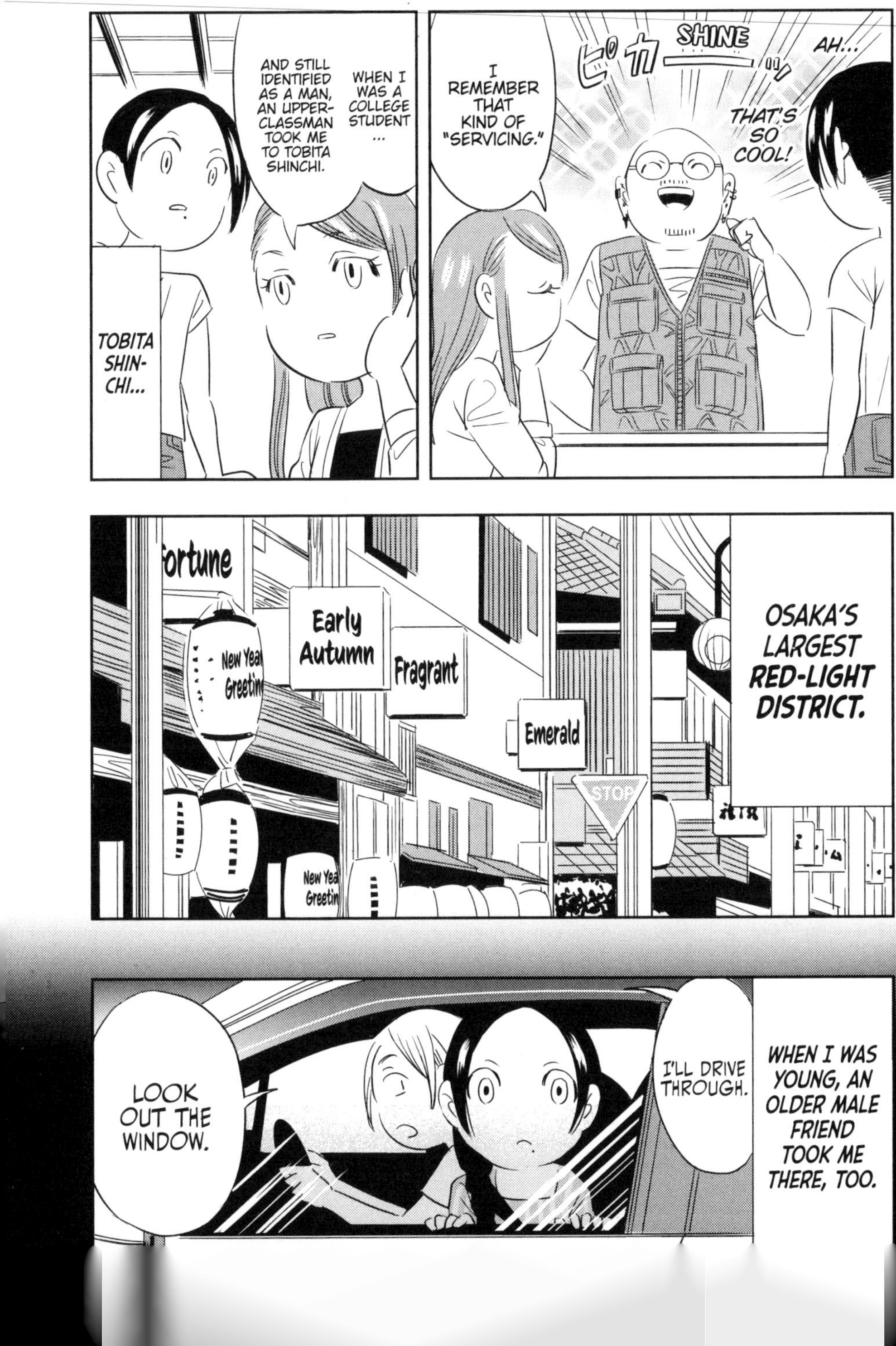

ピカー
SHINE
AH... THAT'S SO COOL!
I REMEMBER THAT KIND OF "SERVICING."
WHEN I WAS A COLLEGE STUDENT ...
AND STILL IDENTIFIED AS A MAN, AN UPPER-CLASSMAN TOOK ME TO TOBITA SHINCHI.
TOBITA SHIN-CHI...
OSAKA'S LARGEST RED-LIGHT DISTRICT.
Fortune
Early Autumn
Fragrant
Emerald
STOP
WHEN I WAS YOUNG, AN OLDER MALE FRIEND TOOK ME THERE, TOO.
I'LL DRIVE THROUGH.
LOOK OUT THE WINDOW.

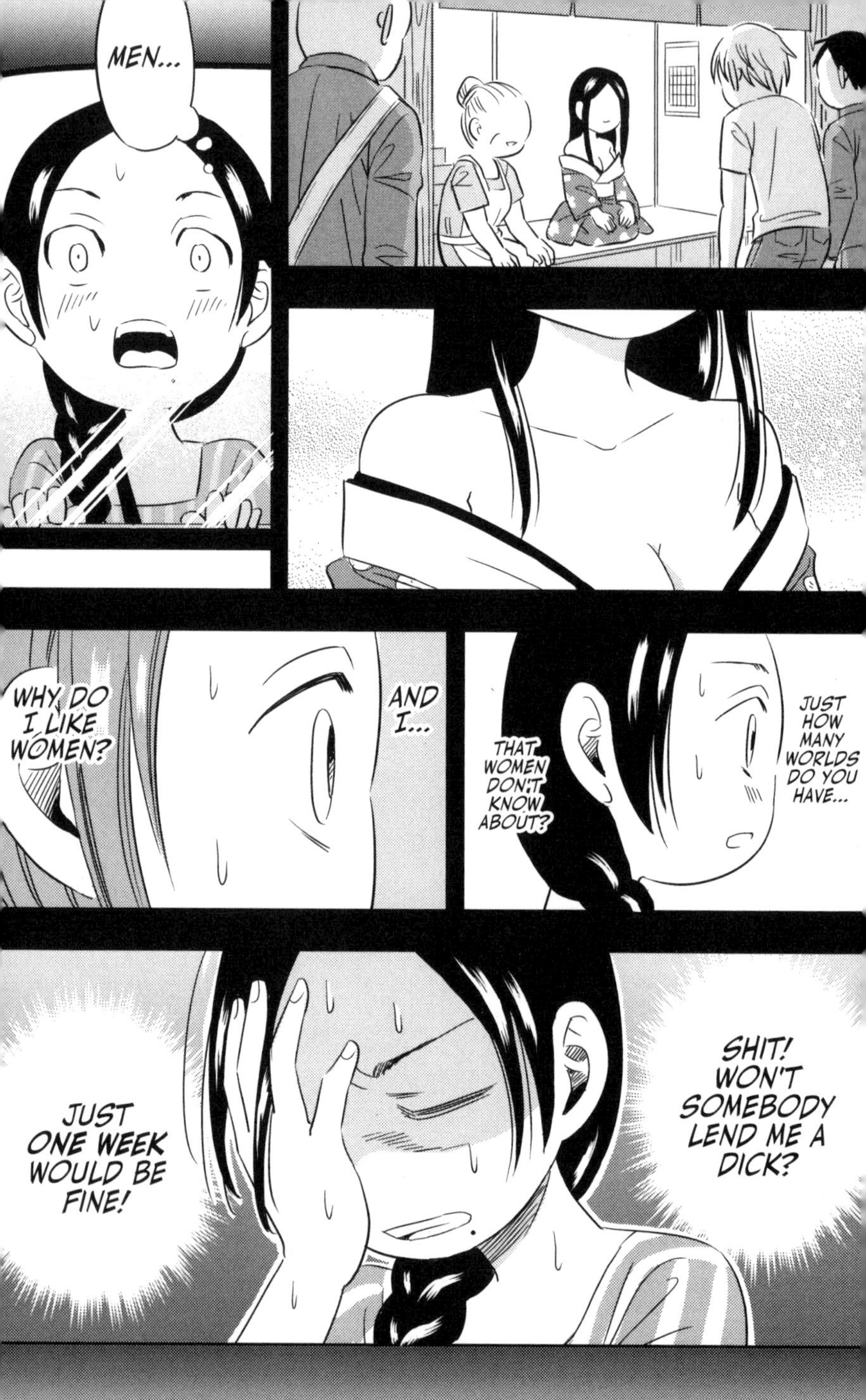
MEN...
JUST HOW MANY WORLDS DO YOU HAVE...
THAT WOMEN DON'T KNOW ABOUT?
AND I...
WHY DO I LIKE WOMEN?
SHIT! WON'T SOMEBODY LEND ME A DICK?
JUST ONE WEEK WOULD BE FINE!

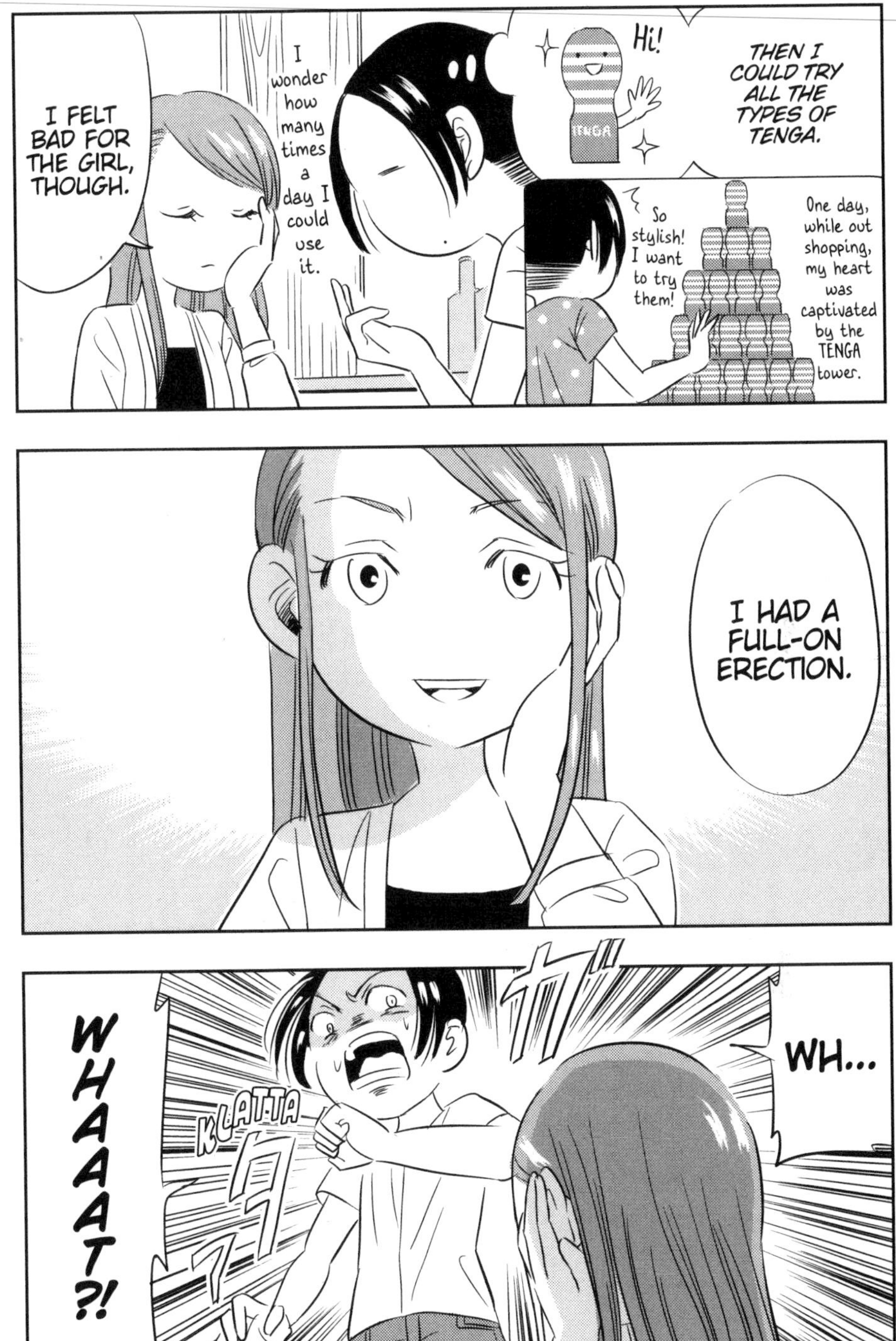

THEN I COULD TRY ALL THE TYPES OF TENGA.
Hi!
TENGA
One day, while out shopping, my heart was captivated by the TENGA tower.
So stylish! I want to try them!
I wonder how many times a day I could use it.
I FELT BAD FOR THE GIRL, THOUGH.
I HAD A FULL-ON ERECTION.
WH...
KLATTA
WHAAAAT?!

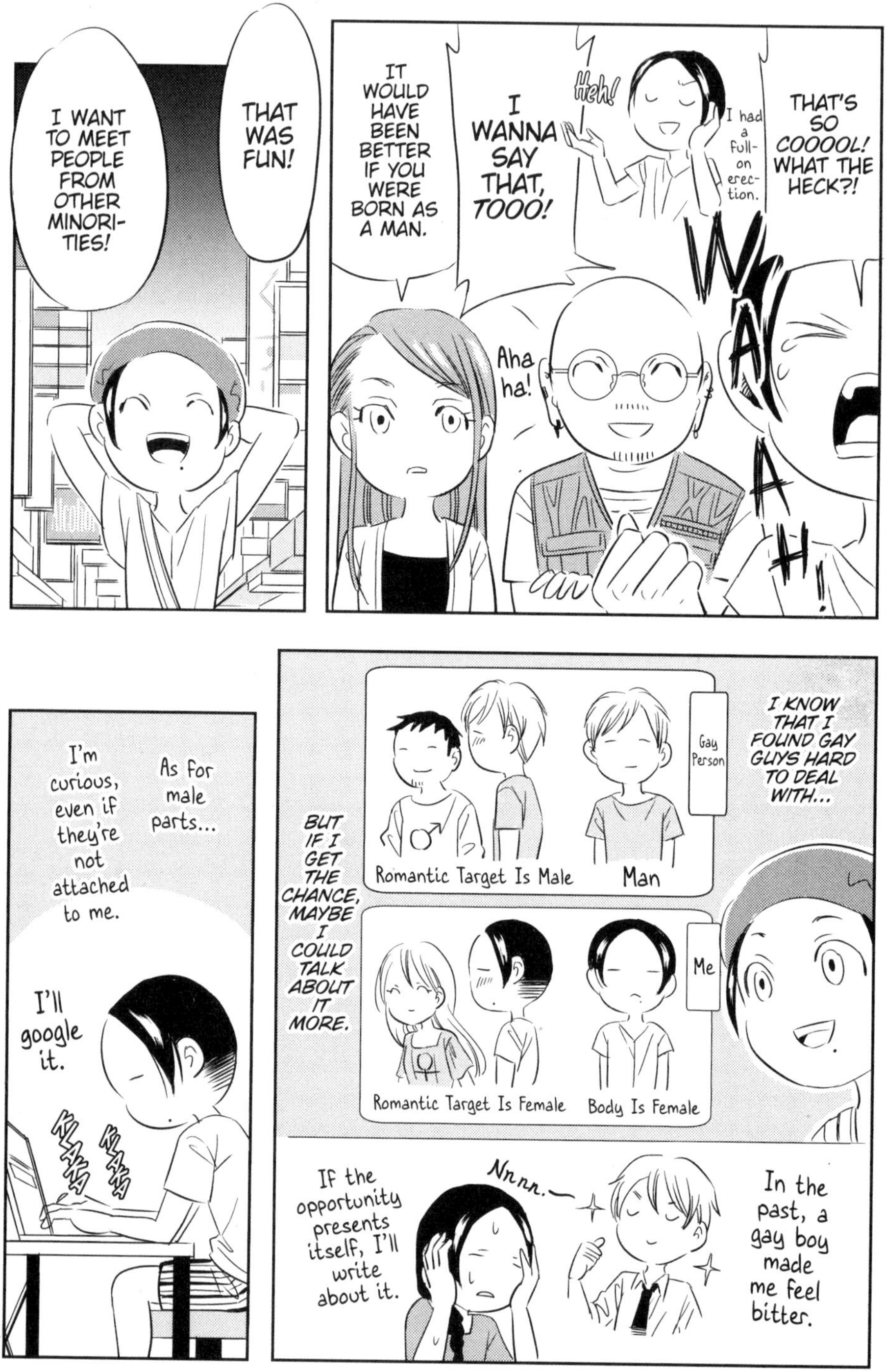
THAT'S SO COOOOL! WHAT THE HECK?!
I had a full-on erection.
Heh!
I WANNA SAY THAT, TOOO!
IT WOULD HAVE BEEN BETTER IF YOU WERE BORN AS A MAN.
WAAAH!!
Aha ha!
THAT WAS FUN!
I WANT TO MEET PEOPLE FROM OTHER MINORITIES!
I KNOW THAT I FOUND GAY GUYS HARD TO DEAL WITH...
Gay Person
Man
Romantic Target Is Male
Me
Body Is Female
Romantic Target Is Female
BUT IF I GET THE CHANCE, MAYBE I COULD TALK ABOUT IT MORE.
In the past, a gay boy made me feel bitter.
Nnnn.
If the opportunity presents itself, I'll write about it.
As for male parts...
I'm curious, even if they're not attached to me.
I'll google it.
KLAKA
KLAKA

Ep. 6: The "Gloomy Person, Cheery Person" Story

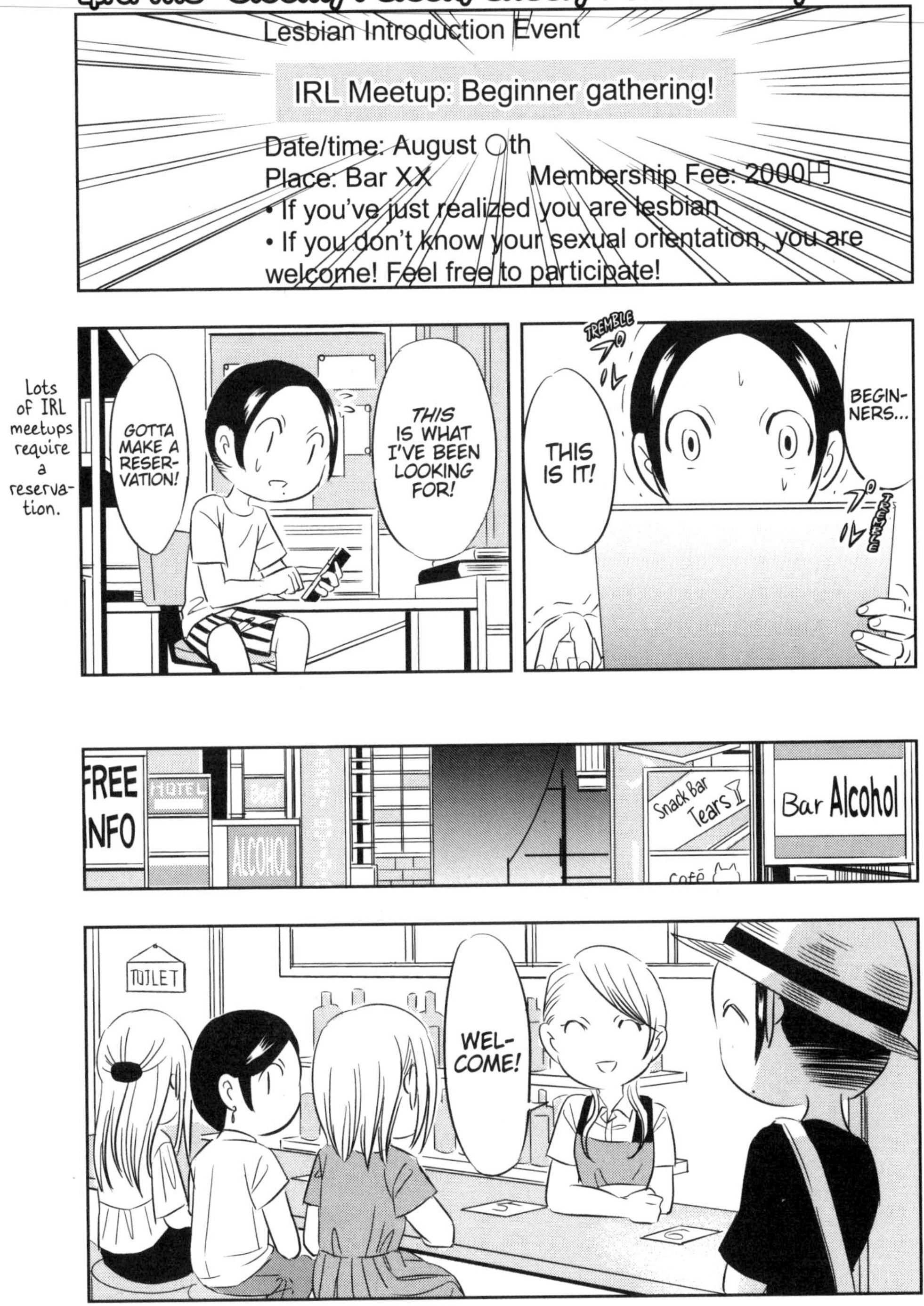
Lesbian Introduction Event
IRL Meetup: Beginner gathering!
Date/time: August ○th
Place: Bar XX Membership Fee: 2000円
• If you've just realized you are lesbian
• If you don't know your sexual orientation, you are welcome! Feel free to participate!
BEGINNERS...
TREMBLE
THIS IS IT!
TREMBLE
THIS IS WHAT I'VE BEEN LOOKING FOR!
GOTTA MAKE A RESERVATION!
Lots of IRL meetups require a reservation.
Bar Alcohol
Snack Bar Tears
Café
ALCOHOL
HOTEL
FREE INFO
WELCOME!
TOILET

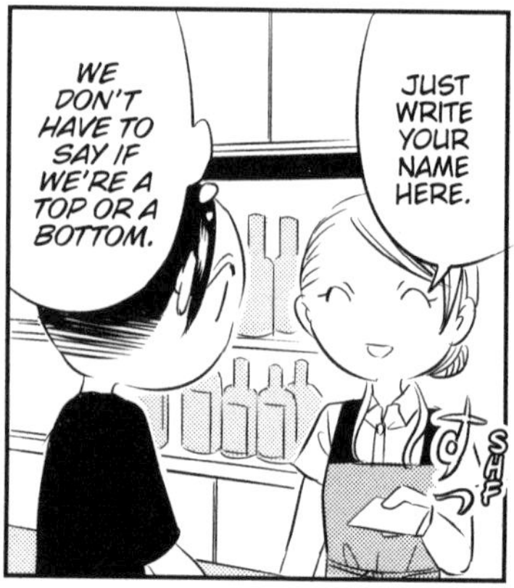
JUST WRITE YOUR NAME HERE.
WE DON'T HAVE TO SAY IF WE'RE A TOP OR A BOTTOM.
SHF

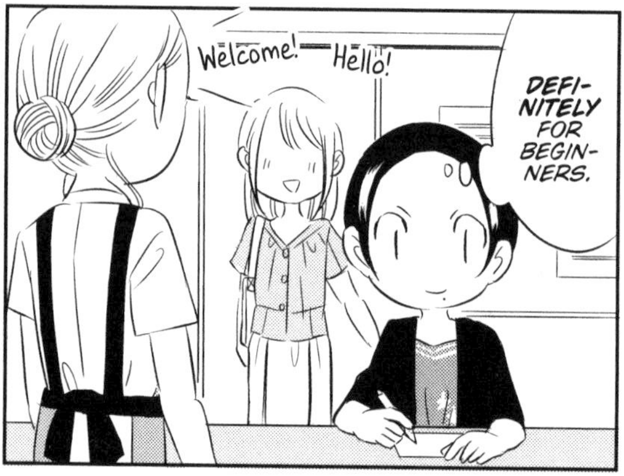
DEFINITELY FOR BEGINNERS.
Welcome!
Hello!

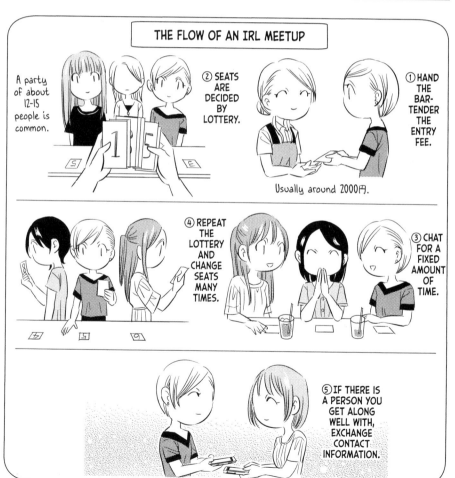

THE FLOW OF AN IRL MEETUP

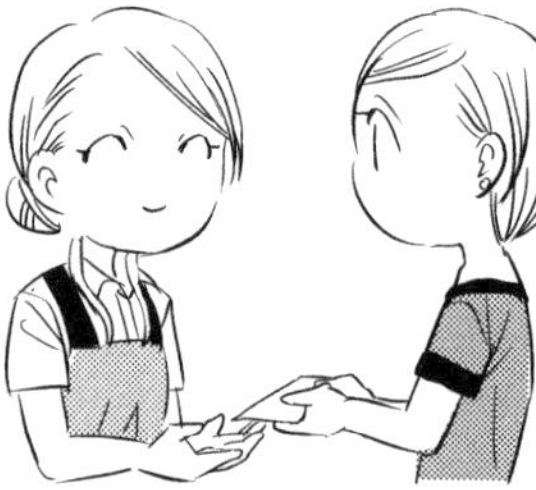

① HAND THE BARTENDER THE ENTRY FEE.

Usually around 2000円.

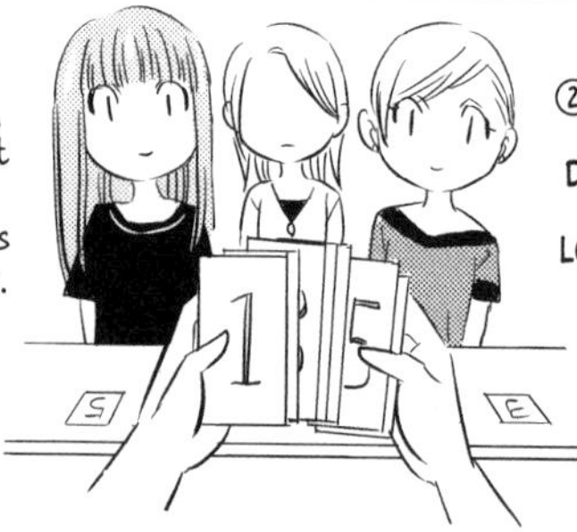
1
5
5
3

② SEATS ARE DECIDED BY LOTTERY.

A party of about 12-15 people is common.

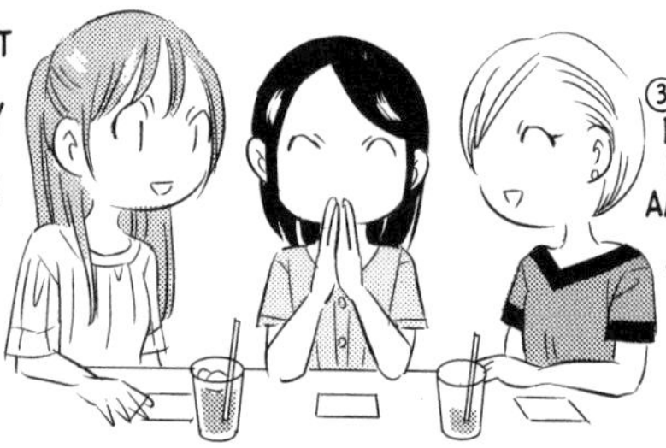

③ CHAT FOR A FIXED AMOUNT OF TIME.

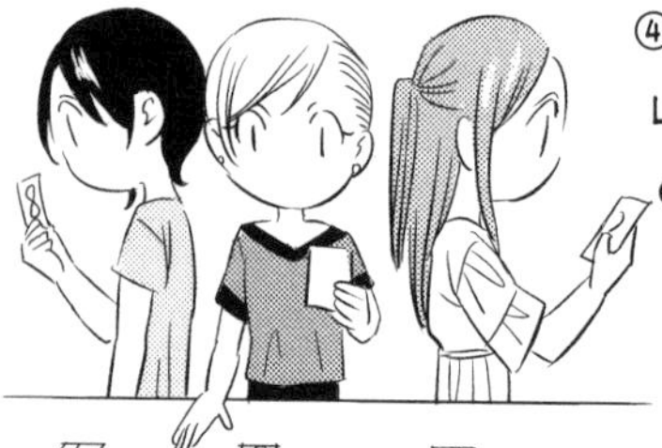

④ REPEAT THE LOTTERY AND CHANGE SEATS MANY TIMES.

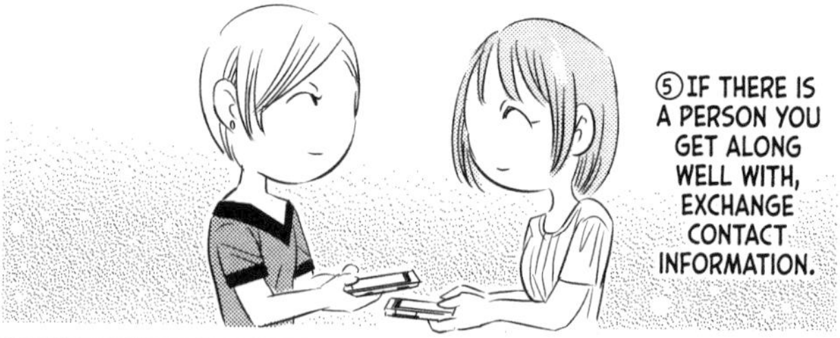

⑤ IF THERE IS A PERSON YOU GET ALONG WELL WITH, EXCHANGE CONTACT INFORMATION.

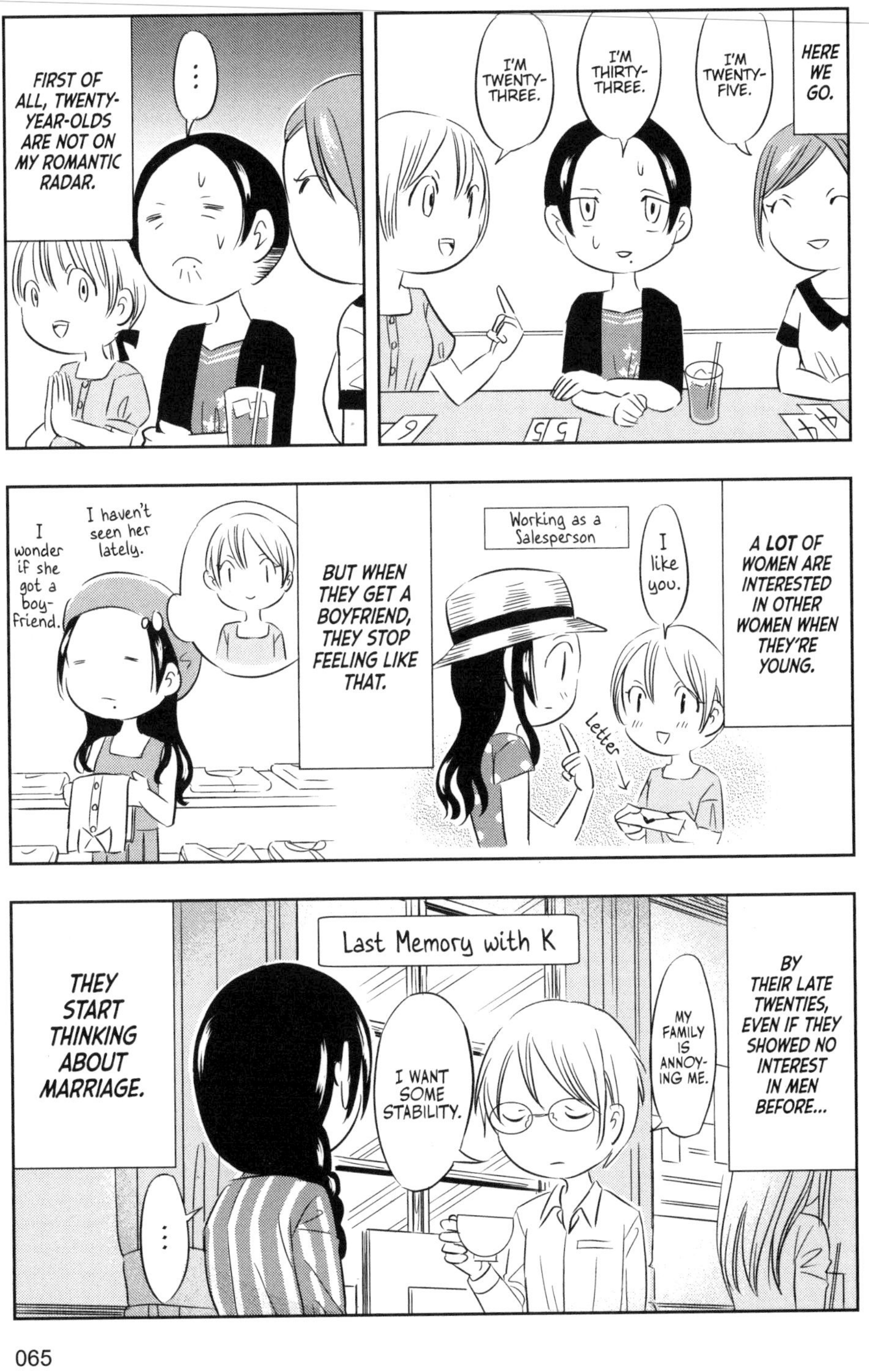
HERE WE GO.
I'M TWENTY-FIVE.
I'M THIRTY-THREE.
I'M TWENTY-THREE.
...
FIRST OF ALL, TWENTY-YEAR-OLDS ARE NOT ON MY ROMANTIC RADAR.
A LOT OF WOMEN ARE INTERESTED IN OTHER WOMEN WHEN THEY'RE YOUNG.
Working as a Salesperson
I like you.
Letter
BUT WHEN THEY GET A BOYFRIEND, THEY STOP FEELING LIKE THAT.
I haven't seen her lately.
I wonder if she got a boy-friend.
BY THEIR LATE TWENTIES, EVEN IF THEY SHOWED NO INTEREST IN MEN BEFORE...
Last Memory with K
MY FAMILY IS ANNOY-ING ME.
I WANT SOME STABILITY.
THEY START THINKING ABOUT MARRIAGE.
...

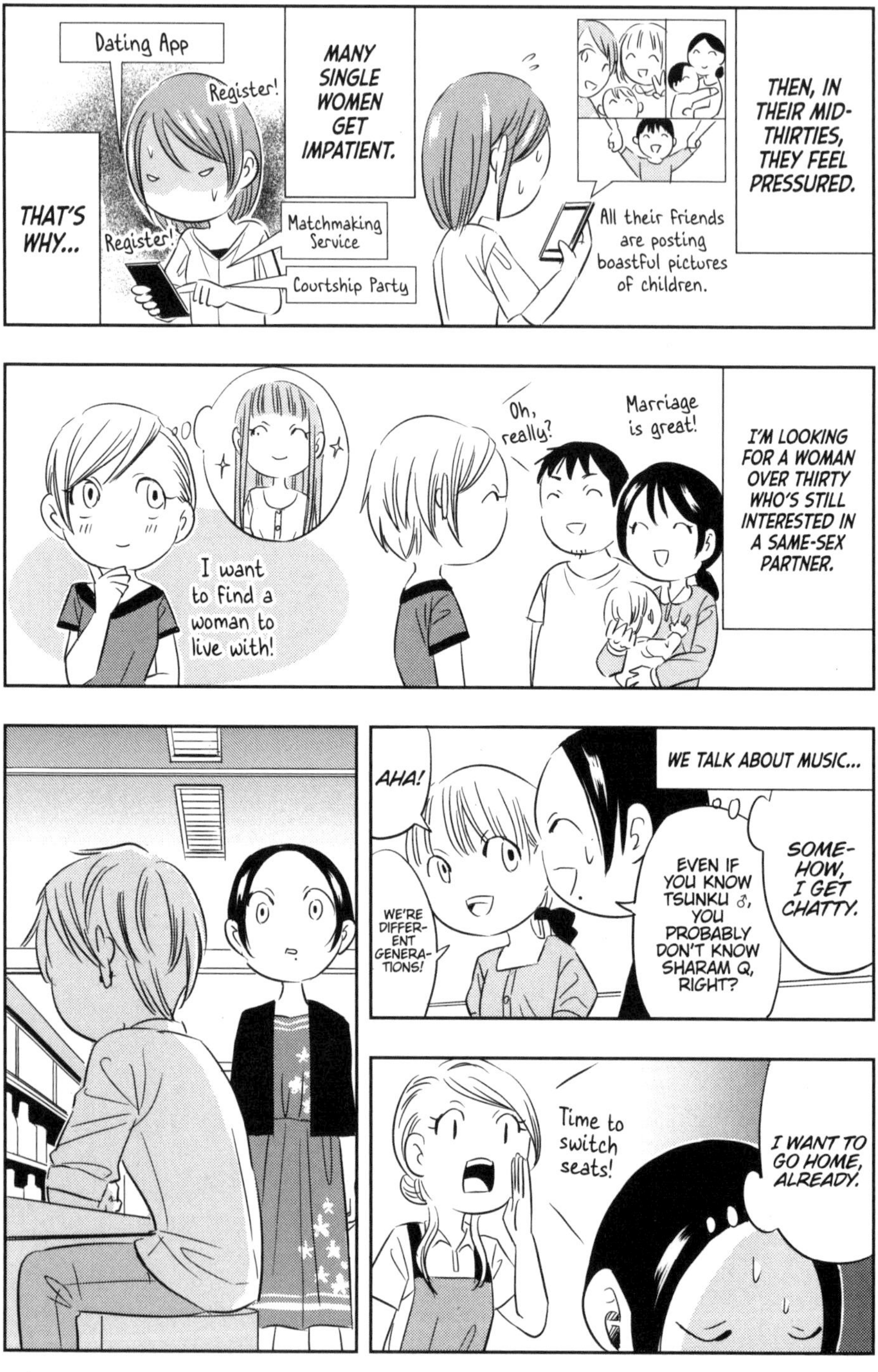
THEN, IN THEIR MID-THIRTIES, THEY FEEL PRESSURED.
All their friends are posting boastful pictures of children.
MANY SINGLE WOMEN GET IMPATIENT.
Dating App
Register!
Matchmaking Service
Register!
Courtship Party
THAT'S WHY...
I'M LOOKING FOR A WOMAN OVER THIRTY WHO'S STILL INTERESTED IN A SAME-SEX PARTNER.
Marriage is great!
Oh, really?
I want to find a woman to live with!
WE TALK ABOUT MUSIC...
SOMEHOW, I GET CHATTY.
EVEN IF YOU KNOW TSUNKU ♂, YOU PROBABLY DON'T KNOW SHARAM Q, RIGHT?
AHA!
WE'RE DIFFERENT GENERATIONS!
I WANT TO GO HOME, ALREADY.
Time to switch seats!

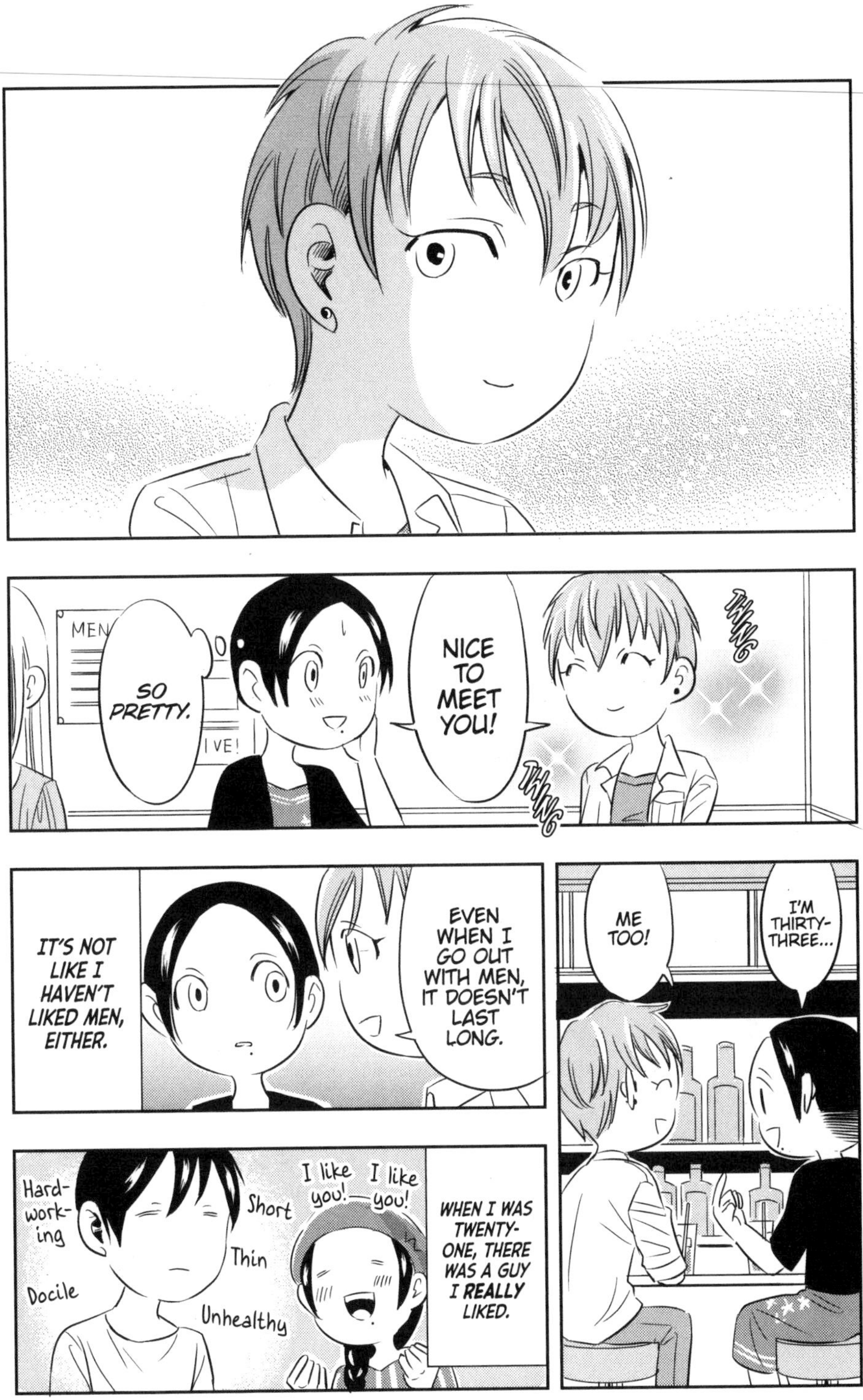
THING
NICE TO MEET YOU!
THING
SO PRETTY.
I'M THIRTY-THREE...
ME TOO!
EVEN WHEN I GO OUT WITH MEN, IT DOESN'T LAST LONG.
IT'S NOT LIKE I HAVEN'T LIKED MEN, EITHER.
WHEN I WAS TWENTY-ONE, THERE WAS A GUY I REALLY LIKED.
I like you!
I like you!
Short
Hard-working
Thin
Docile
Unhealthy

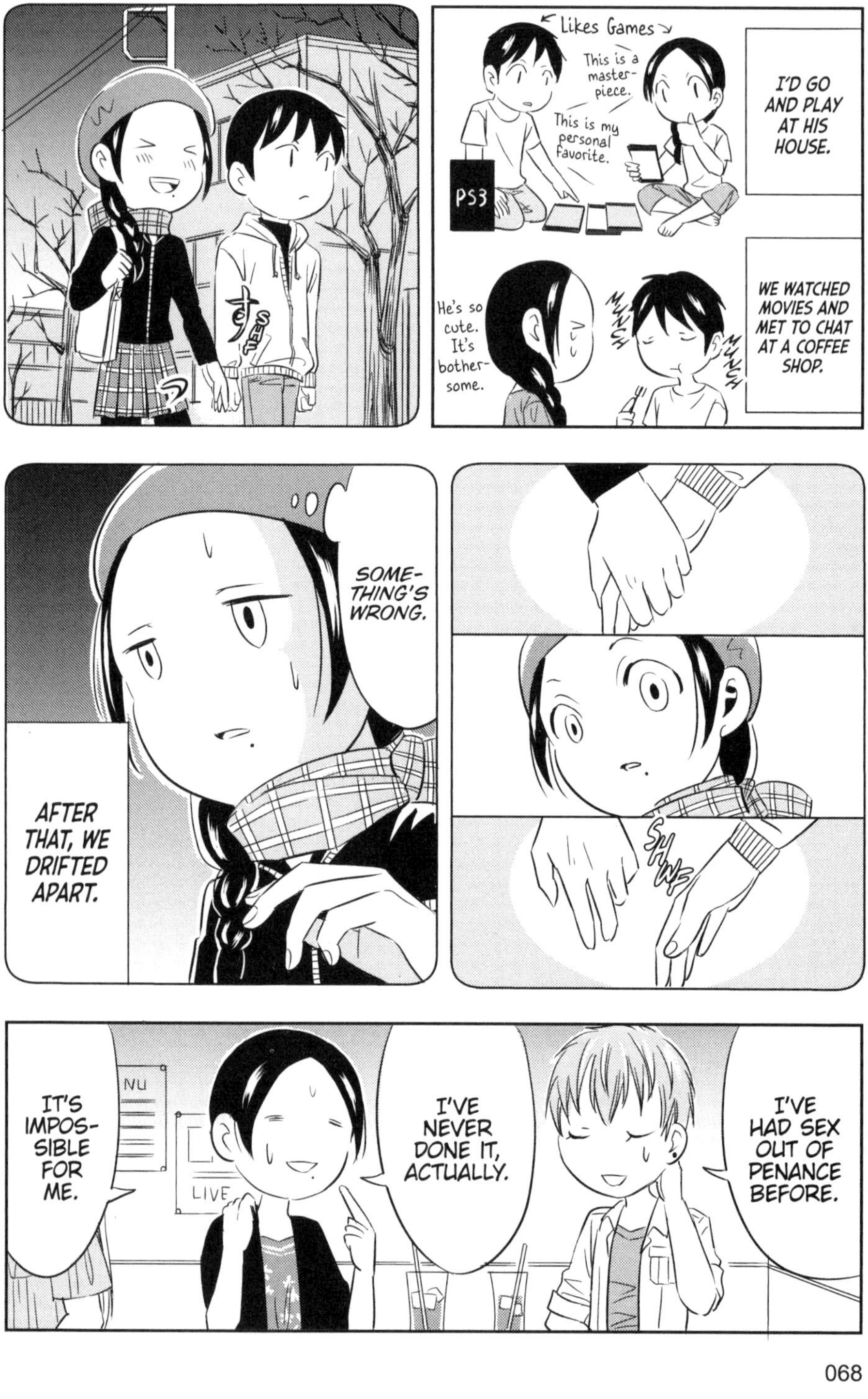
I'D GO AND PLAY AT HIS HOUSE.
Likes Games
This is a masterpiece.
This is my personal favorite.
PS3
WE WATCHED MOVIES AND MET TO CHAT AT A COFFEE SHOP.
MUNCH
MUNCH
He's so cute. It's bothersome.
SHWF
SOMETHING'S WRONG.
AFTER THAT, WE DRIFTED APART.
I'VE HAD SEX OUT OF PENANCE BEFORE.
I'VE NEVER DONE IT, ACTUALLY.
IT'S IMPOSSIBLE FOR ME.
NU
LIVE

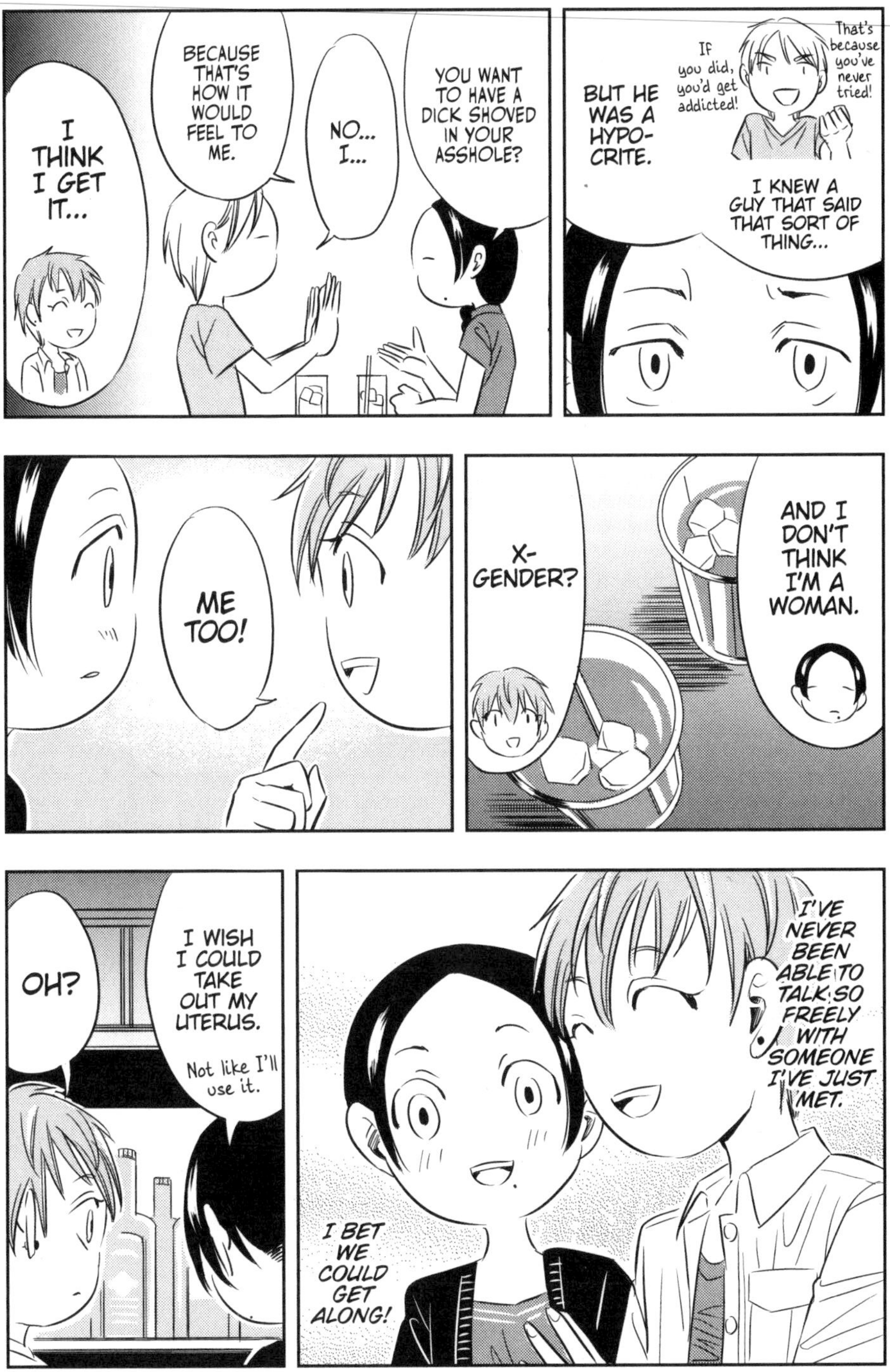
I KNEW A GUY THAT SAID THAT SORT OF THING...
That's because you've never tried!
If you did, you'd get addicted!
BUT HE WAS A HYPOCRITE.
YOU WANT TO HAVE A DICK SHOVED IN YOUR ASSHOLE?
NO... I...
BECAUSE THAT'S HOW IT WOULD FEEL TO ME.
I THINK I GET IT...
AND I DON'T THINK I'M A WOMAN.
X-GENDER?
ME TOO!
I'VE NEVER BEEN ABLE TO TALK SO FREELY WITH SOMEONE I'VE JUST MET.
I BET WE COULD GET ALONG!
I WISH I COULD TAKE OUT MY UTERUS.
Not like I'll use it.
OH?

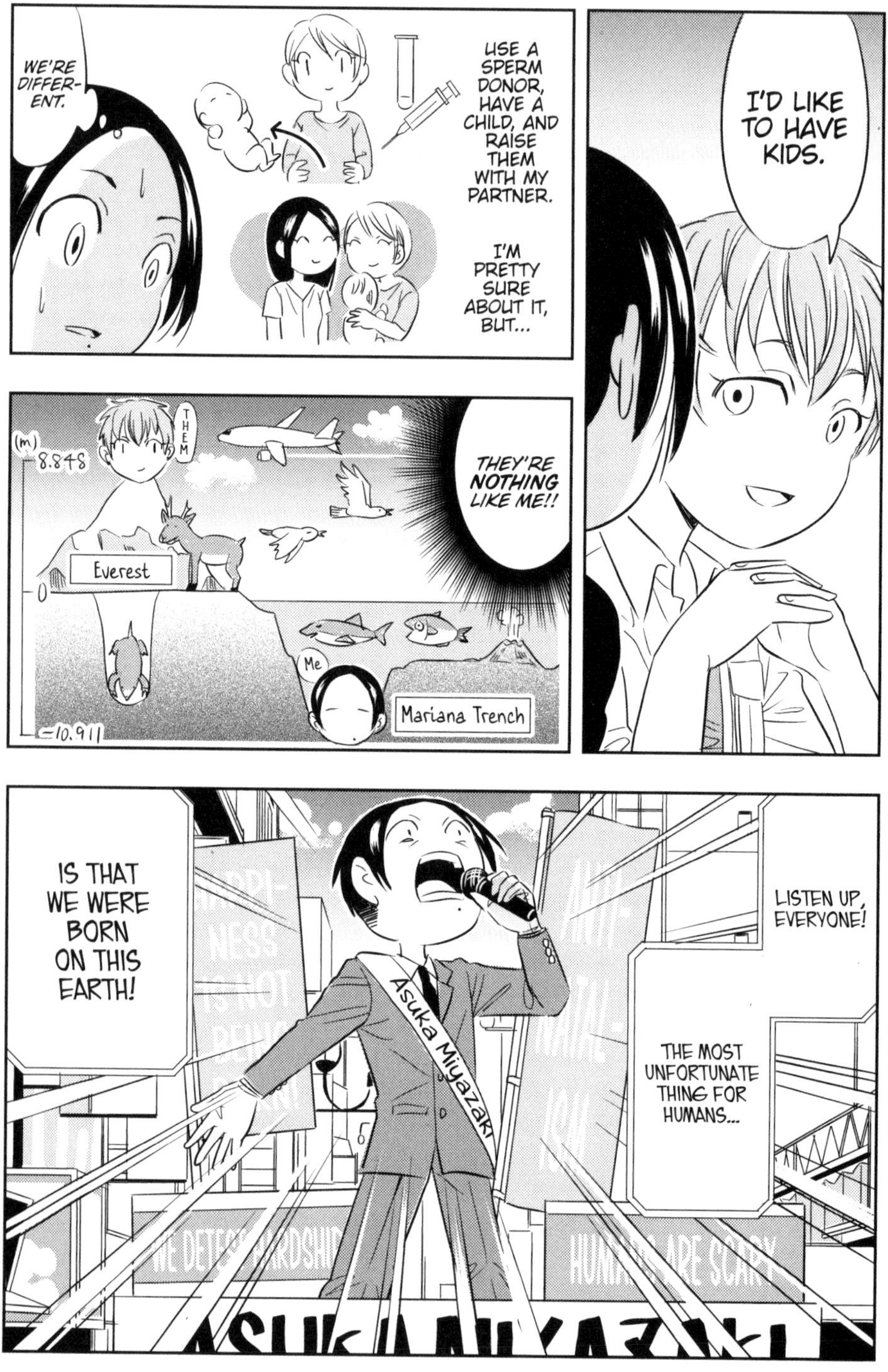
I'D LIKE TO HAVE KIDS.
USE A SPERM DONOR, HAVE A CHILD, AND RAISE THEM WITH MY PARTNER.
I'M PRETTY SURE ABOUT IT, BUT...
WE'RE DIFFER-ENT.
THEY'RE NOTHING LIKE ME!!
THEM
(m)
8.848
Everest
0
Me
Mariana Trench
-10.911
LISTEN UP, EVERYONE!
THE MOST UNFORTUNATE THING FOR HUMANS...
IS THAT WE WERE BORN ON THIS EARTH!
Asuka Miyazaki

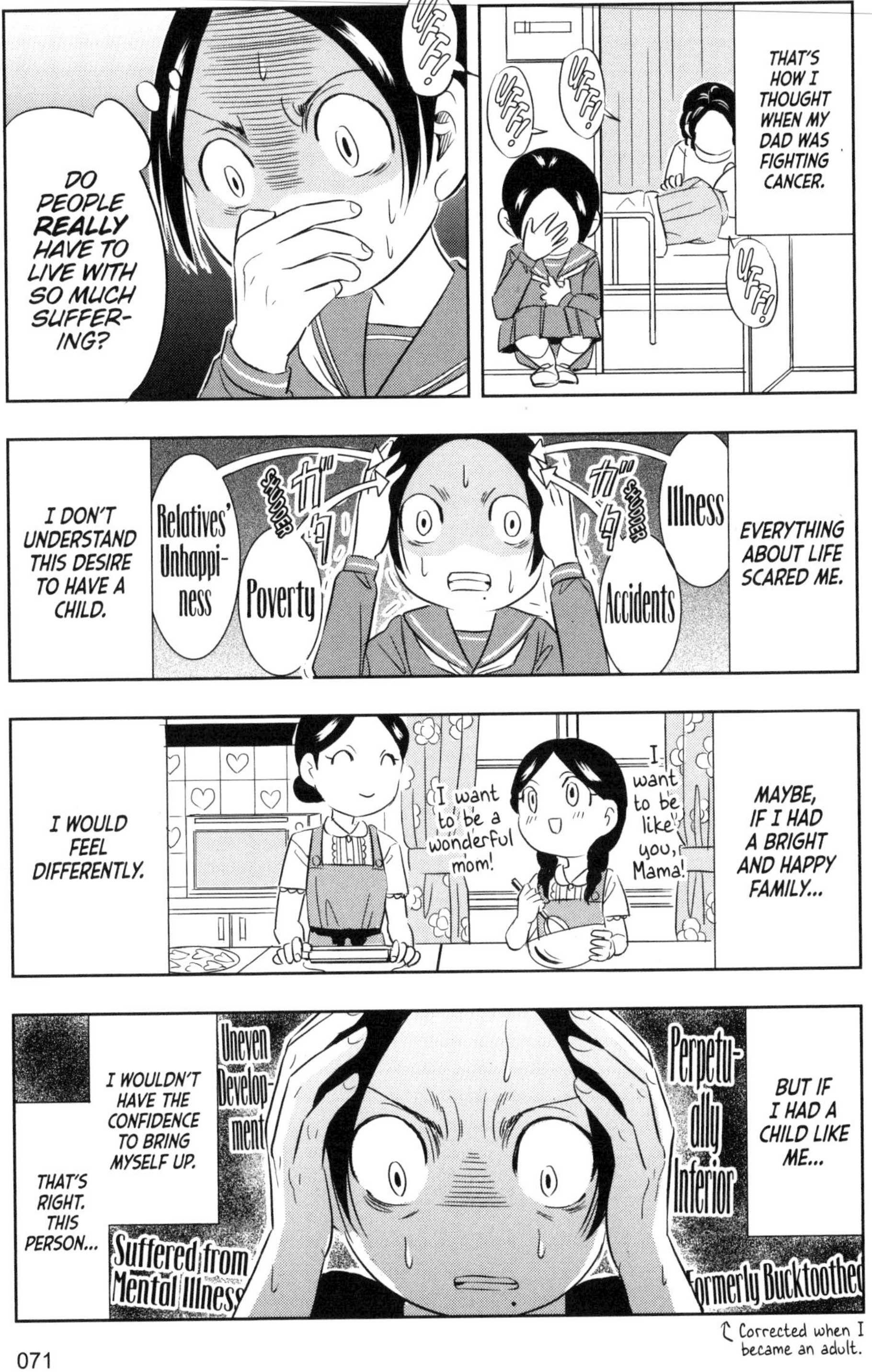
THAT'S HOW I THOUGHT WHEN MY DAD WAS FIGHTING CANCER.
UFF!
UFF!
UFF!
UFF!
DO PEOPLE **REALLY** HAVE TO LIVE WITH SO MUCH SUFFER-ING?
EVERYTHING ABOUT LIFE SCARED ME.
Illness
Accidents
SHUDDER
SHUDDER
Poverty
Relatives' Unhappi-ness
I DON'T UNDERSTAND THIS DESIRE TO HAVE A CHILD.
MAYBE, IF I HAD A BRIGHT AND HAPPY FAMILY...
I want to be like you, Mama!
I want to be a wonderful mom!
I WOULD FEEL DIFFERENTLY.
BUT IF I HAD A CHILD LIKE ME...
Perpetu-ally Inferior
Formerly Bucktoothed
Uneven Develop-ment
I WOULDN'T HAVE THE CONFIDENCE TO BRING MYSELF UP.
THAT'S RIGHT. THIS PERSON...
Suffered from Mental Illness
Corrected when I became an adult.

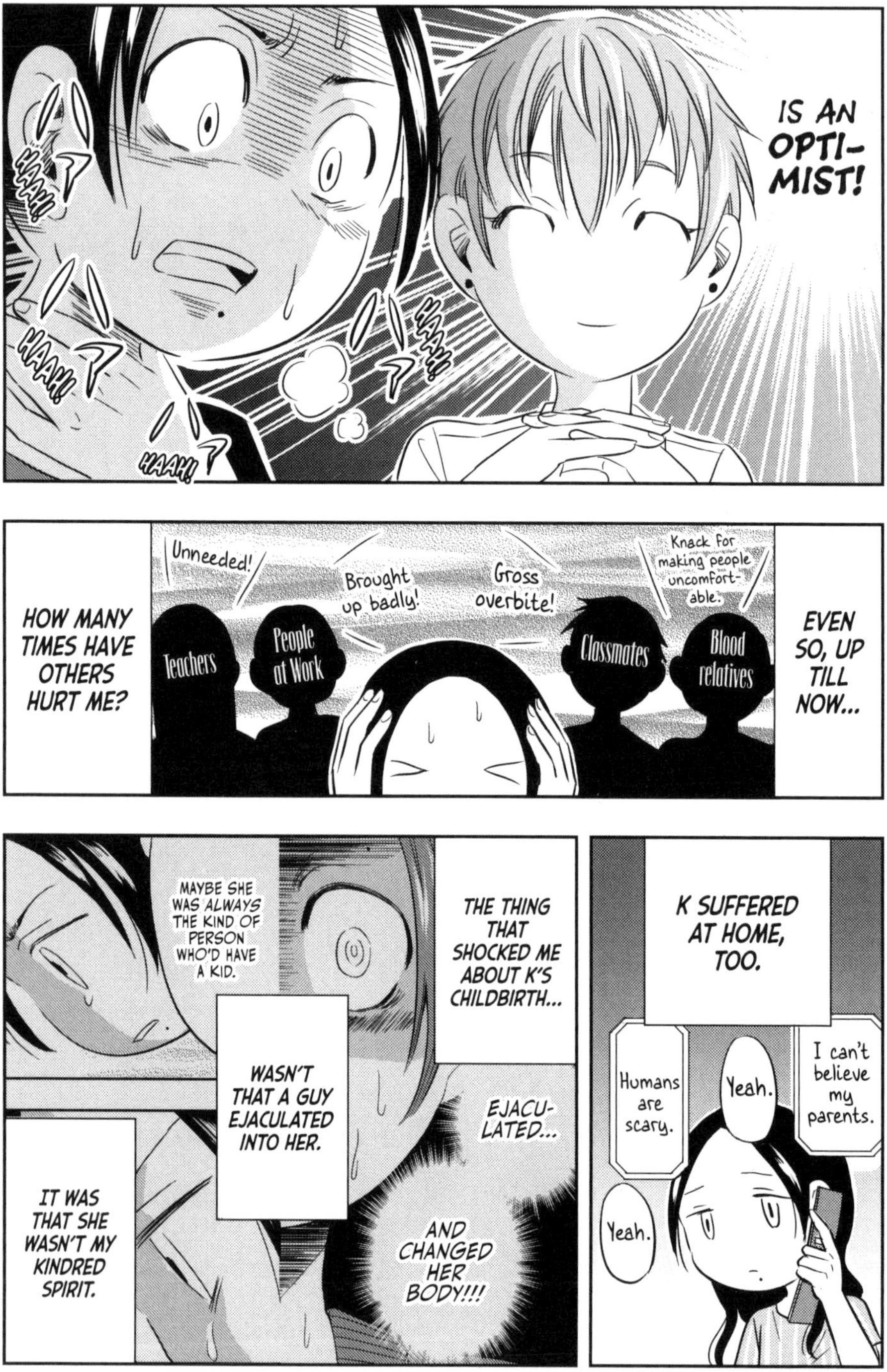
IS AN OPTI-MIST!
HAAH!
HAAH!
HAAH!
HAAH!
EVEN SO, UP TILL NOW...
Knack for making people uncomfort-able.
Blood relatives
Classmates
Gross overbite!
Brought up badly!
People at Work
Unneeded!
Teachers
HOW MANY TIMES HAVE OTHERS HURT ME?
K SUFFERED AT HOME, TOO.
I can't believe my parents.
Yeah.
Humans are scary.
Yeah.
THE THING THAT SHOCKED ME ABOUT K'S CHILDBIRTH...
MAYBE SHE WAS ALWAYS THE KIND OF PERSON WHO'D HAVE A KID.
WASN'T THAT A GUY EJACULATED INTO HER.
EJACU-LATED...
AND CHANGED HER BODY!!!
IT WAS THAT SHE WASN'T MY KINDRED SPIRIT.

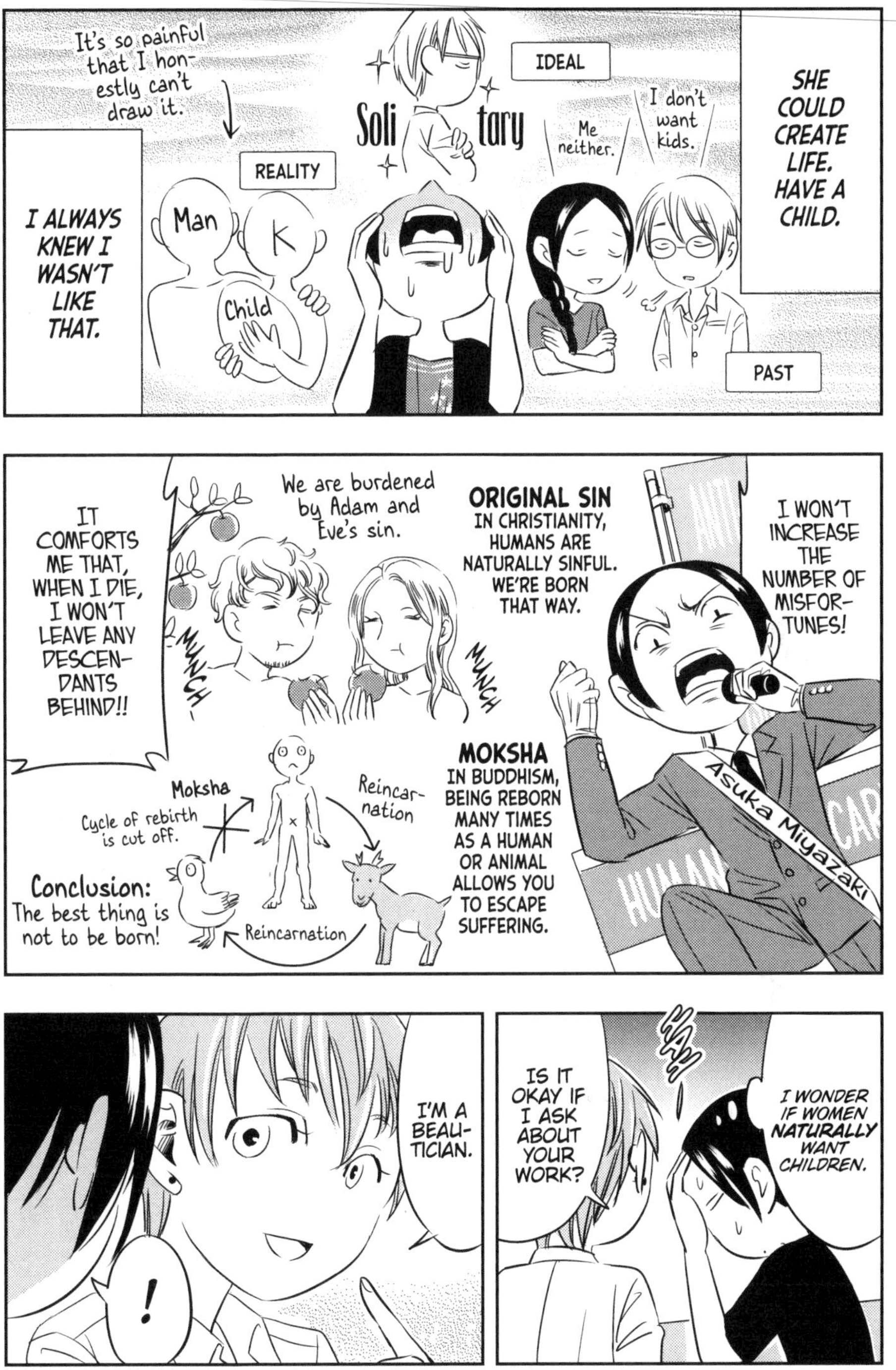
SHE COULD CREATE LIFE. HAVE A CHILD.
IDEAL
Solitary
I don't want kids.
Me neither.
PAST
It's so painful that I honestly can't draw it.
REALITY
Man
K
Child
I ALWAYS KNEW I WASN'T LIKE THAT.
I WON'T INCREASE THE NUMBER OF MISFORTUNES!
Asuka Miyazaki
ORIGINAL SIN
IN CHRISTIANITY, HUMANS ARE NATURALLY SINFUL. WE'RE BORN THAT WAY.
We are burdened by Adam and Eve's sin.
MUNCH
MUNCH
IT COMFORTS ME THAT, WHEN I DIE, I WON'T LEAVE ANY DESCENDANTS BEHIND!!
MOKSHA
IN BUDDHISM, BEING REBORN MANY TIMES AS A HUMAN OR ANIMAL ALLOWS YOU TO ESCAPE SUFFERING.
Reincarnation
Reincarnation
Moksha
Cycle of rebirth is cut off.
Conclusion:
The best thing is not to be born!
I WONDER IF WOMEN NATURALLY WANT CHILDREN.
HAH
IS IT OKAY IF I ASK ABOUT YOUR WORK?
I'M A BEAUTICIAN.
!

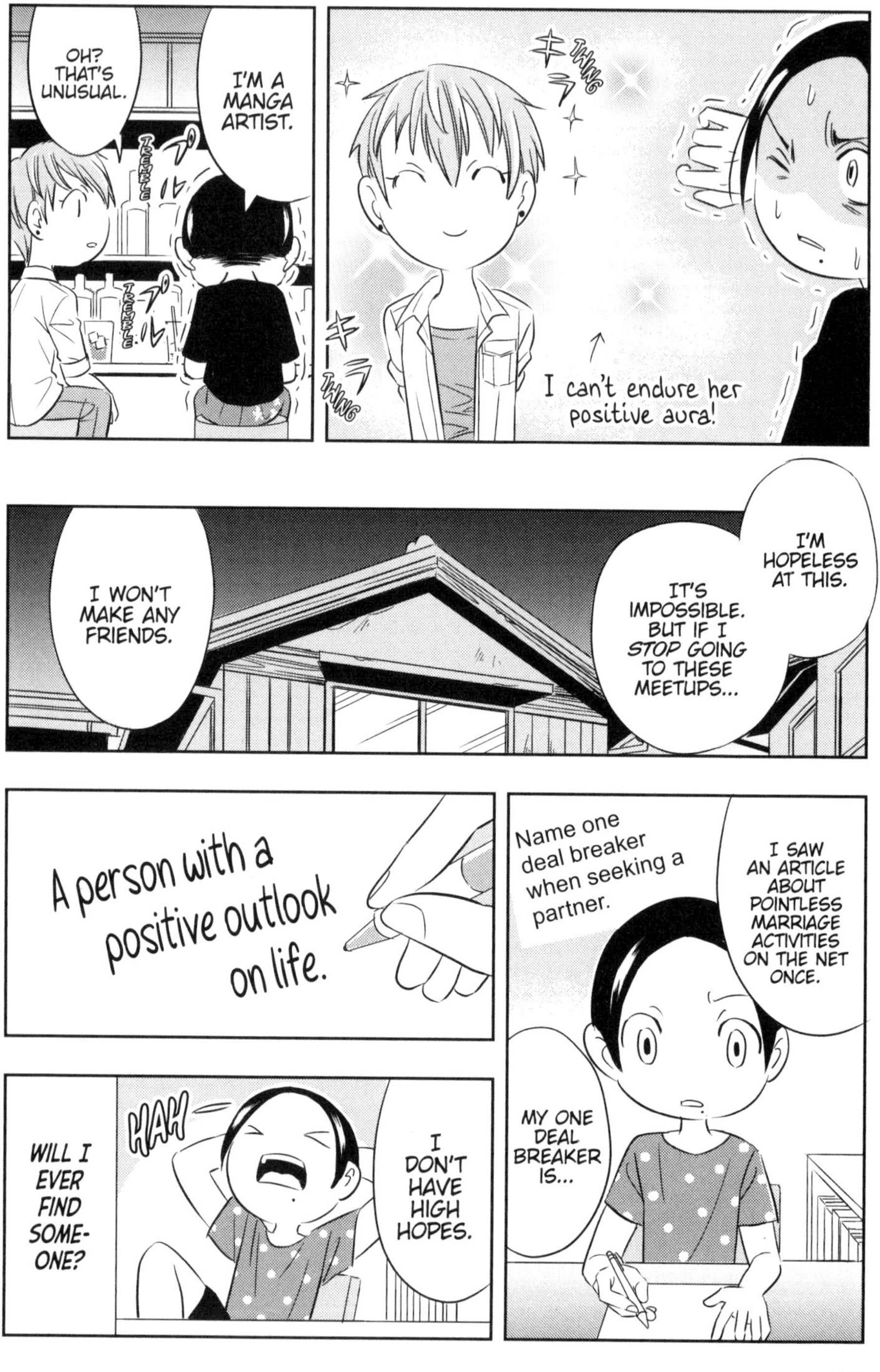
THING
THING
I can't endure her positive aura!
I'M A MANGA ARTIST.
OH? THAT'S UNUSUAL.
TREMBLE
TREMBLE
I'M HOPELESS AT THIS.
IT'S IMPOSSIBLE. BUT IF I *STOP* GOING TO THESE MEETUPS...
I WON'T MAKE ANY FRIENDS.
I SAW AN ARTICLE ABOUT POINTLESS MARRIAGE ACTIVITIES ON THE NET ONCE.
Name one deal breaker when seeking a partner.
MY ONE DEAL BREAKER IS...
A person with a positive outlook on life.
I DON'T HAVE HIGH HOPES.
HAH
WILL I EVER FIND SOME-ONE?

Ep. 7: The "IRL Meetups, Again and Again" Story

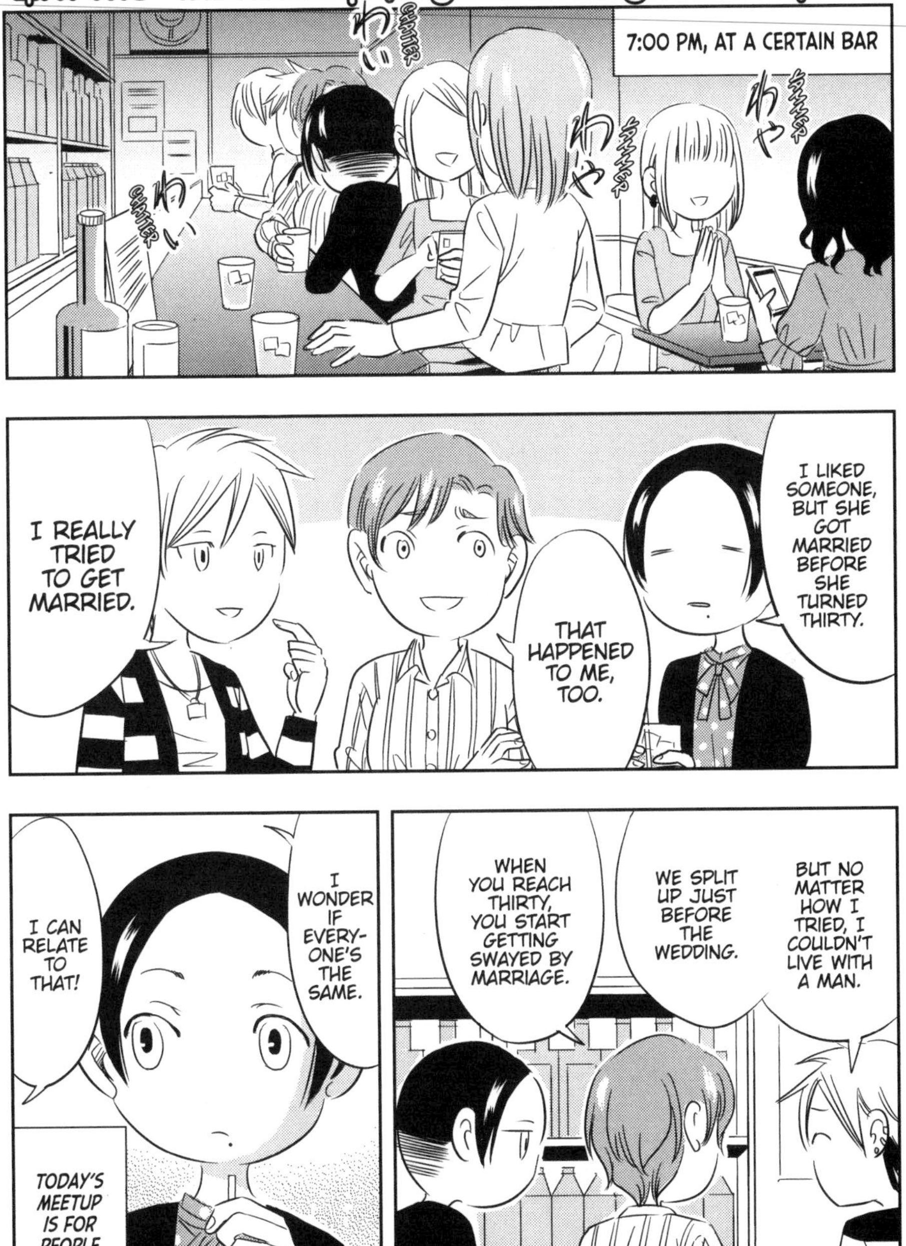
7:00 PM, AT A CERTAIN BAR
CHATTER
CHATTER
CHATTER
CHATTER
I LIKED SOMEONE, BUT SHE GOT MARRIED BEFORE SHE TURNED THIRTY.
THAT HAPPENED TO ME, TOO.
I REALLY TRIED TO GET MARRIED.
BUT NO MATTER HOW I TRIED, I COULDN'T LIVE WITH A MAN.
WE SPLIT UP JUST BEFORE THE WEDDING.
WHEN YOU REACH THIRTY, YOU START GETTING SWAYED BY MARRIAGE.
I WONDER IF EVERY-ONE'S THE SAME.
I CAN RELATE TO THAT!
TODAY'S MEETUP IS FOR PEOPLE IN THEIR THIRTIES AND FORTIES.

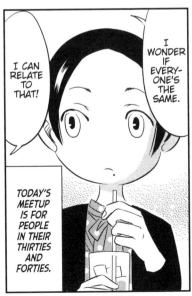

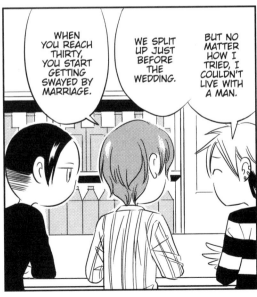

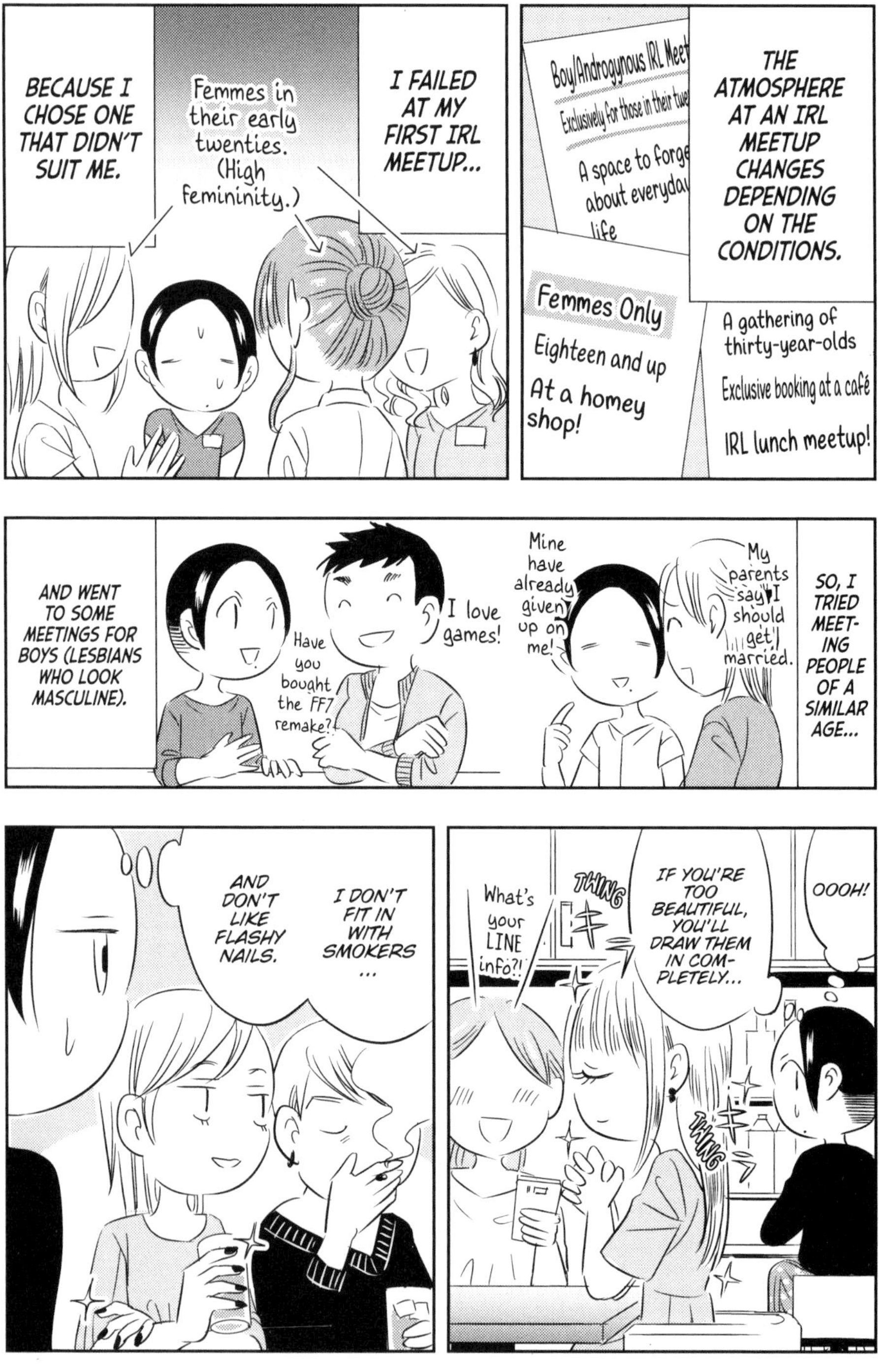
THE ATMOSPHERE AT AN IRL MEETUP CHANGES DEPENDING ON THE CONDITIONS.
Boy/Androgynous IRL Meet
Exclusively for those in their twe
A space to forge about everyday life
A gathering of thirty-year-olds
Exclusive booking at a café
IRL lunch meetup!
Femmes Only
Eighteen and up
At a homey shop!
I FAILED AT MY FIRST IRL MEETUP...
Femmes in their early twenties. (High femininity.)
BECAUSE I CHOSE ONE THAT DIDN'T SUIT ME.
SO, I TRIED MEETING PEOPLE OF A SIMILAR AGE...
My parents say I should get married.
Mine have already given up on me!
I love games!
Have you bought the FF7 remake?
AND WENT TO SOME MEETINGS FOR BOYS (LESBIANS WHO LOOK MASCULINE).
OOOH!
IF YOU'RE TOO BEAUTIFUL, YOU'LL DRAW THEM IN COMPLETELY...
THING
What's your LINE info?!
THING
I DON'T FIT IN WITH SMOKERS...
AND DON'T LIKE FLASHY NAILS.

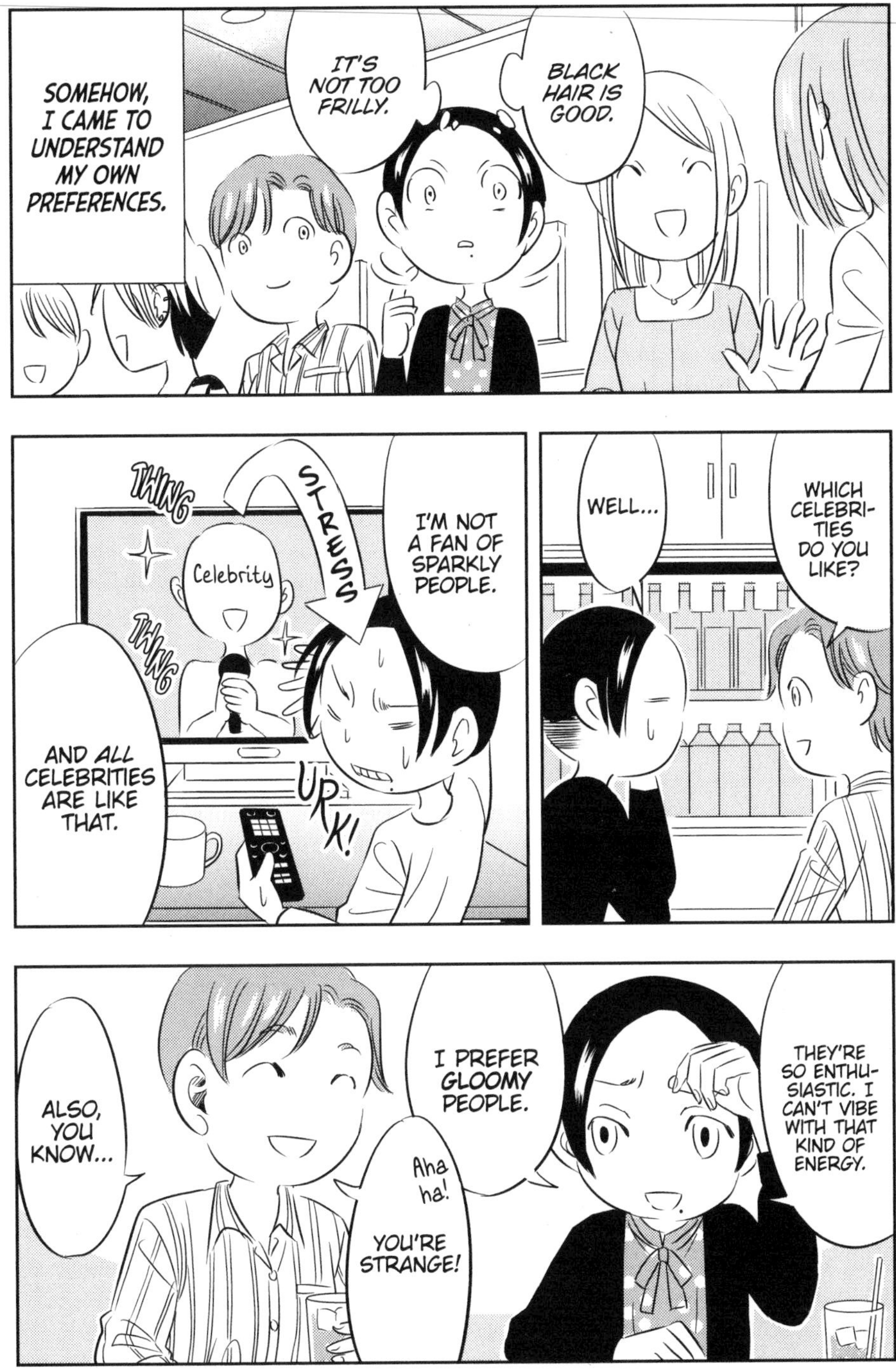
BLACK HAIR IS GOOD.
IT'S NOT TOO FRILLY.
SOMEHOW, I CAME TO UNDERSTAND MY OWN PREFERENCES.
WHICH CELEBRITIES DO YOU LIKE?
WELL...
I'M NOT A FAN OF SPARKLY PEOPLE.
STRESS
THING
Celebrity
THING
URK!
AND ALL CELEBRITIES ARE LIKE THAT.
THEY'RE SO ENTHUSIASTIC. I CAN'T VIBE WITH THAT KIND OF ENERGY.
I PREFER GLOOMY PEOPLE.
Aha ha!
YOU'RE STRANGE!
ALSO, YOU KNOW...

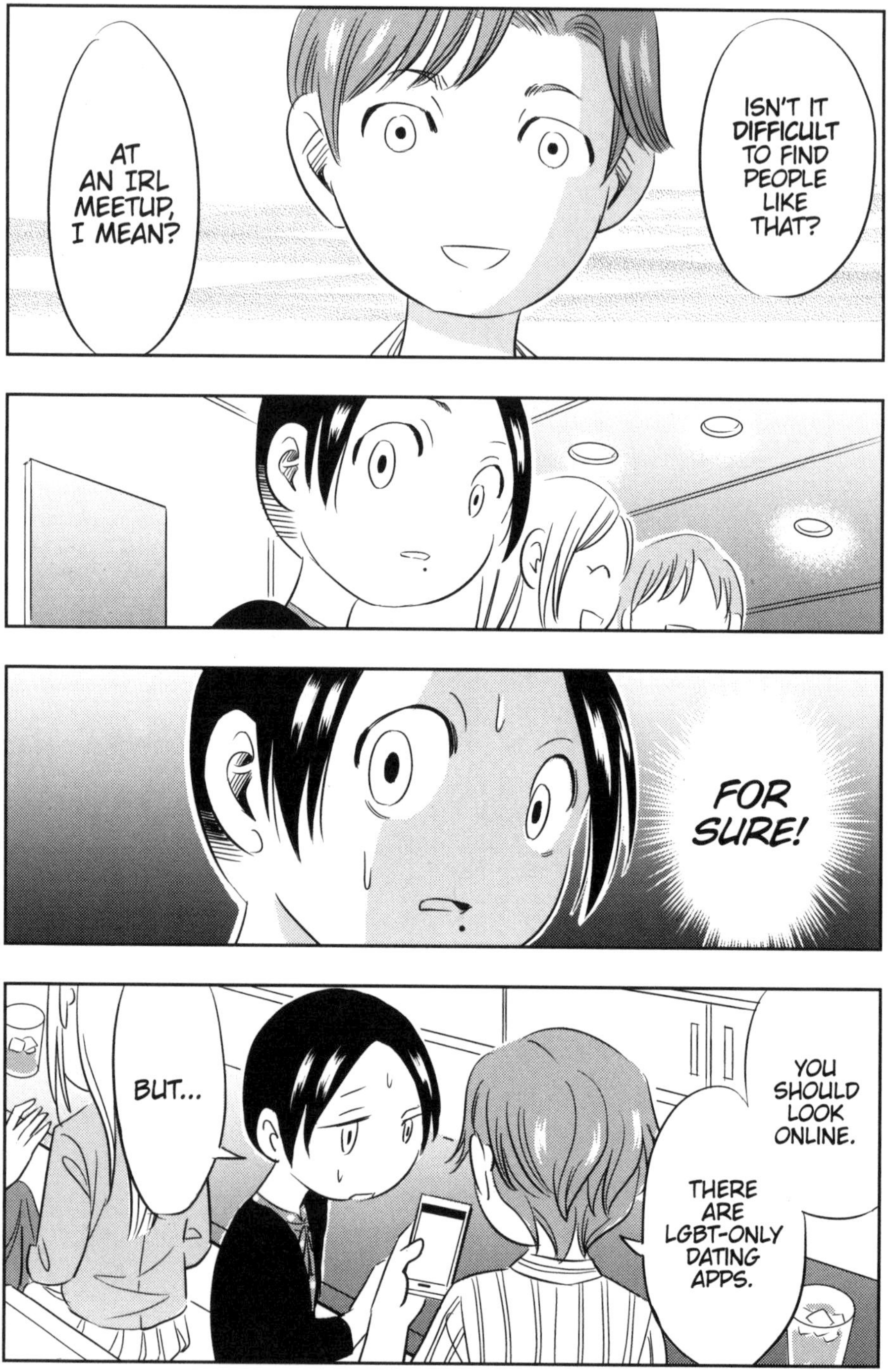
ISN'T IT DIFFICULT TO FIND PEOPLE LIKE THAT?
AT AN IRL MEETUP, I MEAN?
FOR SURE!
YOU SHOULD LOOK ONLINE.
THERE ARE LGBT-ONLY DATING APPS.
BUT...

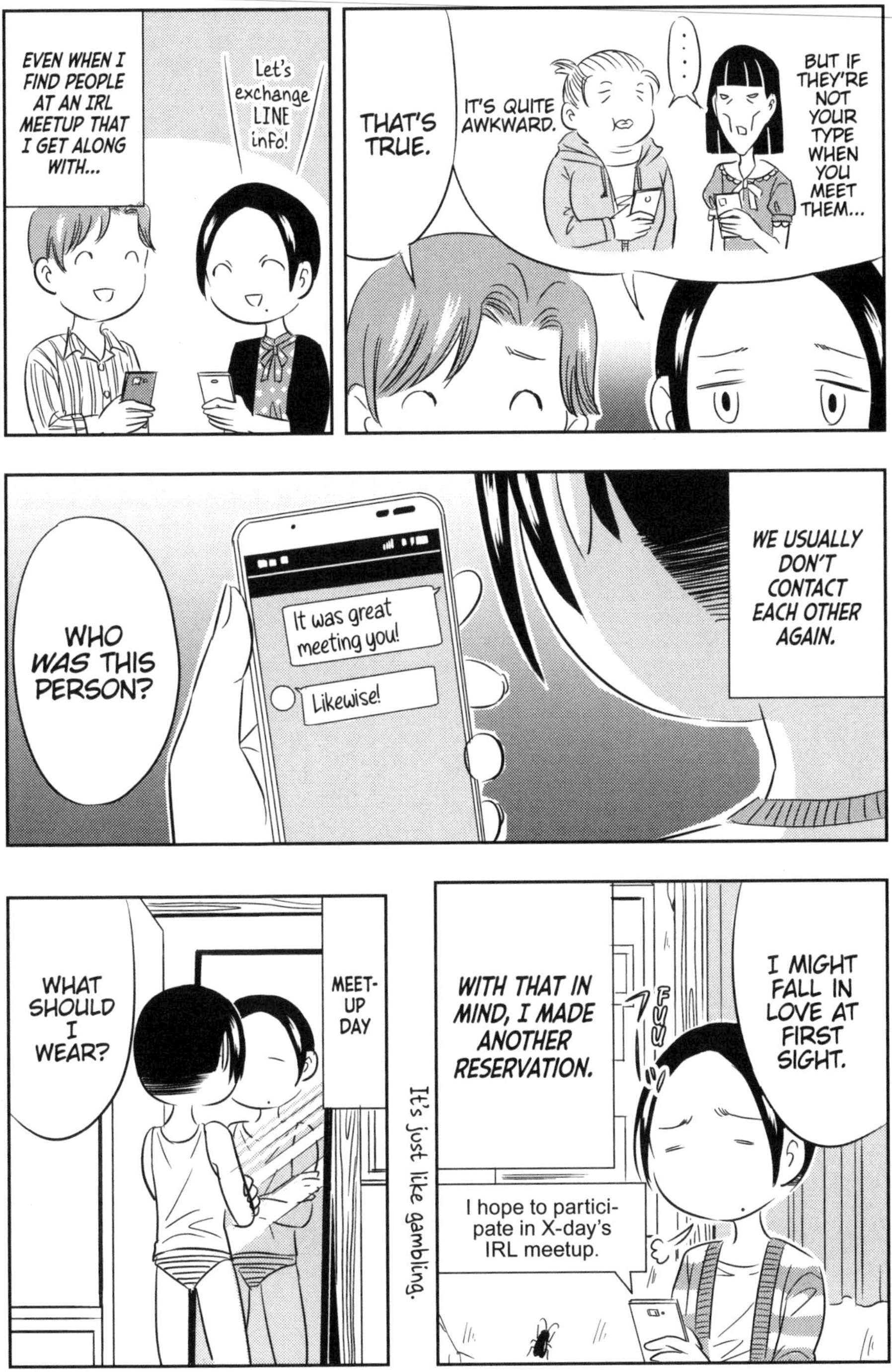
BUT IF THEY'RE NOT YOUR TYPE WHEN YOU MEET THEM...
. . . .
IT'S QUITE AWKWARD.
THAT'S TRUE.
EVEN WHEN I FIND PEOPLE AT AN IRL MEETUP THAT I GET ALONG WITH...
Let's exchange LINE info!
WE USUALLY DON'T CONTACT EACH OTHER AGAIN.
It was great meeting you!
Likewise!
WHO WAS THIS PERSON?
I MIGHT FALL IN LOVE AT FIRST SIGHT.
FUU
WITH THAT IN MIND, I MADE ANOTHER RESERVATION.
I hope to partici-pate in X-day's IRL meetup.
It's just like gambling.
MEET-UP DAY
WHAT SHOULD I WEAR?

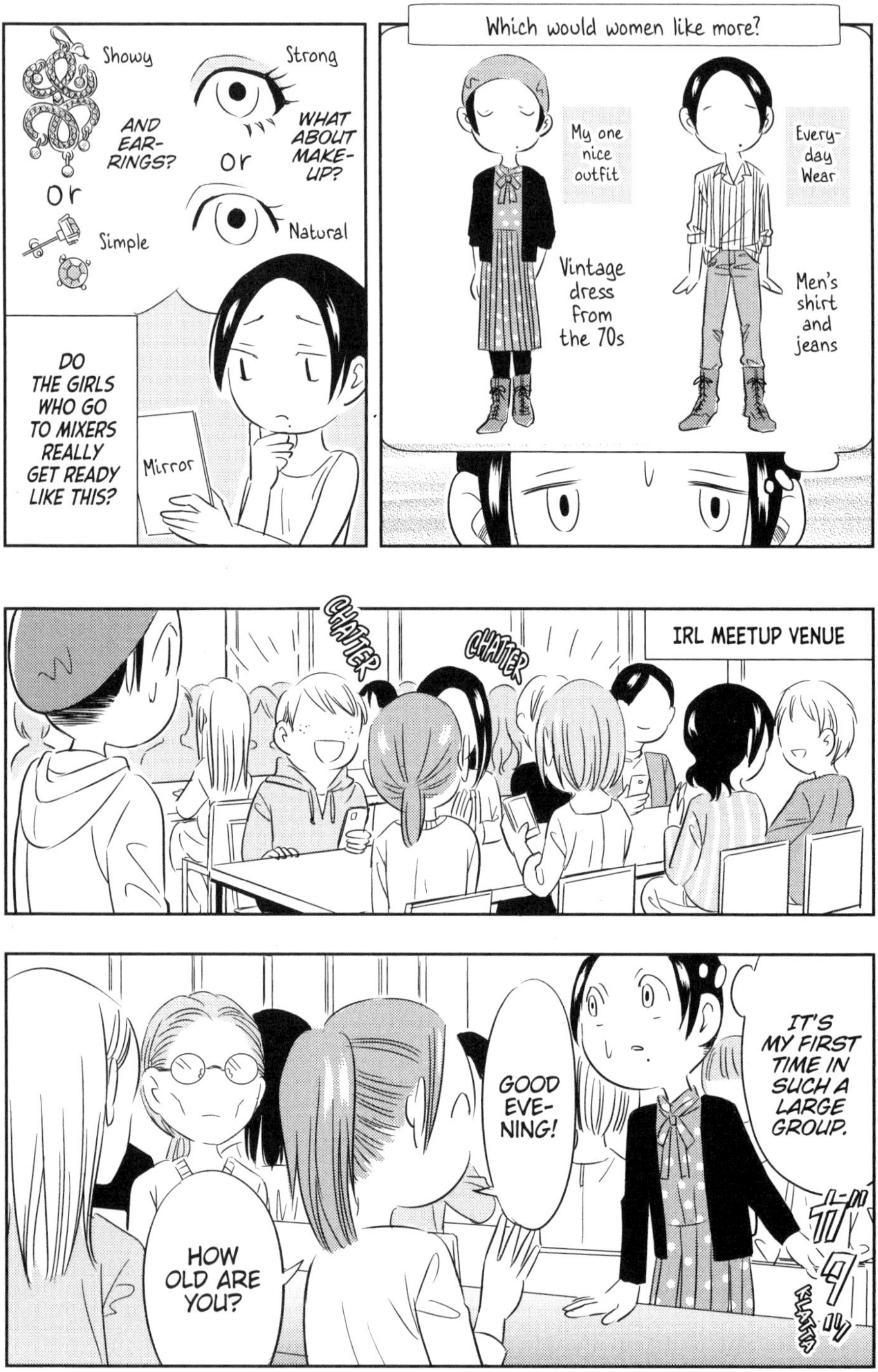

Which would women like more?
Every-day Wear
Men's shirt and jeans
My one nice outfit
Vintage dress from the 70s
Strong
WHAT ABOUT MAKE-UP?
or
Natural
Showy
AND EAR-RINGS?
or
Simple
Mirror
DO THE GIRLS WHO GO TO MIXERS REALLY GET READY LIKE THIS?
IRL MEETUP VENUE
CHATTER
CHATTER
IT'S MY FIRST TIME IN SUCH A LARGE GROUP.
KLATTA
GOOD EVE-NING!
HOW OLD ARE YOU?

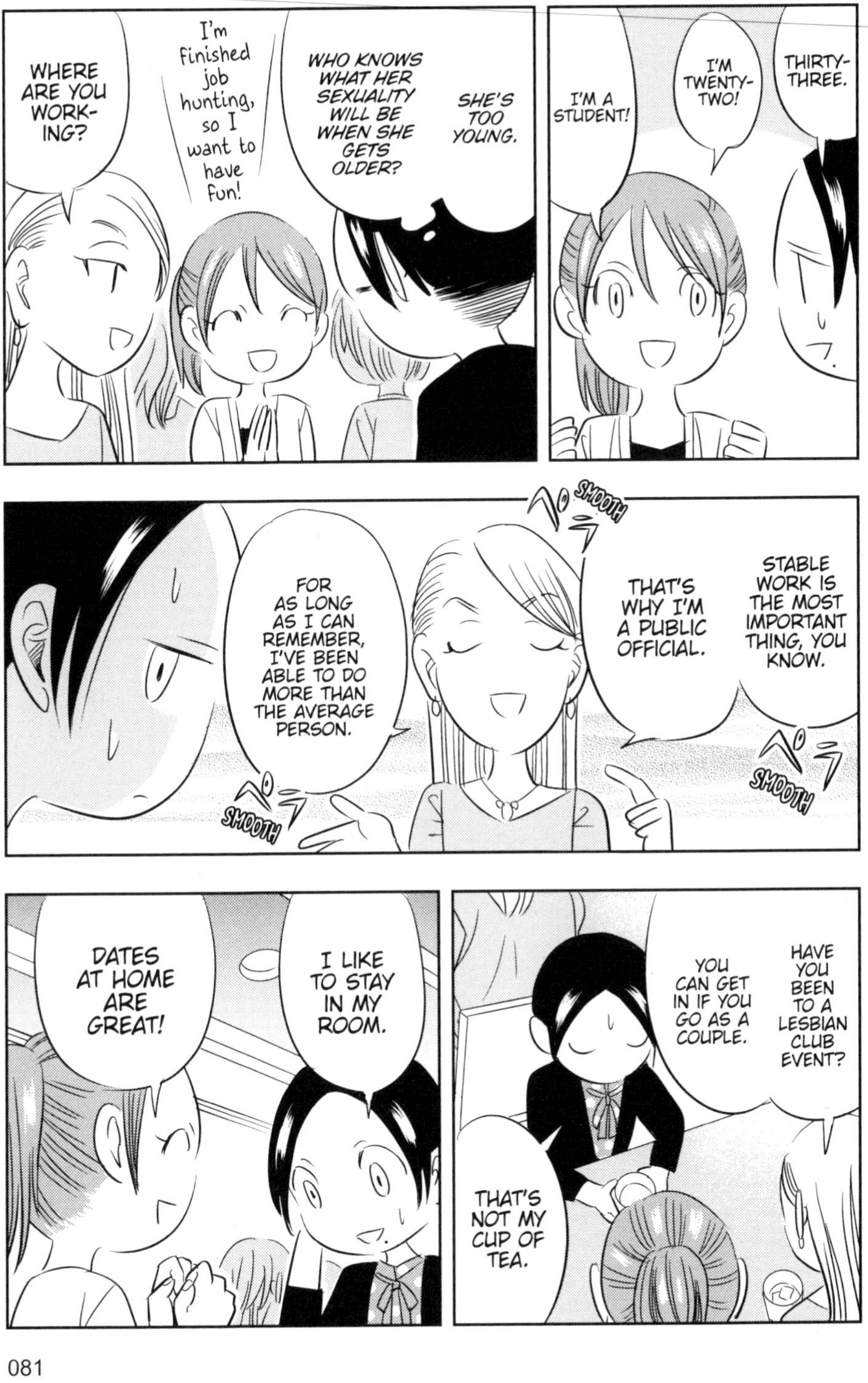
THIRTY-THREE.
I'M TWENTY-TWO!
I'M A STUDENT!
SHE'S TOO YOUNG.
WHO KNOWS WHAT HER SEXUALITY WILL BE WHEN SHE GETS OLDER?
I'm finished job hunting, so I want to have fun!
WHERE ARE YOU WORKING?
SMOOTH
STABLE WORK IS THE MOST IMPORTANT THING, YOU KNOW.
THAT'S WHY I'M A PUBLIC OFFICIAL.
SMOOTH
FOR AS LONG AS I CAN REMEMBER, I'VE BEEN ABLE TO DO MORE THAN THE AVERAGE PERSON.
SMOOTH
HAVE YOU BEEN TO A LESBIAN CLUB EVENT?
YOU CAN GET IN IF YOU GO AS A COUPLE.
THAT'S NOT MY CUP OF TEA.
I LIKE TO STAY IN MY ROOM.
DATES AT HOME ARE GREAT!

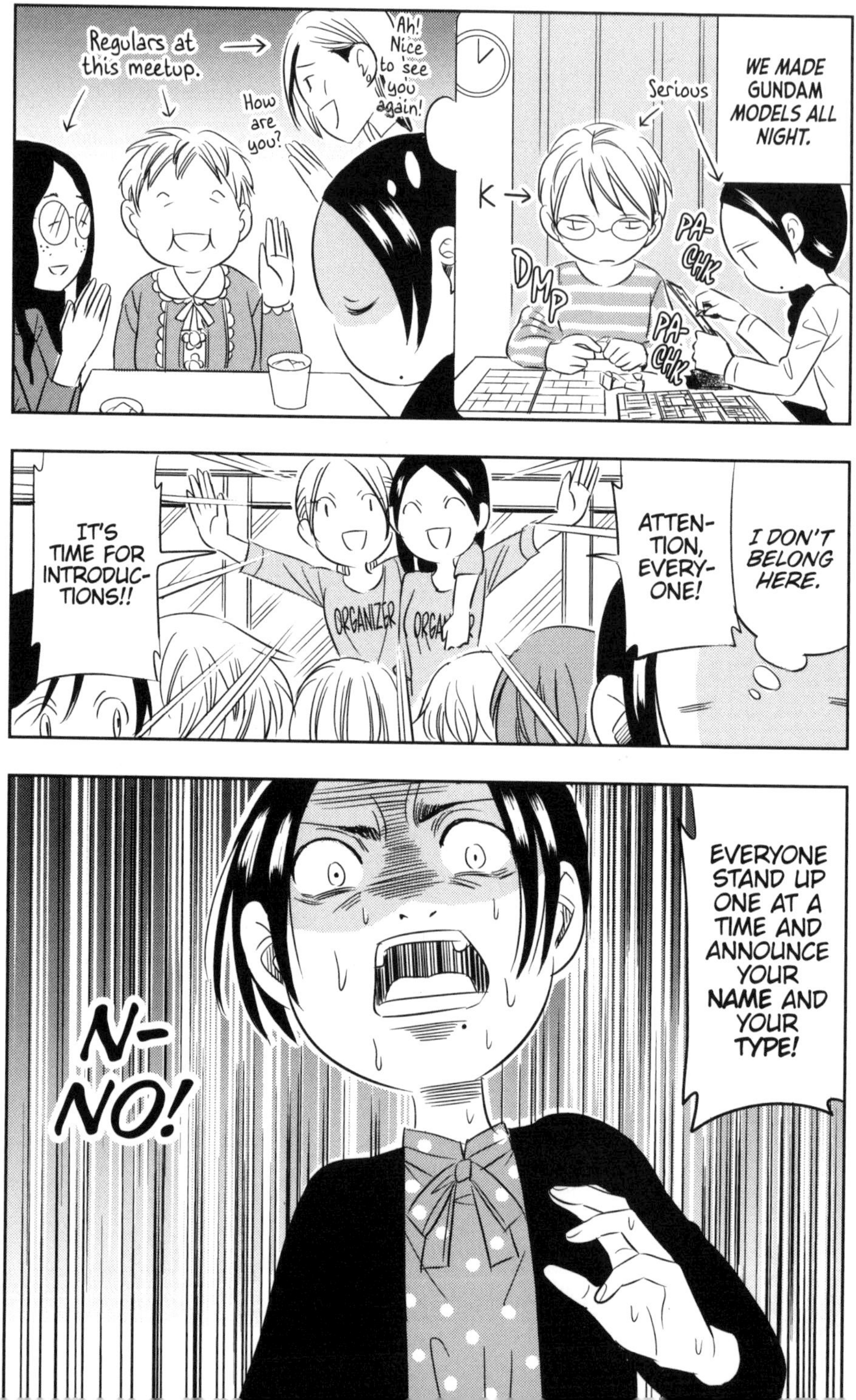
WE MADE GUNDAM MODELS ALL NIGHT.
Serious
K
DMP
PA-CHK
PA-CHK
Ah! Nice to see you again!
How are you?
Regulars at this meetup.
I DON'T BELONG HERE.
ATTENTION, EVERYONE!
IT'S TIME FOR INTRODUCTIONS!!
ORGANIZER
ORGANIZER
EVERYONE STAND UP ONE AT A TIME AND ANNOUNCE YOUR NAME AND YOUR TYPE!
N-NO!

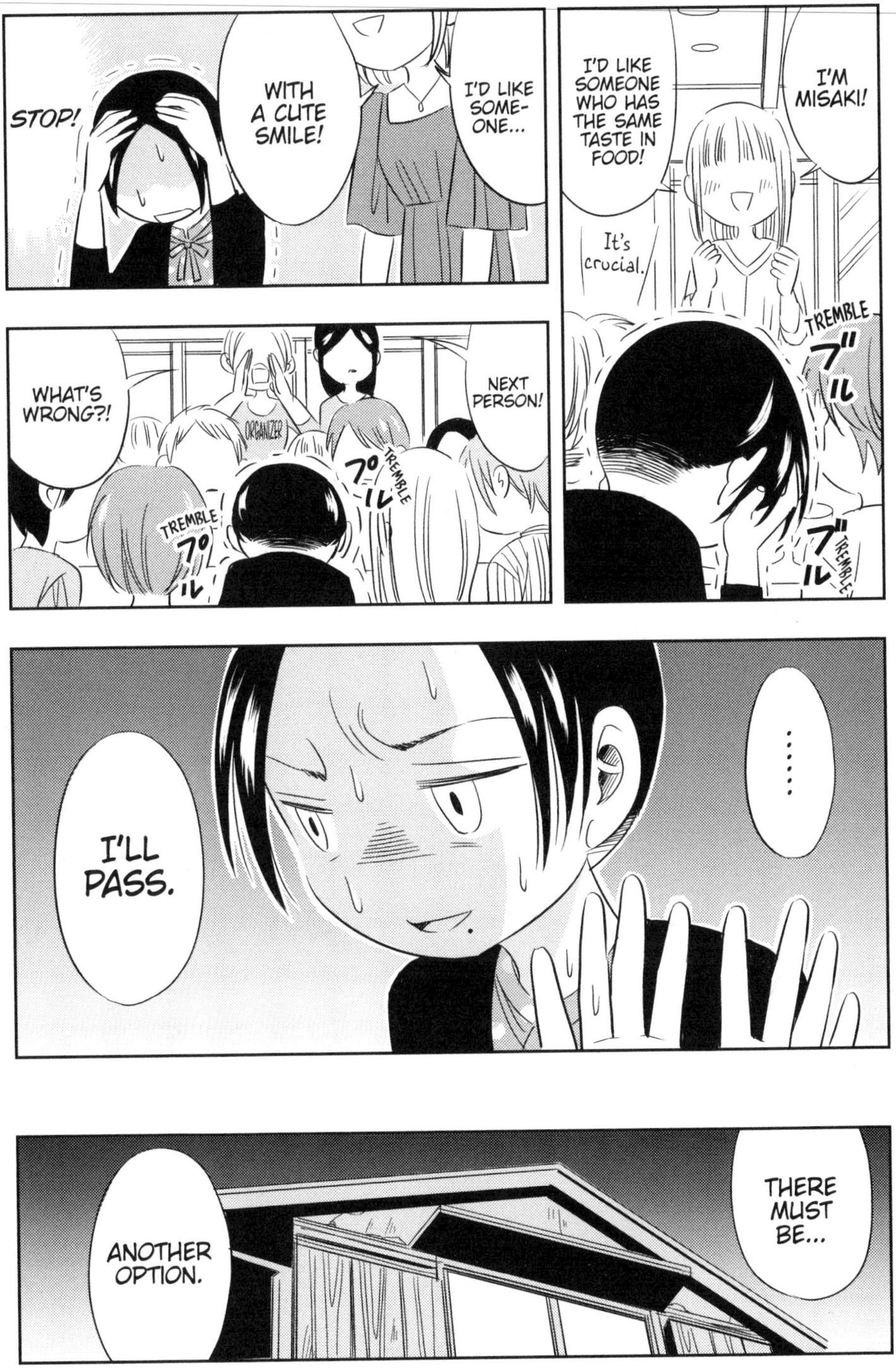
I'M MISAKI!
I'D LIKE SOMEONE WHO HAS THE SAME TASTE IN FOOD!
It's crucial.
TREMBLE
ブル
ブル
TREMBLE
I'D LIKE SOME-ONE...
WITH A CUTE SMILE!
STOP!
NEXT PERSON!
TREMBLE
プル
TREMBLE
プル
WHAT'S WRONG?!
......
I'LL PASS.
THERE MUST BE...
ANOTHER OPTION.

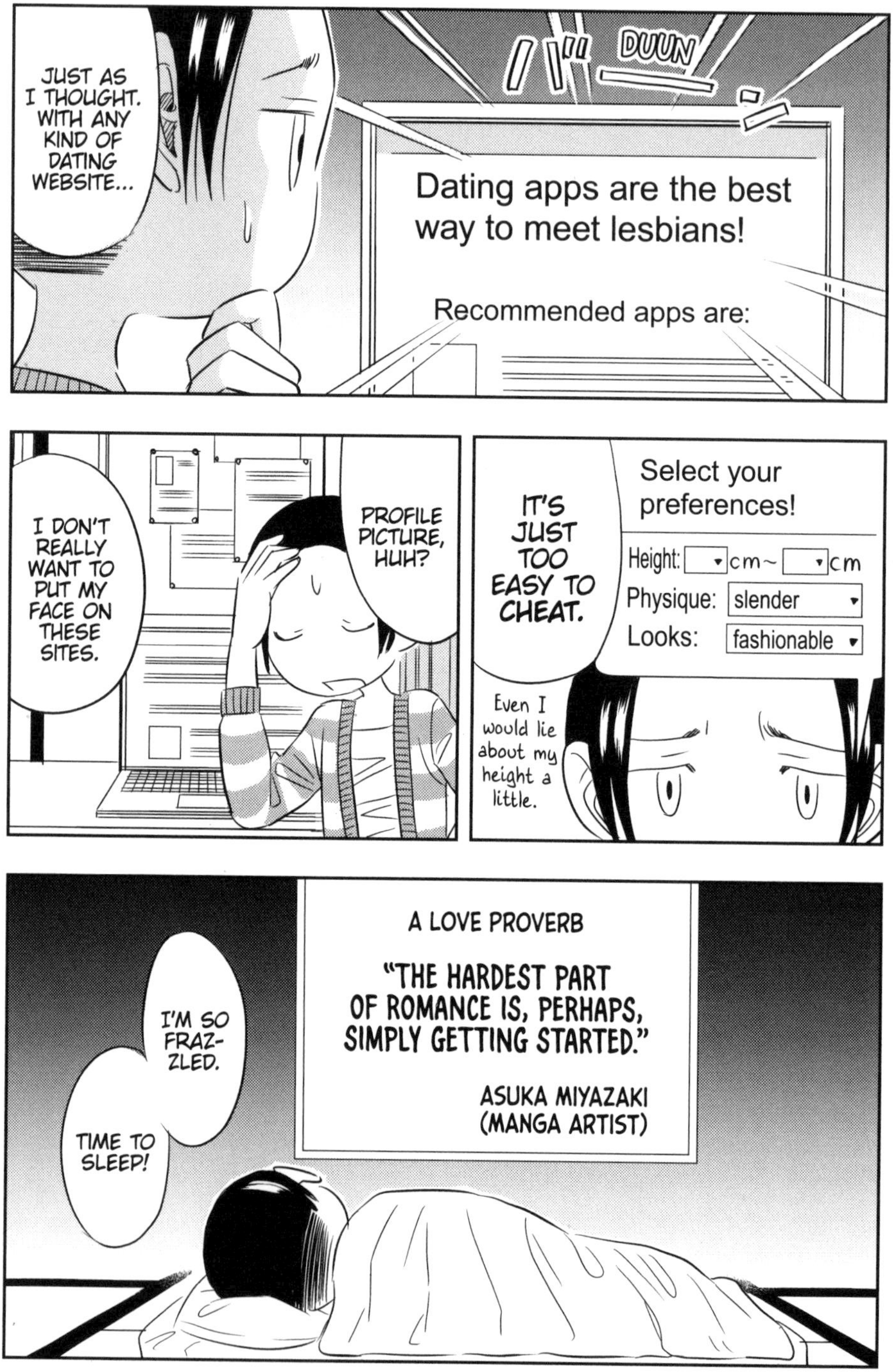
DUUN
Dating apps are the best way to meet lesbians!
Recommended apps are:
JUST AS I THOUGHT. WITH ANY KIND OF DATING WEBSITE...
Select your preferences!
Height: cm~ cm
Physique: slender
Looks: fashionable
IT'S JUST TOO EASY TO CHEAT.
Even I would lie about my height a little.
PROFILE PICTURE, HUH?
I DON'T REALLY WANT TO PUT MY FACE ON THESE SITES.
A LOVE PROVERB
"THE HARDEST PART OF ROMANCE IS, PERHAPS, SIMPLY GETTING STARTED."
ASUKA MIYAZAKI (MANGA ARTIST)
I'M SO FRAZ-ZLED.
TIME TO SLEEP!

Ep. 8: The "I Want to Teach You About Periods" Story

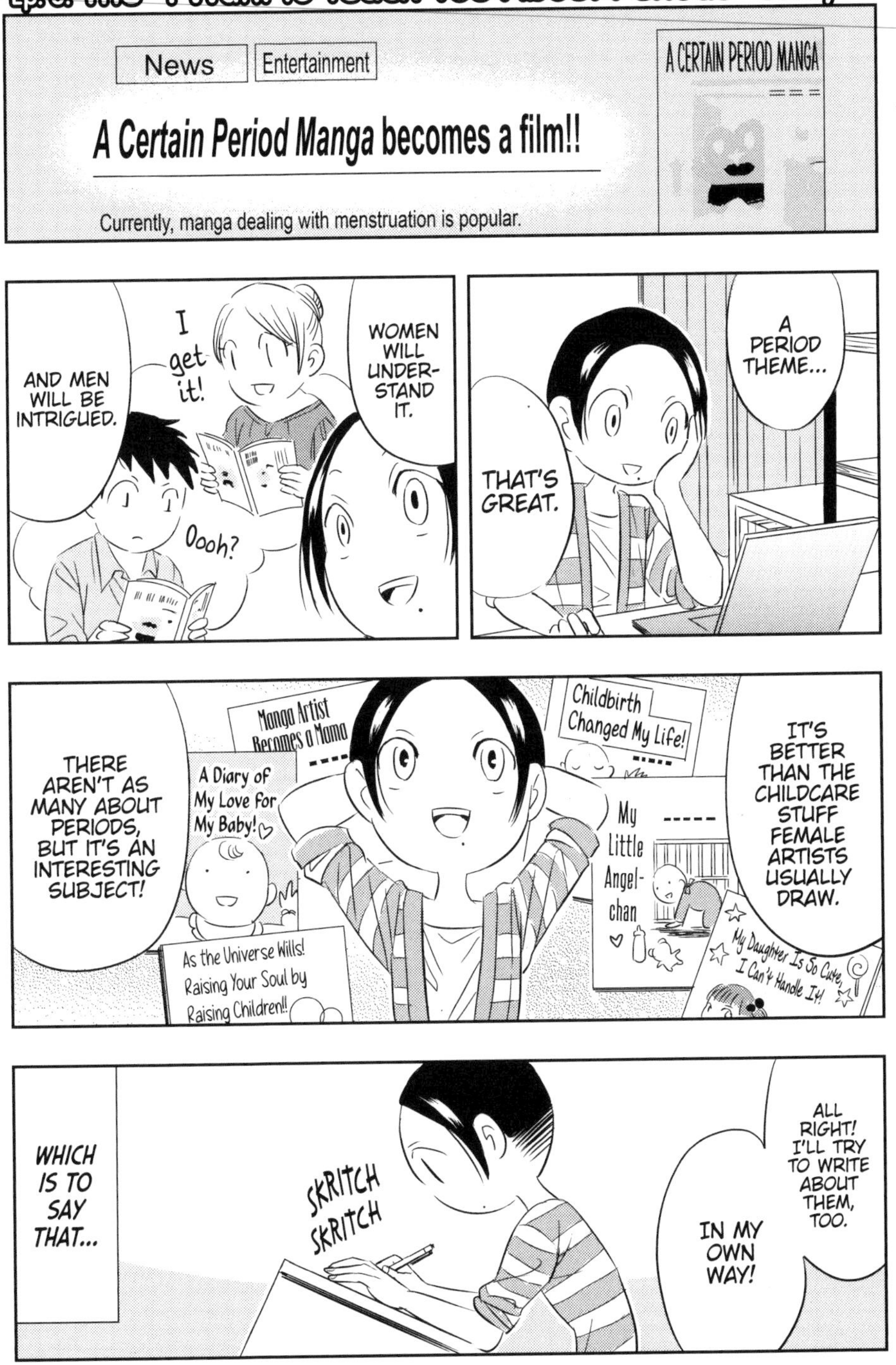

News
Entertainment
A Certain Period Manga becomes a film!!
Currently, manga dealing with menstruation is popular.
A CERTAIN PERIOD MANGA
A PERIOD THEME...
THAT'S GREAT.
WOMEN WILL UNDERSTAND IT.
I get it!
AND MEN WILL BE INTRIGUED.
Oooh?
IT'S BETTER THAN THE CHILDCARE STUFF FEMALE ARTISTS USUALLY DRAW.
Childbirth Changed My Life!
My Little Angel-chan
My Daughter Is So Cute, I Can't Handle It!
Manga Artist Becomes a Mama
A Diary of My Love for My Baby!
As the Universe Wills! Raising Your Soul by Raising Children!!
THERE AREN'T AS MANY ABOUT PERIODS, BUT IT'S AN INTERESTING SUBJECT!
ALL RIGHT! I'LL TRY TO WRITE ABOUT THEM, TOO.
IN MY OWN WAY!
SKRITCH SKRITCH
WHICH IS TO SAY THAT...

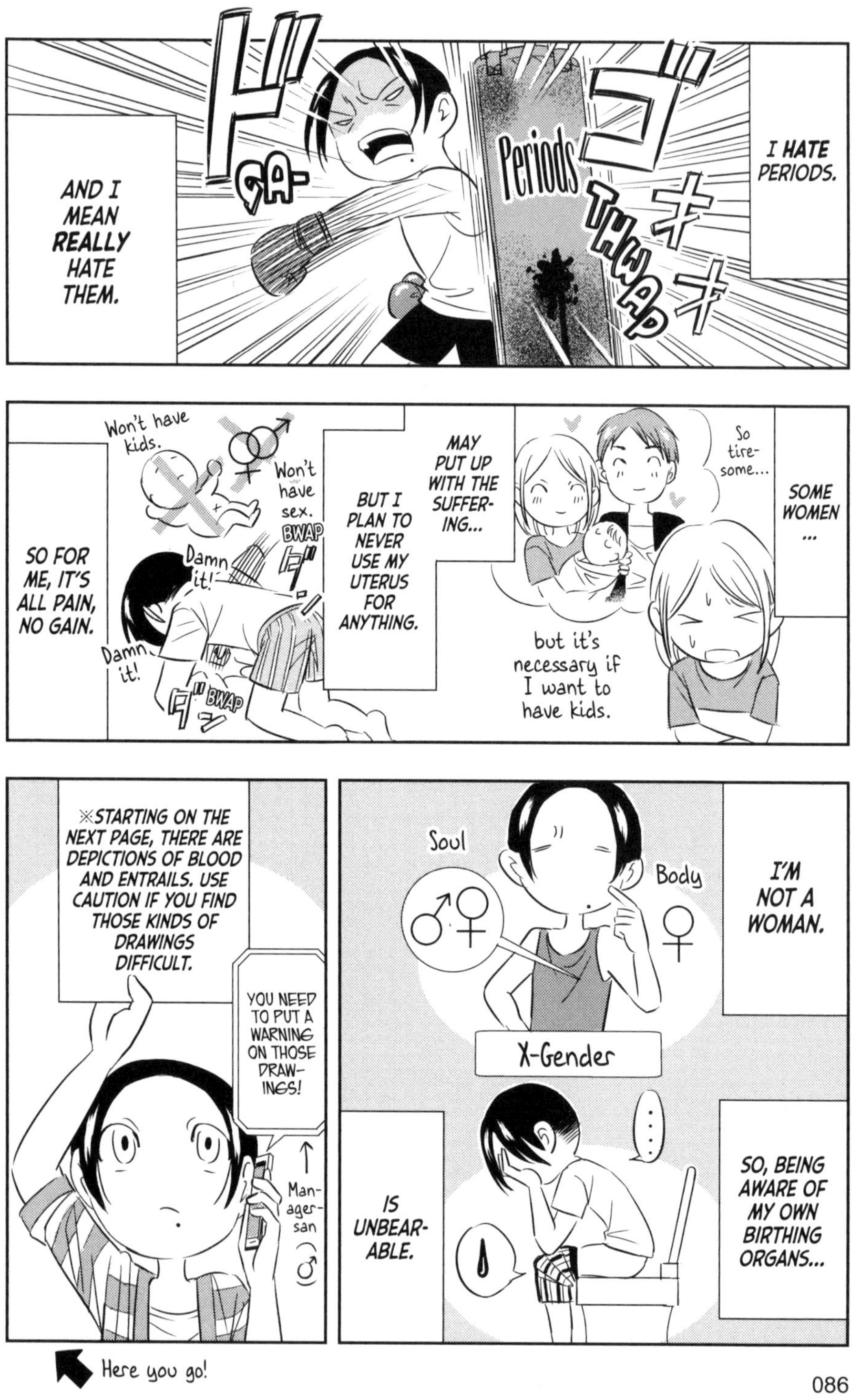
I HATE PERIODS.
THWAP
Periods
GA
AND I MEAN REALLY HATE THEM.
SOME WOMEN...
So tiresome...
but it's necessary if I want to have kids.
MAY PUT UP WITH THE SUFFERING...
BUT I PLAN TO NEVER USE MY UTERUS FOR ANYTHING.
Won't have kids.
Won't have sex.
BWAP
Damn it!
Damn it!
BWAP
SO FOR ME, IT'S ALL PAIN, NO GAIN.
I'M NOT A WOMAN.
Soul
Body
X-Gender
SO, BEING AWARE OF MY OWN BIRTHING ORGANS...
...
IS UNBEARABLE.
※STARTING ON THE NEXT PAGE, THERE ARE DEPICTIONS OF BLOOD AND ENTRAILS. USE CAUTION IF YOU FIND THOSE KINDS OF DRAWINGS DIFFICULT.
YOU NEED TO PUT A WARNING ON THOSE DRAWINGS!
Manager-san
Here you go!

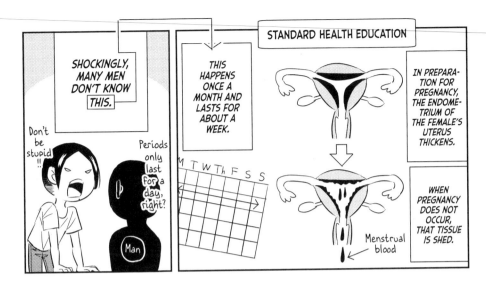

STANDARD HEALTH EDUCATION
IN PREPARATION FOR PREGNANCY, THE ENDOMETRIUM OF THE FEMALE'S UTERUS THICKENS.
WHEN PREGNANCY DOES NOT OCCUR, THAT TISSUE IS SHED.
Menstrual blood
THIS HAPPENS ONCE A MONTH AND LASTS FOR ABOUT A WEEK.
M T W Th F S S
SHOCKINGLY, MANY MEN DON'T KNOW THIS.
Periods only last for a day, right?
Man
Don't be stupid!!
PERIODS ARE DIFFERENT FOR EVERYONE.
Bleeding: heavy
Length: four days
Horrid abdominal pain
Length: six days
Etc...
FROM NOW ON, I'M MOSTLY TALKING ABOUT MYSELF.
PRE-MENSTRUAL
CRAP... I'M GAINING WEIGHT.
AROUND THAT TIME, MORE THAN JUST THE UTERUS GETS HEAVY.
My abdomen is swollen...
Eat! Eat! Eat!
CHIPS
It doesn't matter what I do then.
I can't lose weight.
BECAUSE OF THE HORMONES, THE BODY HOLDS ONTO WATER AND ENERGY.

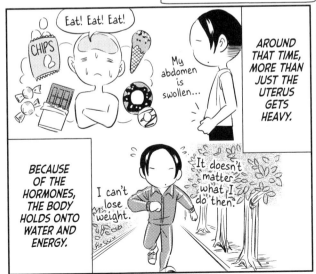

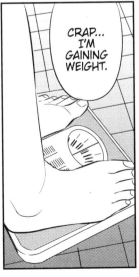

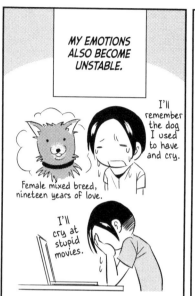

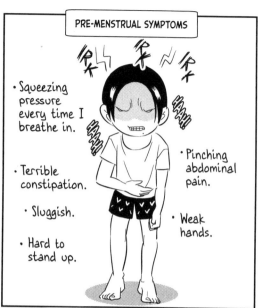

PRE-MENSTRUAL SYMPTOMS
IRK IRK IRK
• Squeezing pressure every time I breathe in.
• Pinching abdominal pain.
• Terrible constipation.
• Sluggish.
• Weak hands.
• Hard to stand up.
MY EMOTIONS ALSO BECOME UNSTABLE.
I'll remember the dog I used to have and cry.
Female mixed breed, nineteen years of love.
I'll cry at stupid movies.
OH!
TOILET
MY PERIOD CAME.
Brown blood
TOILET
I'LL CHANGE FROM A PANTY LINER TO A PAD.
Pads
Panty Liners
SHWP SHWP
I GUESS I NEED TO EXPLAIN VAGINAL DISCHARGE.

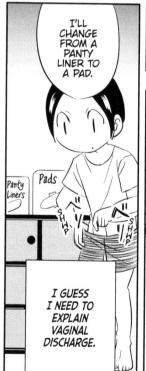

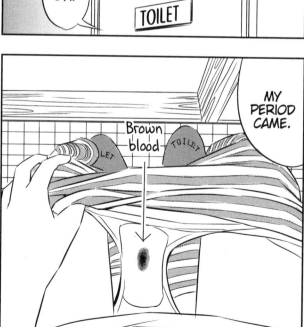

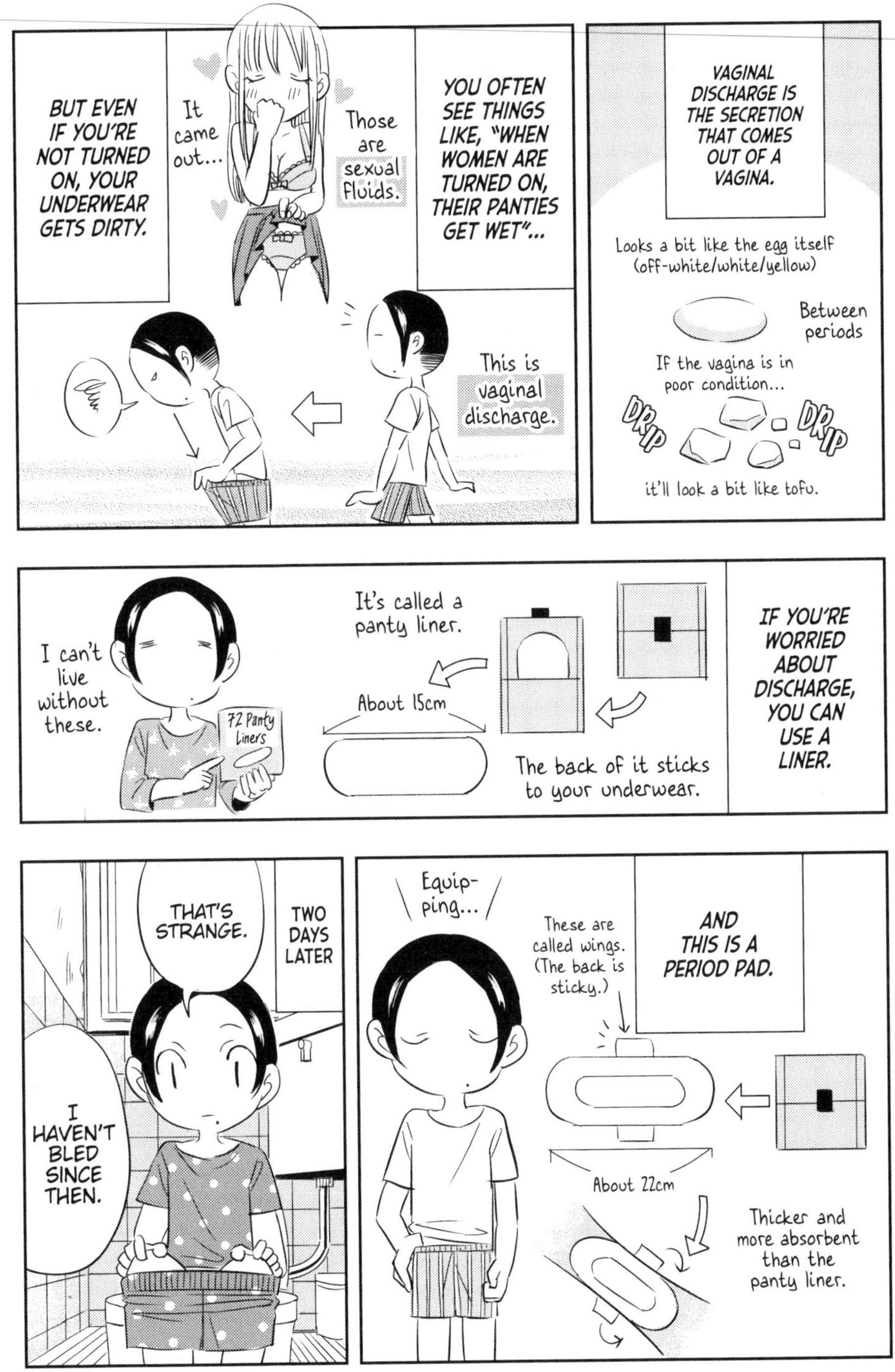

VAGINAL DISCHARGE IS THE SECRETION THAT COMES OUT OF A VAGINA.
Looks a bit like the egg itself (off-white/white/yellow)
Between periods
If the vagina is in poor condition...
DRIP
DRIP
it'll look a bit like tofu.
YOU OFTEN SEE THINGS LIKE, "WHEN WOMEN ARE TURNED ON, THEIR PANTIES GET WET"...
Those are sexual fluids.
It came out...
BUT EVEN IF YOU'RE NOT TURNED ON, YOUR UNDERWEAR GETS DIRTY.
This is vaginal discharge.
IF YOU'RE WORRIED ABOUT DISCHARGE, YOU CAN USE A LINER.
The back of it sticks to your underwear.
It's called a panty liner.
About 15cm
72 Panty Liners
I can't live without these.
AND THIS IS A PERIOD PAD.
These are called wings. (The back is sticky.)
About 22cm
Thicker and more absorbent than the panty liner.
Equip-ping...
TWO DAYS LATER
THAT'S STRANGE.
I HAVEN'T BLED SINCE THEN.

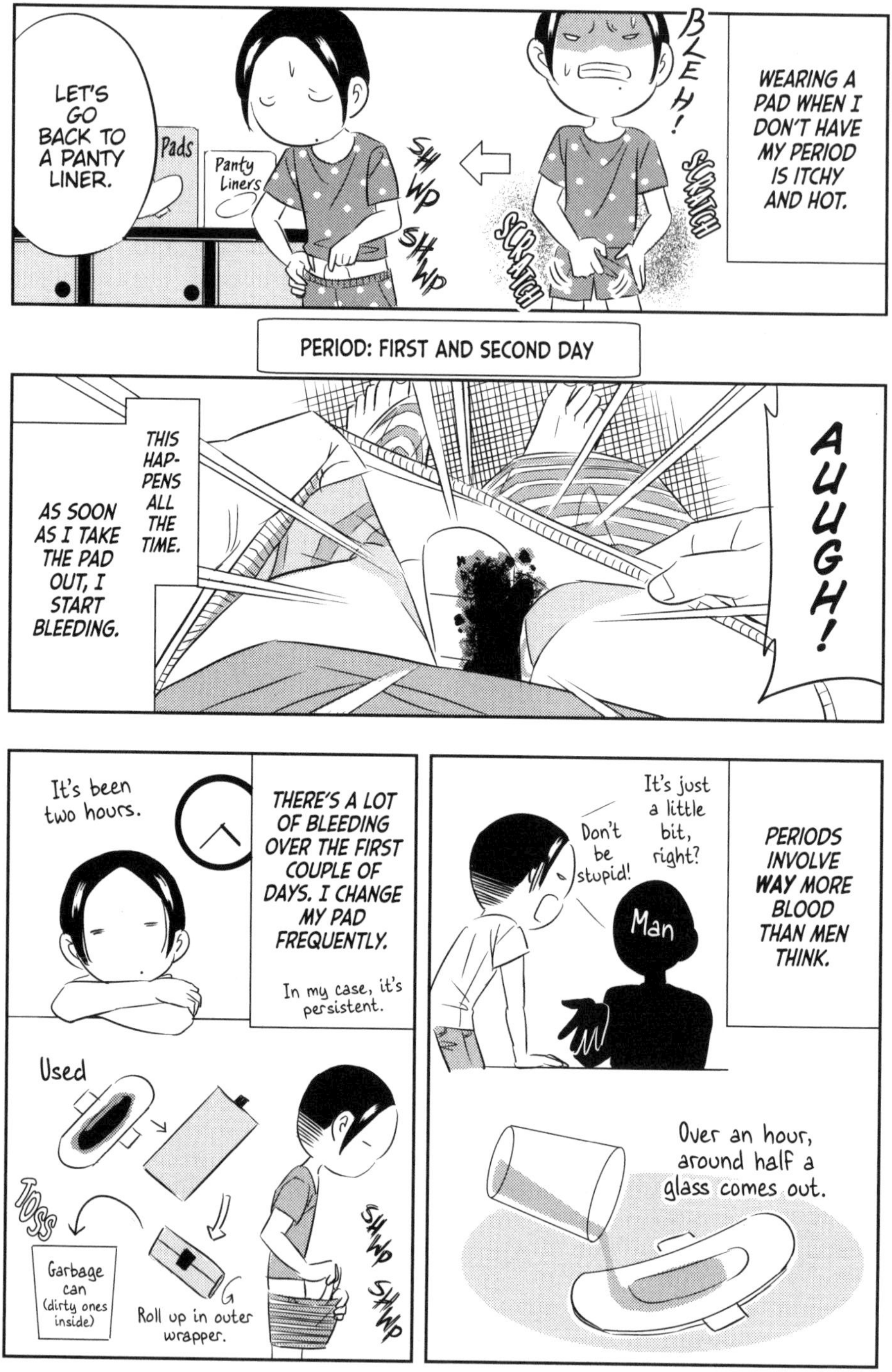
WEARING A PAD WHEN I DON'T HAVE MY PERIOD IS ITCHY AND HOT.
BLEH!
SCRATCH
SCRATCH
SHWP
SHWP
Pads
Panty Liners
LET'S GO BACK TO A PANTY LINER.
PERIOD: FIRST AND SECOND DAY
AUUGH!
THIS HAPPENS ALL THE TIME.
AS SOON AS I TAKE THE PAD OUT, I START BLEEDING.
PERIODS INVOLVE WAY MORE BLOOD THAN MEN THINK.
It's just a little bit, right?
Don't be stupid!
Man
Over an hour, around half a glass comes out.
THERE'S A LOT OF BLEEDING OVER THE FIRST COUPLE OF DAYS. I CHANGE MY PAD FREQUENTLY.
In my case, it's persistent.
It's been two hours.
SHWP
SHWP
Used
Roll up in outer wrapper.
TOSS
Garbage can (dirty ones inside)

They use blue water in pad commercials, so some guys even think that menstrual blood is blue.

※ Again: In my case, the blood is very persistent!

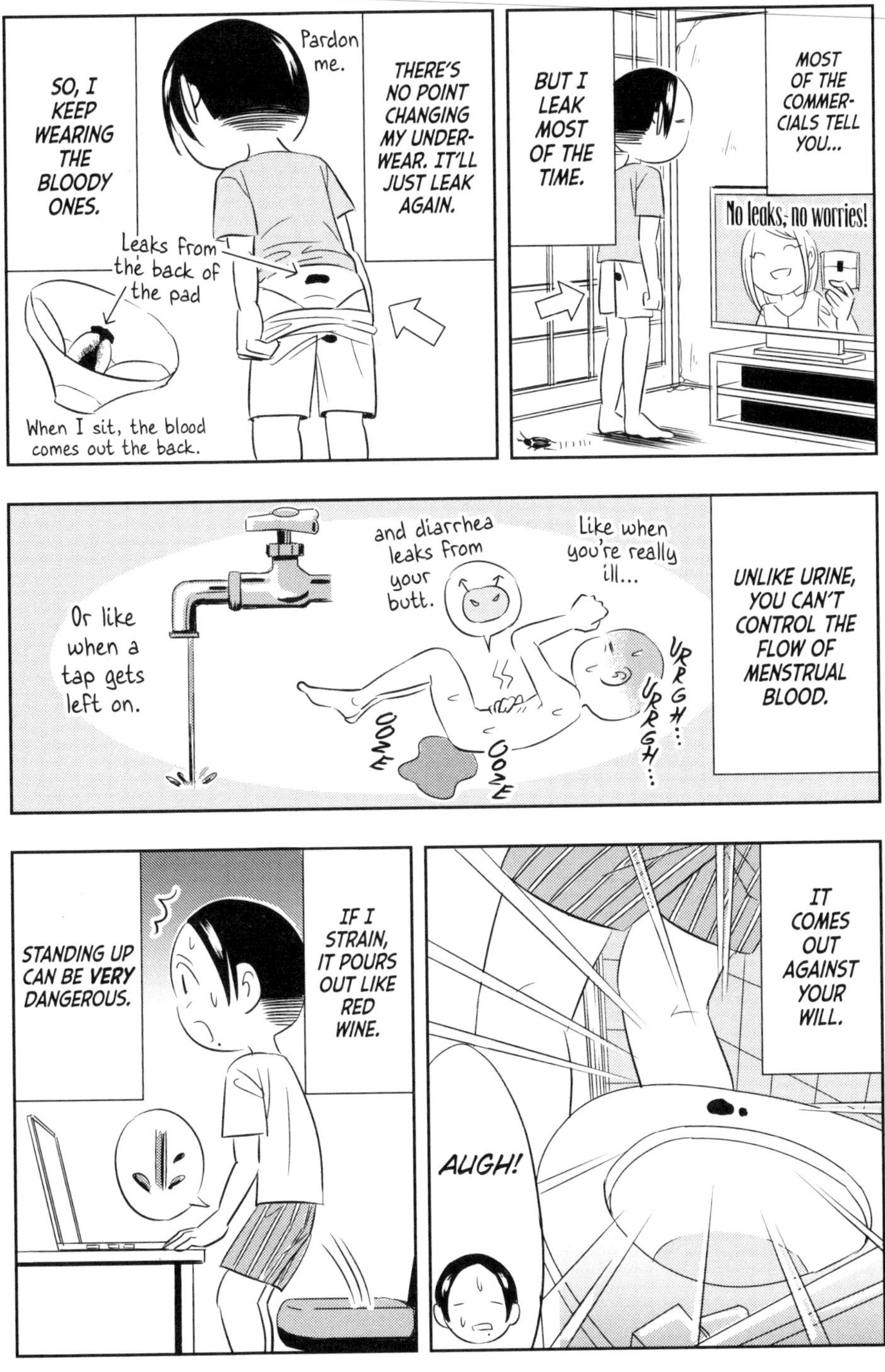
MOST OF THE COMMERCIALS TELL YOU...
No leaks, no worries!
BUT I LEAK MOST OF THE TIME.
THERE'S NO POINT CHANGING MY UNDERWEAR. IT'LL JUST LEAK AGAIN.
Pardon me.
SO, I KEEP WEARING THE BLOODY ONES.
Leaks from the back of the pad
When I sit, the blood comes out the back.
UNLIKE URINE, YOU CAN'T CONTROL THE FLOW OF MENSTRUAL BLOOD.
Like when you're really ill...
URRGH...
URRGH...
and diarrhea leaks from your butt.
OOZE
OOZE
Or like when a tap gets left on.
IT COMES OUT AGAINST YOUR WILL.
AUGH!
IF I STRAIN, IT POURS OUT LIKE RED WINE.
STANDING UP CAN BE VERY DANGEROUS.

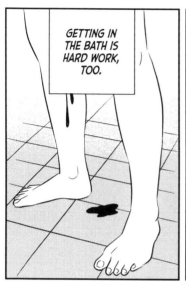

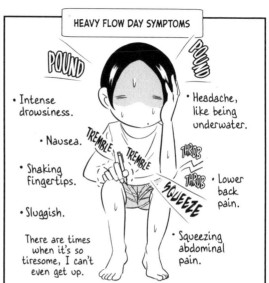

HEAVY FLOW DAY SYMPTOMS
POUND
POUND
• Headache, like being underwater.
• Intense drowsiness.
• Nausea.
TREMBLE
TREMBLE
THROB
THROB
• Lower back pain.
• Shaking fingertips.
SQUEEZE
• Sluggish.
• Squeezing abdominal pain.
There are times when it's so tiresome, I can't even get up.
GETTING IN THE BATH IS HARD WORK, TOO.
I have no idea how women wash their lower bodies.
① WASH BETWEEN THE LEGS.
Wash the left side, wash the right...
SCRUB
Bubbles turn red
SCRUB
② SAND-WICH THE PAD IN AND PUT ON UNDER-WEAR.
Pad
If I don't, my underwear will get blood on them.
FUU
③ WASH THE LEGS.
SO, SO TIRED.
NOD うと
NOD うと
ぐったり‥
EXHAUSTED
NO! I CAN'T...
FALL ASLEEP THIS WAY.

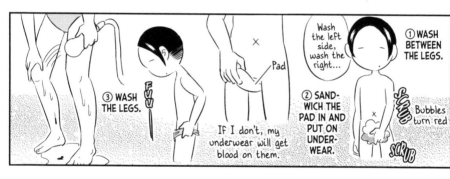

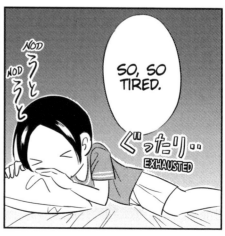

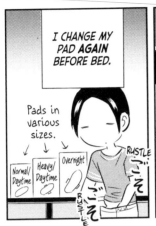

TREMBLE
ブル
I'LL LEAK.
TREMBLE
ブル
I CHANGE MY PAD AGAIN BEFORE BED.
Pads in various sizes.
Normal/ Daytime
Heavy/ Daytime
Overnight
RUSTLE
ごそ
RUSTLE
ごそ
Over-night Pad
About 40cm
Basically a diaper.
There's also overnight under-wear.
Even then, leaks can happen.
PERIOD: DAYS THREE AND FOUR
A LOT OF THE BLOOD HAS GONE, AND I FEEL BETTER...
Just a little head-ache.
SKRITCH
SKRITCH
BUT THE BLOOD BECOMES DARKER.
IT GETS STICKY AND HAS A UNIQUE SMELL.
MENSTRUAL BLOOD ISN'T JUST MADE OF BLOOD. IT ALSO CONTAINS THE UNNEEDED ENDOMETRIUM.
Muddy red-black blood
Reddish-black clot

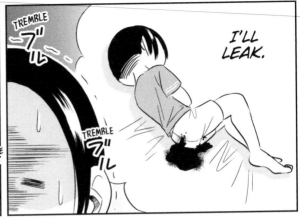

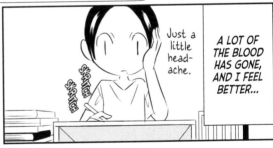

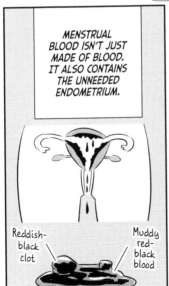

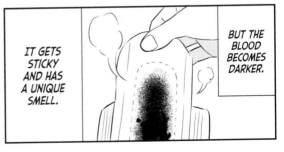

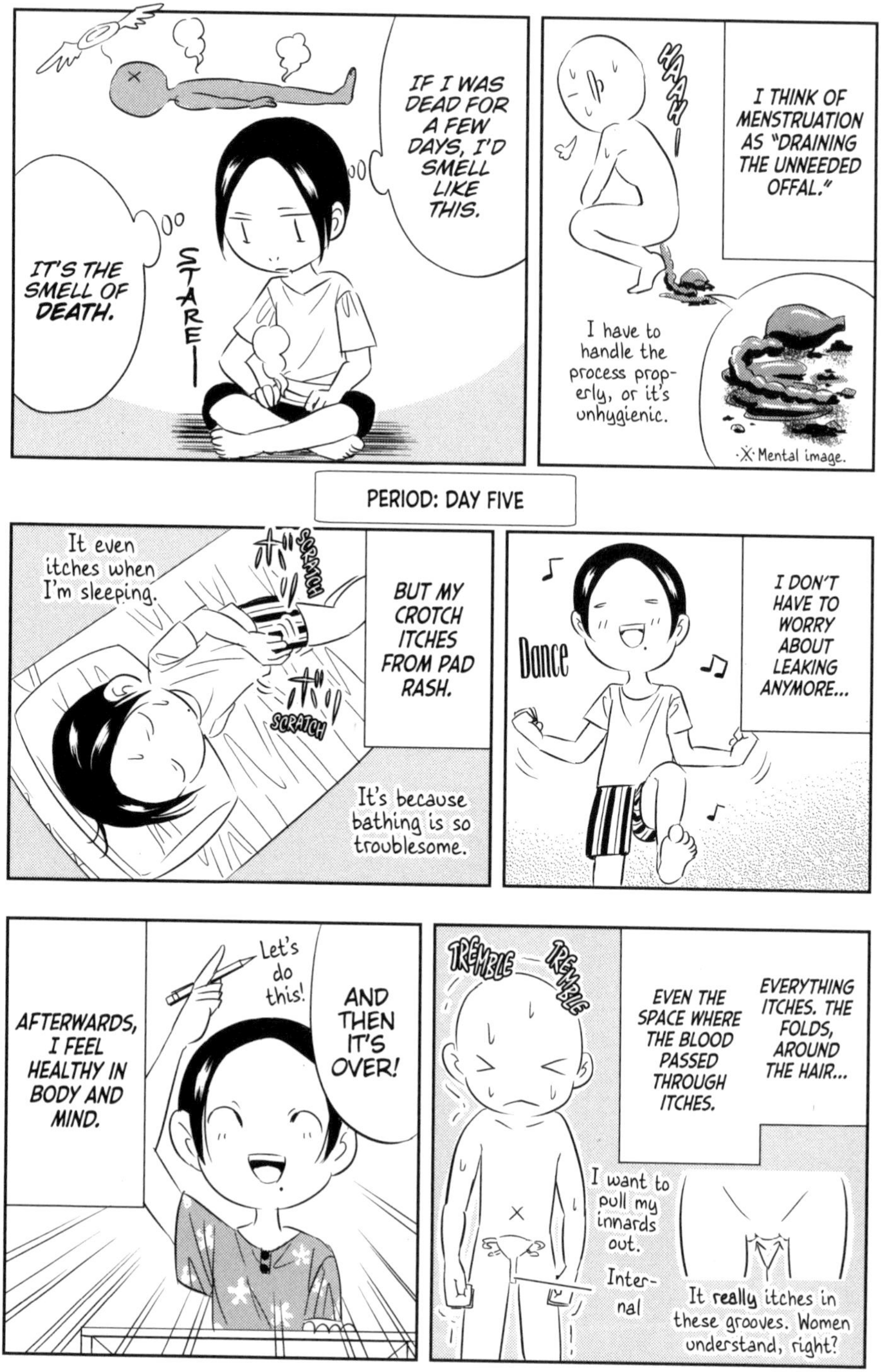
I THINK OF MENSTRUATION AS "DRAINING THE UNNEEDED OFFAL."
HAAAH
I have to handle the process properly, or it's unhygienic.
※ Mental image.
IF I WAS DEAD FOR A FEW DAYS, I'D SMELL LIKE THIS.
STARE
IT'S THE SMELL OF DEATH.
PERIOD: DAY FIVE
I DON'T HAVE TO WORRY ABOUT LEAKING ANYMORE...
Dance
BUT MY CROTCH ITCHES FROM PAD RASH.
SCRATCH
It even itches when I'm sleeping.
SCRATCH
It's because bathing is so troublesome.
EVERYTHING ITCHES. THE FOLDS, AROUND THE HAIR...
EVEN THE SPACE WHERE THE BLOOD PASSED THROUGH ITCHES.
TREMBLE TREMBLE
I want to pull my innards out.
Internal
It **really** itches in these grooves. Women understand, right?
AND THEN IT'S OVER!
Let's do this!
AFTERWARDS, I FEEL HEALTHY IN BODY AND MIND.

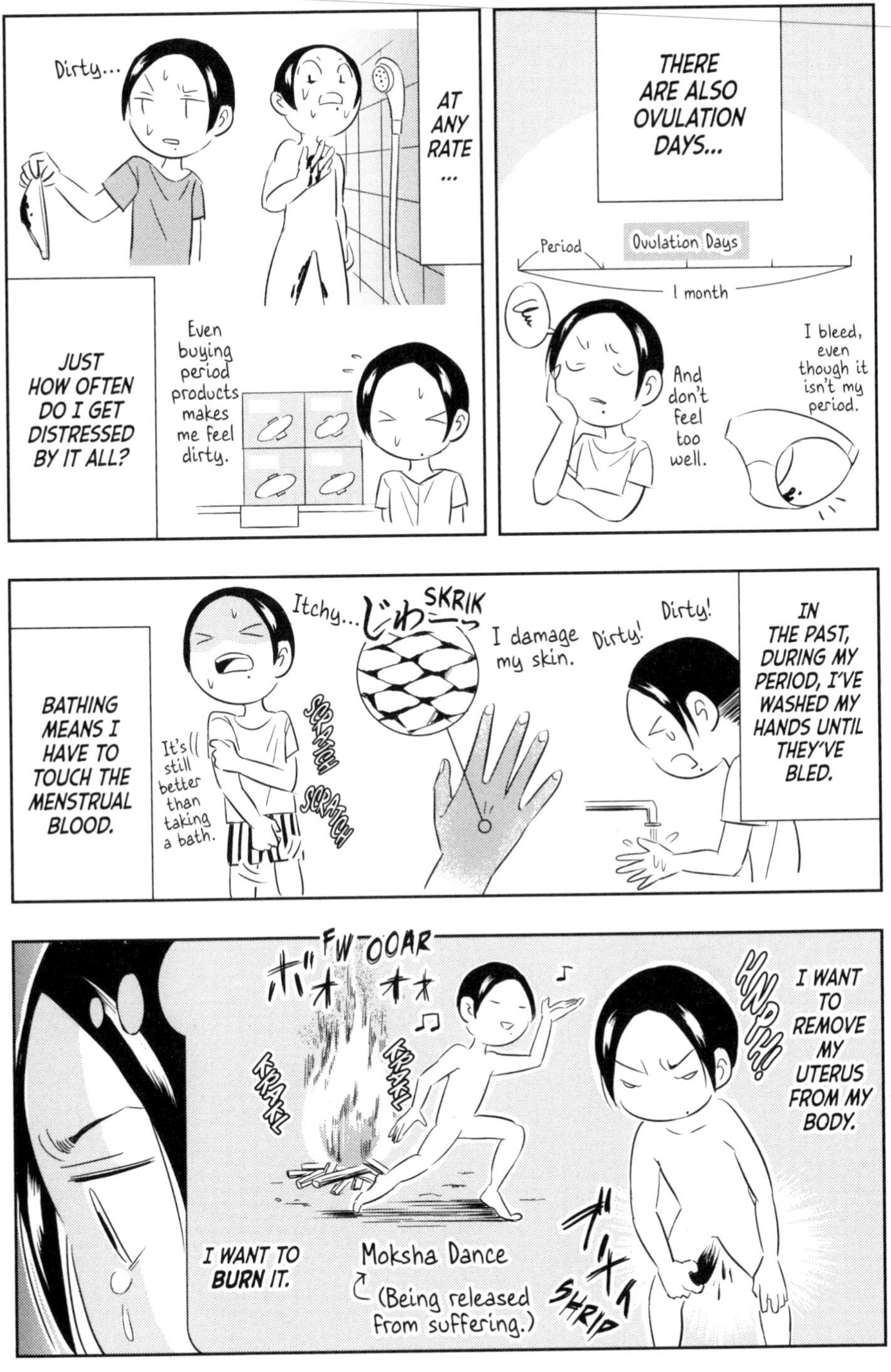
THERE ARE ALSO OVULATION DAYS...
Period
Ovulation Days
1 month
I bleed, even though it isn't my period.
And don't feel too well.
AT ANY RATE...
Dirty...
JUST HOW OFTEN DO I GET DISTRESSED BY IT ALL?
Even buying period products makes me feel dirty.
IN THE PAST, DURING MY PERIOD, I'VE WASHED MY HANDS UNTIL THEY'VE BLED.
Dirty!
Dirty!
I damage my skin.
SKRIK
Itchy...
SCRATCH
SCRATCH
It's still better than taking a bath.
BATHING MEANS I HAVE TO TOUCH THE MENSTRUAL BLOOD.
I WANT TO REMOVE MY UTERUS FROM MY BODY.
SHRIP
FWOOAR
KRAKL
KRAKL
Moksha Dance
(Being released from suffering.)
I WANT TO BURN IT.

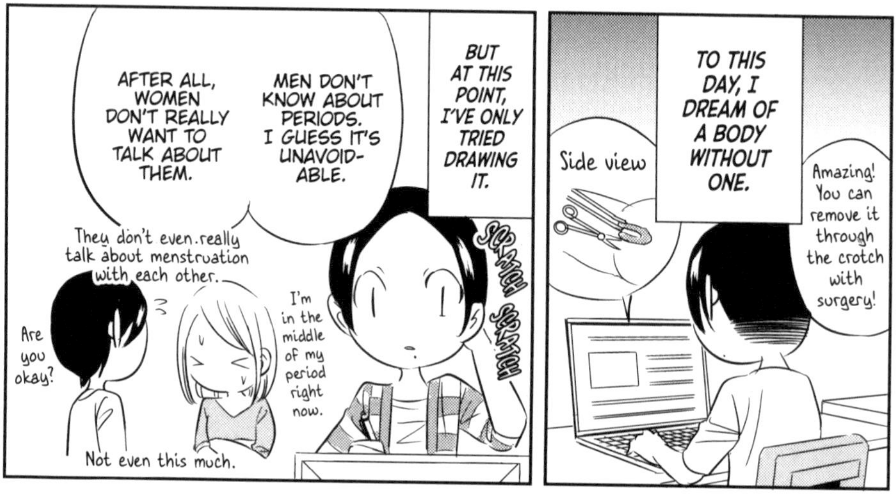
TO THIS DAY, I DREAM OF A BODY WITHOUT ONE.
Amazing! You can remove it through the crotch with surgery!
Side view
BUT AT THIS POINT, I'VE ONLY TRIED DRAWING IT.
SCRATCH SCRATCH
MEN DON'T KNOW ABOUT PERIODS. I GUESS IT'S UNAVOIDABLE.
AFTER ALL, WOMEN DON'T REALLY WANT TO TALK ABOUT THEM.
I'm in the middle of my period right now.
They don't even really talk about menstruation with each other.
Are you okay?
Not even this much.

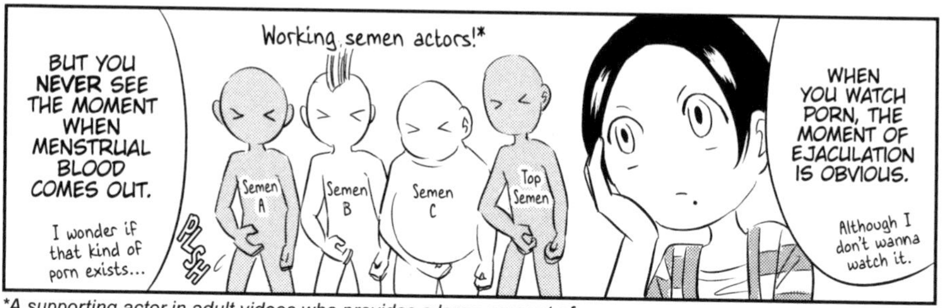
WHEN YOU WATCH PORN, THE MOMENT OF EJACULATION IS OBVIOUS.
Although I don't wanna watch it.
Working semen actors!*
Top Semen
Semen C
Semen B
Semen A
BUT YOU NEVER SEE THE MOMENT WHEN MENSTRUAL BLOOD COMES OUT.
PLSH
I wonder if that kind of porn exists...

*A supporting actor in adult videos who provides a large amount of semen.

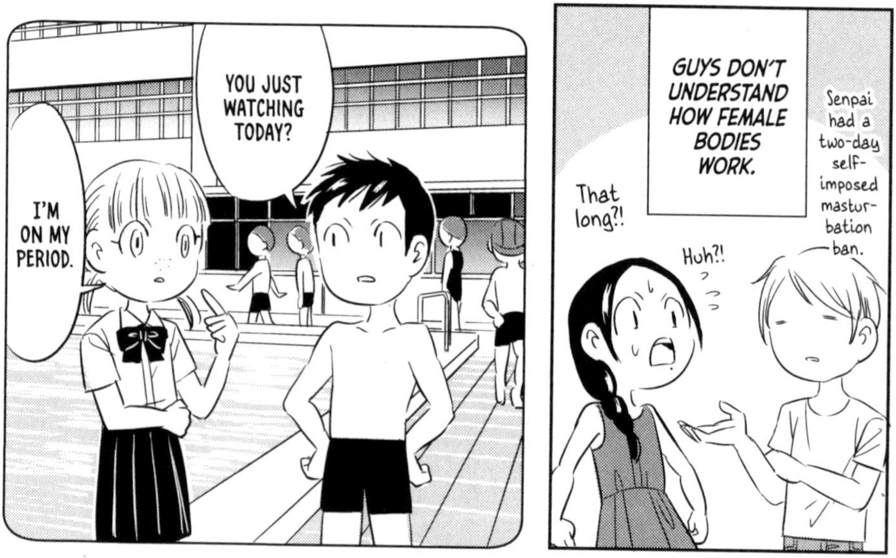
GUYS DON'T UNDERSTAND HOW FEMALE BODIES WORK.
Senpai had a two-day self-imposed mastur-bation ban.
Huh?!
That long?!
YOU JUST WATCHING TODAY?
I'M ON MY PERIOD.

Me, around twenty.

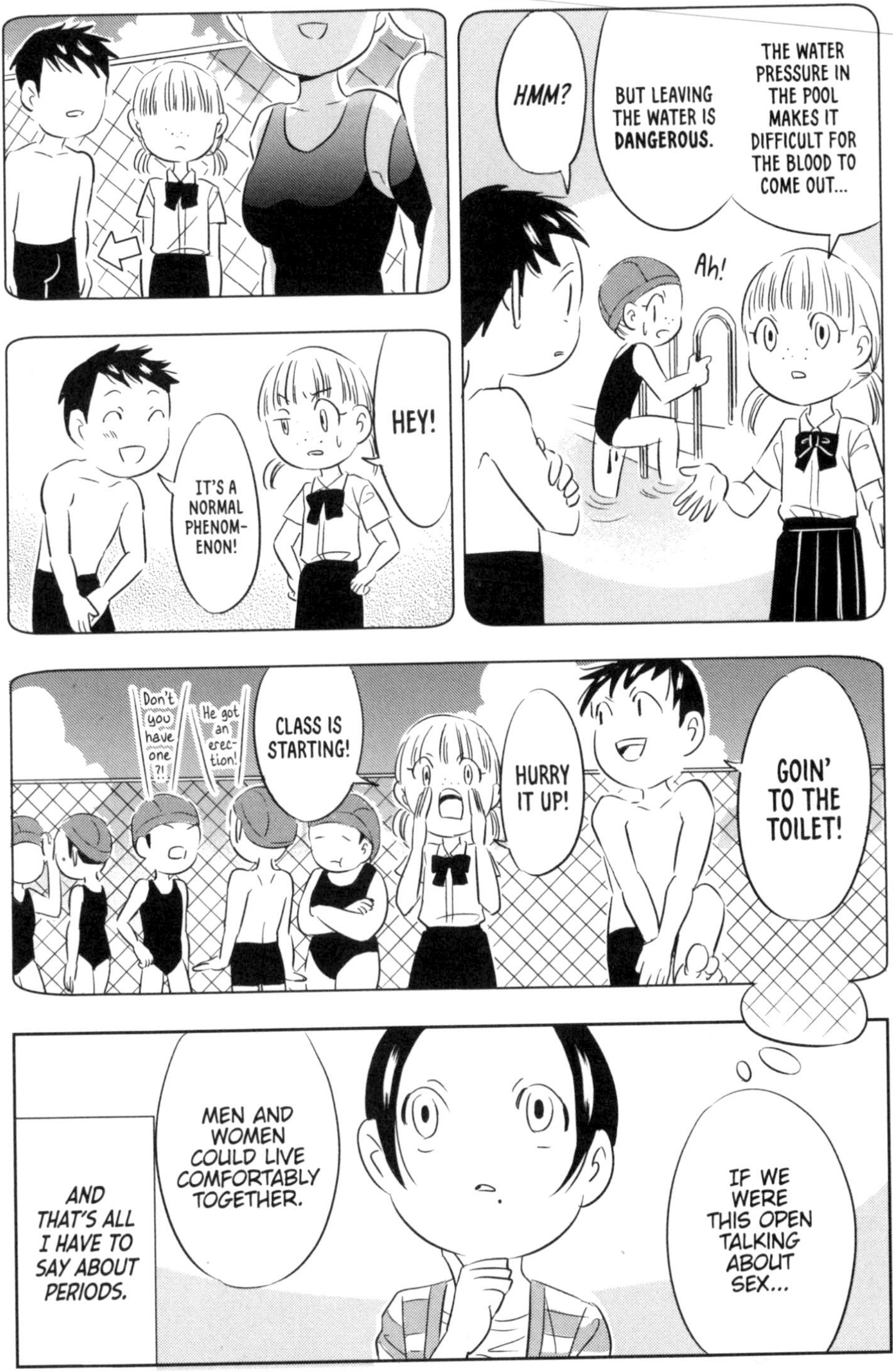
THE WATER PRESSURE IN THE POOL MAKES IT DIFFICULT FOR THE BLOOD TO COME OUT...
BUT LEAVING THE WATER IS **DANGEROUS.**
HMM?
Ah!
HEY!
IT'S A NORMAL PHENOM-ENON!
GOIN' TO THE TOILET!
HURRY IT UP!
CLASS IS STARTING!
He got an erec-tion!
Don't you have one ?!
IF WE WERE THIS OPEN TALKING ABOUT SEX...
MEN AND WOMEN COULD LIVE COMFORTABLY TOGETHER.
AND THAT'S ALL I HAVE TO SAY ABOUT PERIODS.

Ep. 9: The "That Girl of My Memories" Story

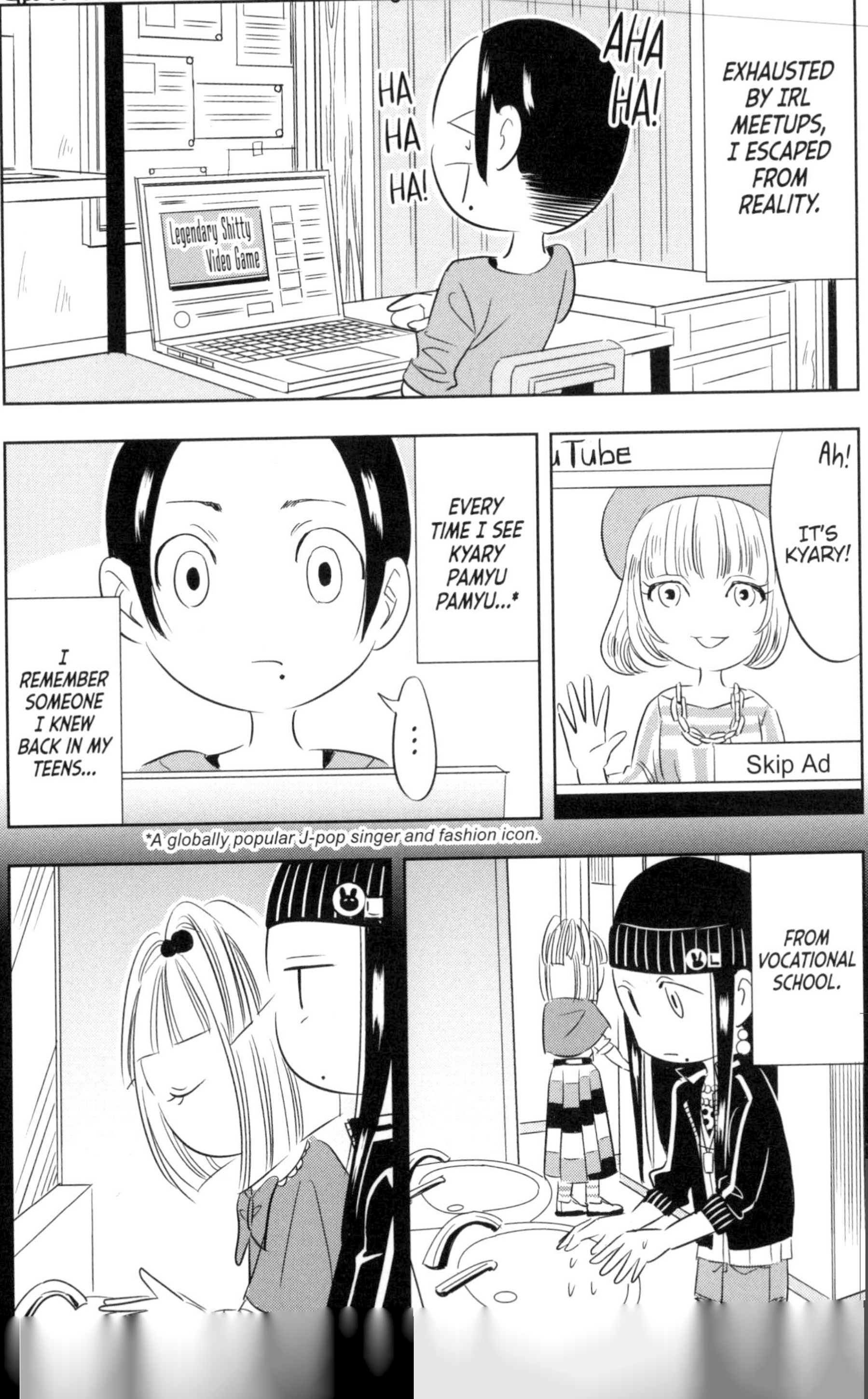
EXHAUSTED BY IRL MEETUPS, I ESCAPED FROM REALITY.
AHA HA!
HA HA HA!
Legendary Shitty Video Game
uTube
Ah!
IT'S KYARY!
Skip Ad
EVERY TIME I SEE KYARY PAMYU PAMYU...*
...
I REMEMBER SOMEONE I KNEW BACK IN MY TEENS...
FROM VOCATIONAL SCHOOL.

*A globally popular J-pop singer and fashion icon.

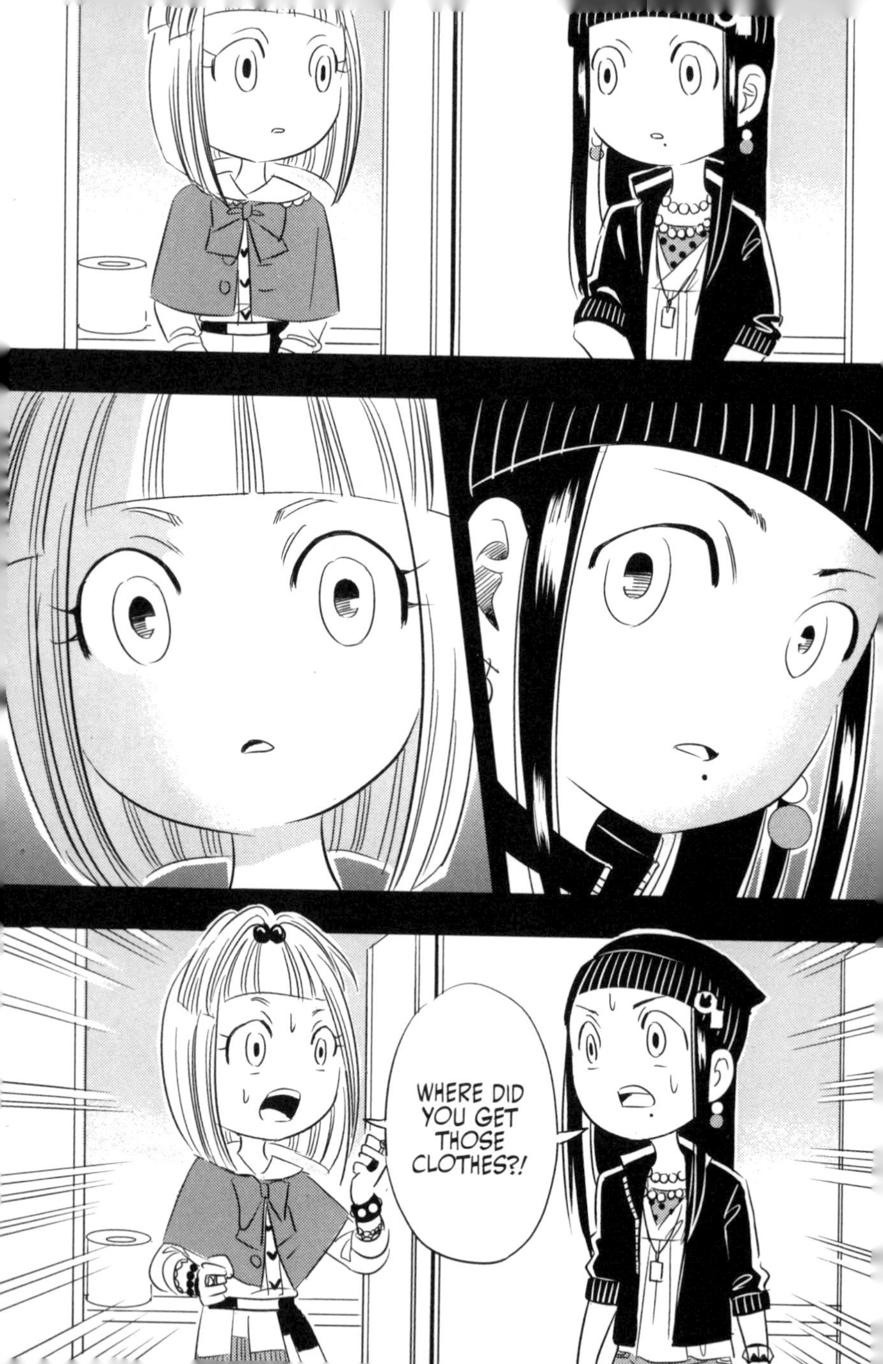
WHERE DID YOU GET THOSE CLOTHES?!

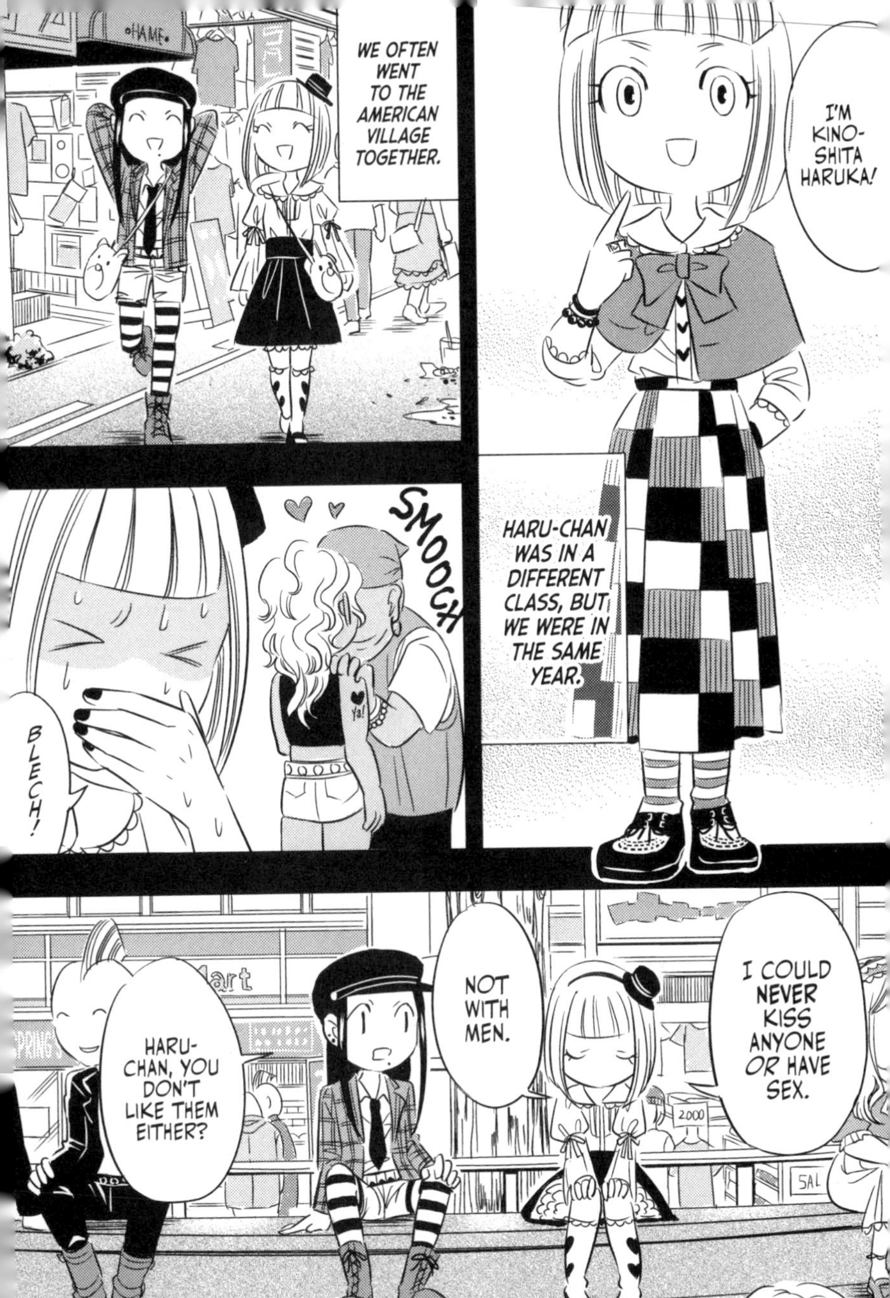
I'M KINO-SHITA HARUKA!
HARU-CHAN WAS IN A DIFFERENT CLASS, BUT WE WERE IN THE SAME YEAR.
WE OFTEN WENT TO THE AMERICAN VILLAGE TOGETHER.
SMOOCH
BLECH!
I COULD NEVER KISS ANYONE OR HAVE SEX.
NOT WITH MEN.
HARU-CHAN, YOU DON'T LIKE THEM EITHER?

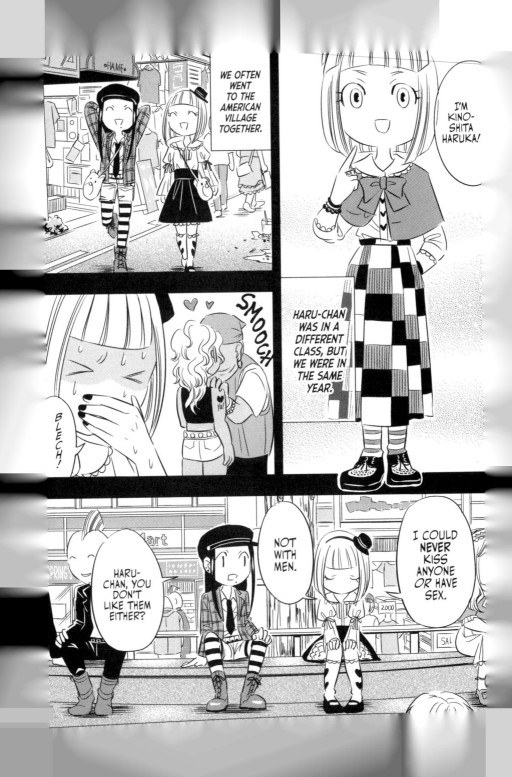

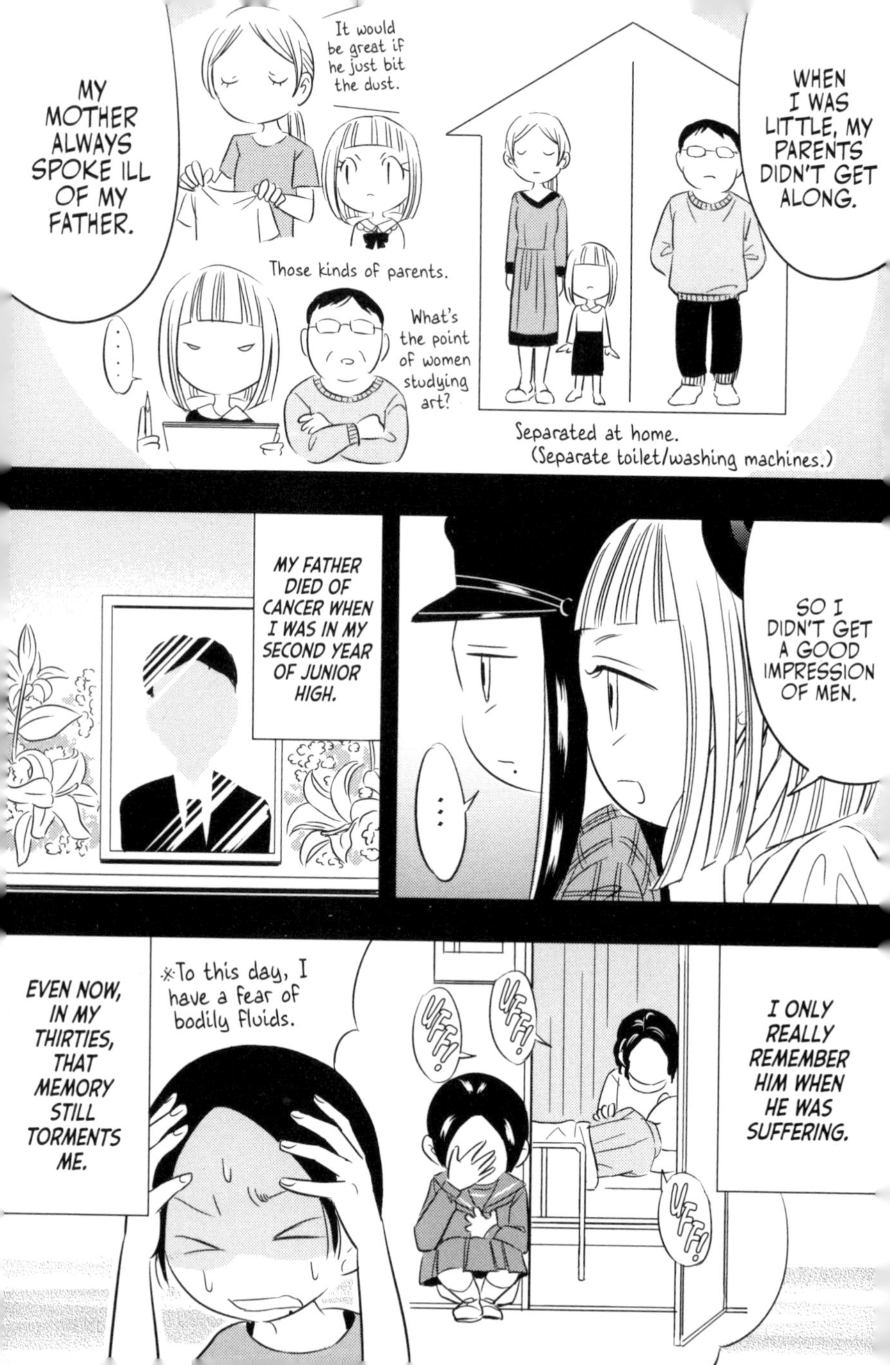

WHEN I WAS LITTLE, MY PARENTS DIDN'T GET ALONG.
Separated at home. (Separate toilet/washing machines.)
MY MOTHER ALWAYS SPOKE ILL OF MY FATHER.
It would be great if he just bit the dust.
Those kinds of parents.
What's the point of women studying art?
...
SO I DIDN'T GET A GOOD IMPRESSION OF MEN.
...
MY FATHER DIED OF CANCER WHEN I WAS IN MY SECOND YEAR OF JUNIOR HIGH.
I ONLY REALLY REMEMBER HIM WHEN HE WAS SUFFERING.
UFF!
UFF!
UFF!
EVEN NOW, IN MY THIRTIES, THAT MEMORY STILL TORMENTS ME.
※To this day, I have a fear of bodily fluids.

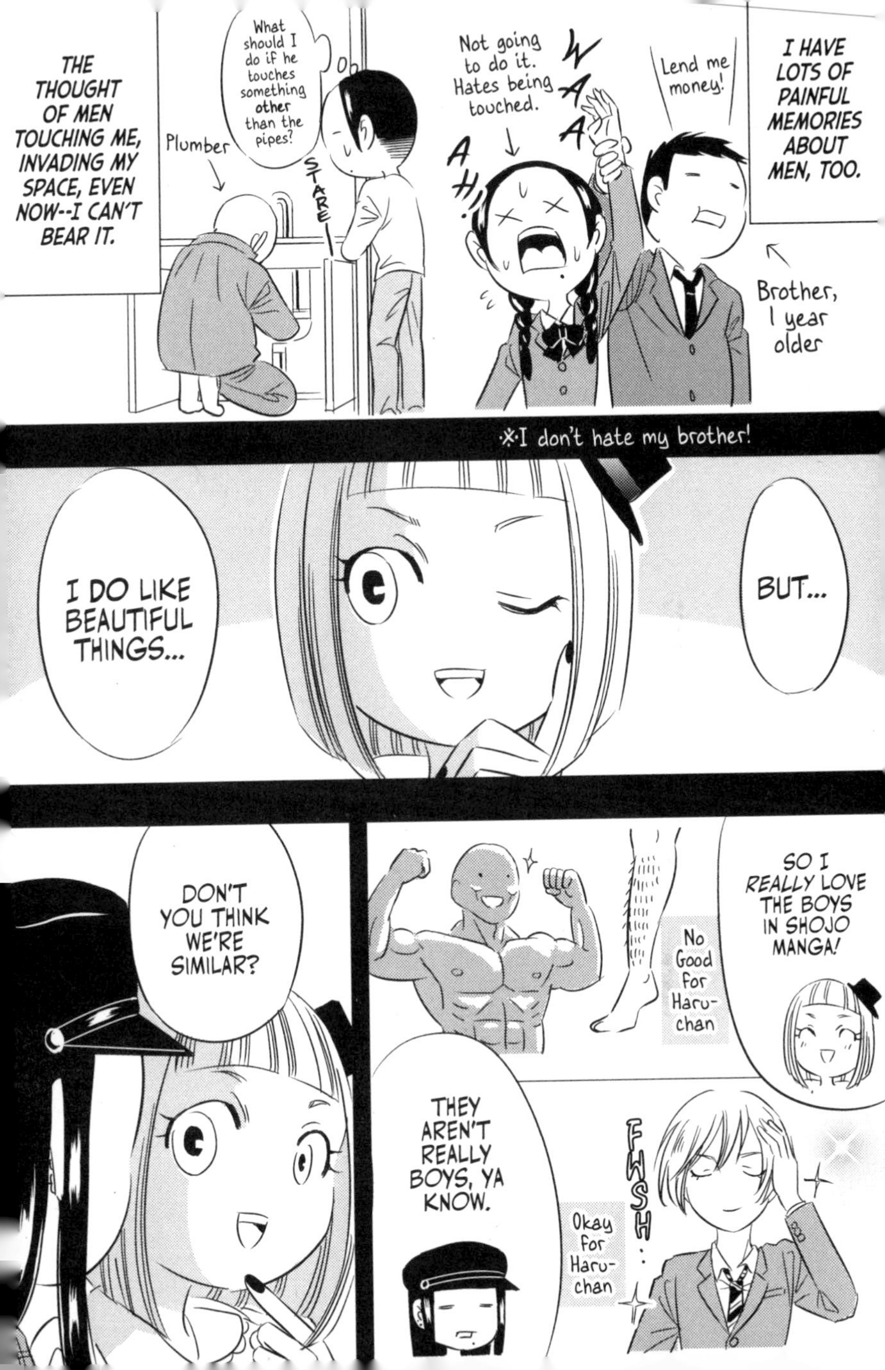
I HAVE LOTS OF PAINFUL MEMORIES ABOUT MEN, TOO.
Lend me money!
Brother, 1 year older
WAAAAH!
Not going to do it. Hates being touched.
What should I do if he touches something other than the pipes?
STARE
Plumber
THE THOUGHT OF MEN TOUCHING ME, INVADING MY SPACE, EVEN NOW--I CAN'T BEAR IT.
※I don't hate my brother!
I DO LIKE BEAUTIFUL THINGS...
BUT...
SO I REALLY LOVE THE BOYS IN SHOJO MANGA!
No Good for Haru-chan
THEY AREN'T REALLY BOYS, YA KNOW.
FWSH...
Okay for Haru-chan
DON'T YOU THINK WE'RE SIMILAR?

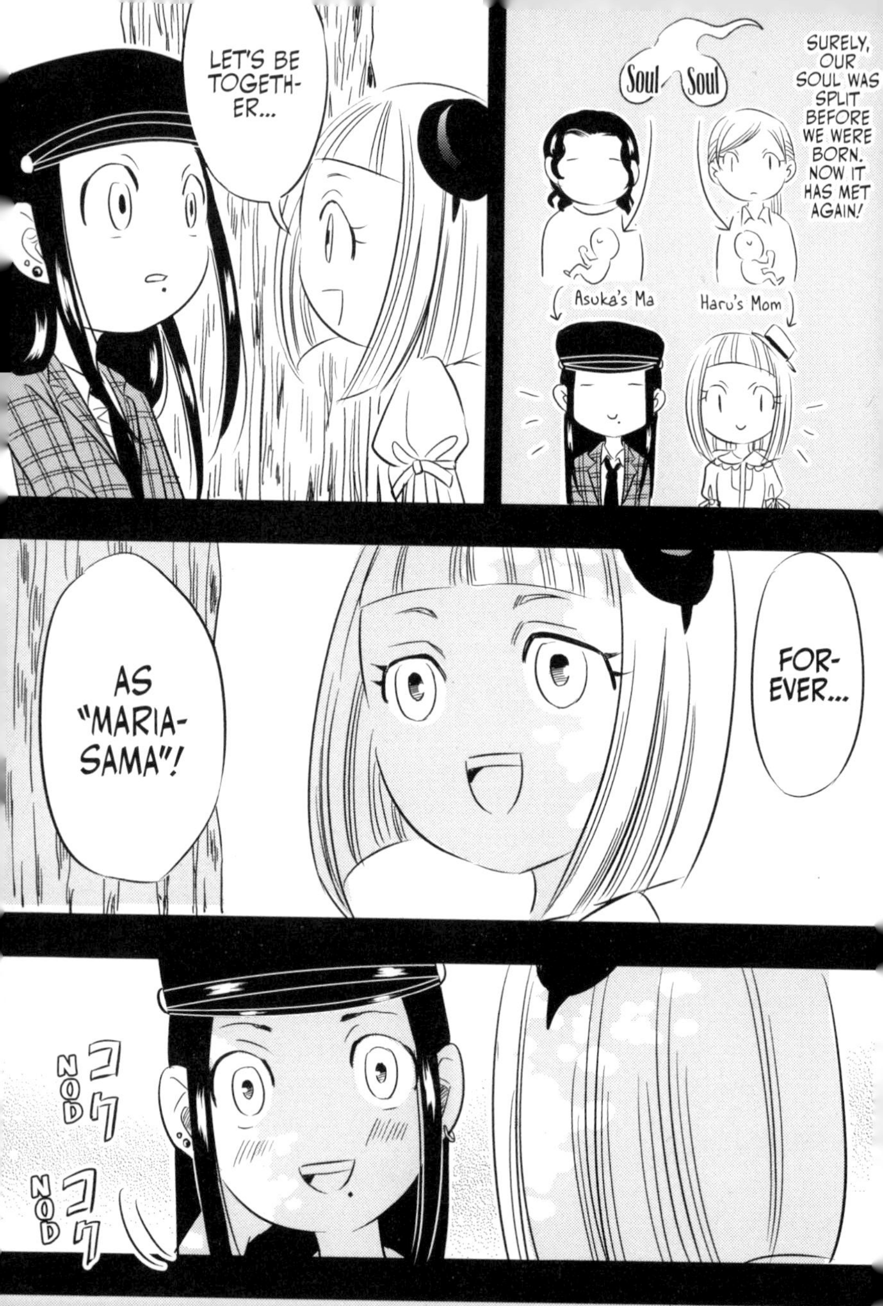
SURELY, OUR SOUL WAS SPLIT BEFORE WE WERE BORN. NOW IT HAS MET AGAIN!
Soul
Soul
Asuka's Ma
Haru's Mom
LET'S BE TOGETH-ER...
FOR-EVER...
AS "MARIA-SAMA"!
NOD
NOD

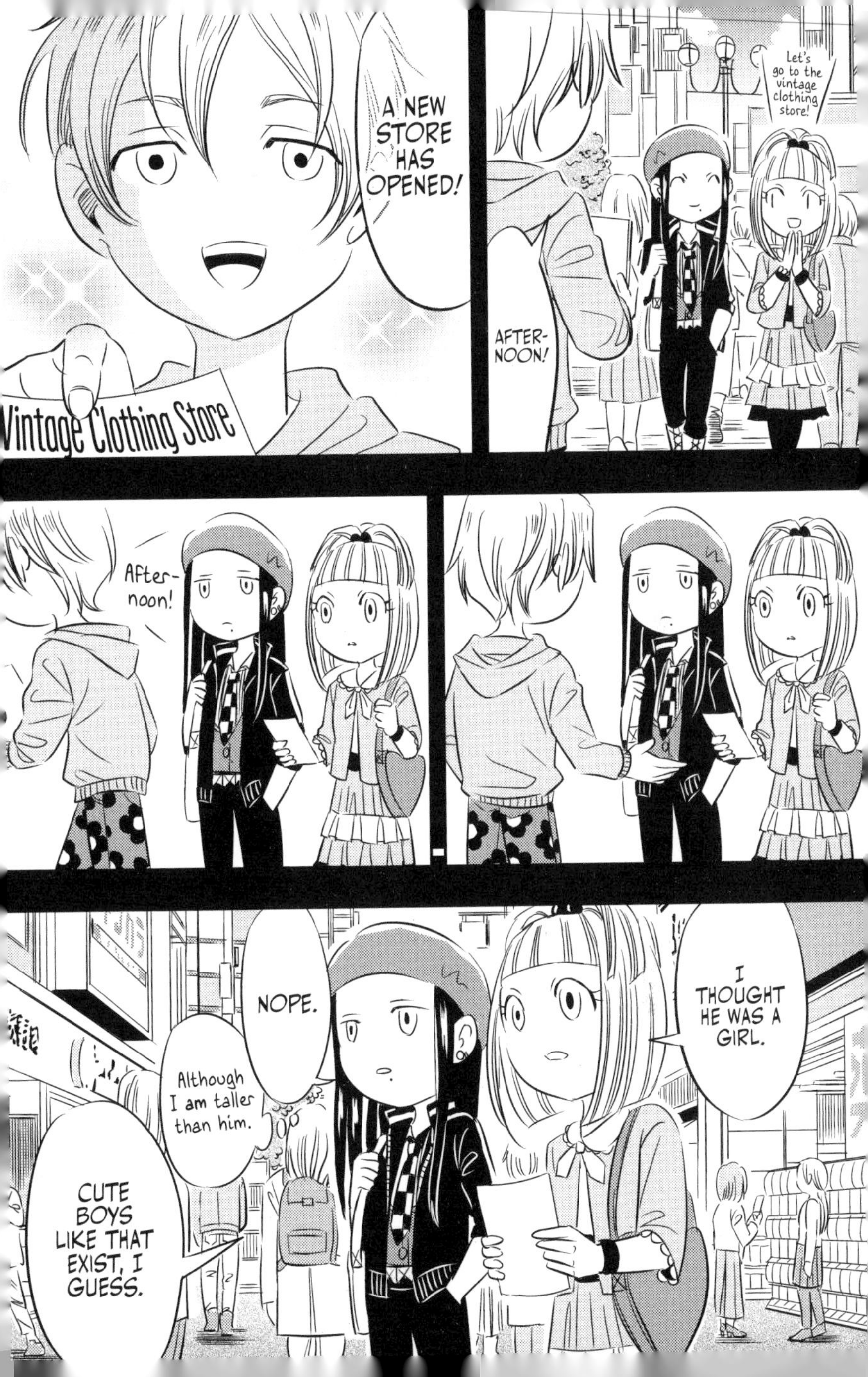

Let's go to the vintage clothing store!
AFTER-NOON!
A NEW STORE HAS OPENED!
Vintage Clothing Store
After-noon!
I THOUGHT HE WAS A GIRL.
NOPE.
Although I am taller than him.
CUTE BOYS LIKE THAT EXIST, I GUESS.

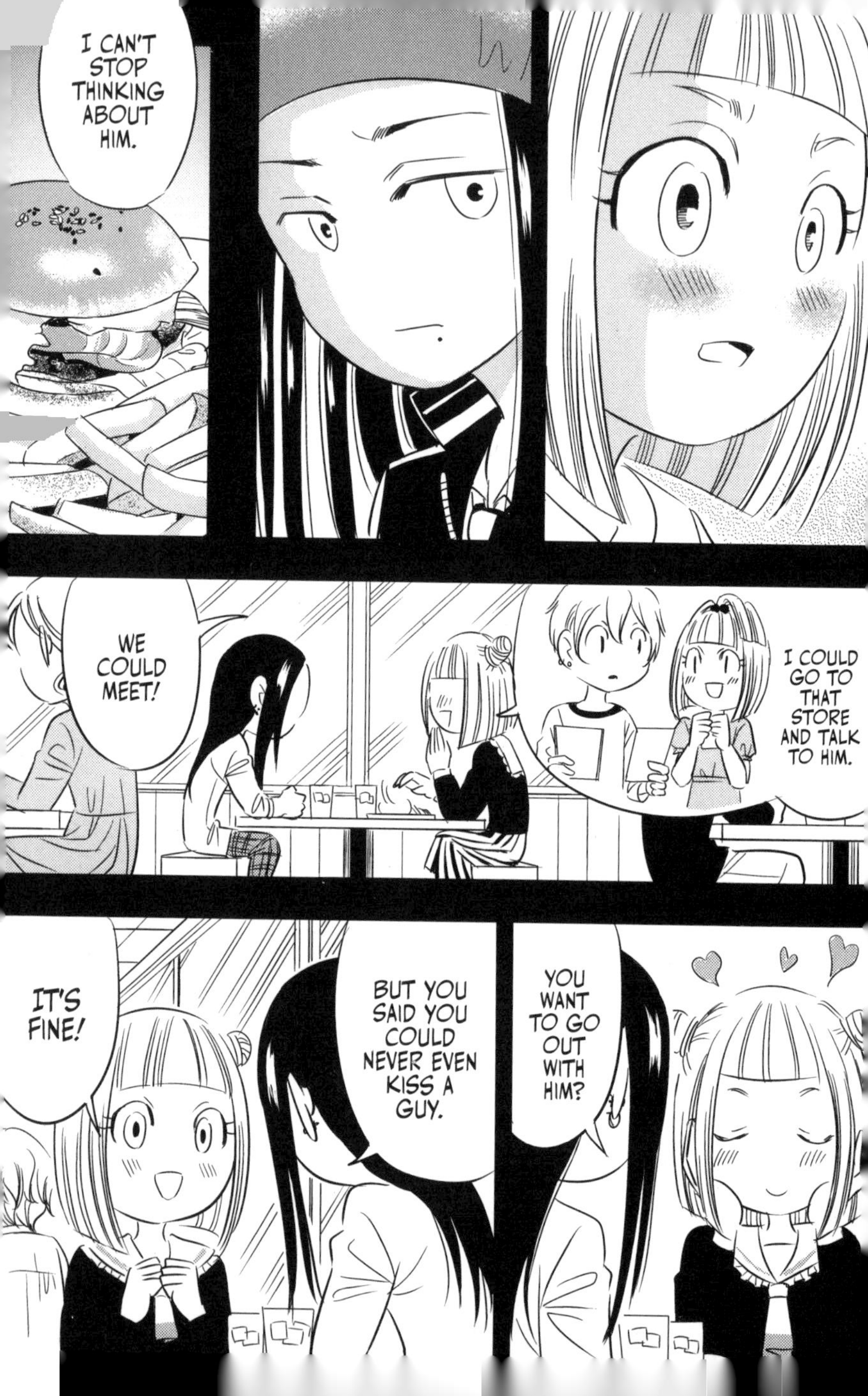
I CAN'T STOP THINKING ABOUT HIM.
I COULD GO TO THAT STORE AND TALK TO HIM.
WE COULD MEET!
YOU WANT TO GO OUT WITH HIM?
BUT YOU SAID YOU COULD NEVER EVEN KISS A GUY.
IT'S FINE!

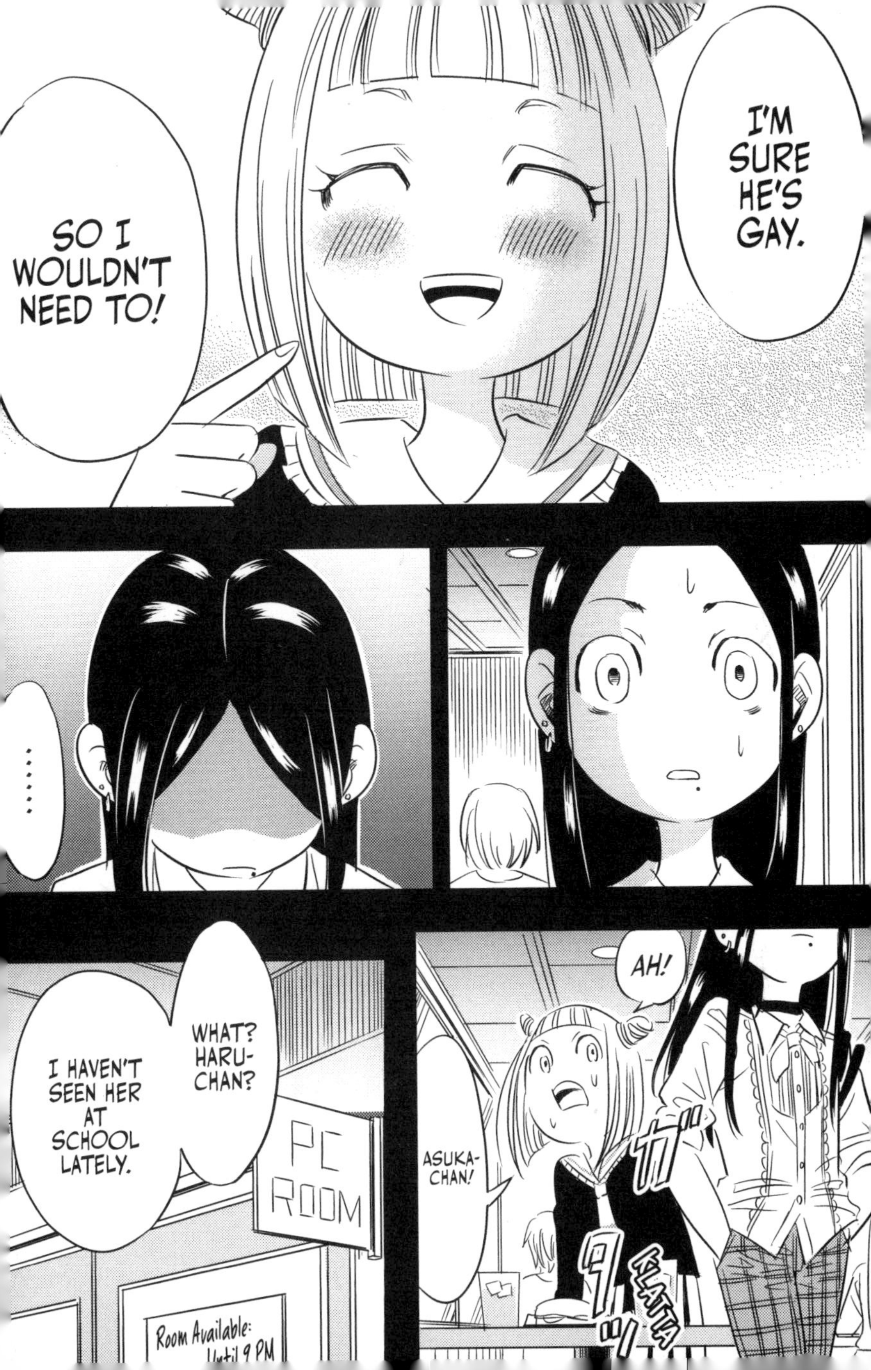
I'M SURE HE'S GAY.
SO I WOULDN'T NEED TO!
......
AH!
ASUKA-CHAN!
KLATTA
WHAT? HARU-CHAN?
I HAVEN'T SEEN HER AT SCHOOL LATELY.
PC ROOM
Room Available: Until 9 PM

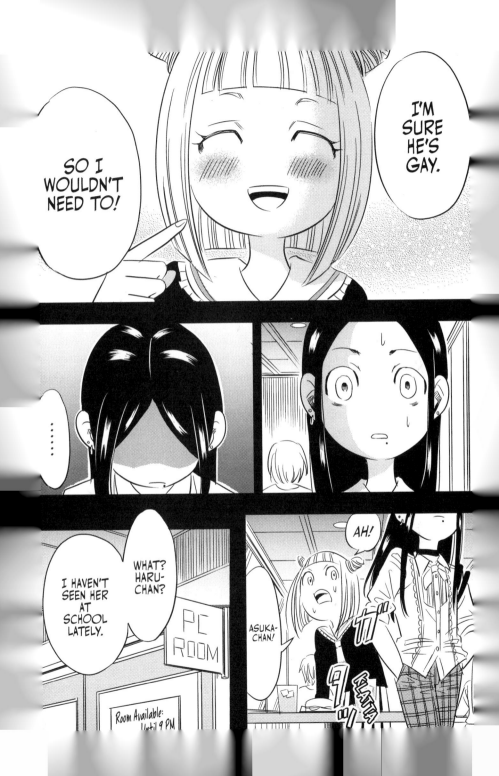

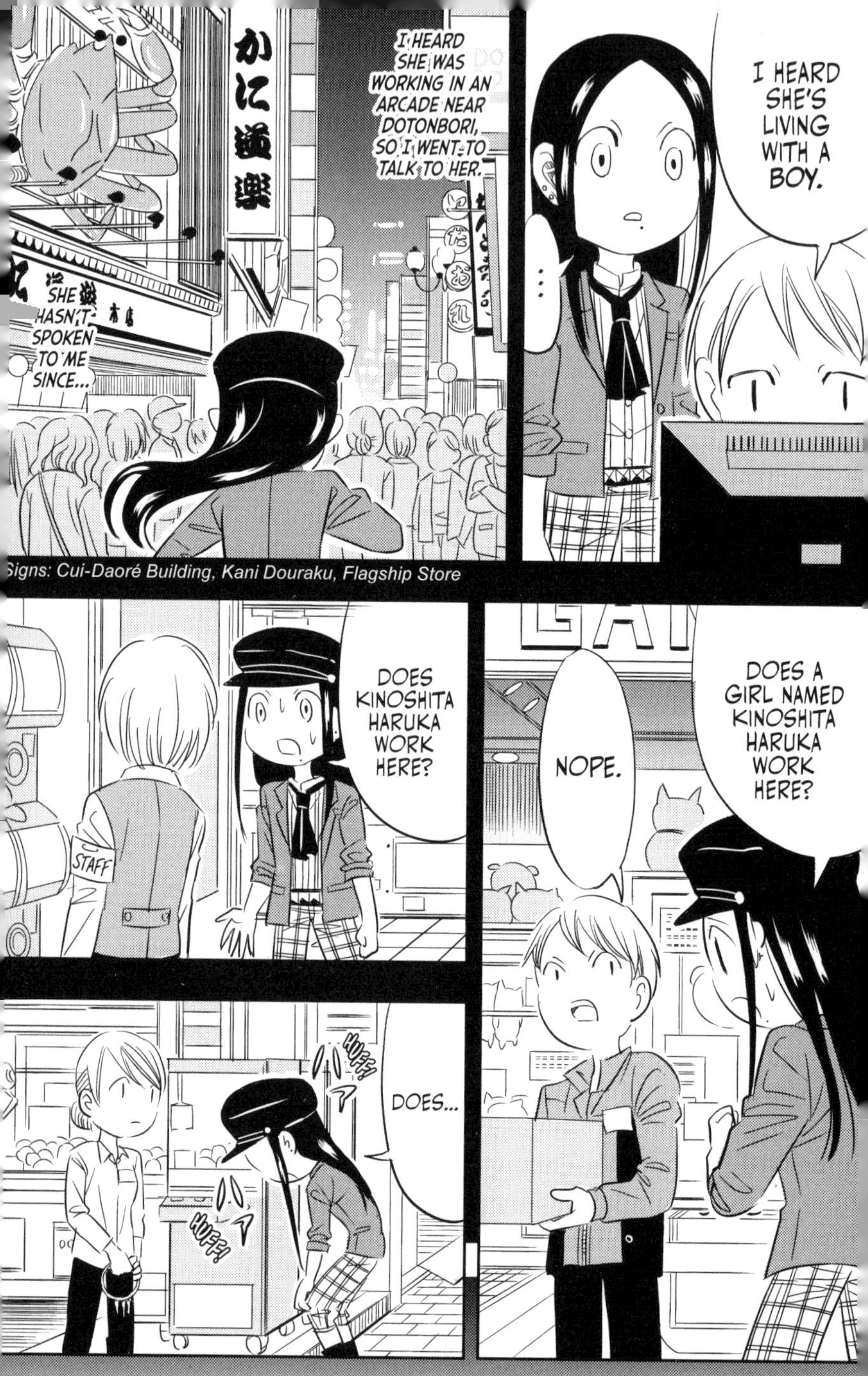
I HEARD SHE'S LIVING WITH A BOY.
...
I HEARD SHE WAS WORKING IN AN ARCADE NEAR DOTONBORI, SO I WENT TO TALK TO HER.
かに道楽
SHE HASN'T SPOKEN TO ME SINCE...
Signs: Cui-Daoré Building, Kani Douraku, Flagship Store
DOES A GIRL NAMED KINOSHITA HARUKA WORK HERE?
NOPE.
DOES KINOSHITA HARUKA WORK HERE?
STAFF
HUFF!
HUFF!
DOES...

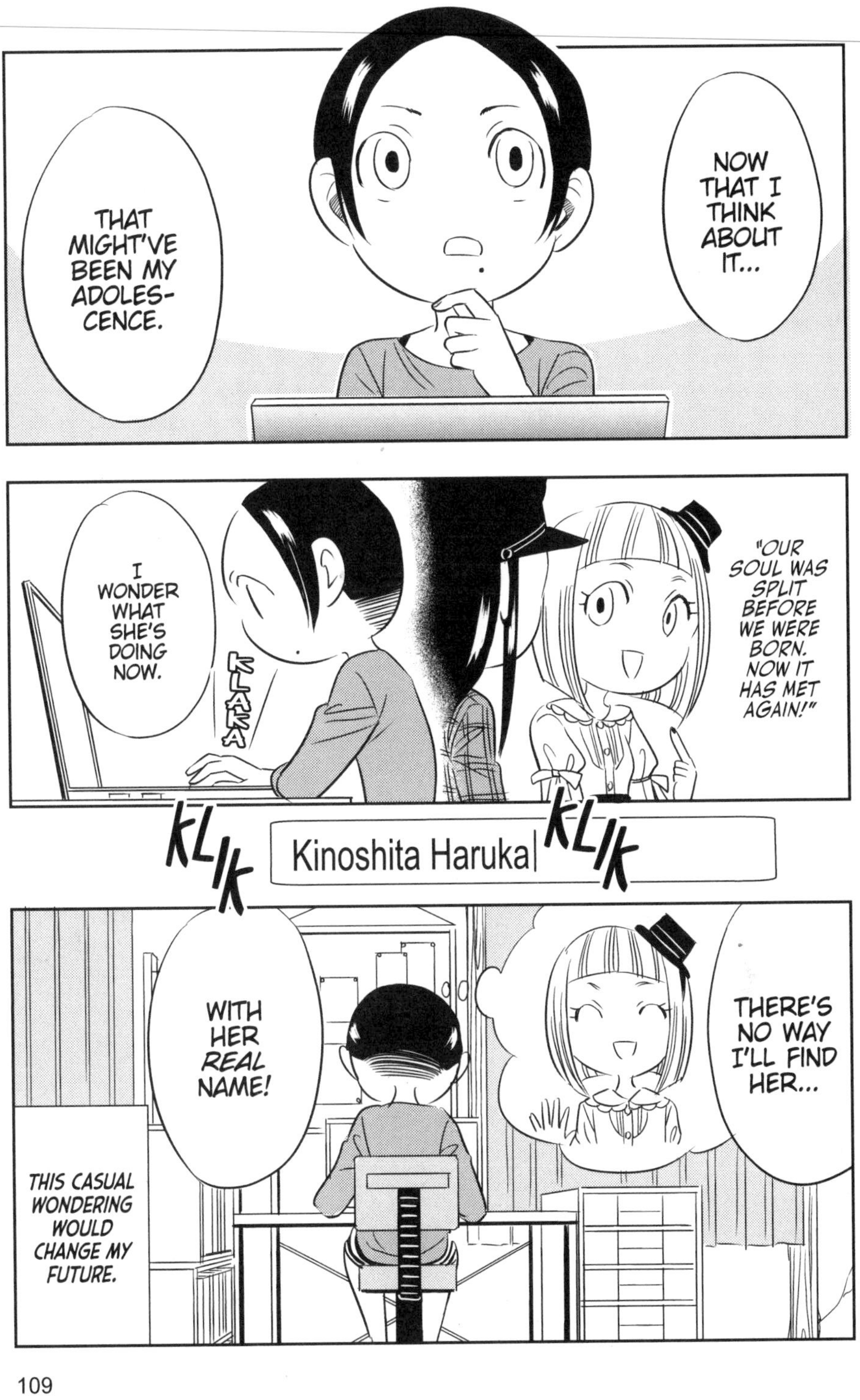
NOW THAT I THINK ABOUT IT...
THAT MIGHT'VE BEEN MY ADOLES-CENCE.
"OUR SOUL WAS SPLIT BEFORE WE WERE BORN. NOW IT HAS MET AGAIN!"
I WONDER WHAT SHE'S DOING NOW.
KLAKA
KLIK
Kinoshita Haruka
KLIK
THERE'S NO WAY I'LL FIND HER...
WITH HER REAL NAME!
THIS CASUAL WONDERING WOULD CHANGE MY FUTURE.

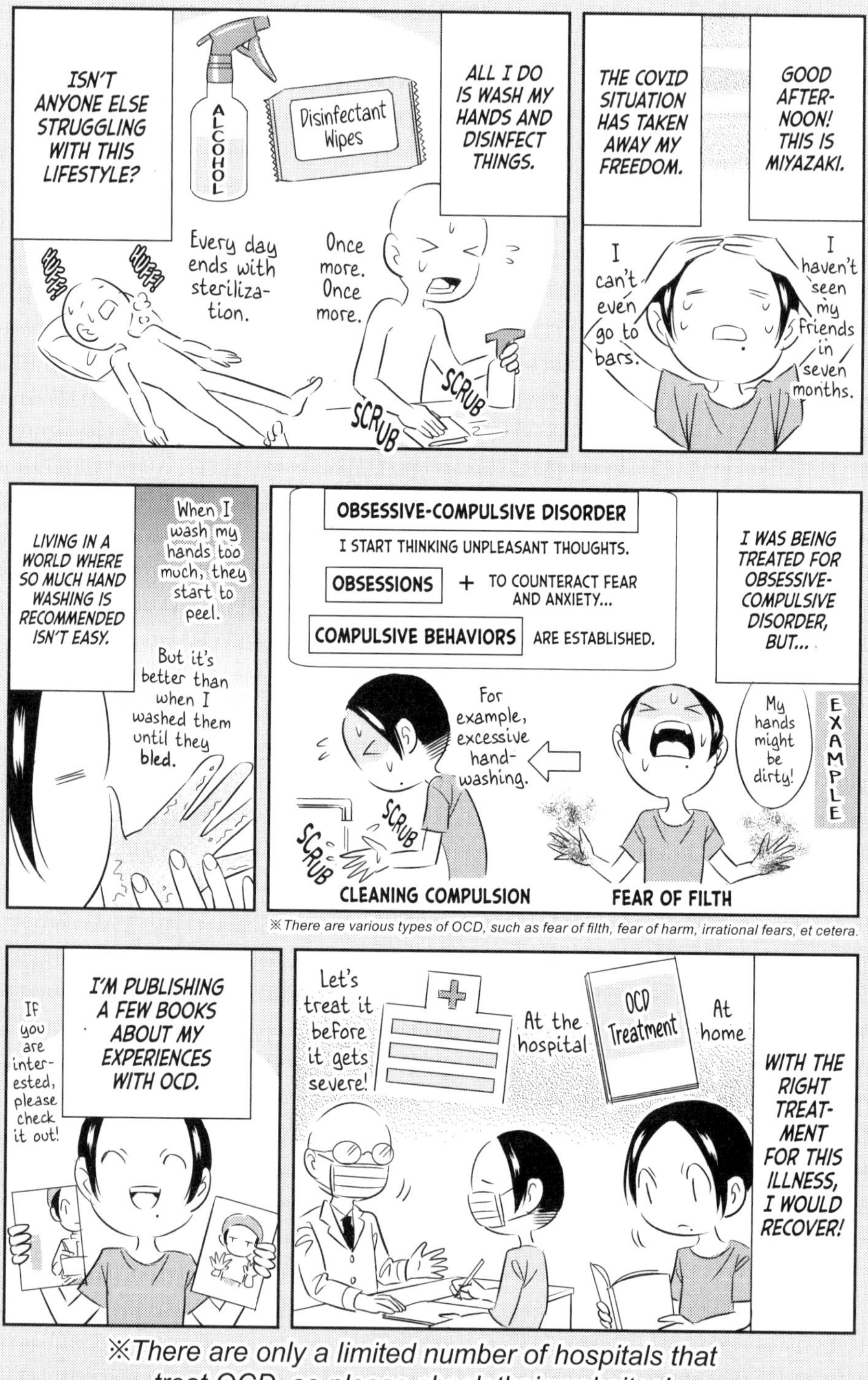
GOOD AFTER-NOON! THIS IS MIYAZAKI.
THE COVID SITUATION HAS TAKEN AWAY MY FREEDOM.
I haven't seen my friends in seven months.
I can't even go to bars.
ALL I DO IS WASH MY HANDS AND DISINFECT THINGS.
Once more. Once more.
SCRUB
SCRUB
Disinfectant Wipes
ALCOHOL
ISN'T ANYONE ELSE STRUGGLING WITH THIS LIFESTYLE?
Every day ends with steriliza-tion.
HUFF
HUFF
I WAS BEING TREATED FOR OBSESSIVE-COMPULSIVE DISORDER, BUT...
OBSESSIVE-COMPULSIVE DISORDER
I START THINKING UNPLEASANT THOUGHTS.
OBSESSIONS + TO COUNTERACT FEAR AND ANXIETY...
COMPULSIVE BEHAVIORS ARE ESTABLISHED.
EXAMPLE
My hands might be dirty!
For example, excessive hand-washing.
SCRUB
SCRUB
FEAR OF FILTH
CLEANING COMPULSION
When I wash my hands too much, they start to peel.
LIVING IN A WORLD WHERE SO MUCH HAND WASHING IS RECOMMENDED ISN'T EASY.
But it's better than when I washed them until they bled.
WITH THE RIGHT TREATMENT FOR THIS ILLNESS, I WOULD RECOVER!
At home
OCD Treatment
At the hospital
Let's treat it before it gets severe!
I'M PUBLISHING A FEW BOOKS ABOUT MY EXPERIENCES WITH OCD.
If you are inter-ested, please check it out!

※There are various types of OCD, such as fear of filth, fear of harm, irrational fears, et cetera.

※There are only a limited number of hospitals that treat OCD, so please check their websites!

This is OCD! by Asuka Miyazaki, Published by Seiwa Shoten
OCD Treatment Diary by Asuka Miyazaki, Published by Seiwa Shoten

Ep. 10: The "Love Story" Story

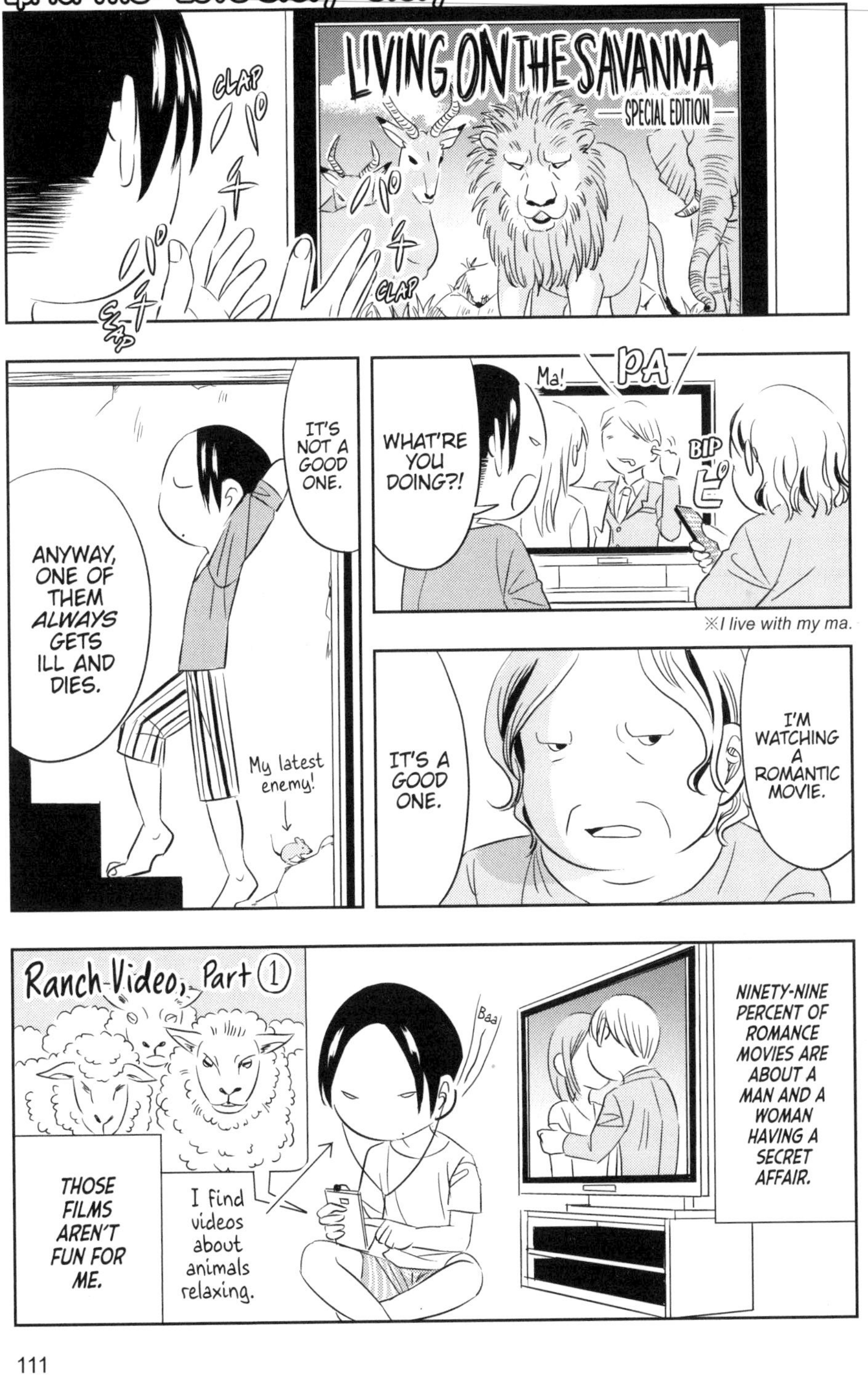
LIVING ON THE SAVANNA
SPECIAL EDITION
CLAP
CLAP
CLAP
Ma!
PA
WHAT'RE YOU DOING?!
BIP
ピ
※I live with my ma.
I'M WATCHING A ROMANTIC MOVIE.
IT'S A GOOD ONE.
IT'S NOT A GOOD ONE.
ANYWAY, ONE OF THEM *ALWAYS* GETS ILL AND DIES.
My latest enemy!
NINETY-NINE PERCENT OF ROMANCE MOVIES ARE ABOUT A MAN AND A WOMAN HAVING A SECRET AFFAIR.
Ranch-Video, Part ①
Baa
I find videos about animals relaxing.
THOSE FILMS AREN'T FUN FOR ME.

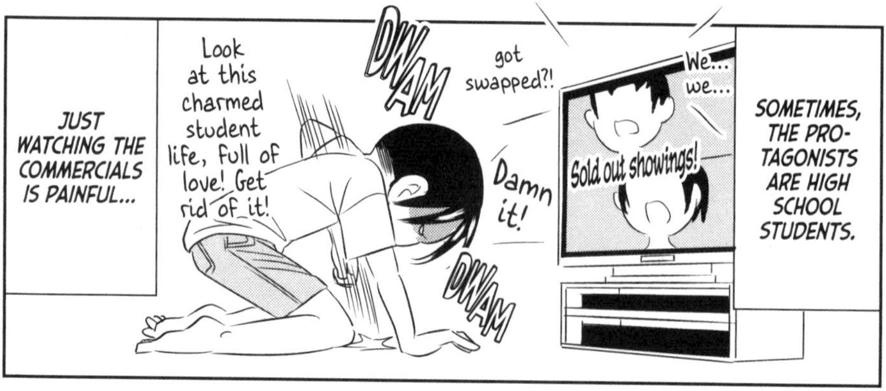
SOMETIMES, THE PRO-TAGONISTS ARE HIGH SCHOOL STUDENTS.
We... we...
got swapped?!
Sold out showings!
DWAM
Damn it!
DWAM
Look at this charmed student life, full of love! Get rid of it!
JUST WATCHING THE COMMERCIALS IS PAINFUL...

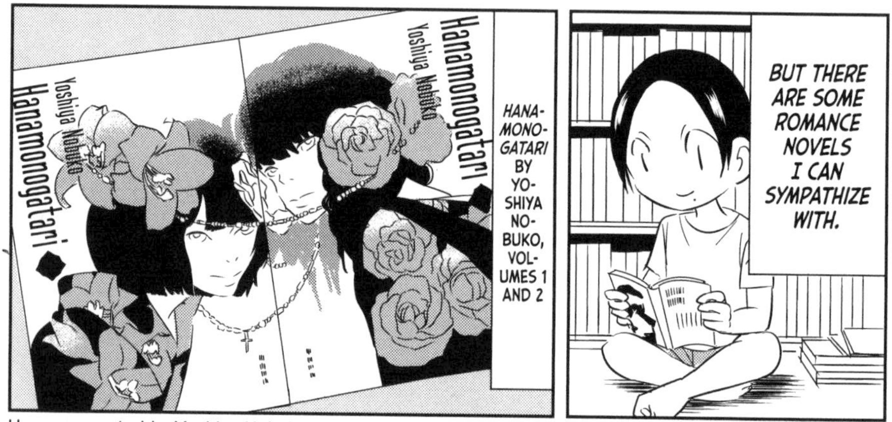
BUT THERE ARE SOME ROMANCE NOVELS I CAN SYMPATHIZE WITH.
HANA-MONO-GATARI BY YO-SHIYA NO-BUKO, VOL-UMES 1 AND 2
Hanamonogatari
Yoshiya Nobuko
Yoshiya Nobuko
Hanamonogatari

Hanamonogatari *by Yoshiya Nobuko (published by Kawade Bunko)*

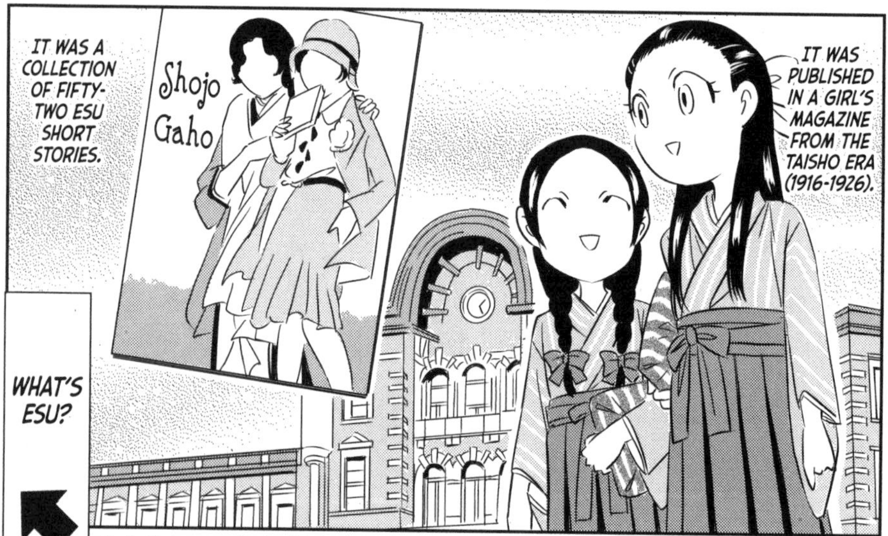
IT WAS PUBLISHED IN A GIRL'S MAGAZINE FROM THE TAISHO ERA (1916-1926).
Shojo Gaho
IT WAS A COLLECTION OF FIFTY-TWO ESU SHORT STORIES.
WHAT'S ESU?

Shojo Gaho *was first published in 1912 (Tokyo ~ Shinsensha).*

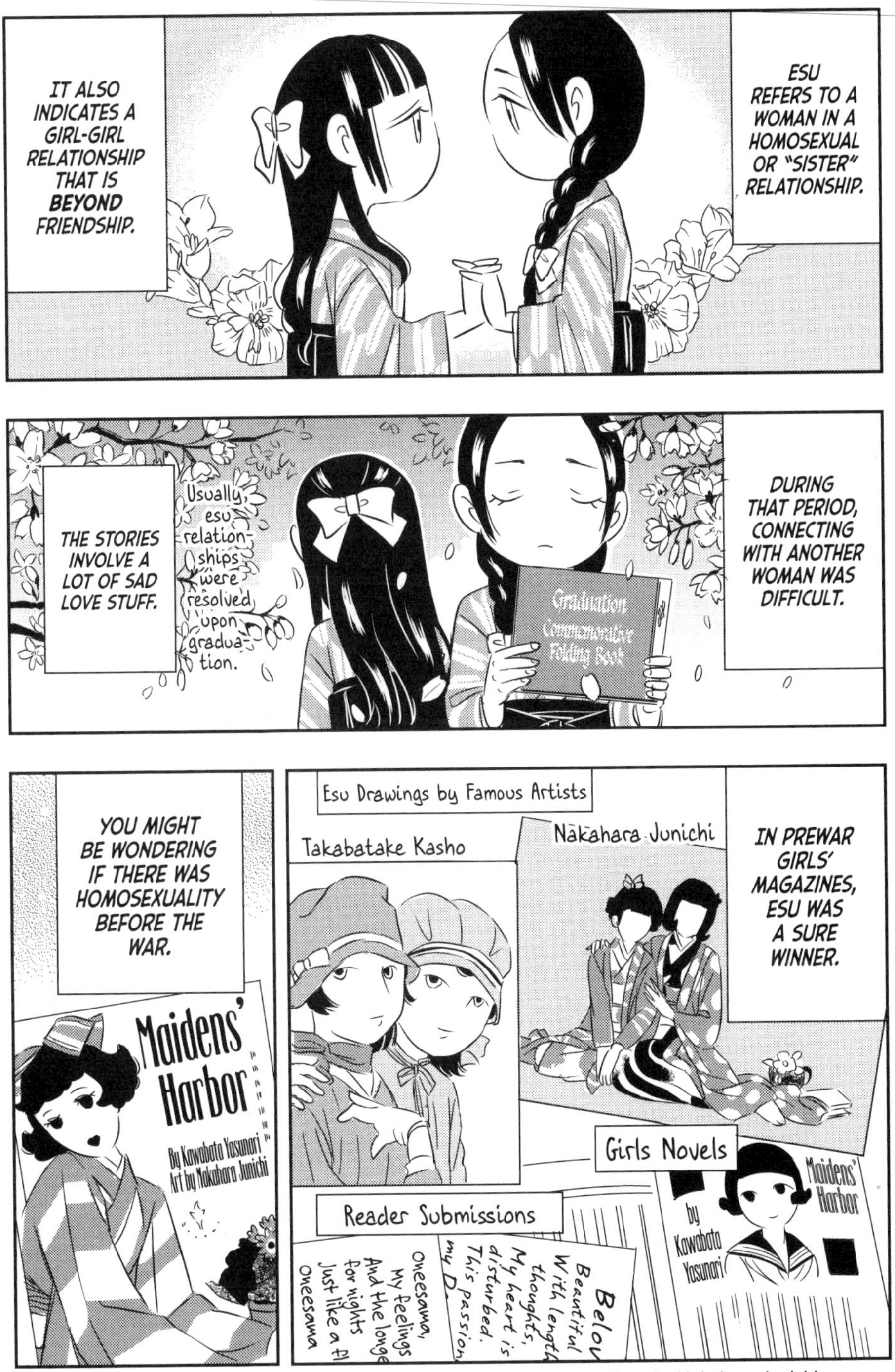
ESU REFERS TO A WOMAN IN A HOMOSEXUAL OR "SISTER" RELATIONSHIP.
IT ALSO INDICATES A GIRL-GIRL RELATIONSHIP THAT IS **BEYOND** FRIENDSHIP.
DURING THAT PERIOD, CONNECTING WITH ANOTHER WOMAN WAS DIFFICULT.
Graduation Commemorative Folding Book
Usually, esu relationships were resolved upon graduation.
THE STORIES INVOLVE A LOT OF SAD LOVE STUFF.
IN PREWAR GIRLS' MAGAZINES, ESU WAS A SURE WINNER.
Esu Drawings by Famous Artists
Nakahara Junichi
Takabatake Kasho
Girls Novels
Maidens' Harbor
by Kawabata Yasunari
Reader Submissions
Belov
Beautiful
With length
thoughts,
My heart is
disturbed.
This passion
my D
Oneesama,
My feelings
And the longe
for nights
Just like a fl
Oneesama
YOU MIGHT BE WONDERING IF THERE WAS HOMOSEXUALITY BEFORE THE WAR.
Maidens' Harbor
By Kawabata Yasunari
Art by Nakahara Junichi

Maidens' Harbor by Kawabata Yasunari, art by Nakahara Junichi (Published by Jitsugyo no Nihon Sha)

In truth, some of Kawabata Yasunari's esu pieces may have been ghostwritten.

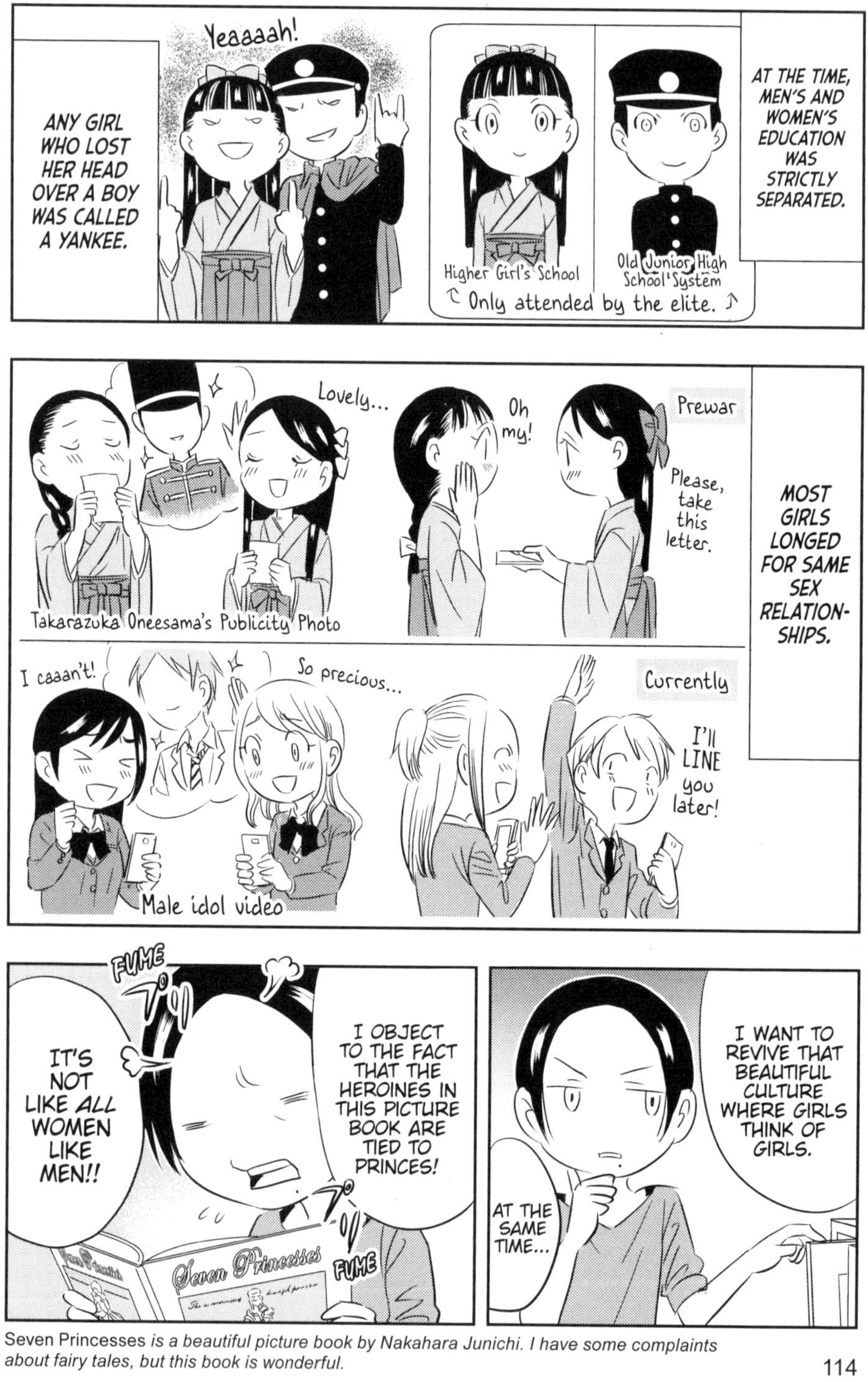
AT THE TIME, MEN'S AND WOMEN'S EDUCATION WAS STRICTLY SEPARATED.
Old Junior High School System
Higher Girl's School
Only attended by the elite.
Yeaaaah!
ANY GIRL WHO LOST HER HEAD OVER A BOY WAS CALLED A YANKEE.
MOST GIRLS LONGED FOR SAME SEX RELATIONSHIPS.
Prewar
Please, take this letter.
Oh my!
Lovely...
Takarazuka Oneesama's Publicity Photo
Currently
I'll LINE you later!
So precious...
I caaan't!
Male idol video
I WANT TO REVIVE THAT BEAUTIFUL CULTURE WHERE GIRLS THINK OF GIRLS.
AT THE SAME TIME...
I OBJECT TO THE FACT THAT THE HEROINES IN THIS PICTURE BOOK ARE TIED TO PRINCES!
IT'S NOT LIKE *ALL* WOMEN LIKE MEN!!
FUME
Seven Princesses
FUME

Seven Princesses *is a beautiful picture book by Nakahara Junichi. I have some complaints about fairy tales, but this book is wonderful.*

Everyone on the dating scene is so competitive.

THE PRINCE FROM *THE LITTLE MERMAID* IS SO CRAPPY.
The prince from The Little Mermaid.
ALL RIGHT!
The literary world's three biggest bastards.
Toyotarō from "The Dancing Girl."*
Yōzō from No Longer Human.**
I'LL DRAW *THE LITTLE MERMAID* FOR REIWA-ERA GIRLS!
AND I'LL BRAINWASH THEM INTO BEING ESU FROM BIRTH!!

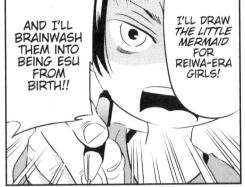

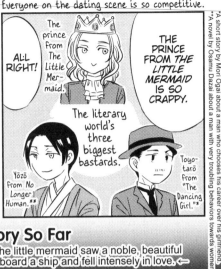

*A short story by Mori Ogai about a man who chooses his career over his girlfriend.
**A novel by Osamu Dazai about a man with very troubling behaviors towards women.

The Little Mermaid
(Asuka Miyazaki Edition)
※*Please read the extra-long sentences if you can, generous readers!*

The Story So Far
One day, the little mermaid saw a noble, beautiful princess aboard a ship and fell intensely in love. ⟵

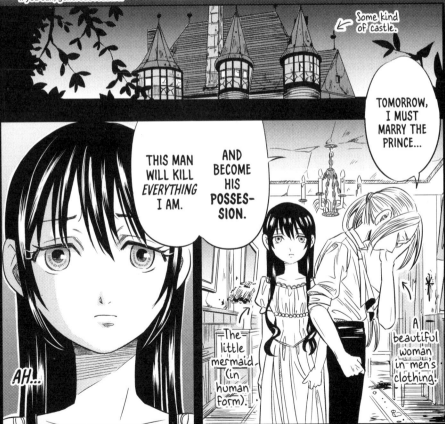

The little mermaid wished to become human to be with her princess, so she visited a witch and exchanged her beautiful voice for legs. The princess picked up the little mermaid, and they lived together in the castle like sisters. For a while, they were happy.

Some kind of castle.
TOMORROW, I MUST MARRY THE PRINCE...
AND BECOME HIS POSSESSION.
THIS MAN WILL KILL *EVERYTHING* I AM.
A beautiful woman in men's clothing.
The little mermaid (in human form).
AH...

However, the little mermaid worried about the shadow on the face of the woman she loved. The princess was fighting against her own fate, but it was in vain. Soon, she would be married to the

Nothing is more important than the first page of a story, but let's start when these two beautiful people wake up in bed under the morning sun and exchange greetings. I'll draw a summary of the first episode, leading up to that relationship.

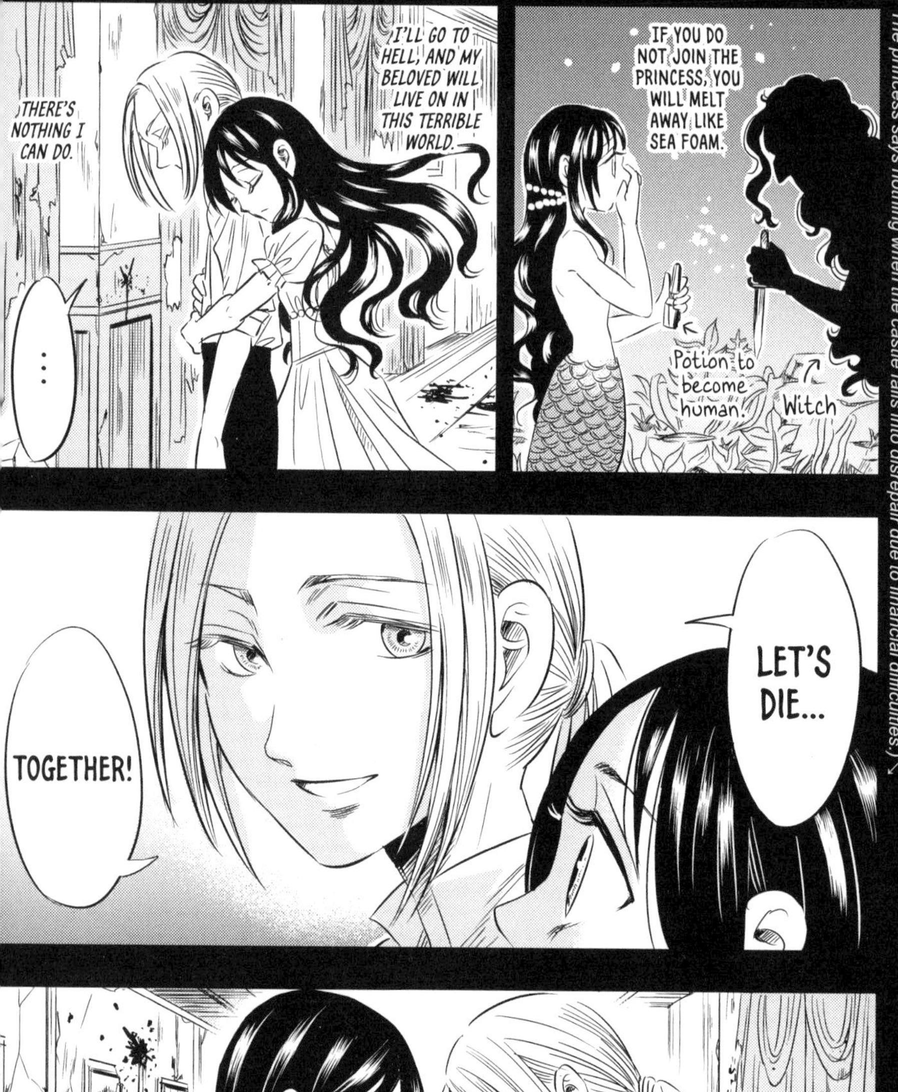
IF YOU DO NOT JOIN THE PRINCESS, YOU WILL MELT AWAY LIKE SEA FOAM.
Potion to become human.
Witch
I'LL GO TO HELL, AND MY BELOVED WILL LIVE ON IN THIS TERRIBLE WORLD.
THERE'S NOTHING I CAN DO.
...
LET'S DIE...
TOGETHER!

poke out his eyes. Both the princess and the little mermaid are fierce. (I grew up on yankee manga, so the characters behave badly. The princess says nothing when the castle falls into disrepair due to financial difficulties.)↓

I really want to show the princess combing out the little mermaid's long hair and muttering to herself. Before this scene, they've tried to elope twice already but, after a brawl, were dragged back b[illegible]e of the king's men

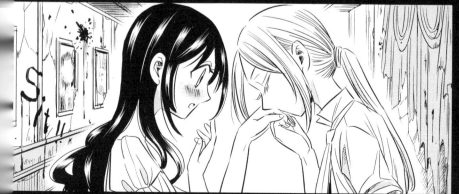

Living is tiresome. They desired death unconsciously and suppressed their suffering... ←

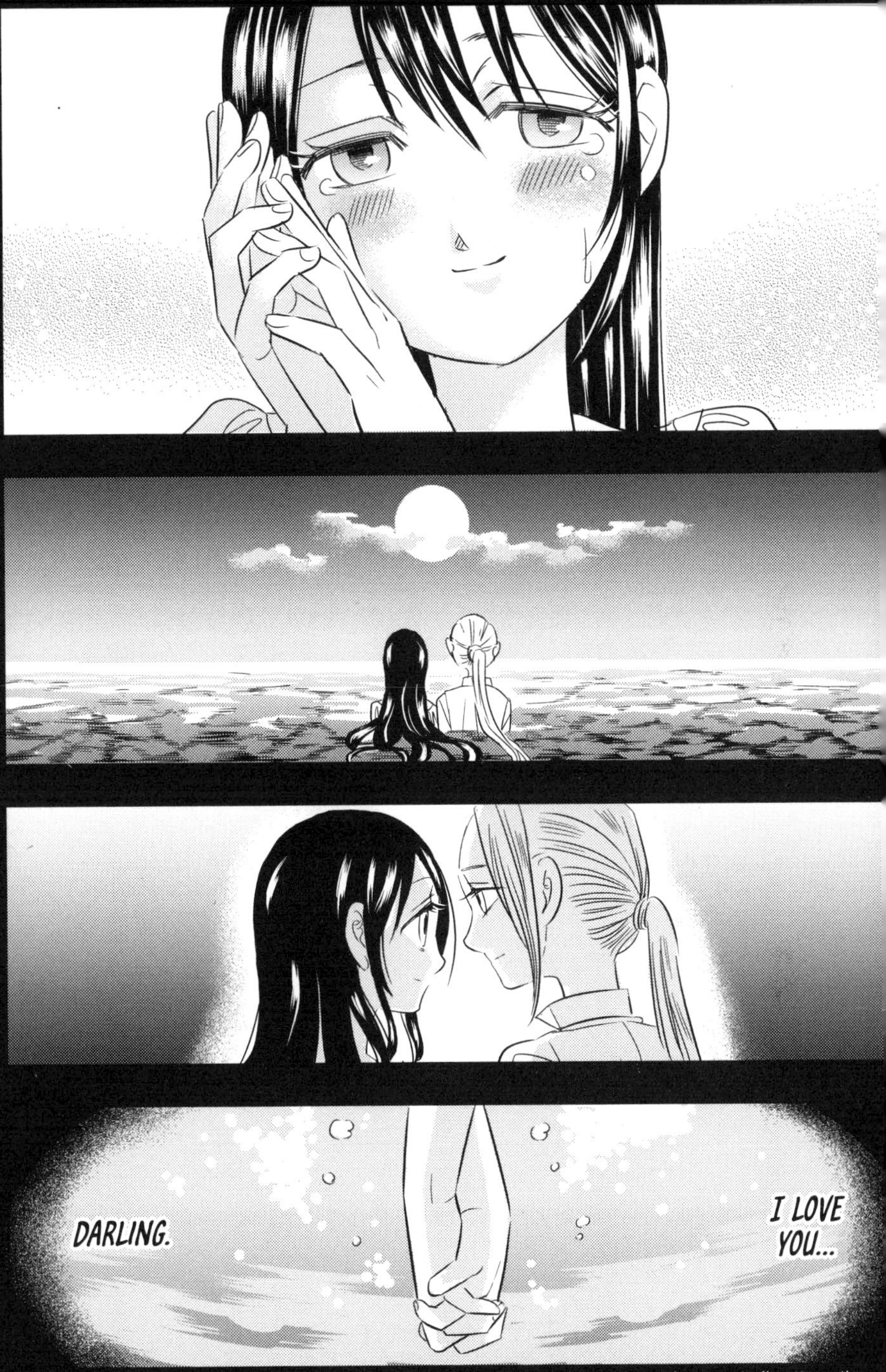
I LOVE YOU...
DARLING.

but then, at last, they lived. It's a motif as old as humankind: two young people realizing the sufferings of life

As a side note, my debut work Heisei Decadence was also about a devoted couple repeatedly attempting

In the original story, the little mermaid helps the prince in a stormy sea and falls deeply in love with him. She wishes to become human and, after having her tongue cut out and losing her voice...↘

she obtains a potion to give her human legs. But each step hurts like she's walking on knives, so the prince picks her up. He loves her, but there is a misunderstanding, and he marries another woman. So, the little mermaid turns into sea foam and disappears.↘

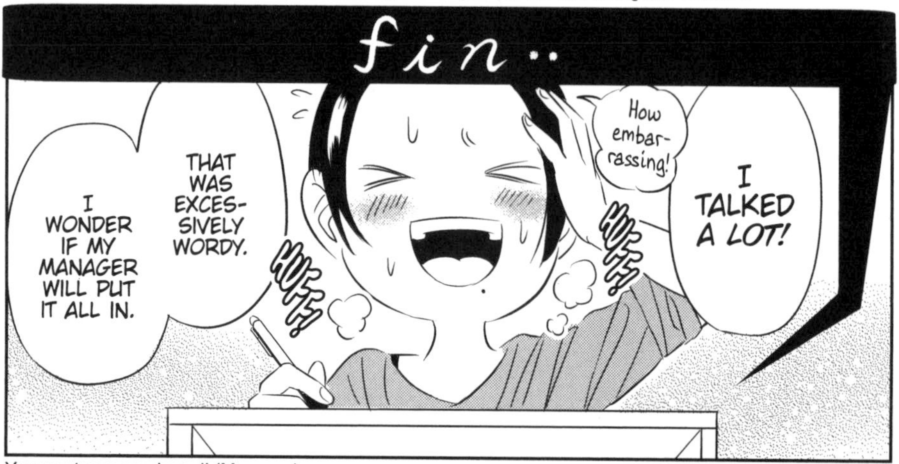
fin..
I TALKED A LOT!
How embarrassing!
HUFF
THAT WAS EXCESSIVELY WORDY.
I WONDER IF MY MANAGER WILL PUT IT ALL IN.
HUFF

You went way overboard! (Manager)

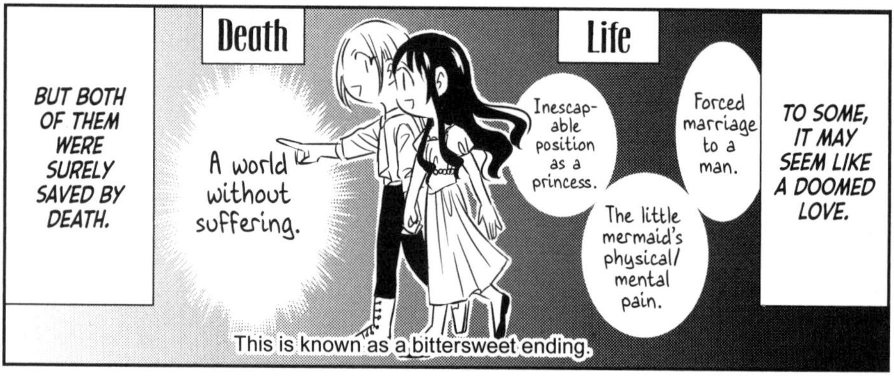
TO SOME, IT MAY SEEM LIKE A DOOMED LOVE.
Life
Forced marriage to a man.
The little mermaid's physical/mental pain.
Inescapable position as a princess.
Death
A world without suffering.
BUT BOTH OF THEM WERE SURELY SAVED BY DEATH.
This is known as a bittersweet ending.

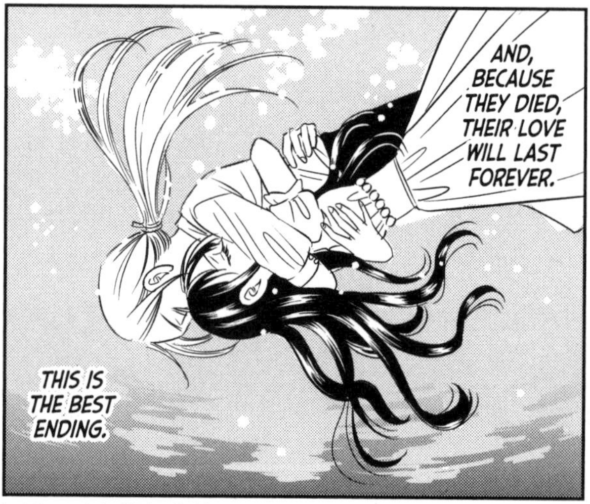
AND, BECAUSE THEY DIED, THEIR LOVE WILL LAST FOREVER.
THIS IS THE BEST ENDING.

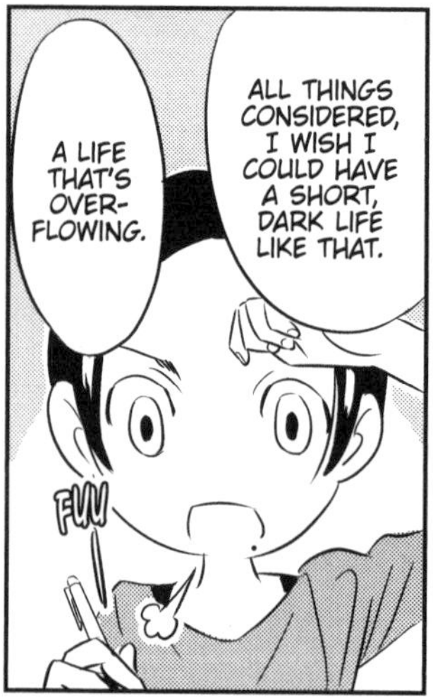
ALL THINGS CONSIDERED, I WISH I COULD HAVE A SHORT, DARK LIFE LIKE THAT.
A LIFE THAT'S OVERFLOWING.
FUU

Even as an adult, I don't understand what the point of it is. But I guess you can take even a story without solace and turn it into a happy animated movie.

Are fairy tale heroines really happy to be bound to inexperienced princes?

It's not something they earn, and it makes their happiness greatly dependent upon men. From now on, I think fairy tales should show women earning success in life, wealth, and their own happy endings. ↗

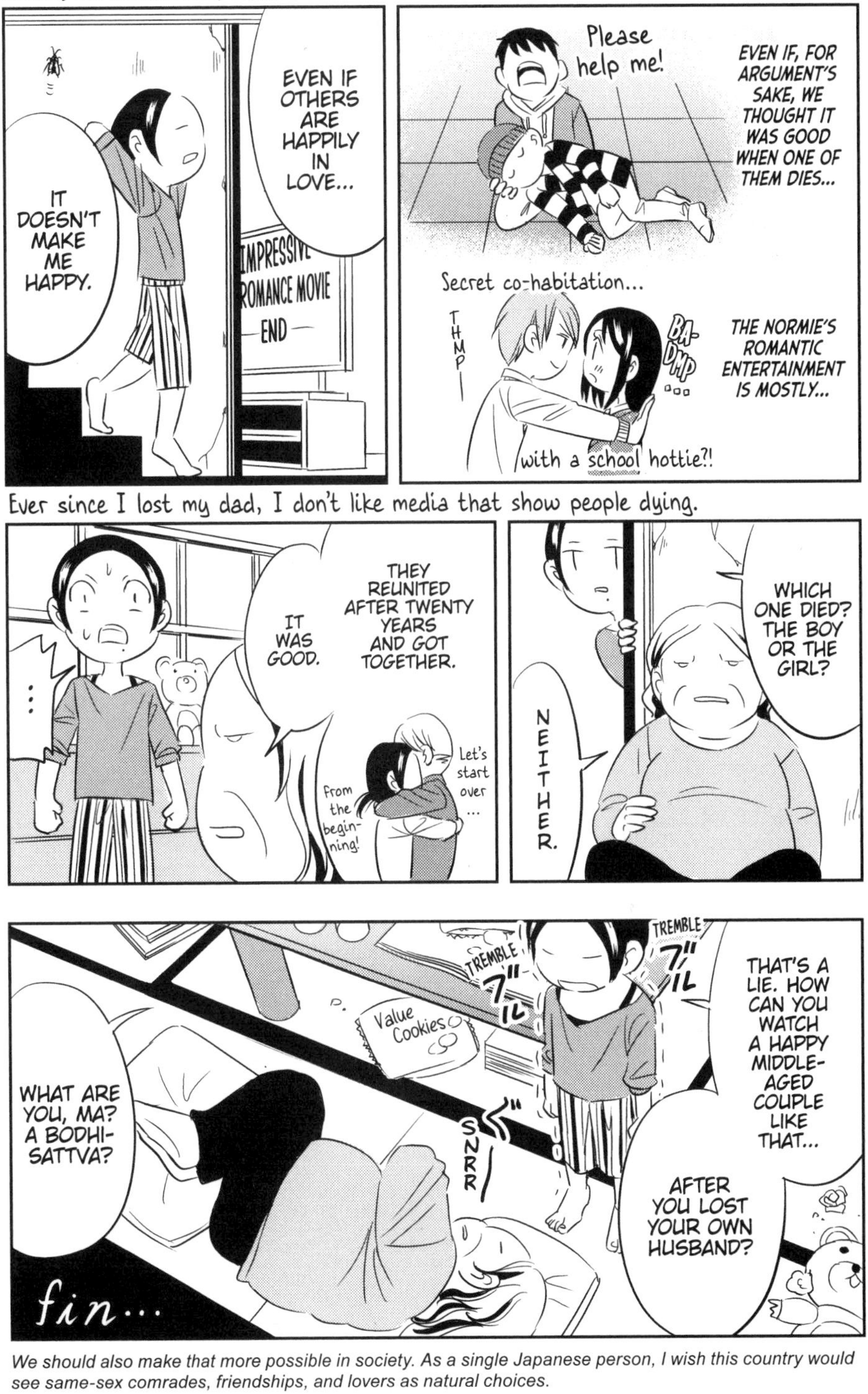
EVEN IF, FOR ARGUMENT'S SAKE, WE THOUGHT IT WAS GOOD WHEN ONE OF THEM DIES...
Please help me!
THE NORMIE'S ROMANTIC ENTERTAINMENT IS MOSTLY...
BA-DMP...
Secret co-habitation...
THMP
with a school hottie?!
EVEN IF OTHERS ARE HAPPILY IN LOVE...
IMPRESSIVE ROMANCE MOVIE
END
IT DOESN'T MAKE ME HAPPY.
Ever since I lost my dad, I don't like media that show people dying.
WHICH ONE DIED? THE BOY OR THE GIRL?
NEITHER.
THEY REUNITED AFTER TWENTY YEARS AND GOT TOGETHER.
IT WAS GOOD.
Let's start over...
From the beginning!
...
THAT'S A LIE. HOW CAN YOU WATCH A HAPPY MIDDLE-AGED COUPLE LIKE THAT...
TREMBLE
AFTER YOU LOST YOUR OWN HUSBAND?
TREMBLE
Value Cookies
SNRR
WHAT ARE YOU, MA? A BODHI-SATTVA?
fin...

We should also make that more possible in society. As a single Japanese person, I wish this country would see same-sex comrades, friendships, and lovers as natural choices.

Ep. 11: The "That Girl Again" Story

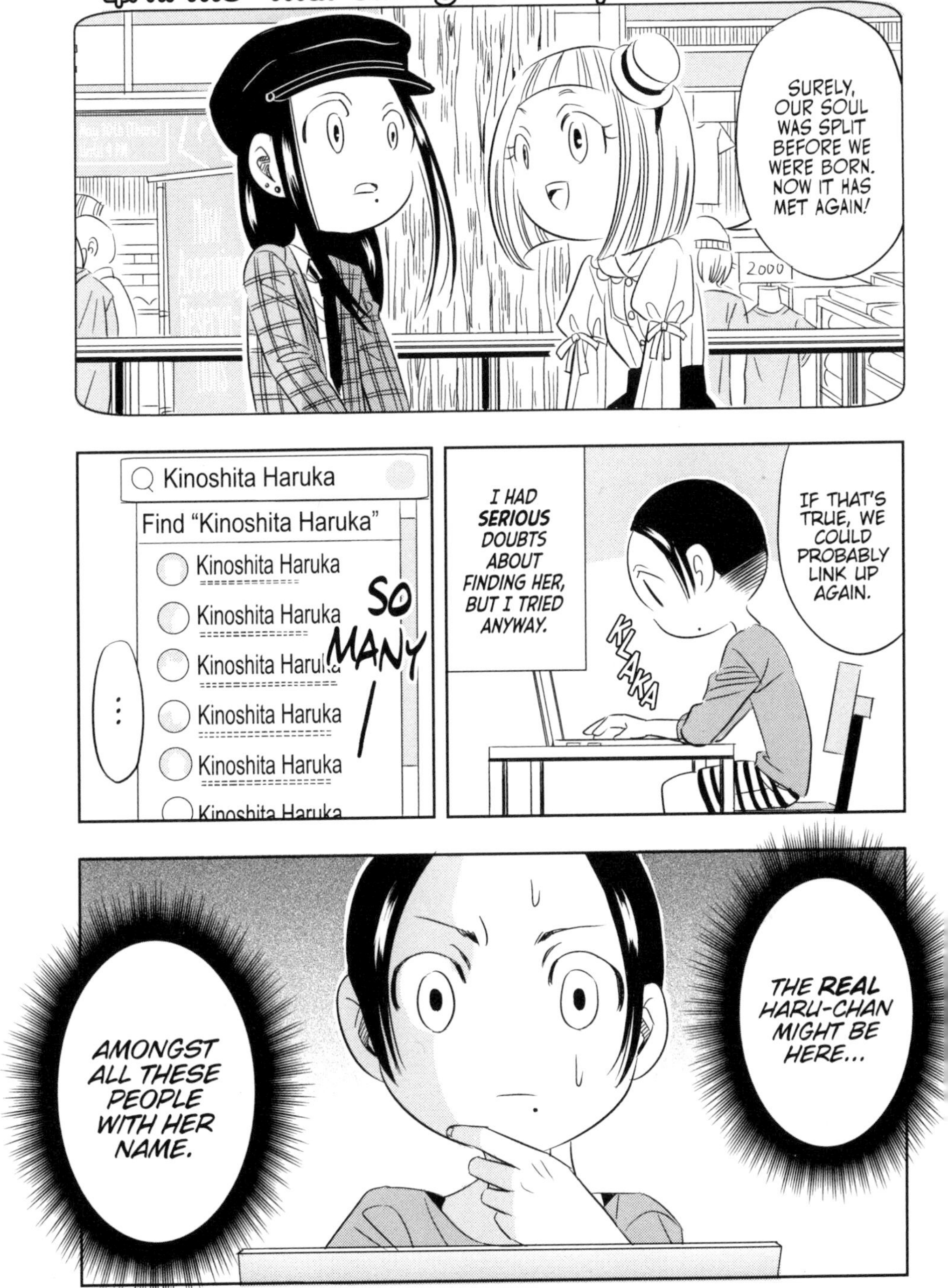
SURELY, OUR SOUL WAS SPLIT BEFORE WE WERE BORN. NOW IT HAS MET AGAIN!
2000
IF THAT'S TRUE, WE COULD PROBABLY LINK UP AGAIN.
I HAD SERIOUS DOUBTS ABOUT FINDING HER, BUT I TRIED ANYWAY.
KLAKA
Kinoshita Haruka
Find "Kinoshita Haruka"
Kinoshita Haruka
Kinoshita Haruka
Kinoshita Haruka
Kinoshita Haruka
Kinoshita Haruka
Kinoshita Haruka
SO MANY!
...
THE REAL HARU-CHAN MIGHT BE HERE...
AMONGST ALL THESE PEOPLE WITH HER NAME.

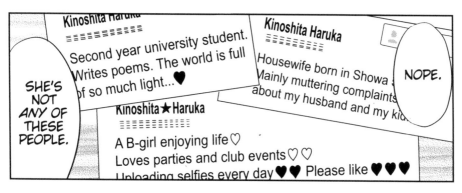

Kinoshita Haruka
Housewife born in Showa
Mainly muttering complaints
about my husband and my kid
NOPE.
Kinoshita Haruka
Second year university student.
Writes poems. The world is full
of so much light...♥
Kinoshita★Haruka
A B-girl enjoying life♡
Loves parties and club events♡♡
Uploading selfies every day♥♥ Please like♥♥♥
SHE'S NOT ANY OF THESE PEOPLE.
NOT THIS ONE, EITHER.
KLAKA
KLAKA
OR THIS ONE.
Kinoshita Haruka
○○ × ●● is the best yuri pairing!!
I have such a crush on ○○-san and ●●-san!!
...
Kinoshita Haruka
I'm a designer.
Graduated from a painting school.

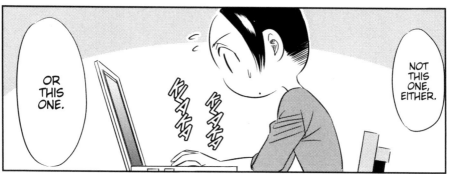

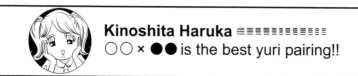

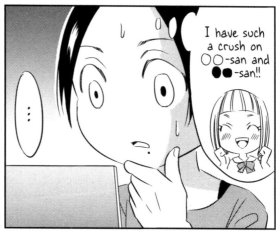

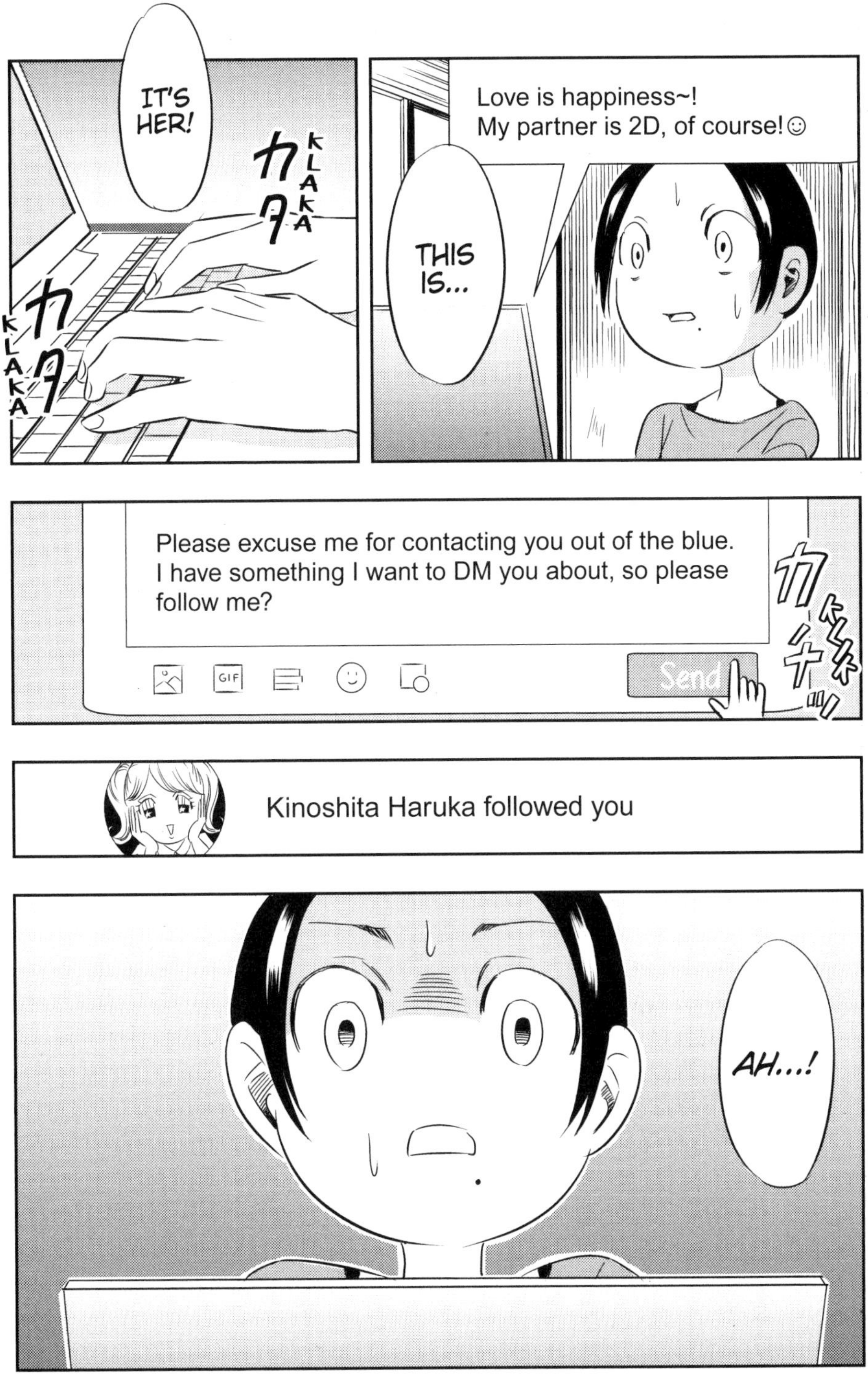
Love is happiness~!
My partner is 2D, of course!☺
THIS IS...
IT'S HER!
カタ KLAKA
カタ KLAKA
Please excuse me for contacting you out of the blue. I have something I want to DM you about, so please follow me?
Send
カチッ KLIK
Kinoshita Haruka followed you
AH...!

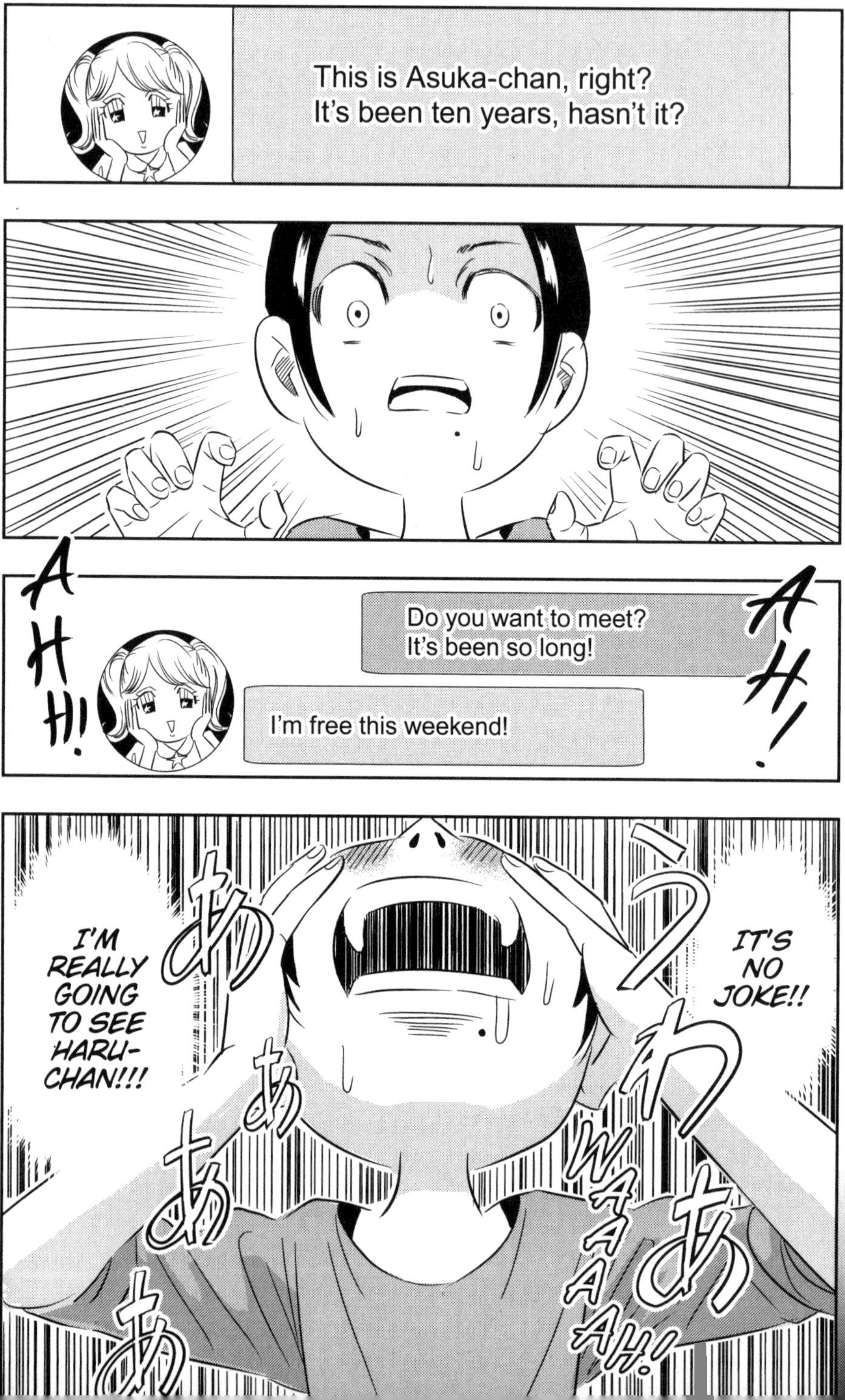
This is Asuka-chan, right?
It's been ten years, hasn't it?
AHH!
AHH!
Do you want to meet?
It's been so long!
I'm free this weekend!
IT'S NO JOKE!!
うわあ
WAAAAH!
I'M REALLY GOING TO SEE HARU-CHAN!!!
あああああ

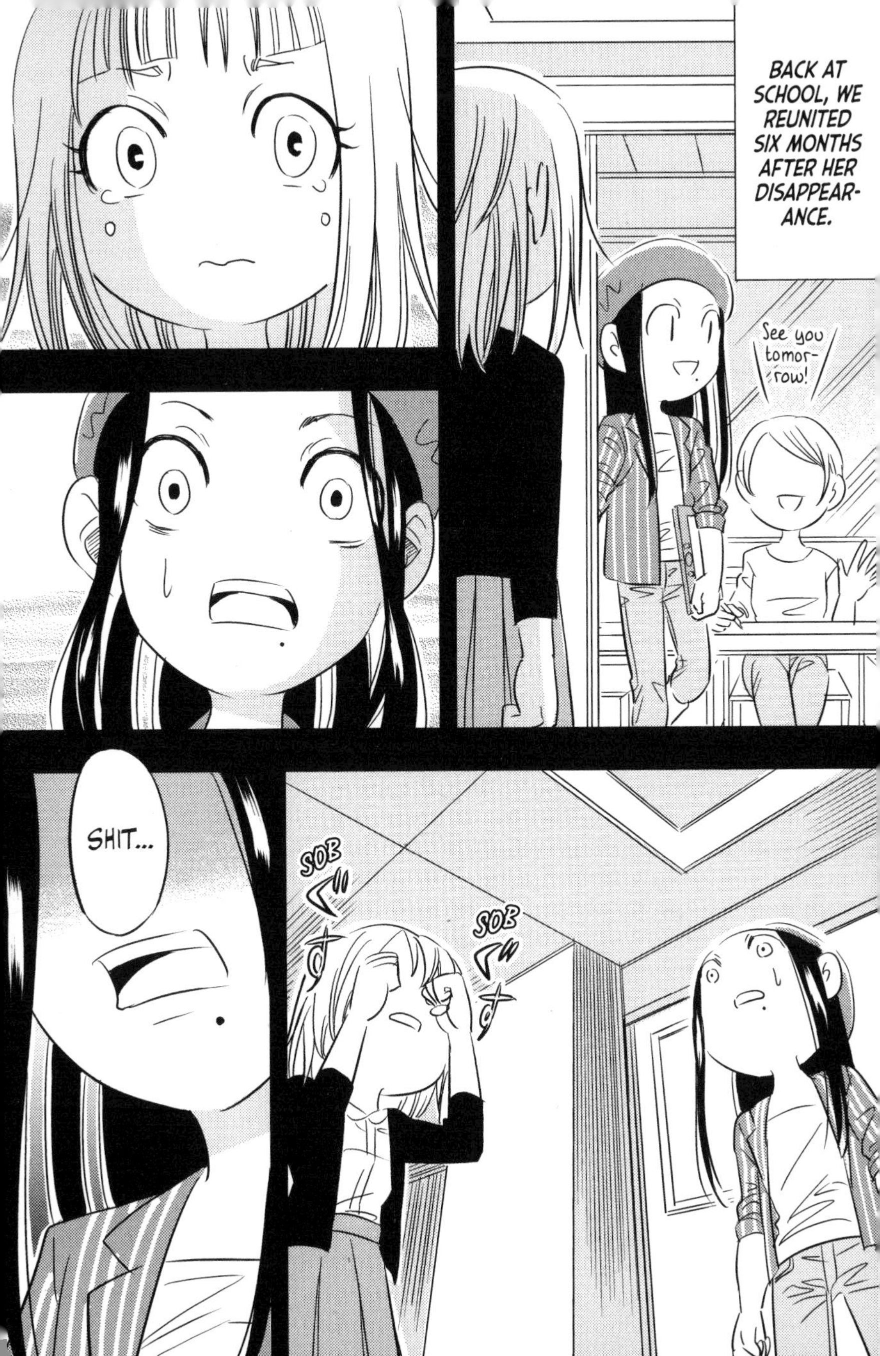
BACK AT SCHOOL, WE REUNITED SIX MONTHS AFTER HER DISAPPEARANCE.
See you tomorrow!
SOB
SOB
SHIT...

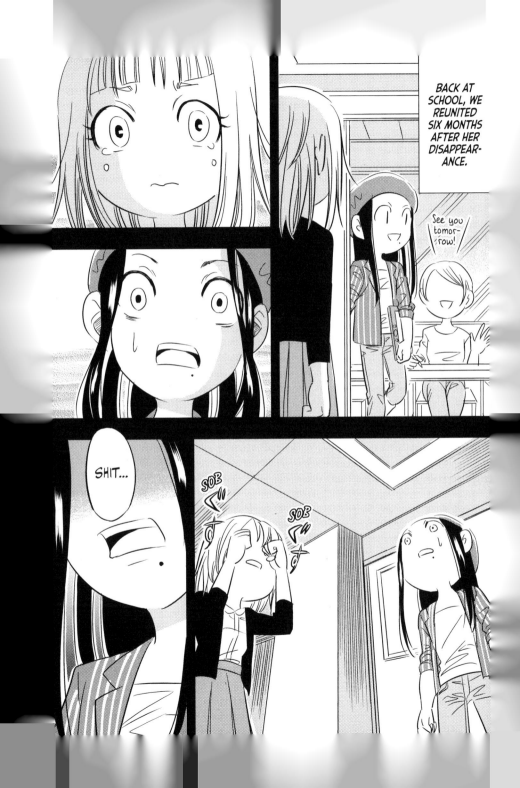

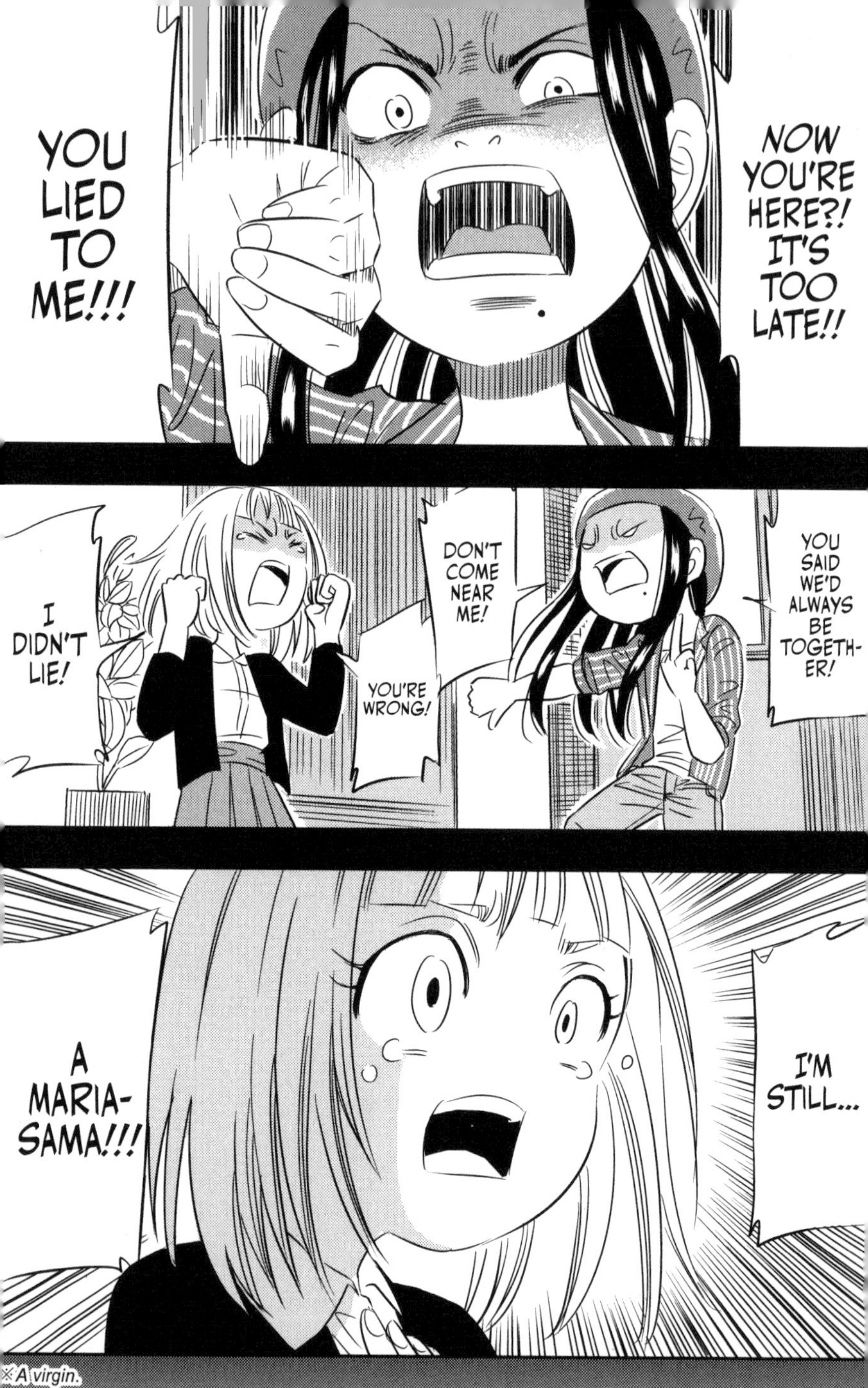
NOW YOU'RE HERE?! IT'S TOO LATE!!
YOU LIED TO ME!!!
YOU SAID WE'D ALWAYS BE TOGETH-ER!
DON'T COME NEAR ME!
YOU'RE WRONG!
I DIDN'T LIE!
I'M STILL...
A MARIA-SAMA!!!

※A virgin.

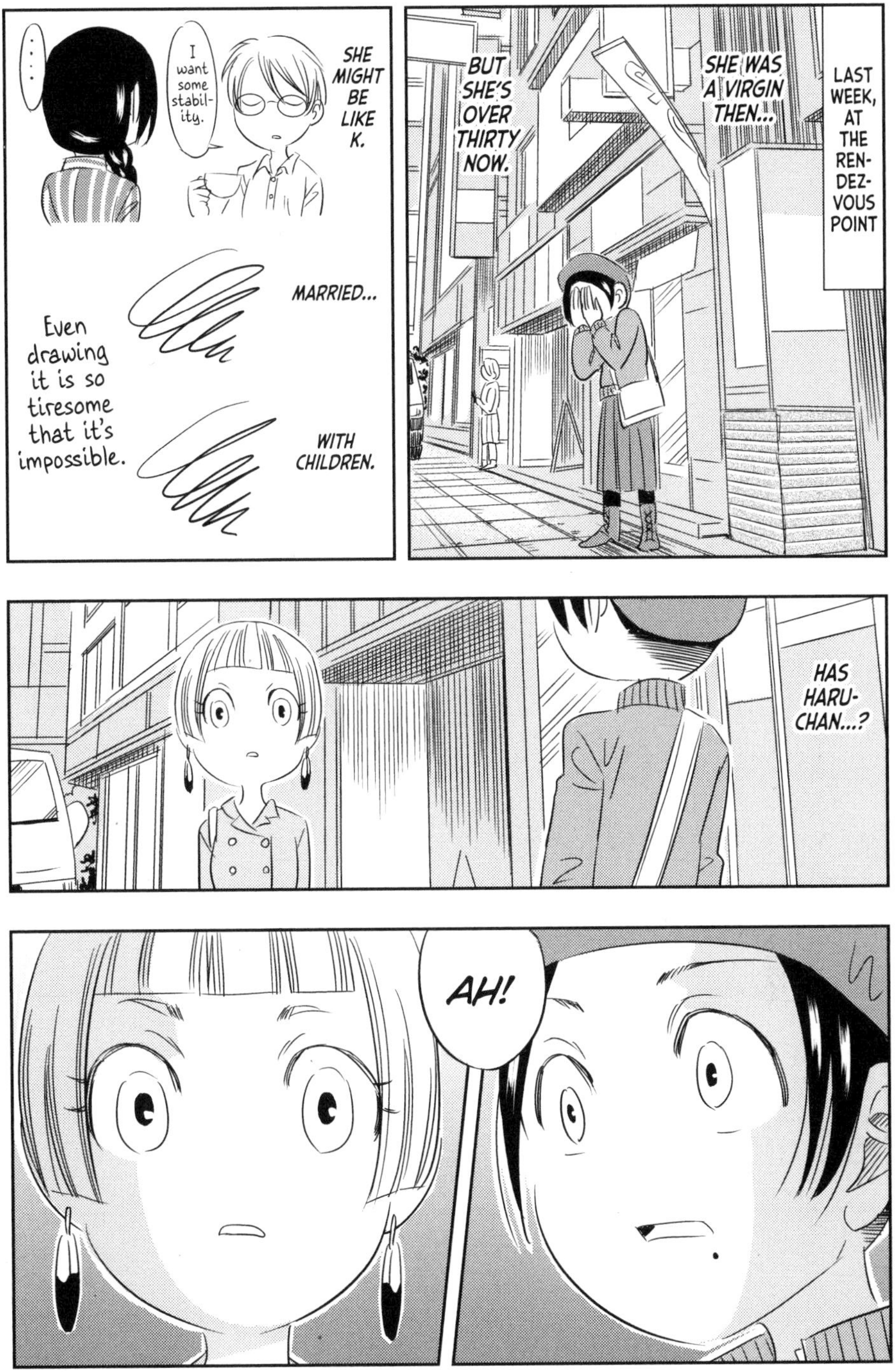
LAST WEEK, AT THE REN-DEZ-VOUS POINT
SHE WAS A VIRGIN THEN...
BUT SHE'S OVER THIRTY NOW.
SHE MIGHT BE LIKE K.
I want some stabil-ity.
...
MARRIED...
WITH CHILDREN.
Even drawing it is so tiresome that it's impossible.
HAS HARU-CHAN...?
AH!

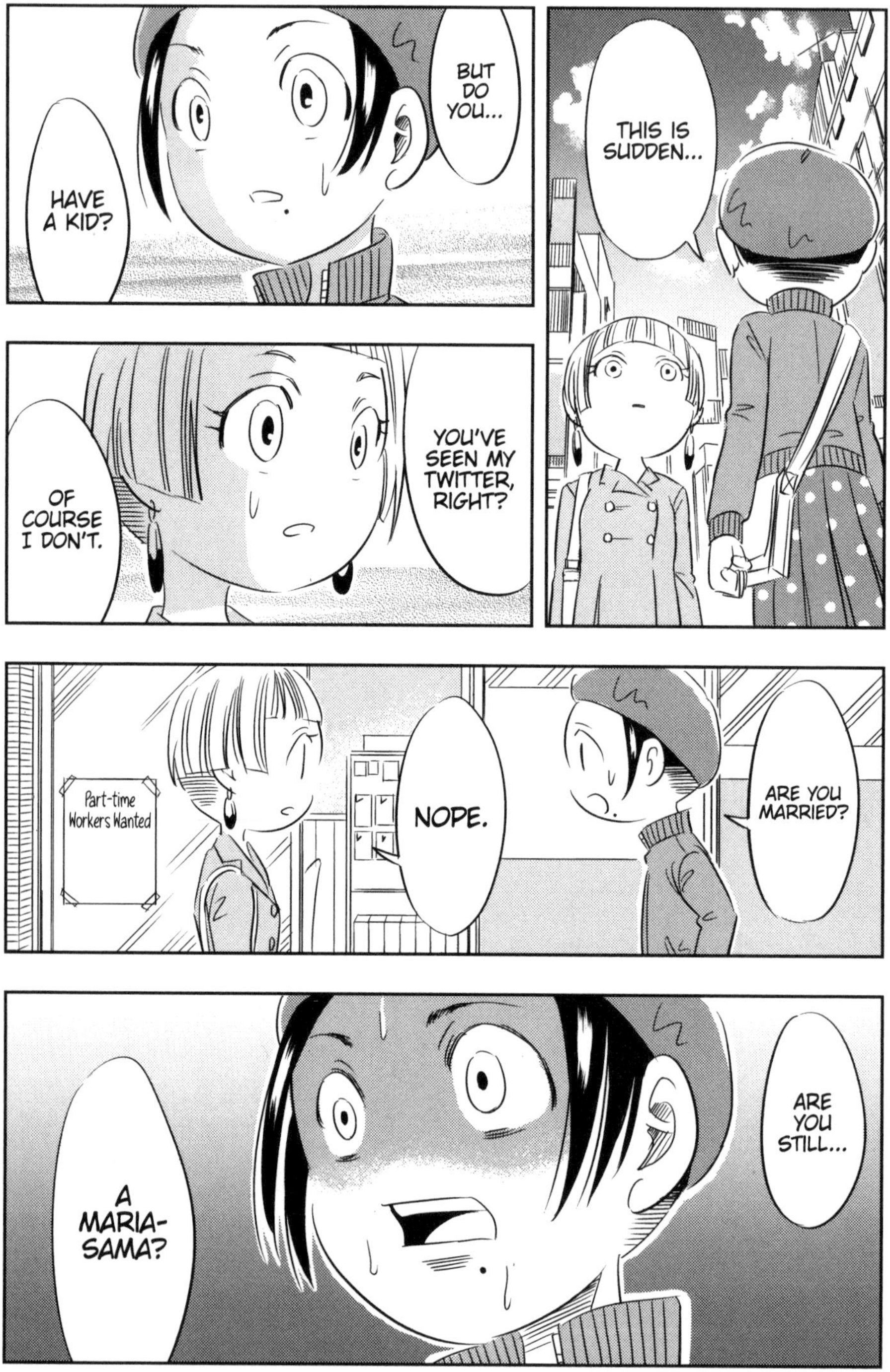
THIS IS SUDDEN...
BUT DO YOU...
HAVE A KID?
YOU'VE SEEN MY TWITTER, RIGHT?
OF COURSE I DON'T.
ARE YOU MARRIED?
NOPE.
Part-time Workers Wanted
ARE YOU STILL...
A MARIA-SAMA?

YUP.

. . . .

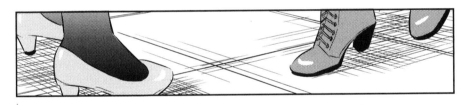

WE MEET AGAIN...

HARU-CHAN!!

One-Page Column About "Q"

ALTHOUGH THE LGBT ACRONYM IS COMMON, DO YOU KNOW WHAT LGBTQ MEANS?

SOME PEOPLE WHO ARE NOT HETEROSEXUAL OR CISGENDER USE Q/QUEER TO DESCRIBE THEMSELVES.

Q A PERSON WHO IDENTIFIES AS QUEER.

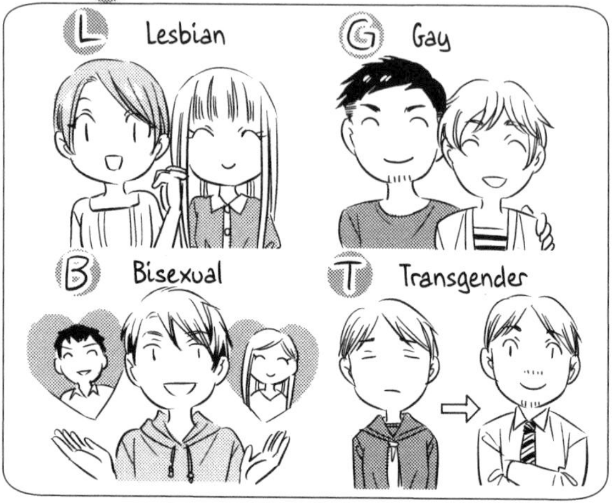
L Lesbian
G Gay
B Bisexual
T Transgender

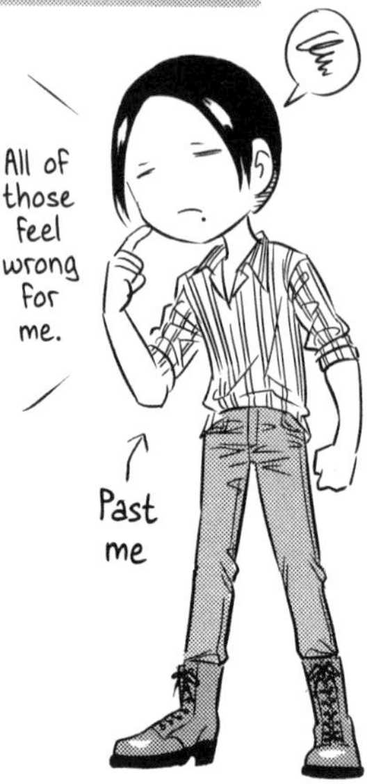
All of those feel wrong for me.
Past me

I'M NOT REPRESENTED HERE.

Q HAS TWO MEANINGS.

① **QUEER:** SOMETIMES USED AS A COLLECTIVE TERM FOR SEXUAL MINORITIES. THE WORD WAS ORIGINALLY DISCRIMINATORY WITH CONNOTATIONS OF PERVERSION, BUT QUEER PEOPLE HAD PRIDE IN THEMSELVES AND RECLAIMED THE WORD. MANY PEOPLE NOW USE IT TO DESCRIBE THEMSELVES.

Miyazaki and the General are both queer. Various other genders and sexualities also fall under the queer umbrella!

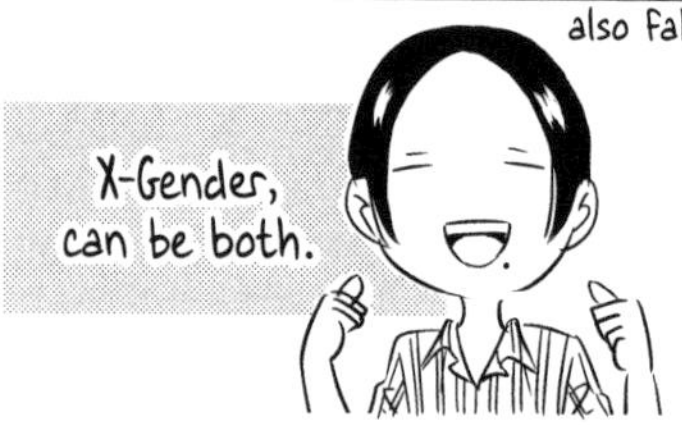
X-Gender, can be both.

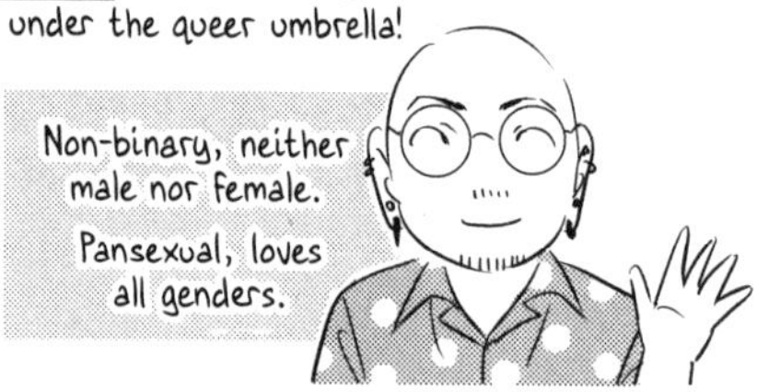
Non-binary, neither male nor female.
Pansexual, loves all genders.

② **QUESTIONING:** DESCRIBES PEOPLE WHO DON'T KNOW THEIR GENDER IDENTITY, ARE LOST, OR DO NOT WISH TO DECIDE.

I'VE ALWAYS FELT DIFFERENT FROM OTHERS, BUT BECAUSE I DIDN'T KNOW THE WORD FOR MY GENDER, IT TOOK ME A WHILE TO REALIZE I'M IN A MINORITY. THE TERM "X-GENDER" GIVES ME AN IDENTITY AND SOME SECURITY THAT THERE ARE OTHER PEOPLE LIKE ME OUT THERE. OF COURSE, I DON'T THINK YOU NEED TO FORCE A DEFINITION ON YOURSELF. HOWEVER, I THINK THAT AS THESE WORDS BECOME MORE WIDELY KNOWN, THE NUMBER OF PEOPLE WHO ARE QUESTIONING, OR WONDERING WHERE THEY FIT IN, WILL DECREASE.

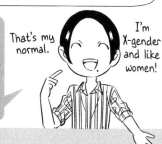

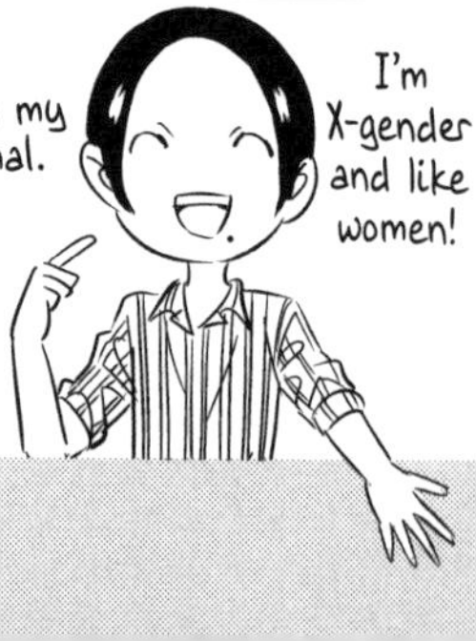
I'm X-gender and like women!
That's my normal.

Reference Site: JobRainbow

Ep. 12: The "Getting Over It" Story

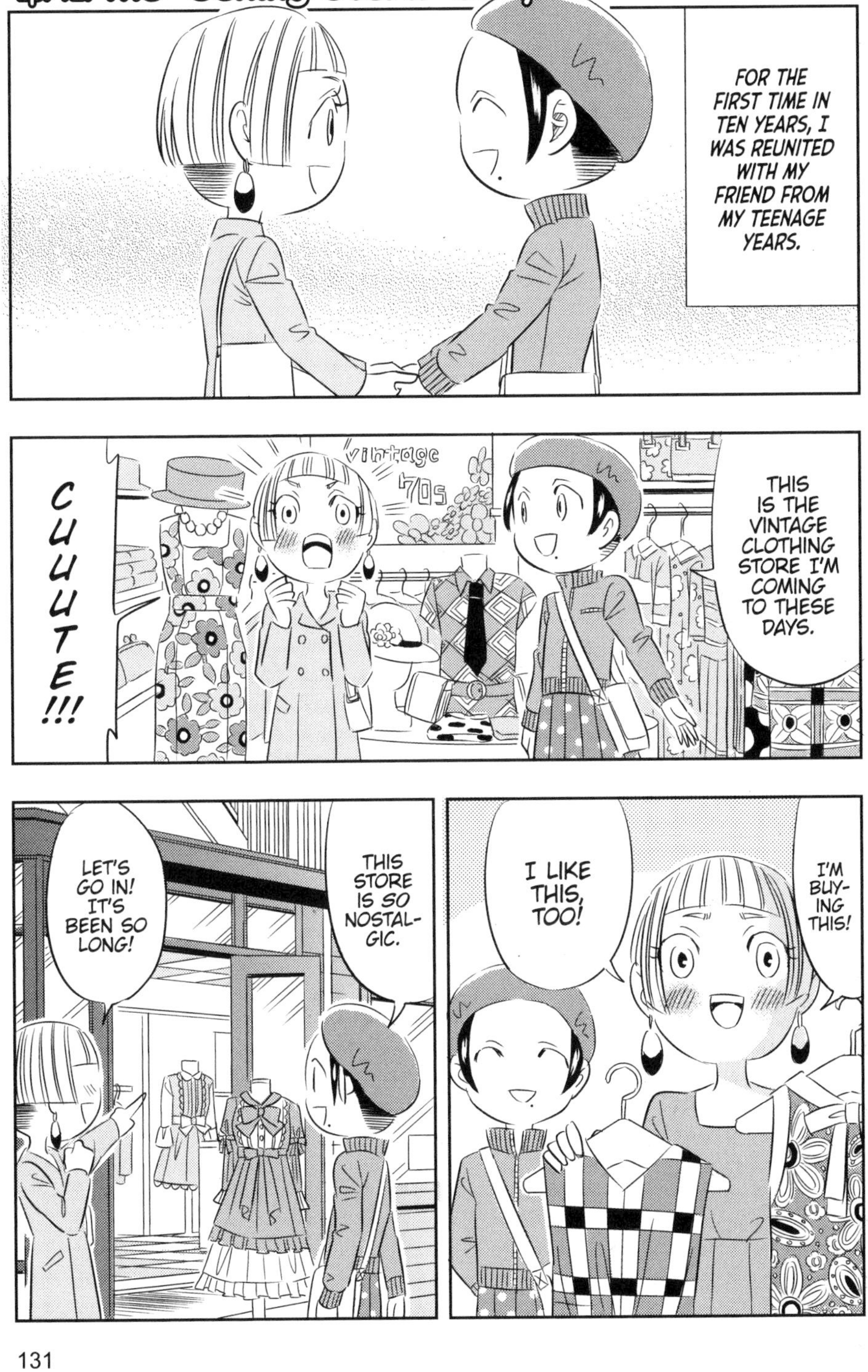
FOR THE FIRST TIME IN TEN YEARS, I WAS REUNITED WITH MY FRIEND FROM MY TEENAGE YEARS.
THIS IS THE VINTAGE CLOTHING STORE I'M COMING TO THESE DAYS.
vintage
'70s
CUUUTE!!!
I'M BUYING THIS!
I LIKE THIS, TOO!
THIS STORE IS SO NOSTALGIC.
LET'S GO IN! IT'S BEEN SO LONG!

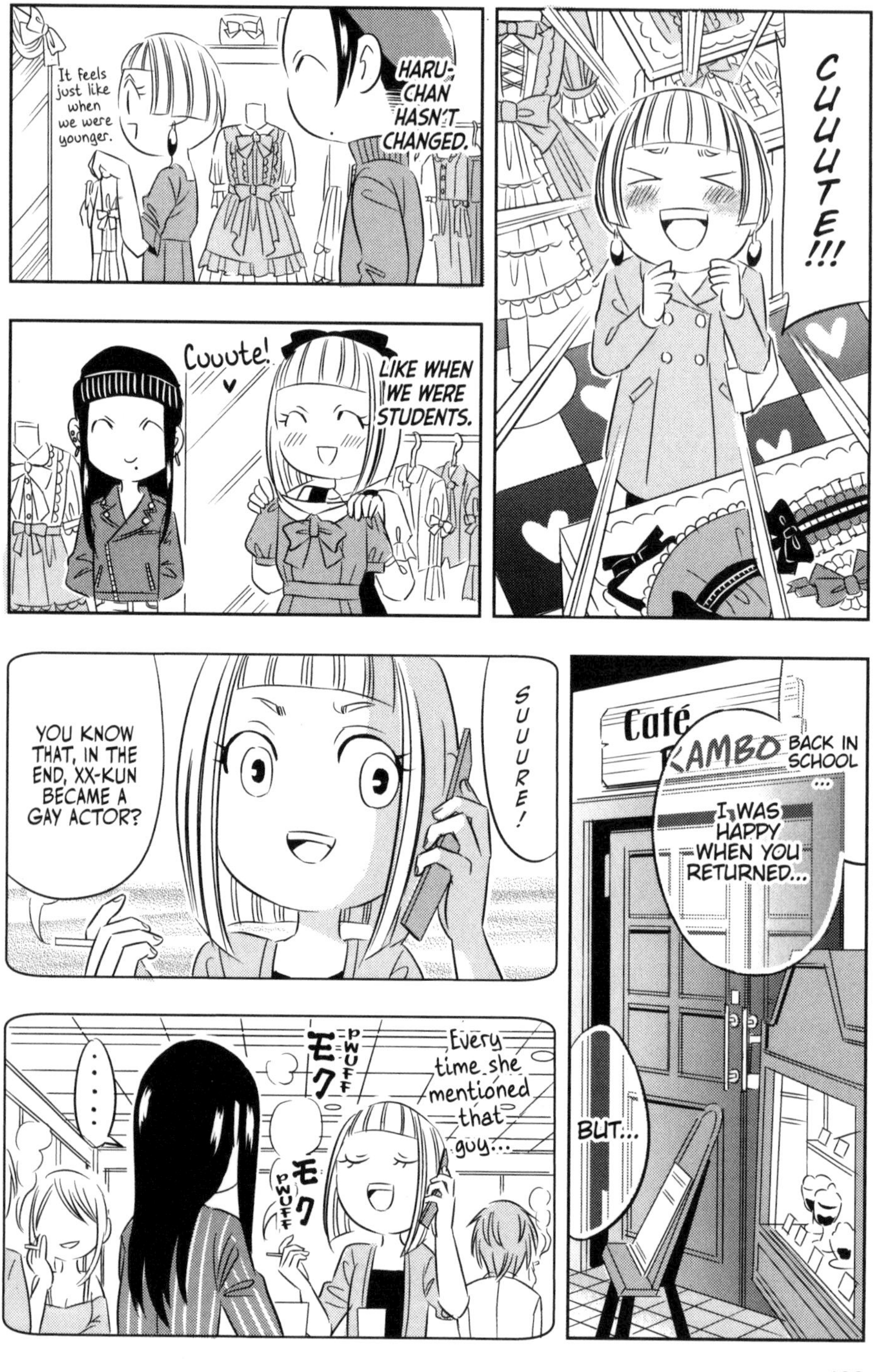
CUUUTE!!!
HARU-CHAN HASN'T CHANGED.
It feels just like when we were younger.
LIKE WHEN WE WERE STUDENTS.
Cuuute!
Café RAMBO
BACK IN SCHOOL...
I WAS HAPPY WHEN YOU RETURNED...
BUT...
SUUURE!
YOU KNOW THAT, IN THE END, XX-KUN BECAME A GAY ACTOR?
Every time she mentioned that guy...
モク PWUFF
モク PWUFF
.....

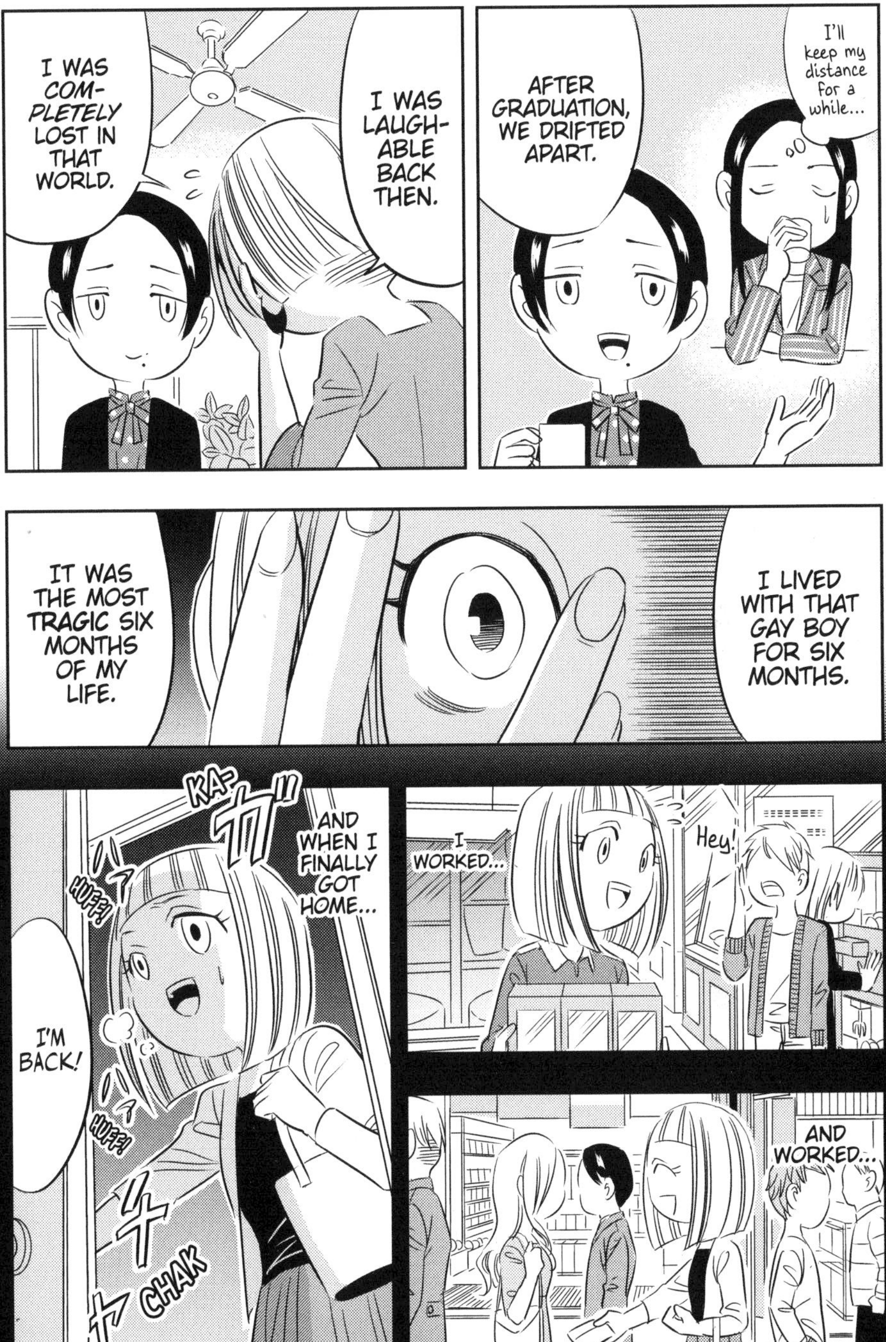
I'll keep my distance for a while...
AFTER GRADUATION, WE DRIFTED APART.
I WAS LAUGHABLE BACK THEN.
I WAS COMPLETELY LOST IN THAT WORLD.
I LIVED WITH THAT GAY BOY FOR SIX MONTHS.
IT WAS THE MOST TRAGIC SIX MONTHS OF MY LIFE.
Hey!
I WORKED...
AND WORKED...
AND WHEN I FINALLY GOT HOME...
KA-
HUFF!
I'M BACK!
HUFF!
CHAK

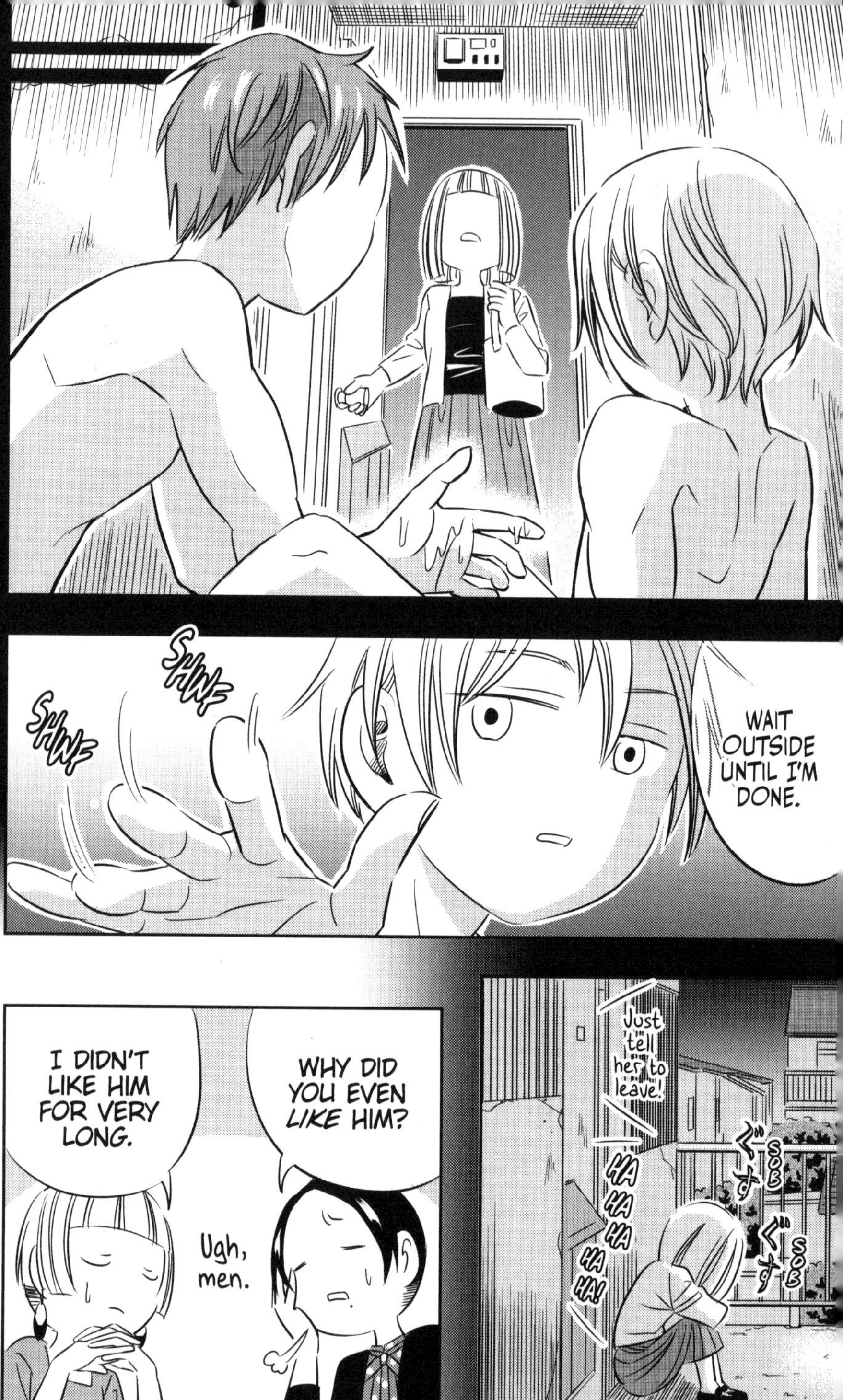
WAIT OUTSIDE UNTIL I'M DONE.
SHWF
SHWF
Just tell her to leave!
HA HA HA HA HA!
SOB ぐす
SOB ぐす
WHY DID YOU EVEN *LIKE* HIM?
I DIDN'T LIKE HIM FOR VERY LONG.
Ugh, men.

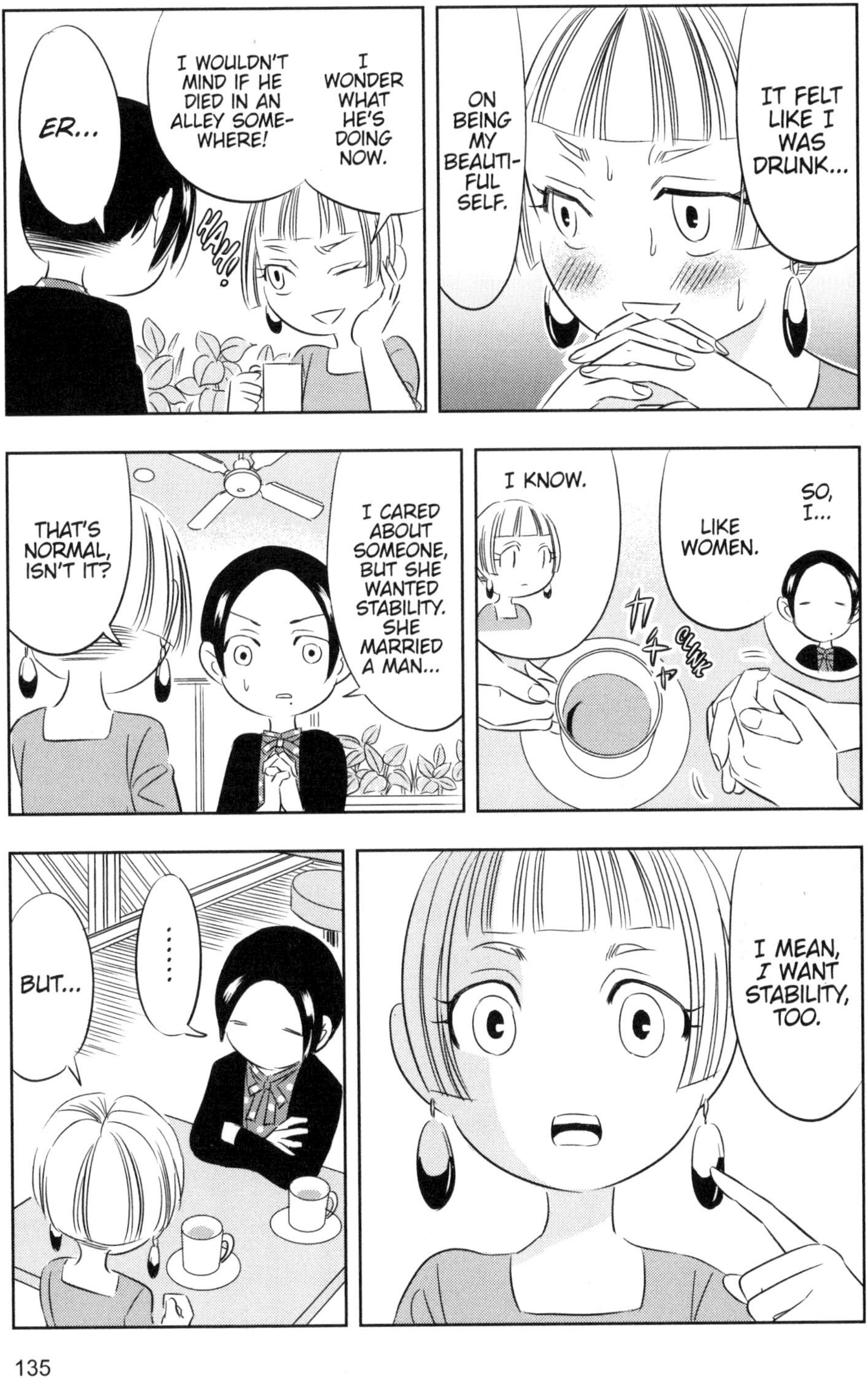
IT FELT LIKE I WAS DRUNK...
ON BEING MY BEAUTIFUL SELF.
I WONDER WHAT HE'S DOING NOW.
I WOULDN'T MIND IF HE DIED IN AN ALLEY SOMEWHERE!
HAH!
ER...
SO, I...
LIKE WOMEN.
CLINK
I KNOW.
I CARED ABOUT SOMEONE, BUT SHE WANTED STABILITY. SHE MARRIED A MAN...
THAT'S NORMAL, ISN'T IT?
I MEAN, *I* WANT STABILITY, TOO.
......
BUT...

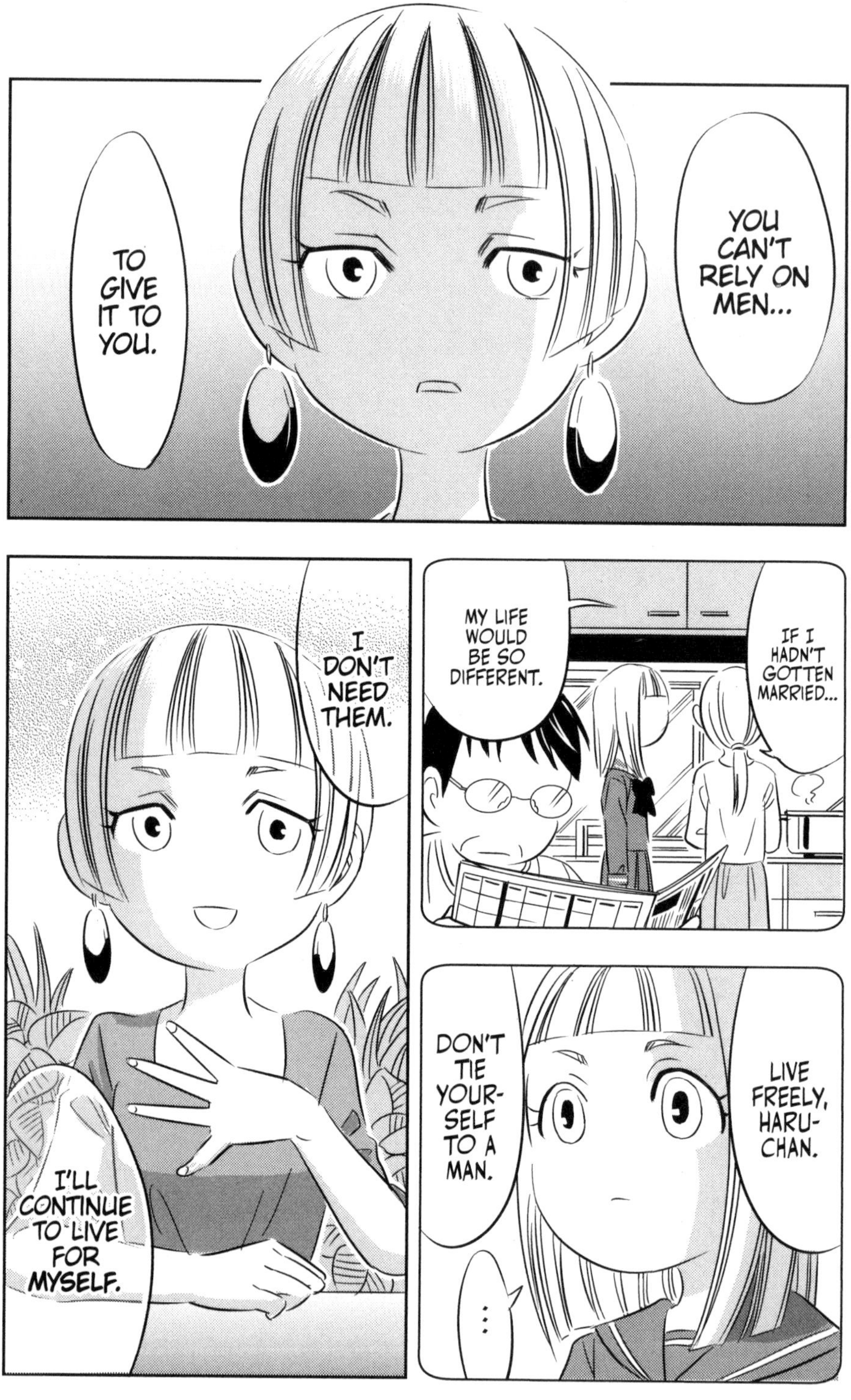
YOU CAN'T RELY ON MEN...
TO GIVE IT TO YOU.
IF I HADN'T GOTTEN MARRIED...
MY LIFE WOULD BE SO DIFFERENT.
LIVE FREELY, HARU-CHAN.
DON'T TIE YOUR-SELF TO A MAN.
...
I DON'T NEED THEM.
I'LL CONTINUE TO LIVE FOR MYSELF.

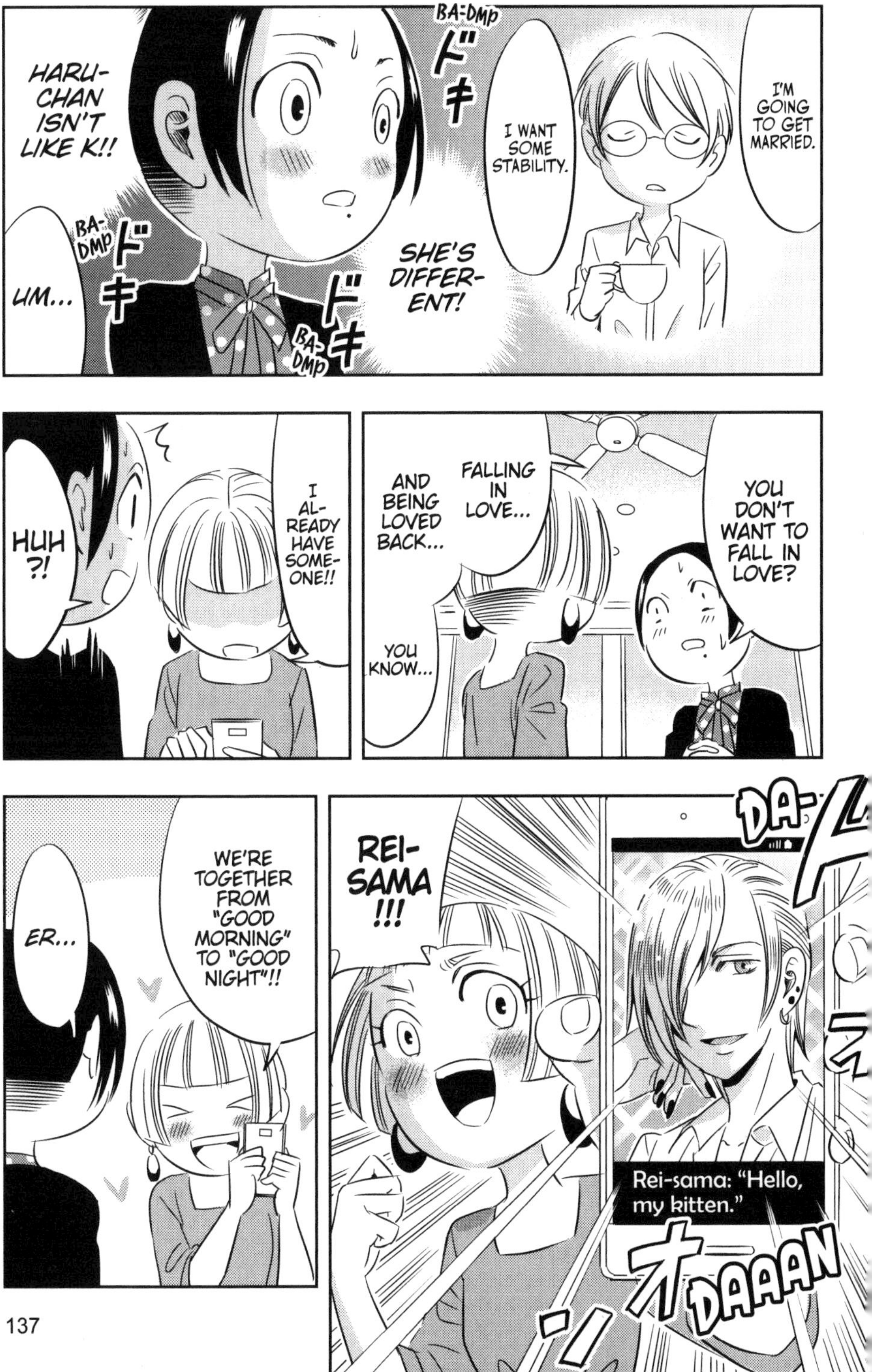

I'M GOING TO GET MARRIED.
I WANT SOME STABILITY.
BA-DMP ドキ
SHE'S DIFFERENT!
HARU-CHAN ISN'T LIKE K!!
BA-DMP ドキ
BA-DMP ドキ
UM...
YOU DON'T WANT TO FALL IN LOVE?
FALLING IN LOVE...
AND BEING LOVED BACK...
YOU KNOW...
I ALREADY HAVE SOMEONE!!
HUH?!
DA-
REI-SAMA!!!
Rei-sama: "Hello, my kitten."
DAAAN
WE'RE TOGETHER FROM "GOOD MORNING" TO "GOOD NIGHT"!!
ER...

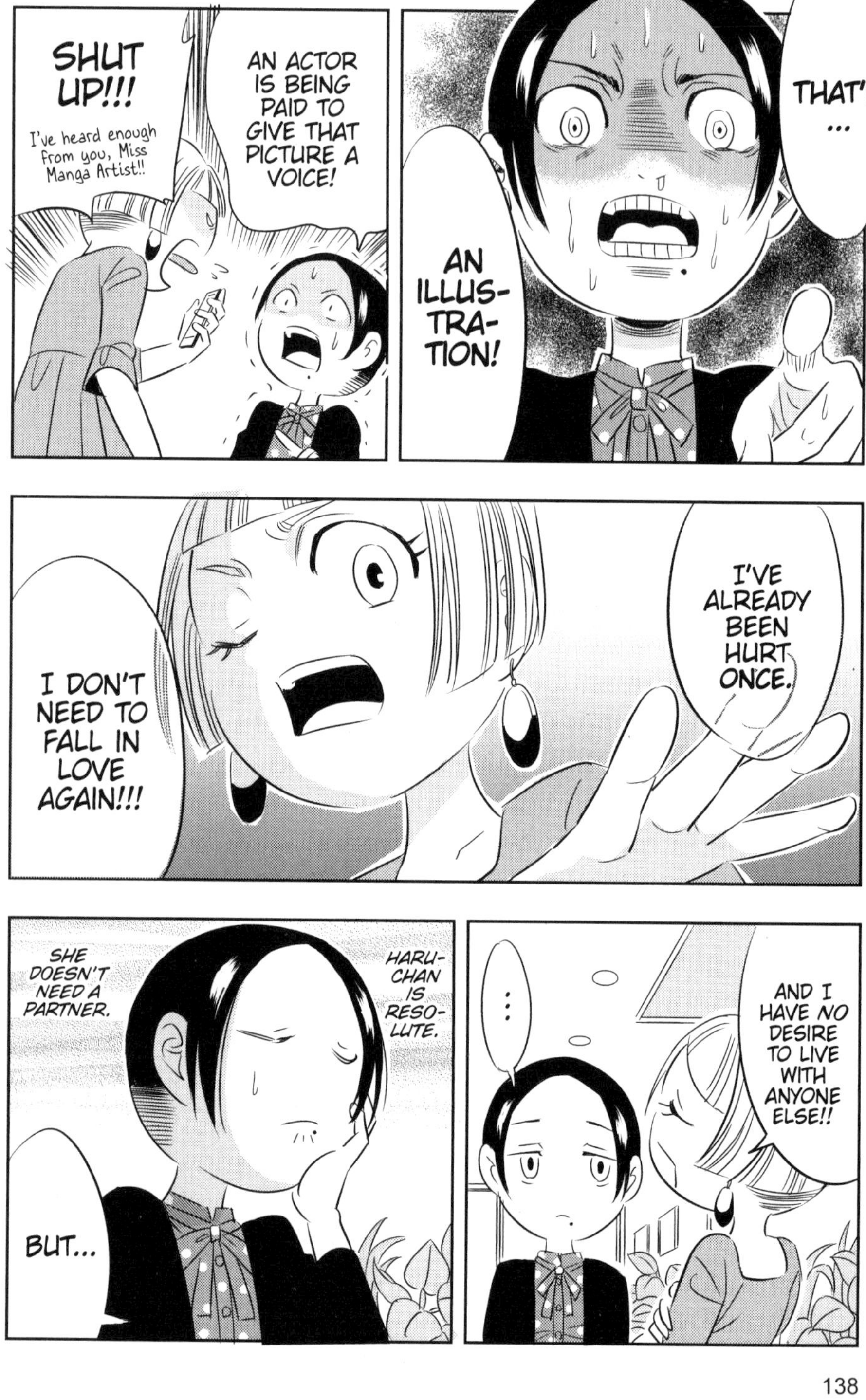
THAT'S ...
AN ILLUS- TRA- TION!
AN ACTOR IS BEING PAID TO GIVE THAT PICTURE A VOICE!
SHUT UP!!!
I've heard enough from you, Miss Manga Artist!!
I'VE ALREADY BEEN HURT ONCE.
I DON'T NEED TO FALL IN LOVE AGAIN!!!
AND I HAVE *NO* DESIRE TO LIVE WITH ANYONE ELSE!!
...
HARU- CHAN IS RESO- LUTE.
SHE DOESN'T NEED A PARTNER.
BUT...

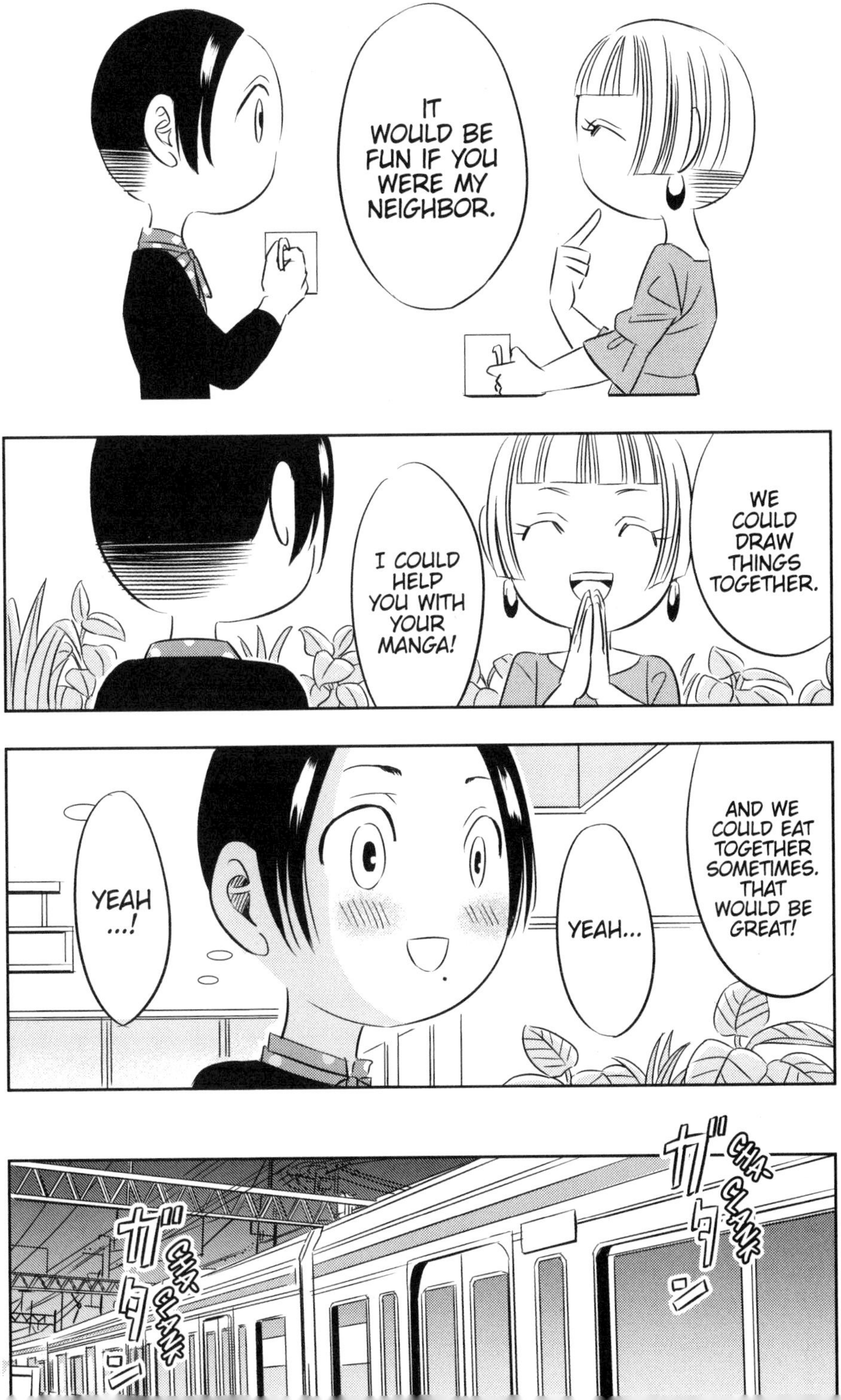
IT WOULD BE FUN IF YOU WERE MY NEIGHBOR.
WE COULD DRAW THINGS TOGETHER.
I COULD HELP YOU WITH YOUR MANGA!
AND WE COULD EAT TOGETHER SOMETIMES. THAT WOULD BE GREAT!
YEAH...
YEAH ...!
ガタン
CHA CLANK
ガタン
CHA CLANK

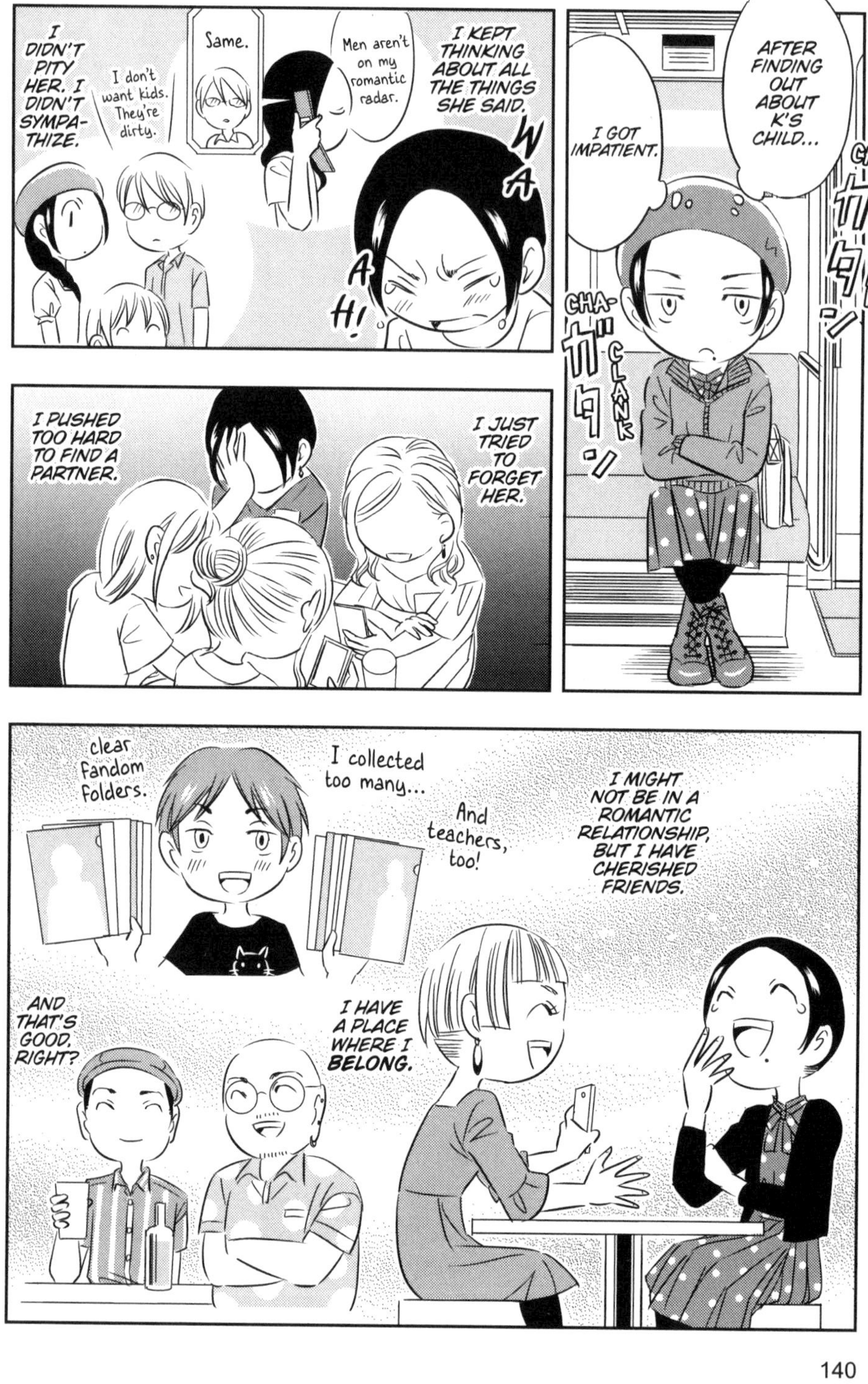
AFTER FINDING OUT ABOUT K'S CHILD...
I GOT IMPATIENT.
ガタッ
CHA-CLANK
ガタッ
CHA-CLANK
I KEPT THINKING ABOUT ALL THE THINGS SHE SAID.
WAAH!
Men aren't on my romantic radar.
Same.
I don't want kids. They're dirty.
I DIDN'T PITY HER. I DIDN'T SYMPATHIZE.
I JUST TRIED TO FORGET HER.
I PUSHED TOO HARD TO FIND A PARTNER.
I MIGHT NOT BE IN A ROMANTIC RELATIONSHIP, BUT I HAVE CHERISHED FRIENDS.
I collected too many...
And teachers, too!
clear fandom folders.
I HAVE A PLACE WHERE I BELONG.
AND THAT'S GOOD, RIGHT?

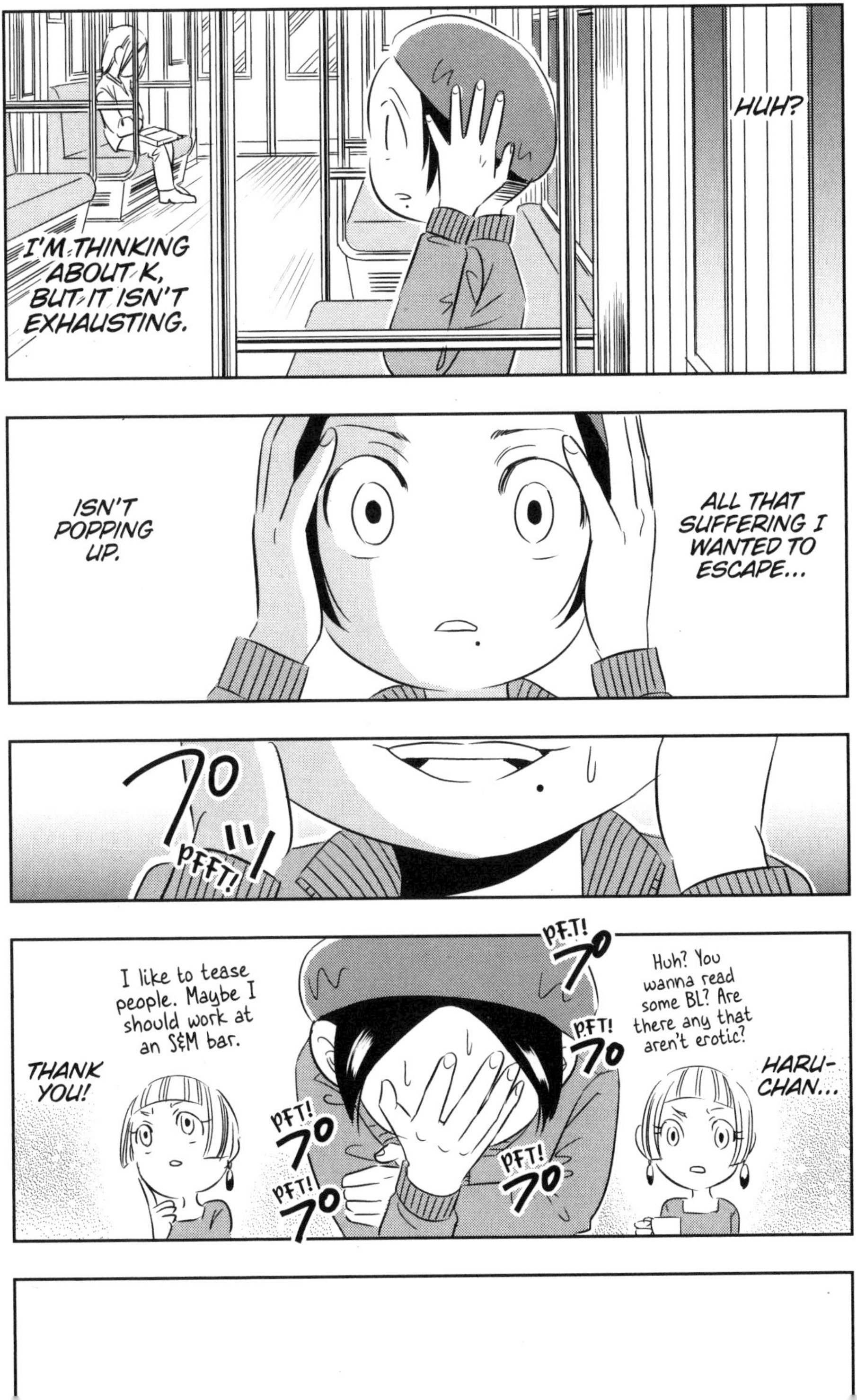
HUH?
I'M THINKING ABOUT K, BUT IT ISN'T EXHAUSTING.
ALL THAT SUFFERING I WANTED TO ESCAPE...
ISN'T POPPING UP.
PFFT!
Huh? You wanna read some BL? Are there any that aren't erotic?
HARU-CHAN...
PFT!
PFT!
PFT!
I like to tease people. Maybe I should work at an S&M bar.
THANK YOU!
PFT!
PFT!

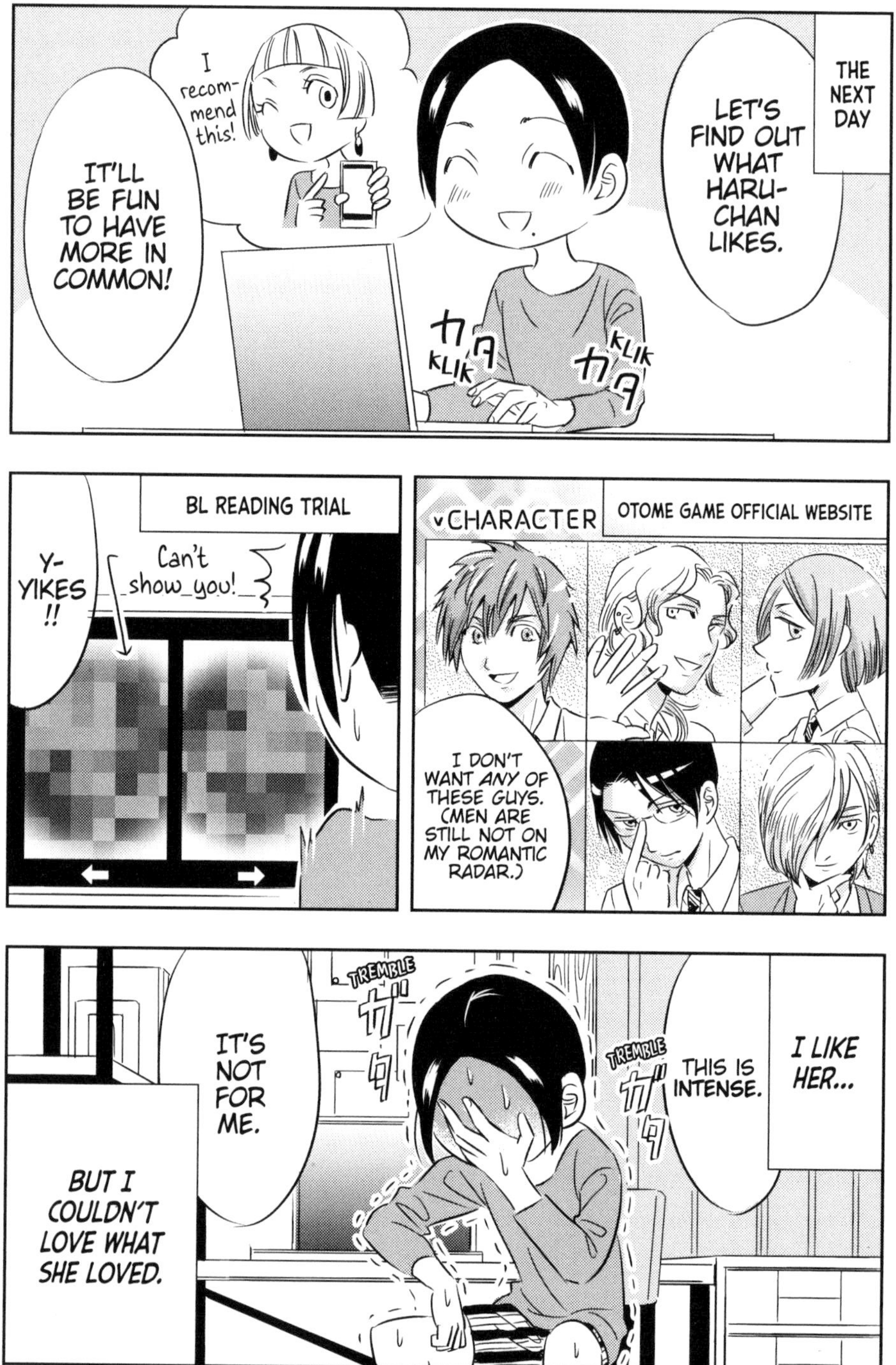
THE NEXT DAY
LET'S FIND OUT WHAT HARU-CHAN LIKES.
カタ KLIK
カタ KLIK
I recommend this!
IT'LL BE FUN TO HAVE MORE IN COMMON!
OTOME GAME OFFICIAL WEBSITE
vCHARACTER
I DON'T WANT ANY OF THESE GUYS. (MEN ARE STILL NOT ON MY ROMANTIC RADAR.)
BL READING TRIAL
Can't show you!
Y-YIKES!!
I LIKE HER...
THIS IS INTENSE.
TREMBLE ガタ
TREMBLE ガタ
IT'S NOT FOR ME.
BUT I COULDN'T LOVE WHAT SHE LOVED.

※*I don't like the intense sexual depictions, but BL is a fun genre! (Asuka Miyazaki)*

X-GENDER

Ep. 13: The "X-Gender" Story

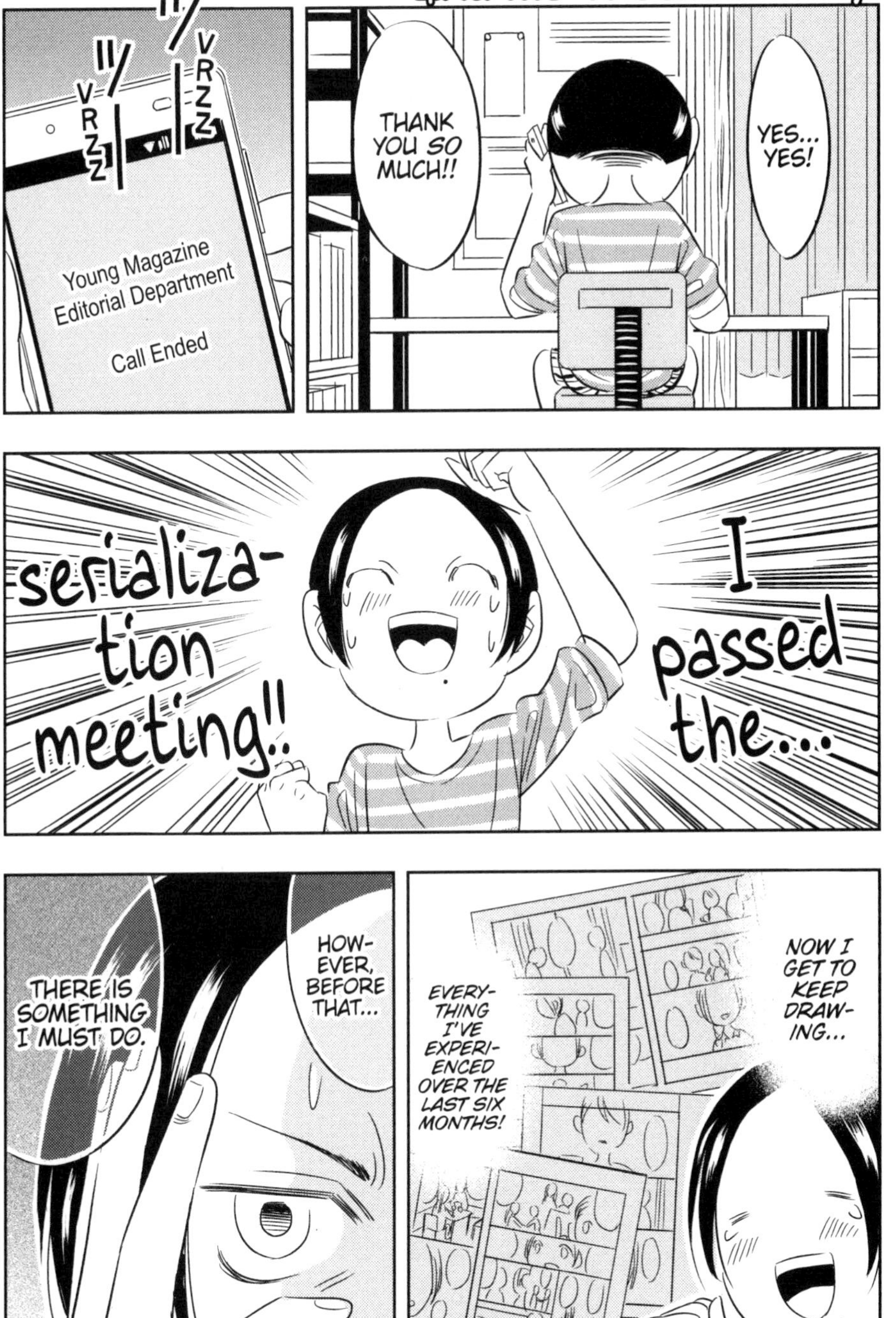
YES... YES!
THANK YOU SO MUCH!!
VRZZ
VRZZ
Young Magazine Editorial Department
Call Ended
I passed the...
serialization meeting!!
NOW I GET TO KEEP DRAWING...
EVERYTHING I'VE EXPERIENCED OVER THE LAST SIX MONTHS!
HOWEVER, BEFORE THAT...
THERE IS SOMETHING I MUST DO.

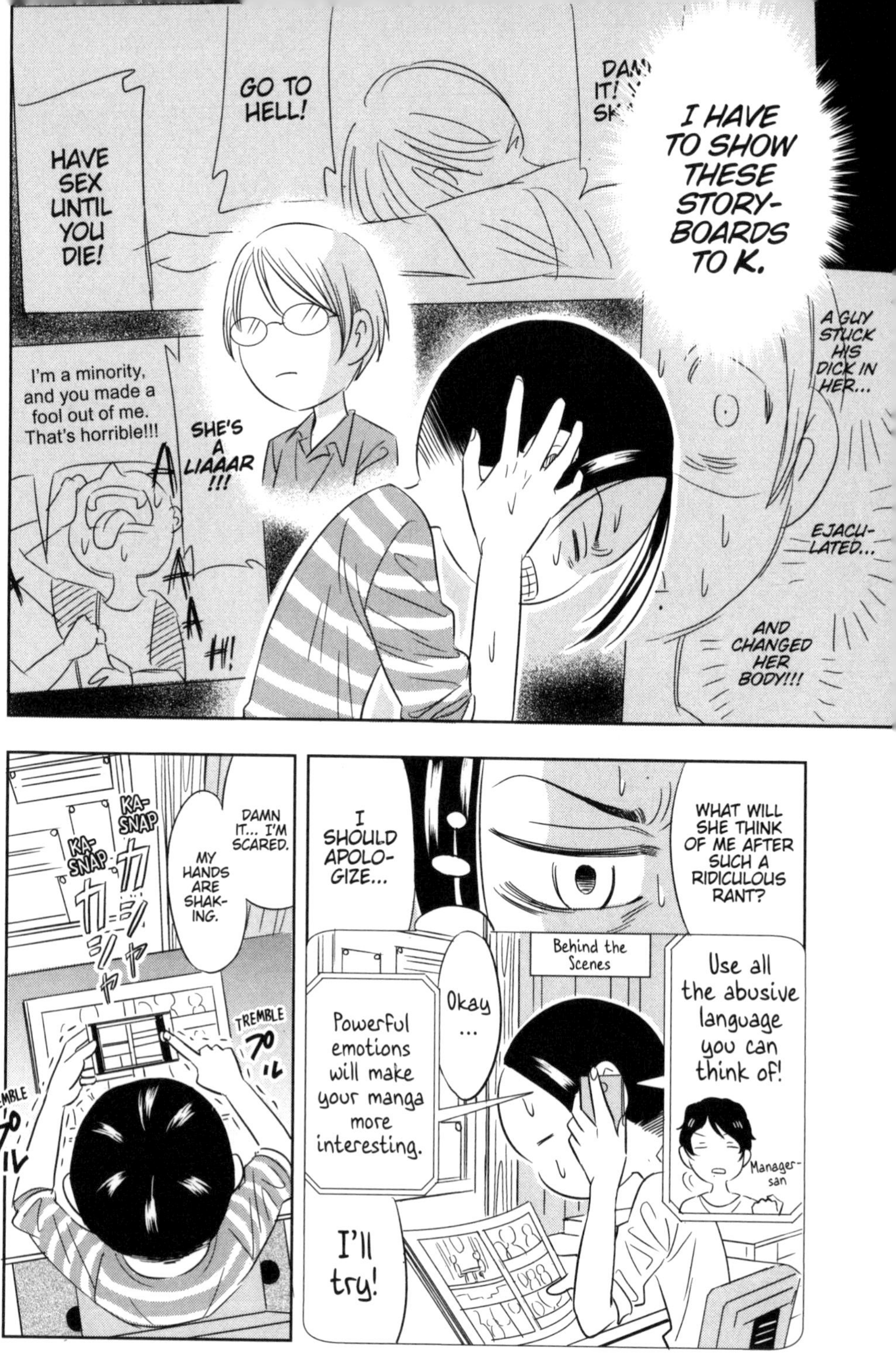
I HAVE TO SHOW THESE STORY-BOARDS TO K.
A GUY STUCK HIS DICK IN HER...
EJACULATED...
AND CHANGED HER BODY!!!
GO TO HELL!
HAVE SEX UNTIL YOU DIE!
SHE'S A LIAAAR!!!
I'm a minority, and you made a fool out of me. That's horrible!!!
AAAAH!
WHAT WILL SHE THINK OF ME AFTER SUCH A RIDICULOUS RANT?
I SHOULD APOLOGIZE...
Behind the Scenes
Use all the abusive language you can think of!
Okay...
Powerful emotions will make your manga more interesting.
I'll try!
Manager-san
DAMN IT... I'M SCARED.
MY HANDS ARE SHAKING.
KA-SNAP
KA-SNAP
TREMBLE
TREMBLE

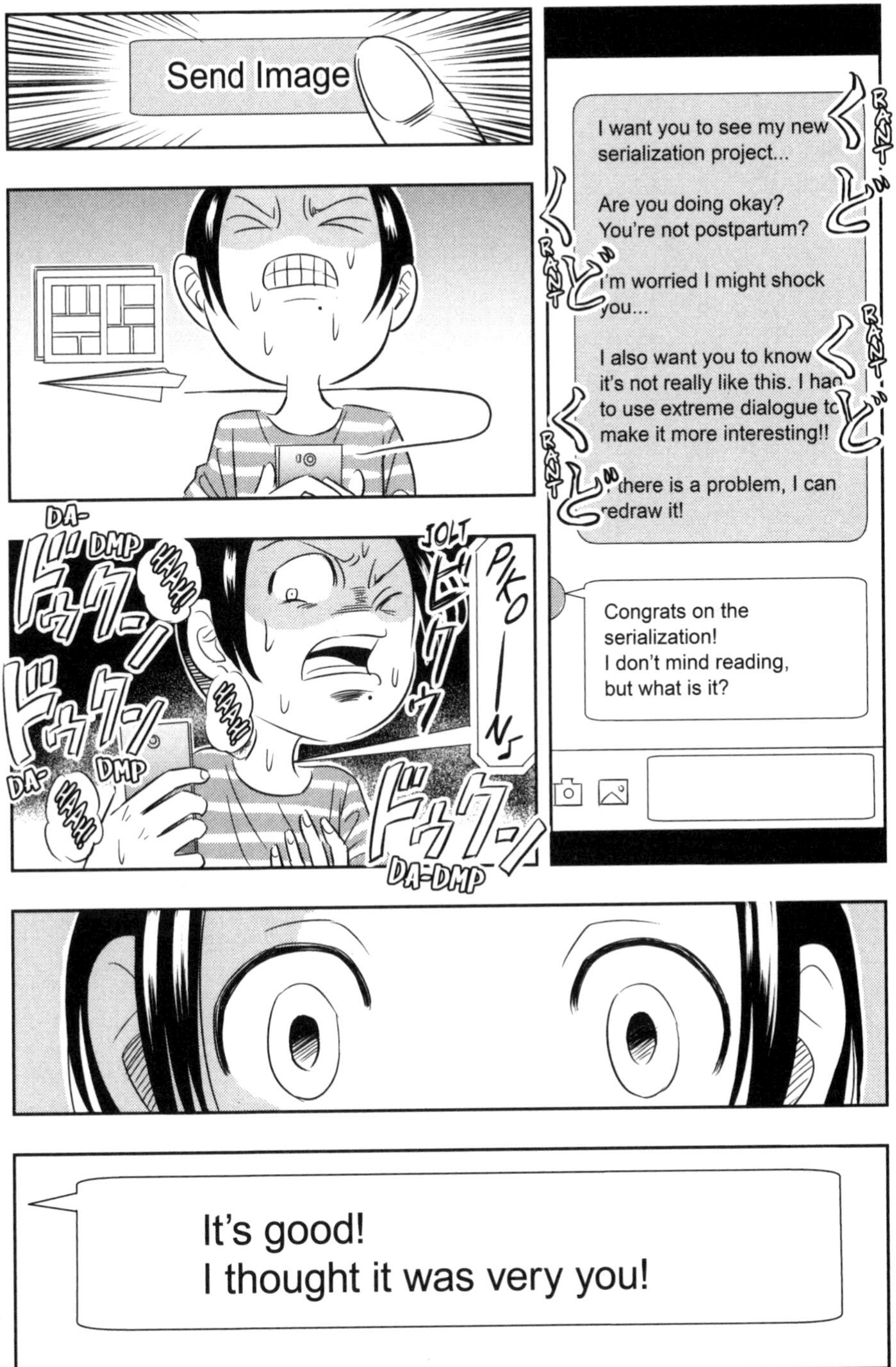

I want you to see my new serialization project...
Are you doing okay? You're not postpartum?
I'm worried I might shock you...
I also want you to know it's not really like this. I had to use extreme dialogue to make it more interesting!!
If there is a problem, I can redraw it!
RANT
RANT
RANT
RANT
Congrats on the serialization! I don't mind reading, but what is it?
Send Image
JOLT
PIKO-N
DA-DMP
HAAH
HAAH
HAAH
DA-DMP
DA-DMP
It's good! I thought it was very you!

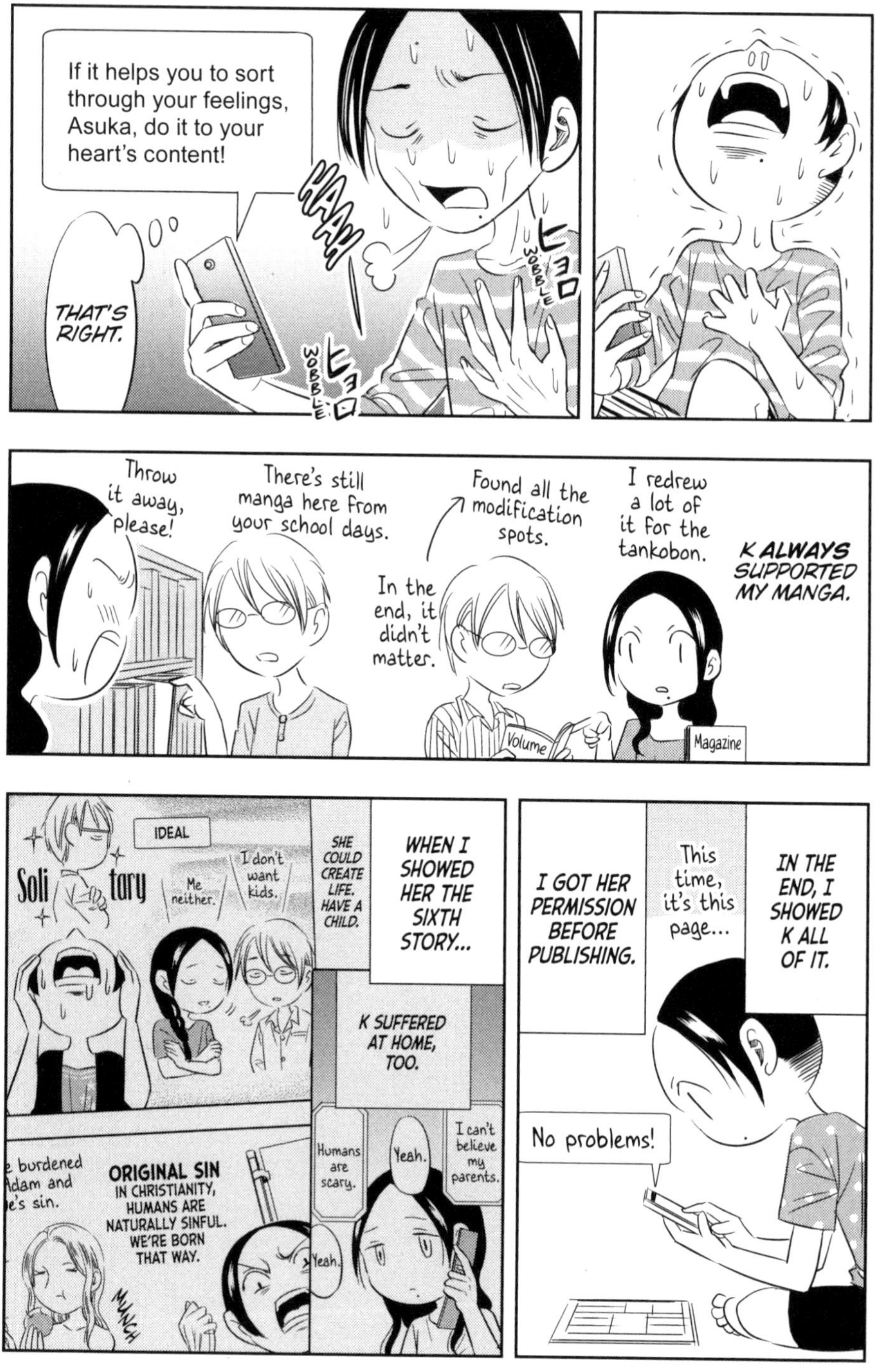
HAA!
WOBBLE
If it helps you to sort through your feelings, Asuka, do it to your heart's content!
WOBBLE
THAT'S RIGHT.
K ALWAYS SUPPORTED MY MANGA.
I redrew a lot of it for the tankobon.
Magazine
Found all the modification spots.
In the end, it didn't matter.
Volume
There's still manga here from your school days.
Throw it away, please!
IN THE END, I SHOWED K ALL OF IT.
This time, it's this page...
I GOT HER PERMISSION BEFORE PUBLISHING.
No problems!
WHEN I SHOWED HER THE SIXTH STORY...
SHE COULD CREATE LIFE. HAVE A CHILD.
K SUFFERED AT HOME, TOO.
I can't believe my parents.
Yeah.
Humans are scary.
Yeah.
IDEAL
Soli tary
I don't want kids.
Me neither.
ORIGINAL SIN
IN CHRISTIANITY, HUMANS ARE NATURALLY SINFUL. WE'RE BORN THAT WAY.
MUNCH

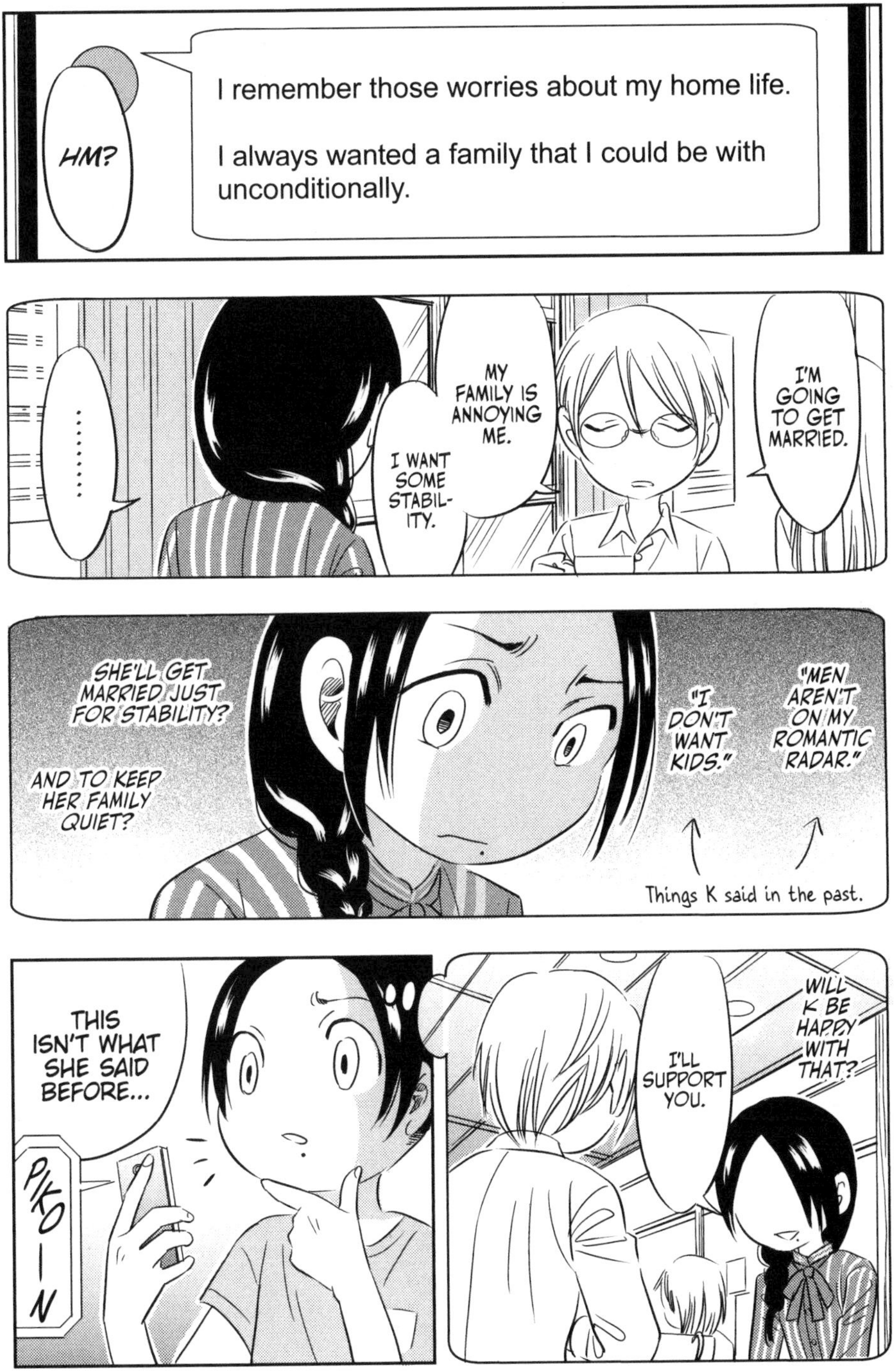
I remember those worries about my home life.
I always wanted a family that I could be with unconditionally.
HM?
I'M GOING TO GET MARRIED.
MY FAMILY IS ANNOYING ME.
I WANT SOME STABIL-ITY.
....
"MEN AREN'T ON MY ROMANTIC RADAR."
"I DON'T WANT KIDS."
Things K said in the past.
SHE'LL GET MARRIED JUST FOR STABILITY?
AND TO KEEP HER FAMILY QUIET?
WILL K BE HAPPY WITH THAT?
I'LL SUPPORT YOU.
THIS ISN'T WHAT SHE SAID BEFORE...
PIKO-I-N

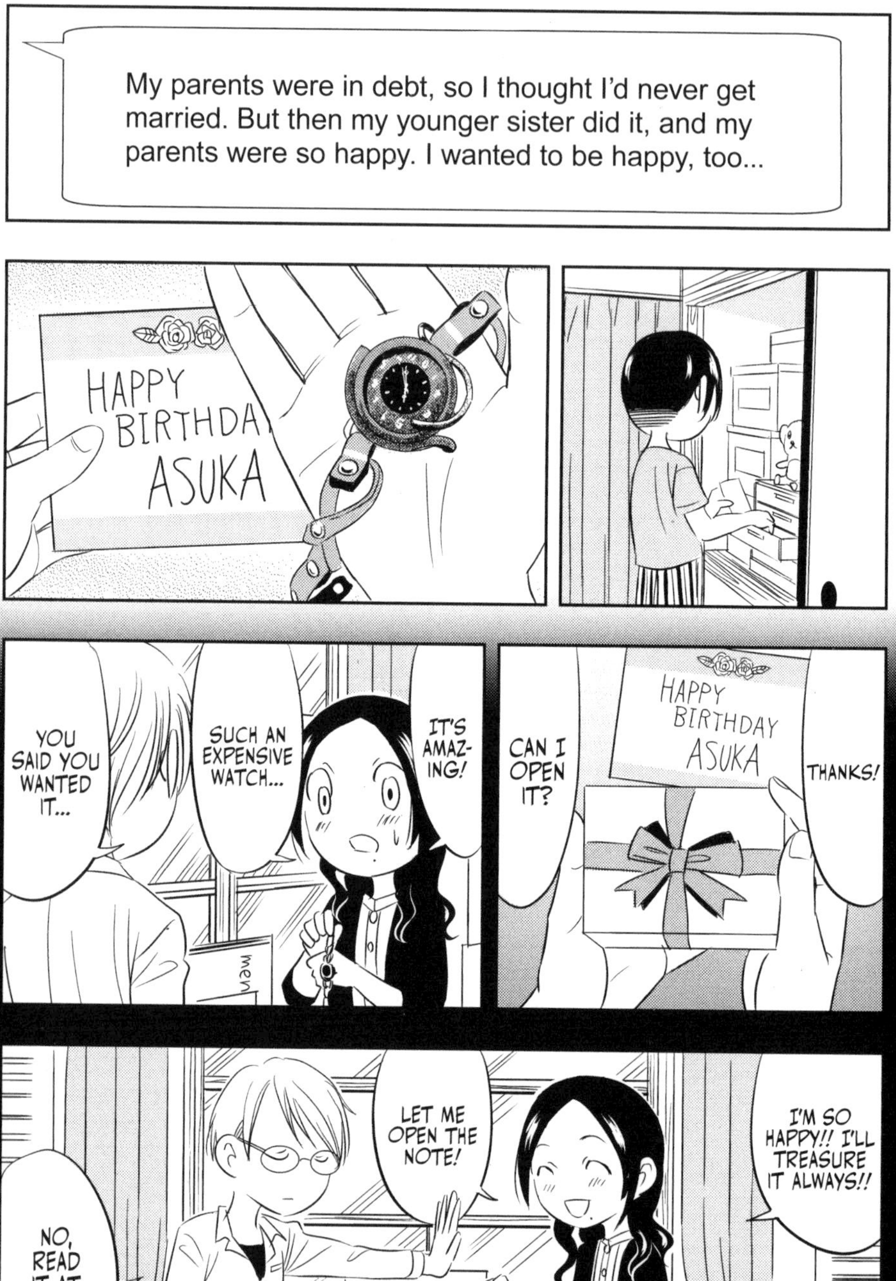
My parents were in debt, so I thought I'd never get married. But then my younger sister did it, and my parents were so happy. I wanted to be happy, too...
HAPPY BIRTHDAY ASUKA
THANKS!
HAPPY BIRTHDAY ASUKA
CAN I OPEN IT?
IT'S AMAZ-ING!
SUCH AN EXPENSIVE WATCH...
YOU SAID YOU WANTED IT...
I'M SO HAPPY!! I'LL TREASURE IT ALWAYS!!
menu
LET ME OPEN THE NOTE!
NO, READ IT AT HOME.

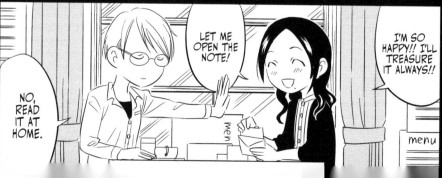

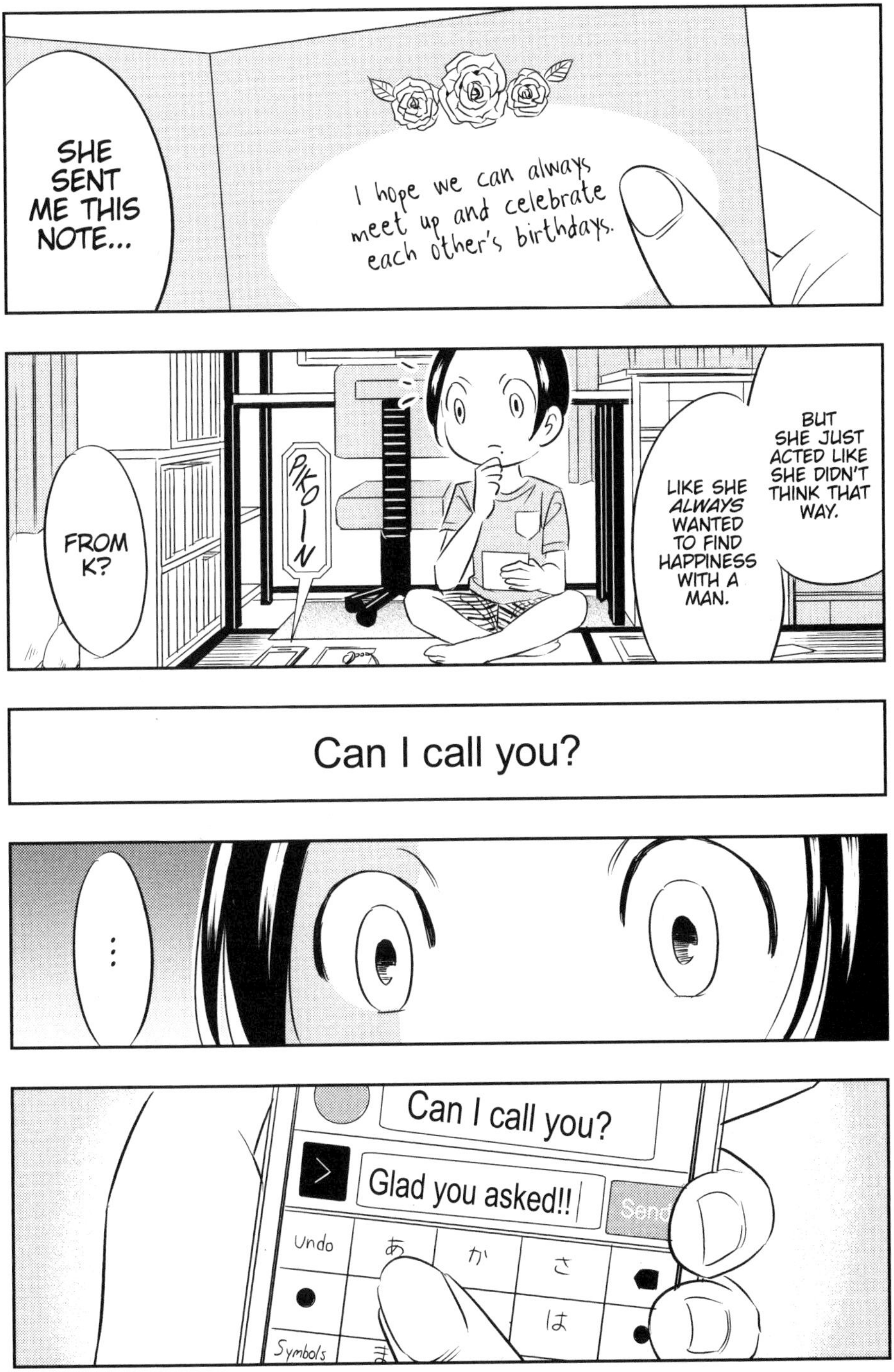

I hope we can always meet up and celebrate each other's birthdays.
SHE SENT ME THIS NOTE...
BUT SHE JUST ACTED LIKE SHE DIDN'T THINK THAT WAY.
LIKE SHE *ALWAYS* WANTED TO FIND HAPPINESS WITH A MAN.
PIKO-IN
FROM K?
Can I call you?
...
Can I call you?
Glad you asked!!
Send
Undo
あ
か
さ
は
Symbols
ま

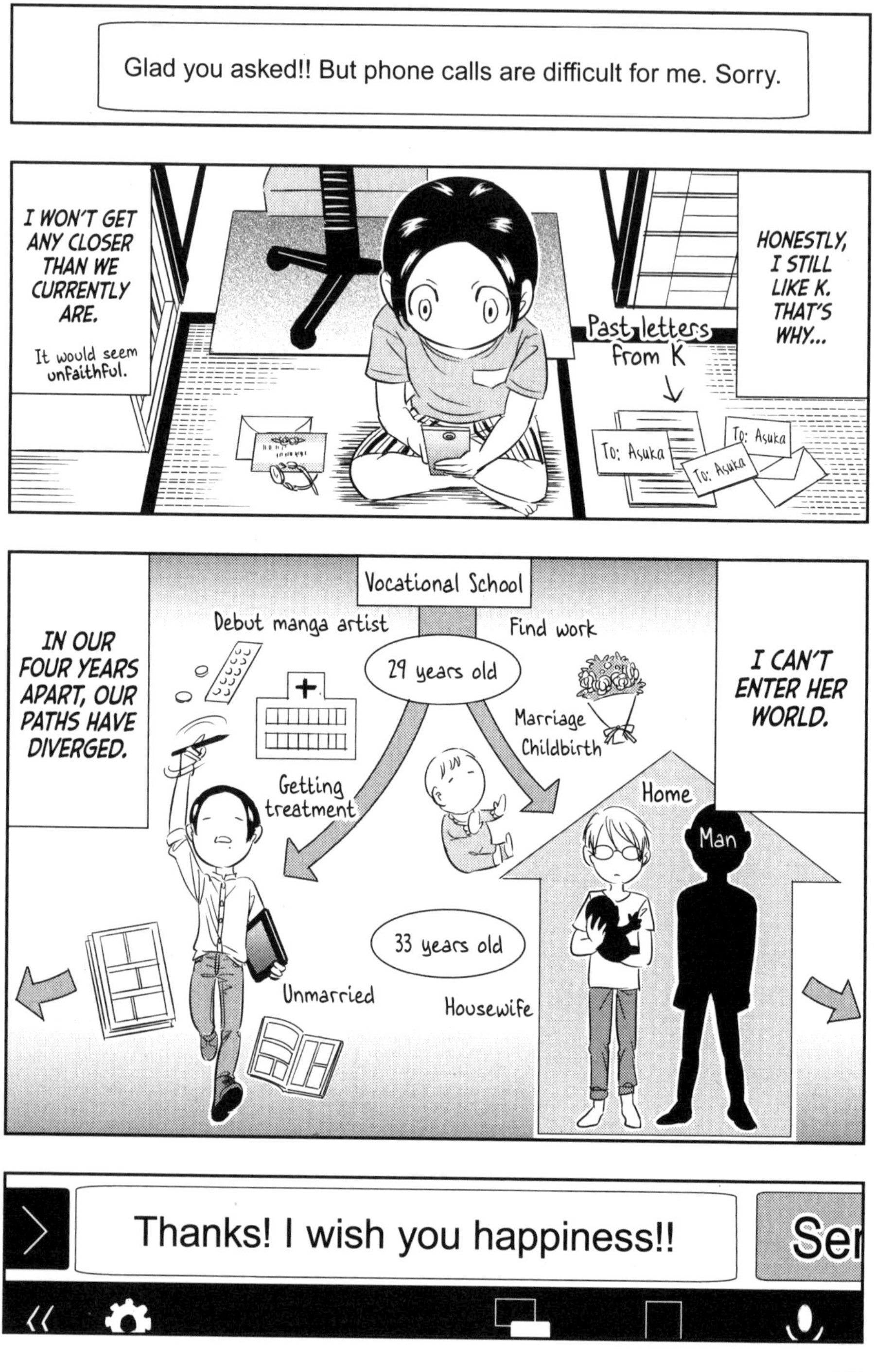

Glad you asked!! But phone calls are difficult for me. Sorry.
HONESTLY, I STILL LIKE K. THAT'S WHY...
Past letters from K
To: Asuka
To: Asuka
To: Asuka
I WON'T GET ANY CLOSER THAN WE CURRENTLY ARE.
It would seem unfaithful.
I CAN'T ENTER HER WORLD.
Vocational School
Find work
Debut manga artist
29 years old
Marriage
Childbirth
Getting treatment
Home
Man
33 years old
Housewife
Unmarried
IN OUR FOUR YEARS APART, OUR PATHS HAVE DIVERGED.
Thanks! I wish you happiness!!
Ser

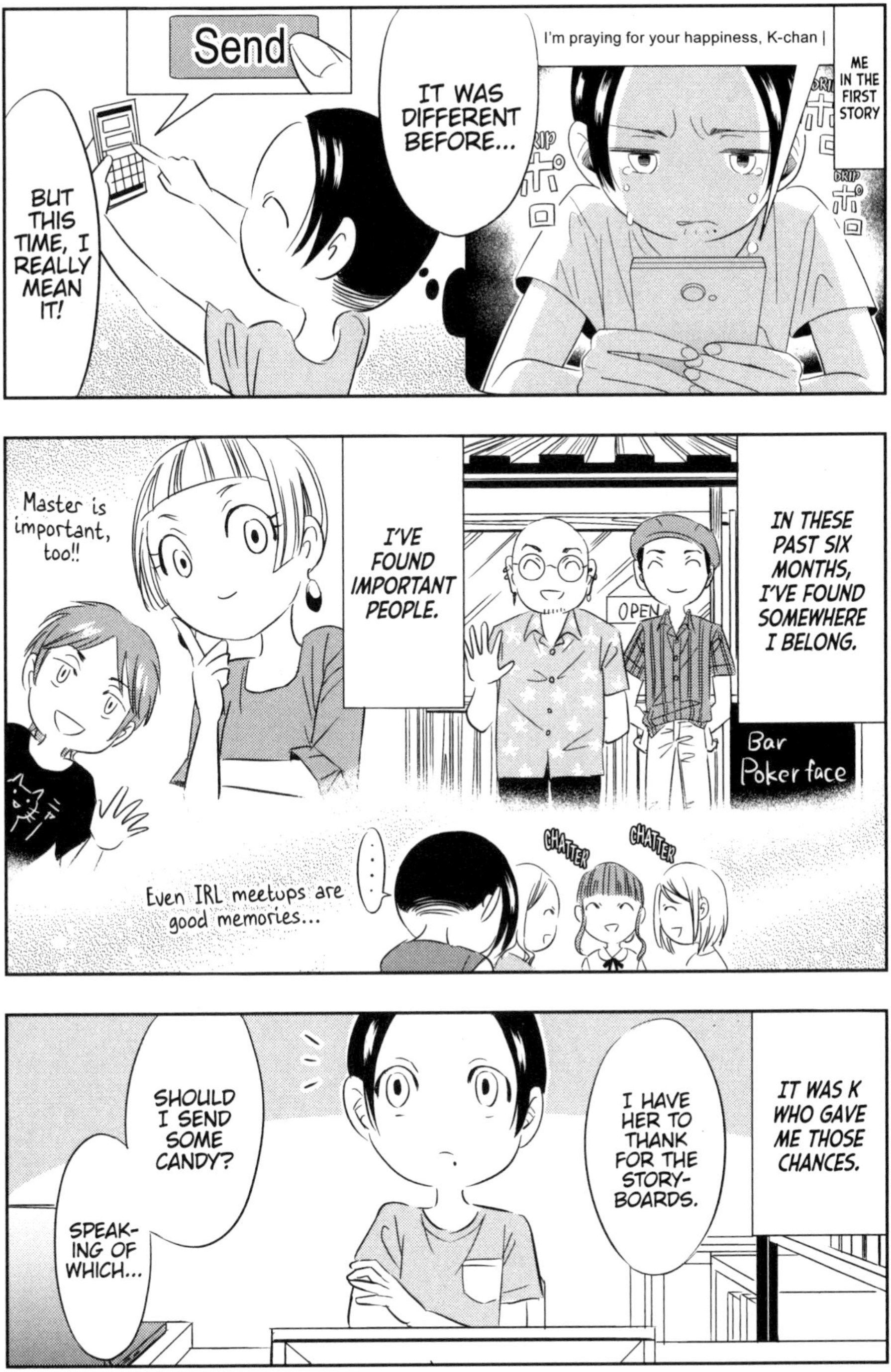
ME IN THE FIRST STORY
I'm praying for your happiness, K-chan |
DRIP
DRIP
DRIP
IT WAS DIFFERENT BEFORE...
Send
BUT THIS TIME, I REALLY MEAN IT!
IN THESE PAST SIX MONTHS, I'VE FOUND SOMEWHERE I BELONG.
Bar Poker face
OPEN
I'VE FOUND IMPORTANT PEOPLE.
Master is important, too!!
CHATTER
CHATTER
...
Even IRL meetups are good memories...
IT WAS K WHO GAVE ME THOSE CHANCES.
I HAVE HER TO THANK FOR THE STORY-BOARDS.
SPEAK-ING OF WHICH...
SHOULD I SEND SOME CANDY?

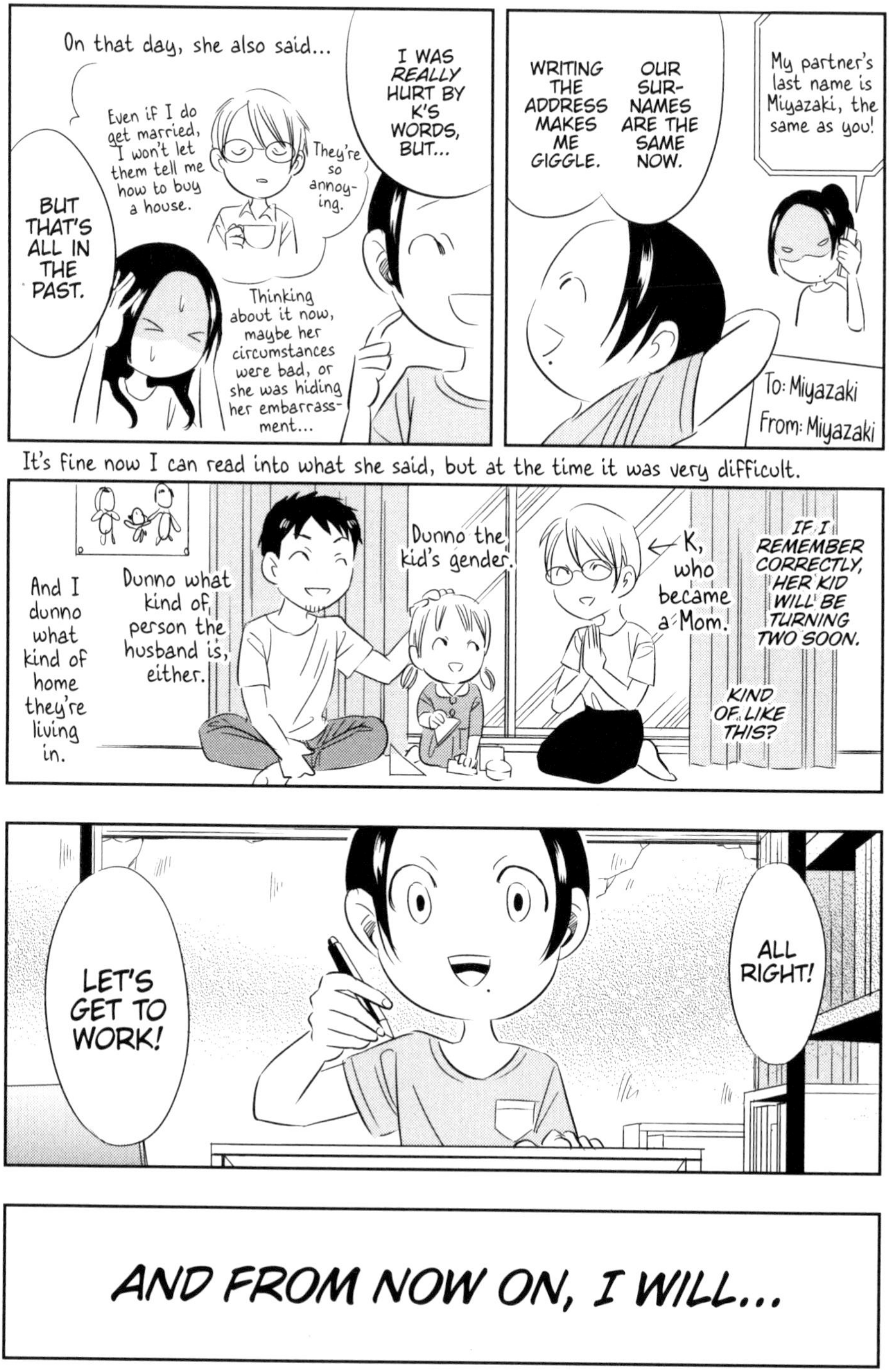
My partner's last name is Miyazaki, the same as you!
OUR SURNAMES ARE THE SAME NOW.
WRITING THE ADDRESS MAKES ME GIGGLE.
To: Miyazaki
From: Miyazaki
I WAS REALLY HURT BY K'S WORDS, BUT...
On that day, she also said...
They're so annoying.
Even if I do get married, I won't let them tell me how to buy a house.
Thinking about it now, maybe her circumstances were bad, or she was hiding her embarrassment...
BUT THAT'S ALL IN THE PAST.
It's fine now I can read into what she said, but at the time it was very difficult.
IF I REMEMBER CORRECTLY, HER KID WILL BE TURNING TWO SOON.
KIND OF LIKE THIS?
← K, who became a Mom.
Dunno the kid's gender.
Dunno what kind of person the husband is, either.
And I dunno what kind of home they're living in.
ALL RIGHT!
LET'S GET TO WORK!
AND FROM NOW ON, I WILL...

X-GENDER

Afterword

Try lining up the back covers of *Young Magazine the Third*. In Issue #5, there was a notice that *X-Gender* would be serialized. My manga appeared in Issues #7, #8, #9, #10, #11, and #12 of 2020, as well as Issue #1 of 2021. It's amazing! The first part is complete. I got it done!

But what about Issue #6?

Do you remember April 7, 2020? That was the day the state of emergency was issued. Schools closed, there were restrictions on using facilities, and people were told not to go out across seven prefectures. On 10th April, I received an email from my manager titled: "Important: Regarding the first issue of serialization." A few days later, the "Postponement of Publication for Ten Kodansha Manga Magazines" was announced on network news. Because of the coronavirus, Issue #6 of *Young Magazine the Third* (where *X-Gender's* serialization was meant to commence) became a phantom issue.

At the same time, my anxiety was as high as it could possibly be. While I was preparing for the serialization, the number of infected people was increasing daily. So, when I received that email, it felt inevitable. I was worried about when my serialization would begin, but also about whether people across the world would be okay.

I've suffered from obsessive-compulsive disorder for a long time, and during the coronavirus, it felt as if the whole world was enveloped by sickness. At that point, we didn't know how the virus was transmitted and every day was filled with fear. That was the environment in which *X-Gender* came into the world. Up to Episode 12, the events of the series were drawn from the second half of 2019.

I only realized that I am part of a sexual minority very recently. In 2020, I spoke with a lot of people and have since gained more awareness about my way of life. But when will I be able to meet people again?

It is the start of January 2021. It's been decided that a second state of emergency will soon be declared.

But there is hope. Vaccines will begin in late February. Until then, we shall have to endure just a little longer. It's dark and lonely now, but surely the light at the end of the tunnel is bright. I hope that, in all of this, my manga can become a companion to you and lighten your heart.

By the way, although I maintained in Volume 1 that IRL meetups weren't for me and wrote about them quite negatively, I'm still in contact with some of the people I met there! We haven't been able to meet again due to the coronavirus, but I hope they'll let me draw them one day!

Last but not least, thank you so much for reading X-Gender! And look out for my other works!

May you live as your most authentic self!

Asuka Miyazaki
January 2021

NEXT VOLUME ANNOUNCEMENT!

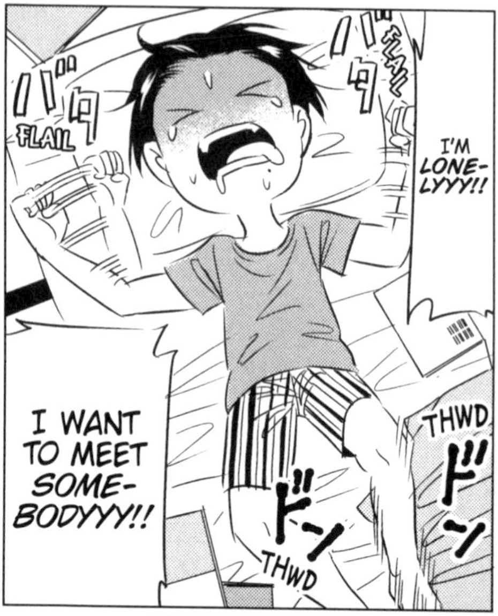
FLAIL
I'M LONE-LYYY!!
FLAIL
THWD
I WANT TO MEET SOME-BODYYY!!
THWD

During the...

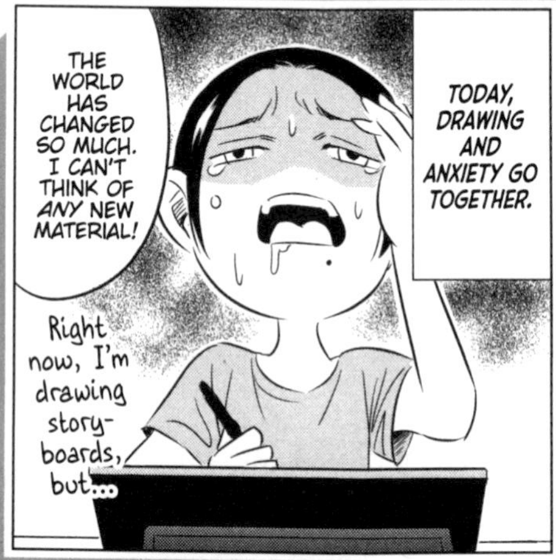
TODAY, DRAWING AND ANXIETY GO TOGETHER.
THE WORLD HAS CHANGED SO MUCH. I CAN'T THINK OF ANY NEW MATERIAL!
Right now, I'm drawing story-boards, but...

corona-virus disaster...

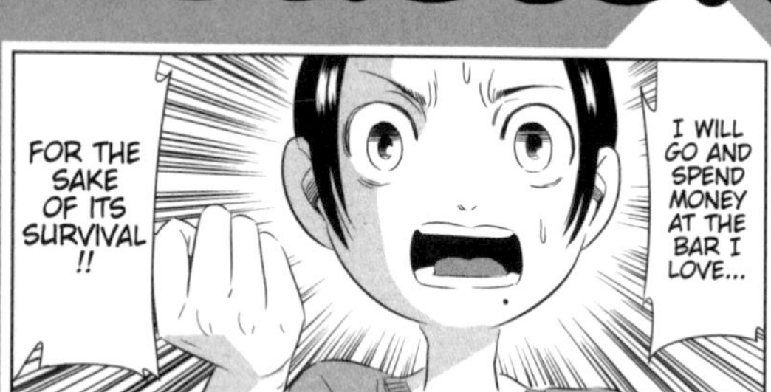
I WILL GO AND SPEND MONEY AT THE BAR I LOVE...
FOR THE SAKE OF ITS SURVIVAL!!

Coming soon!

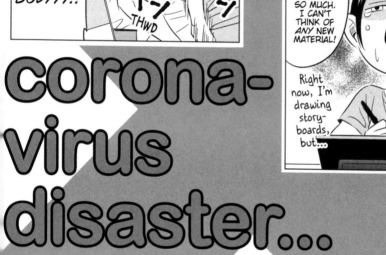

I'll do my best to keep writing!

IT'S REMARKABLE TO SEE A MAN BEING TIED UP AND SUSPENDED LIKE THAT.

IT'S A WORLD I KNEW NOTHING ABOUT.

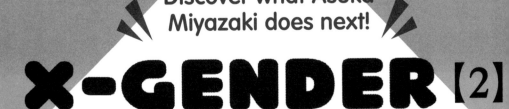

Discover what Asuka Miyazaki does next!

X-GENDER [2]

SEVEN SEAS ENTERTAI

X-GENDER

story and art by **ASUKA MIYAZAKI**

VOLUME 1

TRANSLATION
Kathryn Henzler

ADAPTATION
Cae Hawksmoor

LETTERING
Vanessa Satone

COVER DESIGN
H. Qi

PROOFREADER
Leighanna DeRouen

COPY EDITOR
Dawn Davis

SENIOR EDITOR
Jenn Grunigen

PRODUCTION MANAGER
Lissa Pattillo

PREPRESS TECHNICIAN
Melanie Ujimori

PRINT MANAGER
Rhiannon Rasmussen-Silverstein

EDITOR-IN-CHIEF
Julie Davis

ASSOCIATE PUBLISHER
Adam Arnold

PUBLISHER
Jason DeAngelis

Seibetsu X
©2021 Asuka Miyazaki. All rights reserved.
First published in Japan in 2021 by Kodansha Ltd., Tokyo.
Publication rights for this English edition arranged through Kodansha Ltd., Tokyo.

Seven Seas press and purchase enquiries can be sent to Marketing Manager Lianne Sentar at press@gomanga.com. Information regarding the distribution and purchase of digital editions is available from Digital Manager CK Russell at digital@gomanga.com.

Seven Seas and the Seven Seas logo are trademarks of Seven Seas Entertainment. All rights reserved.

ISBN: 978-1-63858-399-8
Printed in Canada
First Printing: June 2022
10 9 8 7 6 5 4 3 2 1

READING DIRECTIONS

This book reads from *right to left*, Japanese style. If this is your first time reading manga, you start reading from the top right panel on each page and take it from there. If you get lost, just follow the numbered diagram here. It may seem backwards at first, but you'll get the hang of it! Have fun!!

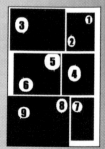

Follow us online: www.SevenSeasEntertainment.com